For reference

Not to be taken from the room.

DICTIONARY
OF
RETAILING
AND
MERCHANDISING

The National Retail Federation Series

The National Retail Federation Series comprises books on retail store management, for stores of all sizes and for all management responsibilities. The National Retail Federation is the world's largest retail trade association, with membership that includes the leading department, specialty, discount, mass merchandise, and independent stores, as well as 30 national and 50 state associations. NRF members represent an industry that encompasses more that 1.4 million U.S. retail establishments and employs nearly 20 million people—1 in 5 American workers. The NRF's international members operate stores in more than 50 nations.

The National Retail Federation Series includes the following books.

Published Books:

FOR 1994: Financial & Operating Results of Retail Stores in 1993
    National Retail Federation
MOR 1994: Merchandising & Operating Results of Retail Stores in 1993
    National Retail Federation
Competing with the Retail Giants: How to Survive in the New Retail Landscape
    Kenneth E. Stone
Value Retailing in the 1990s: Off-Pricers, Factory Outlets, and Closeout Stores
    Packaged Facts, Inc.
Credit Card Marketing
    Bill Grady
Loss Prevention Guide for Retail Businesses
    Rudolph C. Kimiecik
Management of Retail Buying, Third Edition
    R. Patrick Cash, John W. Wingate, and Joseph S. Friedlander
Dictionary of Retailing and Merchandising
    Jerry M. Rosenberg
Retail Store Planning & Design Manual, Second Edition
    Michael Lopez

Forthcoming Books:

Practical Merchandising Math
    Leo Gafney
FOR 1995: Financial & Operating Results of Retail Stores in 1994
    National Retail Federation
MOR 1995: Merchandising & Operating Results of Retail Stores in 1994
    National Retail Federation
The U.S. Electronic Retailing Market
    Packaged Facts, Inc.

Other Books by the Author

Dictionary of Business and Management (Wiley)

Dictionary of Banking (Wiley)

Dictionary of Investing (Wiley)

Business Dictionary of Computers (Wiley)

Dictionary of International Trade (Wiley)

Dictionary of Marketing and Advertising (Wiley)

Dictionary of Artificial Intelligence and Robotics (Wiley)

Automation, Manpower and Education (Random House)

The Computer Prophets (Macmillan)

The Death of Privacy: Do Government and Industrial Computers Threaten Our Personal Freedom? (Random House)

Inside *The Wall Street Journal:* The History and Power of Dow Jones & Company and America's Most Influential Newspaper (Macmillan)

The New Europe: An A to Z Compendium on the European Community (Bureau of National Affairs)

Dictionary of Business Acronyms, Initials, and Abbreviations (McGraw-Hill)

Dictionary of Wall Street Acronyms, Initials, and Abbreviations (McGraw-Hill)

Dictionary of Information Technology and Computer Acronyms, Initials, and Abbreviations (McGraw-Hill)

The New American Community: The U.S. Response to the European and Asian Economic Challenge (Praeger)

Encyclopedia of the North American Free Trade Agreement, the New American Community and Latin-American Trade (Greenwood Press)

DICTIONARY
OF
RETAILING
AND
MERCHANDISING

Jerry M. Rosenberg
Professor, Graduate School
of Management, and
School of Business
RUTGERS UNIVERSITY

John Wiley & Sons, Inc.
New York • Chichester • Brisbane • Toronto • Singapore

Library of Congress Cataloging-in-Publication Data:

Rosenberg, Jerry Martin.
    Dictionary of retailing and merchandising / Jerry M. Rosenberg.
        p.   cm. — (National Retail Federation series)
    Includes bibliographical references.
    ISBN 0-471-11023-X (cloth : alk. paper)
    1. Retail trade—Dictionaries.   2. Merchandising—Dictionaries.
    I. Title. II. Series.
    HF1001.R793   1995
    381′ .1′ 03—dc20   95-17899

Printed in the United States of America

10 9 8 7 6 5 4 3 2 1

This volume is dedicated with love to the most inspiring forces in my life:
Ellen, Liz, Lauren, Bob and Bess.

ACKNOWLEDGMENTS

To prepare this volume, considerable assistance has come indirectly from authors of books, journal articles, and reference materials. They are too numerous to be named here. On a more personal level, I thank the various individuals who were my sounding boards and who helped clarify my ideas and approach; they offered valuable suggestions and encouraged me to go on with this project.

Without the confidence of Stephen Kippur, a friend of many years since the first of my eight Wiley dictionaries appeared in 1978, and presently, senior vice president of John Wiley & Sons; and my newest editor Ruth Mills, this Dictionary would never have appeared. In addition, the assistance from executives of the National Retail Federation and the incorporation of materials from their monthly magazine *Stores* was most welcomed and beneficial.

Last, but truly first, there is my wife Ellen, for 35 years the closest of companions, and other supporters Liz, Lauren, and son-in-law Bob, who collectively continue to lend their reinforcement and share my interest in the meaning and usage of words. Once again, I look forward to hearing from readers with suggestions, both for changes and for future entries.

JERRY M. ROSENBERG

New York, New York

PREFACE

The retail landscape remains fiercely competitive and complex. The explosion of new terms are indicators, in part, of how retailers and merchandisers are facing the challenge of this harsh environment. In the 1990s, with slow economic growth, a decrease in consumer spending for nondurable goods, and a surfeit of retail space put American retailers to the test. Successful retailers are adopting new strategies to deliver lower price merchandise while increasing profitability.

Outlet malls, for example, are luring customers away from department stores and other retailers; superstores have entered fragmented markets and are increasing market share; catalog retailing is expanding; and home shopping via cable television is projected for the future.

Advances in information systems and communications technology are significantly enhancing the prospects for retail productivity improvements and promises to alter the practice of retailing and merchandising. Electronic retailing, electronic vendor catalogs, and bar codes are samples of the dynamic changes already impacting on the field.

With roughly 18 percent of working Americans employed in retailing, store operations have undergone and will continue to undergo massive restructuring over the coming years. In a short time, new technologies, concepts, and opportunities have created unparalleled challenges for these industries. At the same time, reorganization forges ahead with mergers accompanied by a search for new global markets. Some older approaches are floundering in the face of international competition, while others, proven to be effective over decades of practice, survive. Creative merchandising and the skill to keep pace with the fashions of the times will remain an important component for a retailer's success. In short, change is not only inevitable, but change is occurring at a faster pace. Only retailers and merchandisers who are prepared will prosper.

This lexicon on retailing and merchandising includes terms from cousin fields of marketing, advertising, wholesaling, direct marketing, and buying. In addition, special treatment will be given to stores, shopping centers, retail advertising, mail-order, displaying, retail data processing, retail accounting, personnel aspects of retailing, retailing and merchandising research, transactions with manufacturers and vendors, promoting and selling via television, and many more.

CONTENTS

INTRODUCTION

This work of approximately 4,500 entries has been prepared with the hope that awareness of the accepted meaning of terms may enhance the process of sharing information and ideas. Though it cannot eliminate the need for the user to determine how a writer or speaker treats a word, such a dictionary shows what usages exist. It should assist in stabilizing terminology. More important, it should aid people in saying and writing exactly what they intend with greater clarity.

A word can take on different meanings in different contexts. There may be as many meanings as there are areas of specialty. A goal of this dictionary is to establish core definitions that represent the variety of individual meanings to enhance parsimony and clearness in the communications process.

Many terms are used in different ways. I have tried to unite them without giving one advantage or dominance over another. Whenever possible (without creating a controversy), I have stated the connection among multiple usages.

Commonly used acronyms and abbreviations are included. Foreign words and phrases are given only if they have become an integral part of our English vocabulary.

This work reaches throughout the world, incorporating terms from both government and private-sector organizations, making this dictionary an all-inclusive lexicon of international retailing and merchandising.

ORGANIZATION

This is a defining work rather than a compilation of facts. This line is not easy to draw because in the final analysis meanings are based on facts. Consequently, factual information is used where necessary to make a term more easily understood. All terms are presented in the language of those who use them. The level of complexity needed for a definition will vary with the user; one person's complexity is another's precise and parsimonious statement. Sometimes, several meanings are given—one relatively simple for the layperson, and a more developed and technical one for the specialist.

I have organized the dictionary to provide information easily and rapidly, while keeping in mind two categories of user: the experienced person who demands precise information about a particular word, and the newcomer, support member, teacher, or student who seeks general explanation. I have, in most cases, supplied both general and specialized entries to make this dictionary a useful reference source.

FORMAT

Alphabetization. Words are presented alphabetically. Compound terms are placed where the reader is most likely to look for them. They are entered under their most distinctive component, usually a noun. Should you fail to locate a word where you initially look for it, turn to a variant spelling, a synonym, or a different word of the compound term.

Entries containing mutual concepts are usually grouped for comparison. They are then given in inverted order; that is, the expected order of words is reversed to allow the major word of the phrase to appear at the beginning of the term. These entries precede those that are given in the expected order. The terms are alphabetized up to the first comma and then by words following the comma, thus establishing clusters of related terms.

Headings. The current popular term is usually given as the principal entry, with other terms cross-referenced to it. Some terms have been included for historical significance, even though they are no longer in common use.

Cross-References. Cross-references go from the general to the specific. Occasionally, "see" references from the specific to the general are used to inform the user of words related to particular entries. "See" references to currently accepted terminology are made wherever possible. The use of "Cf." suggests words to be compared with the original entry.

Synonyms. The phrase "Synonymous with" following a definition does not imply that the term is *exactly* equivalent to the principal entry under which it appears. Frequently, the term only approximates the primary sense of the original entry.

Disciplines. Many words are given multiple definitions based on their utilization in various fields of activity. The definition with the widest application is given first, with the remaining definitions listed by areas of specialty. Since the areas may overlap, the reader should examine all multiple definitions.

DICTIONARY
OF
RETAILING
AND
MERCHANDISING

AAMA: See *American Apparel Manufacturers Association.*

abandonment:

(1) *retailing:* the final stage in a product's life cycle, when the profit potential is such that management decides that the best course is to discontinue selling it.

(2) *transportation:* damaged cargo in transit on a public carrier that is refused at its destination.

ABC: See *Audit Bureau of Circulations.*

ABF: See *American Buyers Federation.*

above-the-market strategy: See *market-plus pricing.*

absolute sale: where a buyer and seller agree that under no circumstances will there be any limitations or restrictions affecting the saies transactions. Cf. *approval sale; conditional sale.*

absorption costing: a type of product costing that assigns fixed manufacturing overhead to the units produced as a product cost.

accelerator principle: states that the final consumer demand affects several layers of organizational consumers.

accents: in merchandising fashion items, the specific points of emphasis employed by a designer or company to present the style with a particular viewpoint.

acceptance:

(1) the acknowledged receipt by a shipment's consignee resulting in the termination of the common carrier contract.

(2) a positive reception of an item, brand, or line of products by the public.

accepted fashion: a fashion that receives a favorable reception from the public.

accessible site: where a retail store can be readily reached by customers and employees. Distance is a factor, along with driving time and parking facilities.

accessorial service: a service rendered by a carrier in addition to a transportation service, such as assorting, packaging, precooling, heating, storage, or substitution of tonnage.

accessories:

(1) *general:* any subordinate item that adds to the usefulness or attractiveness of the principal item.

(2) *retailing:* items that coordinate with a basic article of clothing to make it more appealing, and therefore more attractive of the total wearer's image. Includes items such as gloves, stockings, scarves.

accessorize: the choosing of accessory articles to complete or complement a fashion style.

accessory items: See *accessories.*

accommodation area: in retailing, the area devoted to providing additional services to customers, such as wrapping of packages, validating parking tickets. Synonymous with *accommodation desk; service area.*

accommodation desk: Synonymous with *accommodation area.*

accommodation items: goods held by the retailer to fulfill the unique needs of a handful of clients or customers.

accommodation services: services and/or facilities offered to customers including gift wrapping, baby changing facilities.

account:
(1) *general:* a record of all the transactions, and the date of each, affecting a particular phase of a business, expressed in debits and credits, evaluated in money, and showing the current balance, if any.
(2) *retailing:* a customer of a supplier or vendor firm from which the consumer obtains specific materials or services.

account classification: the evaluation of retailers or other buyers according to existing and, in particular, potential business.

account opener: a gift given by a bank or other financial institution to a potential depositor opening a new account or adding funds to an existing account. See *direct premium.*

accounts payable:
(1) *general:* a current liability representing the amount owed by an individual or a business to a creditor for merchandise or services purchased on an open account or short-term credit.
(2) *retailing:* an amount owed to a creditor, created often with the purchase of merchandise or materials and supplies. For example, the amount a retailer pays the vendors for items ordered and ultimately received.

accounts receivable:
(1) *general:* money owed a business enterprise for merchandise bought on open account.
(2) *retailing:* a claim against a debtor often resulting from the sale of items or services rendered, such as the amount of money a vendor collects from the retailer for items sent or the amount a retailer must receive from charge customers.

ACDS: See *Associated Chain Drugstores.*

ACSMA: See *American Cloak and Suit Manufacturers Association.*

action program: Synonymous with *marketing plan.*

act of God: in contractual language, an irresistible superhuman cause, such as no reasonable human foresight, prudence, diligence, and care can anticipate or prevent.

actual cost: the billed cost less any cash discount earned.

actual count: See *periodic actual count.*

actuals: merchandise and other items available for immediate purchase and subsequent sale.

adaptation: a design that reflects the dominant feature of a style that inspired it but is not an exact copy.

adaptive behavior concept: the belief in evolutionary shift in retailing where retailers most able to adapt to shifting conditions within the marketplace will have the better frequency for survival.

adaptive forecasting: forecasting sales where a particular amount of unit sales documentation has been adapted to sales expectations.

adaptive product: See *emulative product.*

added gravy: resulting from added selling, sales resulting from items used to provide satisfaction from another item, such as linens for outfitting a queen-size mattress.

added selling: hoping to sell more products and/or services to a customer who has just made a purchase. See *added gravy.*

added value: See *database marketing.*

additional markup: the increase in the original retail price of merchandise because of errors in the original pricing or to increases in their value within the market.

additional markup cancellation: the decrease in the retail price which trades off against a further markup. Cancellations can adjust for an error in pricing and some end a pre-planned sale. A lowered price is not shown as a markdown. Synonymous with *revision of retail downward.*

additional markup percentage: the percentage calculated as:

$$\frac{\text{additional markup}}{\text{percentage}} = \frac{\text{total additional dollar markup}}{\text{net sales (in \$)}}$$

addition to retail percentage: the total price changes as a percentage of the original price

$$\frac{\text{addition to retail}}{\text{percentage}} = \frac{\text{new price} - \text{original price}}{\text{original price}}$$

add-ons: in retailing, further purchases added to the account of a charge account customer before the previous balance in the account has been completely paid.

add-on sales: See *added gravy; add-ons.*

adjacent stock room: See *stock room.*

adjusted balance procedure: a means where retailers determine the balance in a charge account for which a service charge is to be set. With this procedure, charges are made following payments made in the billing period have been subtracted from the outstanding balance. Cf. *average daily balance method; previous balance method.*

adjusted retail book value: the ending retail book value corrected to reflect all stock shortages and stock overages:

$$\frac{\text{adjusted retail}}{\text{book value}} = \frac{\text{ending retail book value} - \text{stock}}{\text{shortages} + \text{stock overages}}$$

adjustment:

(1) *general:* a change in an account to correct an incorrect entry or for some other sound reason.

(2) *retailing:* the satisfying of a customer's claim that a shipment was not as ordered or that the price was improperly charged, by an agreeable financial settlement.

(3) *retailing:* correcting mistakes involving the wrong recording of invoices or wrong dating of purchases bought on open account.

adjustment allowance: appropriate compensation given to a customer to satisfy a complaint or possibly a claim.

adjustment department: the department within a retail store that is responsible for the resolution of customer complaints, especially when they have failed to be resolved on the selling floor.

administered price:

(1) *general:* the price established under situations of imbalance competition wherein one business has some degree of control. See *price leadership.*

(2) *retailing:* a means of managing the retail price of merchandise contingent upon the store's unique retailing mix. The greater the store differentiation, the greater the control a retailer can have over the asked price.

administered system: the manufacturer's control of one or more lines sold by the retailer. It frequently involves creative or newly refined merchandising plans. See *administered vertical marketing.*

administered vertical marketing: a vertically aligned group of organizations, not necessarily vertically integrated, that performs as a unit to lower the costs inherent in merchandising a line or classification of goods. See *administered system.*

administrative offices: as used by the U.S. Census of Business; the designation of locations that are involved in the performance of management activities for retail organizations.

adoption process: the awareness that occurs when a person first becomes aware of an innovation until he or she is willing to accept it; usually in the instance of real things, purchasing them. See *adoption process segmentation variables.*

adoption process segmentation variables: consumer stages that are completed in the process of becoming a regular user of a product and/or service. The stages include awareness, interest, evaluation, trial, and adoption. See *adoption process.*

advance:
(1) the partial payment made before due, such as wages.
(2) a downpayment on the sale of merchandise.

advance bill:
(1) a bill of exchange drawn prior to the shipment of merchandise.
(2) the invoice presented before the items or services itemized have been delivered or carried out. It is usually requested by purchasers for tax reasons.

advance buying: See *advance order.*

advance dating: the added time allowed by a vendor to pay for goods, enabling the purchaser to receive a cash discount.

Such extensions usually are arranged before the goods are shipped. Synonymous with *seasonal dating.*

advance order: the sales order placed sufficiently ahead of the requested date for delivery, thereby often entitling the buyer to a substantial discount.

advance premium: the premium offered to a potential customer by a home-service route firm in the hope that it will be earned by later purchases.

advertise:
(1) to promote; to solicit, usually without payment, i.e., a radio announcer promoting the qualities of a wine he or she experienced in a restaurant.
(2) applying some form of message or communication to attract attention of an individual or group to a product, service, concept, institutions, etc., with the expectation of some form of behavior or action; usually to purchase the item or service, or gain support for the concept or idea. See *advertised.*

advertised: the promotion of a product or service, without cost, such as hearing a radio announcer praise a bottle of wine that he experienced in a local restaurant. See *advertise.* Cf. *advertisement.*

advertisement (ad): a public announcement or sale offer in a public area or medium, expressed in print, by other visual means, or orally. Major locations of advertisements are in newspapers, magazines, and journals and on signs, billboards, radio, and television. Similar to, but not synonymous with commercial. An advertisement is usually paid for. Cf. *advertise; advertised; commercial.*

advertiser: anyone who engaged to pay for advertising. See *account.*

advertising:
(1) a paid for of nonpersonal presentation or promotion of goods, services, and/or ideas. It is usually paid for by an identifiable sponsor. Decisions evolve

around *what* is to be said and where to *place* the advertising. Cf. *publicity*.
(2) often used to include messages promoting concepts and causes; containing three basic objectives (a) to *inform* consumers about new item, product uses, services available, or other information of use to the consumer, (b) to *persuade* an audience to buy an item, change brand preferences, or perceive an item or service differently, (c) to *remind* consumers about the need for an item or service where it can be bought.

advertising allowance: a discount in price or payment given to a store to help meet the expense of the store's advertising of a product. Such allowances are most often granted when new products are being introduced or when manufacturers are attempting to increase promotion of their products. See *trade promotion*.

advertising appeal: the central concept of an advertisement that communicates to the potential consumer what the advertised item or service provides and gives the reasons why it should be bought.

advertising credit: the mention of a store's name in the advertisement of a producer.

advertising models: today, computerized systems assist in advertising decision making, from helping to determine budgets, media scheduling, and expectations of sales and profits.

advertising plan: a store's projection of its advertising usage during the given time period.

advertising record sheet: a work sheet for monitoring either daily, weekly, monthly, or all three orders for merchandise received as a result of a particular advertisement.

advertising research: See *advertising testing*.

advertising space: the portion of the total page space in print (newspaper, magazine, etc.) allocated to store advertising rather than editorial and/or news matter.

advertising specialty distributor: See *specialty distributor*.

advertising testing: a mean of determining the effectiveness of individual advertisements or full campaigns. There is pretesting to determine the appropriateness and projected effectiveness before placing of a store's advertisements; there is posttesting to determine their impact following an appearance in the marketplace.

advertising theme: a major idea behind an advertising campaign as presented to its potential audience. It purports to prove the superiority of the value of the item, idea, or service being offered.

advice note: a supplier's listing of items that is sent to a customer prior to an invoice, either accompanying the merchandise or preceding it, identifying the nature and quantity of the goods but not giving prices.

advocate channel: an individual communication channel composed of a firm's salesforce contracting purchasers in the target market.

affiliated buying: See *cooperative buying*.

affiliated retailer: a store that is operated and owned by an independent retailer affiliated with a voluntary chain or where the retailer holds stock in a co-op wholesaler organization.

affiliated store:
(1) in retailing, a store that is part of a voluntary chain or a franchise.
(2) in retailing, a store under the name other than that of the controlling store.

affiliated wholesaler:
(1) the wholesaler who acts as initiator of a voluntary chain. See *voluntary chain*.

(2) a wholesaler who has an association with other wholesalers utilizing a common trade name for merchandising purposes.

affinities: retail stores that are traditionally found near each other so as to derive benefits from the flow of customers entering their building from the stores nearby.

AFM: See *Associated Fur Manufacturers.*

AFMA: See *American Fur Merchants' Association.*

AG: See *Apparel Guild.*

agent:
(1) *general:* an individual authorized to act in behalf of another person, the principal.
(2) *wholesaler:* a wholesaling intermediary that does not take title to merchandise, but serves primarily to bring buyers and sellers together and facilitate exchanges.
(3) See *manufacturer's agent; selling agent.*

agent middleperson: See *functional middleperson.*

aggregate demand:
(1) the total spending within an economy.
(2) the total of personal consumption expenditures, business investments, and government spending.

aggregation: a method based on the concept that consumers in a particular market are alike. Mass advertising and mass product distribution often result from this assumption, especially when low price is considered the primary appeal leading to the greatest number of consumers.

aging: in retailing, the length of time that goods have been left in stock.

aging accounts receivable: in determining the amount of uncollectible accounts receivable as of a specific date; the process of classifying accounts receivable based on the time period that they have been outstanding.

AGMAC: See *Association of General Merchandise Chains.*

agree and counterattack technique: See *yes, but technique.*

agreeing and neutralizing technique: See *yes, but technique.*

aided recall: a mean for surveying the impression made by a store's advertisement or other media communication whereby an interviewer presents an advertisement or other aid to memory.

air bubble packing: packing materials made of plastic with air pockets for cushioning.

air curtain: a stream of air used in food retailing stores as a barrier to prevent heat loss or cold to the atmosphere.

airedale: (slang) a high-pressure salesperson who often dresses sharply, talks fast, and is aggressive in behavior. Cf. *bird dog.*

air waybill: a transport document that covers both domestic and international flights transporting goods to a specified destination. This is a nonnegotiable instrument of air transport that serves as a receipt for the shipper, indicating that the carrier has accepted the goods listed and obligates itself to carry the consignment to the airport of destination according to specified conditions.

aisle advertising: a store item display used to attract attention and make the item accessible to purchasers; usually has the same copy and graphics used in other promotional efforts produced by the sponsoring product. See *POP advertising.*

aisle table: See *aisle advertising.*

allied products: in retailing, items associated with one another in the same use category. See *complementary products.*

allocated expense: an expenditure that may benefit the store that is traditionally separated between the departments based on time, space, or capital requirements.

allocation:

(1) *general:* assigning one or more items of cost or revenue to one or more segments of an organization, according to benefits received or other logical measure of use.

(2) *retailing:* the lowering of price to a retailer by the manufacturer or wholesaler based upon some unique agreement. Traditionally, it is used to compensate the retailer for expenses in marketing the item.

allowance:

(1) *merchandising:* a deduction from the weight or value of merchandise; a reduction permitted if the carrier does not supply appropriate equipment and the shipper then produces the equipment for use.

(2) *retailing:* any price reduction.

allowance for bad debts: as contra to accounts receivable these are monthly credit entries that indicate the estimated amount of accounts receivable that will not be collected.

allowance to customers: See *returns and allowances.*

allowance for depreciation: an account indicating the accumulated depreciation taken and used for determining; the net valuation of a store's assets.

allowance for doubtful accounts: See *allowance for bad debts.*

allowance for uncollectables: See *allowance for bad debts.*

allowance from vendor: the price adjustment to a buyer for damaged merchandise or return of unsatisfactory merchandise. See *returns and allowances.*

all-purpose revolving account: in retailing, the charge account for which the agreement with customers provides

that no service charge will be imposed if the account is paid in full within a given time period following the presentation of a statement. Synonymous with *flexible charge account; retail installment credit account; revolving charge account.*

all-you-can-afford method: a technique for evolving a promotional budget where all nonpromotional marketing expenses are budgeted initially, and the remaining funds are allocated to promotional activities.

alteration cost: the expense resulting from changing garments to fit the needs of a customer. It includes labor, materials, supplies, etc.

alteration expense: See *alteration cost.*

alteration room: a department where tailors and other workers redo garments to custom fit customers and for repairing merchandise that may have been torn in stock.

alterations: changes in standard-size garments in order to offer a better fit or present a particular image.

altruistic display:

(1) a display for items other than the ones who pay for the display.

(2) a store-wide occurrence of seasonal items including the advertiser's product without specifically naming it.

American Apparel Manufacturers Association (AAMA): based in Arlington, Virginia, an association of manufacturers of wearing apparel. The AAMA provides numerous services to members, including an annual Financial and Operating Ratio Report.

American Buyers Federation (ABF): a purchasing group that permits its members to buy major or large-ticket items at significant savings. Members are employees of corporations, credit unions, associations, and fraternal organization in the metropolitan Chicago area.

American Cloak and Suit Manufacturers Association (ACSMA): a New York City-based organization of contractors manufacturing women's coats and suits for wholesalers and other manufacturers. ACSMA represents contractors and manufacturers in contractual negotiations with the International Ladies Garment Workers' Union.

American Fur Merchants' Association (AFMA): based in New York, an association of fur dealers, brokers, supply houses, banks, factors, auction companies, wholesalers, importers, and exporters. Acts as a credit agency for members and deals with trade issues.

American Mailorder Association (AMOA): located in Washington, DC, an association of individuals, firms, and organizations utilizing mail order or direct mail marketing. The AMOA disseminates information and acts as a go-between with the government.

American Professional Needlework Retailers Association (APNRA): a Forest View, Illinois-based organization of operators and employees of retail stores that sells yarn, needles, and needlework. Certifies in-shop instructors and maintains a liaison with high school home economics classes.

American Retail Association Executives (ARAE): a New York City-based association of executives of local, state, and national retail merchants associations, chamber of commerce retail departments, credit bureaus, and downtown associations.

American Retail Federation (ARF): a parent institution of state and national organizations of retailers; concerned primarily with national issues affecting retailers, such as legislation and federal regulation. Merged with NRMA to form the National Retail Federation.

American Truck Stop Operators Association (ATSOA): based in North Palm Beach, Florida, an organization of truck stop operators and suppliers; geared to promoting and improving the truck stop industry.

American Women Buyers Club (AWBC): a New York City-based association whose members are women who are buyers of apparel for buying offices and for retail operations.

AMOA: See *American Mail Order Association.*

analysis of accounts: See *aging accounts receivable.*

anchor: as used by consumers to evaluate communications; often employed as a rule-of-thumb concept, such as "the higher the price for an item the better its quality."

anchorless mall: a shopping center containing only small specialty shops, but no large department store(s).

anchor store: a large store located in a shopping mall, that provides the draw required to attract customers.

ancillary customer services: optional services provided for customers to increase the noncompetition activities of the sellers; always of a nonessential variety. Some stores do and other do not charge for such services.

ancillary services: See *ancillary customer services.*

angel: in retailing, an individual who invests capital in a business situation; rarely assumes any management activity within the venture.

anniversary sale: a store-wide promotional happening; usually celebrates the anniversary of the store's founding. It is often scheduled for mid-fall and mid-spring, regardless of actual date of the store's beginning. Synonymous with *birthday sale.*

anticipation: the discount that has been added to the cash discount for payment in advance of the cash discount date.

anticipation dating: See *anticipation.*

anticipation of demand: requires a firm to do consumer research on a regular basis in order to develop and introduce offerings desired by consumers.

antiquated: See *obsolescence; obsolete material.*

apathetic shoppers: one of four classifications of consumers; indicates those with little interest in making comparisons. The consumer here is happy to patronize the most convenient store. See *economic shoppers; ethical shoppers; personalizing shoppers.*

APNRA: See *American Professional Needlework Retailers Associations.*

apparel: all forms of clothing or garments, including those. categories of clothing from intimate apparel to outerwear for men, women, teens, and children.

apparel contractor: an independent manufacturer whose participation includes the sewing (and at times cutting) of garments for one or different apparel manufacturers.

apparel designer: See *designer.*

Apparel Guild (AG): a fraternal benevolent society of wholesale apparel salespeople. AG promotes business relations with manufacturers, retailers, buyers, and salepeople as well as awarding their annual Person of the Year prize.

apparel jobber: See *wholesaler.*

appeal:
(1) the motivation of a sales pitch with the expectation that the potential customers will become favorably disposed toward the product or service.
(2) the advantage of purchasing a product or service as given in the sales message for that item or service.

appraiser: one who determines the value of goods.

approval sale: in retailing, the sale to a customer where the person has unlimited returns privileges. Cf. *absolute sale.* See *on-approval offer.*

apron: an open area within the store where displays are set, either on free-standing units, or built entirely of items from the floor up.

ARAE: See *American Retail Association Executives.*

arcade: in enclosed shopping centers, a covered walk; the popular ways of protecting customers and weather-protecting storefronts. The walkway can be open or glass-enclosed and air-conditioned.

arcade shopping center: See *arcade.*

arc of fashion: Synonymous with *fashion cycle.*

area: See *selling area.*

ARF: See *American Retail Federation.*

arrears: monies due but unpaid; a real or contingent obligation that remains unpaid at the date of maturity.

arrival of goods: a cash discount agreement identifying that a granted cash discount will be made should payment occur within a specified number of days following receipt of the items by the retailer. This method is used primarily to accommodate customers who are far from the store.

artificial obsolescence: the decline in market acceptance of an item brought about because of change in the item or a new version of the item introduced to replace the old one on the belief that it is better to lose sales of a product to a new one of one's own firm than to that of a competitor.

ARTS: See *Association for Retail Technology Standards.*

as is: items that have no warranty and may be damaged or shopworn.

asked price: the price that is officially offered by a seller.

as ready: used by manufacturers to indicating that the items ordered by the retailer will be sent when it is completed. No set delivery date is guaranteed.

asset: any probable future economic benefit obtained or controlled by a particular enterprise as a result of past transactions. Can be tangible, such as merchandise and buildings, or intangible, such as good will.

asset turnover: the ratio of sales to total assets available.

assistant buyer: a buyer-in-training assignment where the person is exposed to all aspects of the buyer's responsibilities, including the department budget, selecting and promoting merchandise, analyzing stock and sales reports, supervising sales and stock employees, etc.

associated buying office: Synonymous with *cooperative buying office.*

Associated Chain Drugstores (ACDS): a New York City-based association of drug chains formed for the exchange of information concerning items for retail sale.

Associated Fur Manufacturers (AFM): a New York City-based organization of manufacturers of fur apparel.

associated independent: a member store in the cooperative ownership of a merchandise buying organization, but is self-managed, self-owned, and traditionally self-merchandised.

associated office: See *cooperative buying office.*

Association for Retail Technology Standards (ARTS): formed in 1993 to help retailers move to "seamless" computing environments; to develop a data model by defining elements in a database. See *Voluntary Interindustry Communications Standard.*

Association of General Merchandise Chains (AGMAC): a Washington, DC based organization composed of independent and chain retail companies operating variety and discount general merchandise stores. Membership also includes firms that supply the variety and discount general merchandisers with goods and services (associate members); association's goals include promoting public awareness of the retailing.

Association of Retail Marketing Services: See *TSIA.*

assorting: performed usually by wholesalers or retailers to supply an assortment of items, e.g., an automotive supply store carrying hundreds of related items for the car user. It purports to evolve a heterogeneous inventory of products for the convenience of customers. Cf. *sort.*

assortment:
(1) various forms of the same general type of item, such as the depth and width of the merchandise offering. *Depth* is about variety, an array of styles, colors, and prices; *width* is about different product categories such as towels, hats, lotions to accompany the sale of bathing suits. See *assortment depth; assortment breadth.*
(2) relating to a specific consumer, the particular combination of items and service seen as needed to maintain or improve one's living standard, e.g., toothbrushes and hair spray.

assortment breadth: a means of describing the number of different categories found in a store or department without reference to the quantity available of any one style. Said to be *broad* when a large variety of different items is available within a classification.

assortment consistency: the way in which different components of the merchandise assortment relate to one another with particular emphasis on how they all relate to one another in the customer's perception. See *assortment.*

assortment deep: See *assortment depth.*

assortment depth: the way of measuring the quantity of each item available in the assortment of goods offered the customer. An assortment containing an item in large quantities with a variety of sizes is said to be *deep*.

assortment display: a method of visual merchandising in which all or most of the merchandise available in a store or department is exhibited, identified, and priced, i.e., a leather goods window.

assortment plan:

(1) a range of merchandise in a category planned at a certain inventory level.

(2) items of one type established to meet the requirements of customers by a determination of inventory levels. See *assortment; basic stock; model stock.*

assortment width: See *assortment breadth.*

assumptive close: in sales, a close accomplished without a buyer's verbal agreement. This becomes presumed when the purchaser fails to protest the salesperson's beginning to prepare the order, or to wrap the merchandise.

at best: in global marketing, the instruction with a buying or selling order indicating that it should be carried out quickly at the best possible price. Synonymous with *at the market.*

atelier: a workshop or facility that is used by a fashion designer in the development of fashion items.

atmosphere: the sum total of the physical characteristics of a retail store or group of stores that are used to develop an image and draw customers.

atmospherics: external factors from the environment that are designed to establish a specific mood, image and/or to stimulate sales. These factors include the store's layout, architecture, colors, and other sensory inputs.

ATR (awareness-trial-repeat): an explanation for the behaviors of a consumer in adopting a service or item. The individual goes from being uninformed of the product or service to becoming a regular user after learning of the item or service's assets and availability (awareness), trying the item or service (trial) and assuming the trial usage is beneficial—purchasing the item or service again (repeat).

ATSOA: See *American Truck Stop Operators Association.*

at the market: Synonymous with *at best.*

at-the-market prices: in retailing, prices that are generally the same for all stores within a location. See *market-minus prices; market-plus pricing.*

attribute-based shopping products: products for which consumers get information about and then evaluate features, warranties, performance, options, and other factors.

auction:

(1) a unique trading market in which there is one seller and many potential buyers.

(2) a means of selling products to the highest bidder.

auction company: a wholesaling intermediary that sells merchandise on an agency basis by means of auctions.

auction house: See *auction company.*

audit: the study of accounting records and of the documentation in support of its correctness. See *internal audit.*

Audit Bureau of Circulations (ABC): an independent nonprofit auditing organization established in 1914 to audit and validate circulation figures for the benefit of its members.

audited net sales: the total amount of sales for a specified period, computed after returns and allowances have been deducted. These totals are circulated by the auditing department of a store and credited to the book inventory of each department.

auditor: the individual who is responsible for checking the accuracy, fairness, and general acceptability of accounting records and statements; can be an executive of the store (internal auditor) or an outside expert or consultant (outside auditor).

augmented product:
(1) the core product together with its attendant benefits and services. Cf. *core product.*
(2) an expected product that has been enhanced by a set of benefits that consumers do not expect or that exceed their expectations.

authorization line: the maximum amount that a customer can charge to a credit card without specific authorization for the purchase by the credit card company. See *floor limit.*

authorized dealer:
(1) *general:* a middleperson who has received a franchise to represent or sell a manufacturer's products.
(2) *retailing:* a person who has, by agreement with a manufacturer, the rights to distribution of a product, or line of products.

authorizing: approving credit sales transactions when the amount of the sale is greater than floor limits or when identification of the buyer and account is needed.

automated markdown: See *price verification procedure.*

automatic basement: the lower level or basement store where prices are successively reduced contingent upon length of time merchandise has remained in stock.

automatic buying procedures: See *automatic reorder.*

automatic cancellation: the latest acceptable shipping date as identified by the buyer on a purchase order.

automatic markdown: the lowering of price taken by a retailer according to a predetermined time schedule.

automatic merchandising: See *automatic selling.*

automatic open-to-buy: central merchandising for multi-unit organizations where funds for items are allotted in part to the central buyer and to the specific store manager. The store manager has some control over reordering while new merchandise is chosen by the central buying staff.

automatic reorder: an order for staple goods issued on the basis for reaching an established minimum inventory quantity. The reorder quantity is predetermined.

automatic selling: the retail sale of items or services through machines operated by the consumer utilizing credit cards, funds, or any other authorized method.

automatic vending: a type of nonstore, nonpersonal retailing of goods and services using coin operated, self-service equipment. Examples of merchandise are cigarettes, candy, condoms, sodas.

autonomous operation: fulfilled by bramore autonomy in their operation, and are looked upon on an "equal stores" basis with the traditional downtown, flagship store.

auxiliary dimensions of a product: those features of a product, other than the item itself, which add to the product's attractiveness, utility, and attraction to the consumer.

available market: people who can afford the item or service, who have ready access to it, and who have shown an interest in using or owning it.

average collection period of receivables: the financial ratio resulting from dividing the number of days in one year (365) by the receivables turnover.

average cost: the sum of all output costs divided by the quantity of production.

average daily balance method: a means by which retailers determine the balance in a charge account upon which a service charge is to be assessed. With this approach, the customer's balance for each day of the billing period is added up and then divided by the number of days in the period. The final figure is used as a basis for setting a service charge. See *adjusted balance procedure; previous balance method.*

average gross sales: the dollar amount of gross sales divided by the number of sales transactions that created the gross sales.

average inventory of item: that amount representing a midpoint between the highest and lowest inventory levels.

average mark-on: the mark-on obtained when the costs and retail prices of several purchases are combined.

average stock: the quantity representing the midpoint between the highest and lowest inventory levels for a stated time period. Average stock is calculated by adding each month's opening stock figure plus the closing stock figure for the last month. The total is divided by the number of months being considered.

awareness-trial-repeat: See *ATR.*

AWBC: See *American Women Buyers Club.*

B

back-door selling: when the salesperson deliberately avoids the purchasing department and calls on people in the department that he or she assumes can use the item.

back end:
(1) following a customer's order, the fulfillment by servicing, delivering of the merchandise.
(2) actions of the consumer after the initial order has been received. Through back-end analysis, the seller examines pay up, cancellation rates, and renewal or reorder rates.

back-end analysis: See *back end.*

back-haul: to reship freight on the same route it has just completed.

back-haul allowance: a price reduction to customers who make their own pickups at the seller's warehouse.

backing activities: activities in a retail store that do not directly involve interfacing with customers.

backlog: the accumulation of unfilled orders.

back order:
(1) a customer's request that is held up the supplier has the capability to ship it.
(2) merchandise ordered but not available for delivery because the supplier does not have it in inventory.

backup merchandise: See *reserve stock.*

bad debt:
(1) *general:* the amount due on an open account that has been proved to be uncollectible; any uncollectible receivable.
(2) *sales:* when the customer fails to pay for products or services received. Synonymous with *bad pay.* See *bad pay list.*

bad faith: to mislead or deceive (Latin: *mala fides*). It does not include misleading by an honest, inadvertent, or uncalled-for misstatement. See *bona fide sale; fraud.*

bad pay: Synonymous with *bad debt.*

bad pay file: Synonymous with *bad pay list.*

bad pay list: people with a poor credit history are withdrawn from a list who would ordinarily receive promotions, advertisements, services, and/or future merchandise. They are purged as people who have a high probability of incurring bad debt expense. These lists can be purchased by advertisers and others. Synonymous with *bad pay file.*

bad risk: a person or organization whose credit record shows that it is unlikely that they will fulfill their financial obligations.

bagel: round plastic markers fitting on hanger rods. They identify clothing by size.

bagger: a supermarket worker who packs groceries into boxes or bags while at the checkout counter.

bailment lease: a retail installment contract where the goods are rented to the purchaser and the rent is paid in installments. When a set number of rental payments has been made, title is then given to the purchaser on the payment of a nominal fee.

bait-and-switch merchandising:
(1) a pricing strategy in which a product is given a low price in order to lure customers into a store, where an attempt is made to persuade them to buy a more expensive model or product.
(2) an unethical and illegal approach in which a retailer advertises a product at a particularly low price with the intention of inducing people who ask for the item to purchase a more costly one. Sometimes the switch is made by the salesperson telling the purchaser that the advertised item is not good or has been sold out. See *switch selling.*

bait-and-switch pricing: See *bait-and-switch merchandising.*

bait merchandising: See *bait-and-switch merchandising.*

bait pricing: Synonymous with *leader pricing.*

balance and mix: combining merchandise in each line of goods to please customers. The correct selection of lines to perpetuate the consistency of the goods with the store image.

balanced selling: the action of selling all products in a vendor's line in proportion to the sales potential found within a stated area, or to the profit associated with the products.

balanced stock: a planned inventory available to customers in proportion to the request for all items they desire in every price range. Synonymous with *ideal stock.* See *model stock.*

balanced tenancy: in retailing, where an area's type and number of stores correspond precisely to the mix proper to meet the needs of that community's population.

balance sheet: in retailing, an itemized statement listing the total assets and total liabilities of a store to portray its net worth at a particular moment in time.

balance sheet close: a closing strategy when confronted with a prospect unable to make up his or her mind about a purchase. The salesperson prepares a list of advantages and disadvantages for both moving quickly or delaying a decision. If the salesperson has been creative, the pluses outweigh the minuses and hopefully become a major reason for the prospect to agree to a transaction.

ballooning: a deterrent to the successful sale of items and services, a price manipulation used to send prices beyond safe or real values.

balloon note: a form of credit agreement where the purchaser pays a series of small installments until, at the end of a specified period, the balance comes due as a single, larger balloon payment.

ballpark pricing: a technique to determine the price for an item by examining the average price level for similar items, choosing a price in this range, and working backwards to set the feasibility of yielding at the cost constraint disclosed.

BAMA: See *Boys' and Young Men's Apparel Manufacturers Association.*

banded pack: items offered at retail that are secured by a tape, string or plastic film strip and therefore sold as one unit. Synonymous with *factory pack.* See *economy pack.*

banded premium: See *on-pack.*

bandwagon impact: when people purchase an item because others are doing the same thing. See *law of demand.*

bangtail: a promotional envelope containing a perforated flap that is torn away and then used as an order form. Often used for placing exposed film to be returned for processing.

Bankcheck Fraud Task Force: represented by members from the American Bankers Association and the National Retail Federation; established in January 1993 to cooperatively examine solutions to check-fraud problems. A goal is to increase the sensitivity of retailers and bankers for each other's check-fraud problems. The task force encourages check printers to prescreen all check orders.

bantam store: a community market that remains open in the late evening or on weekends or holidays when other markets are closed. Cf. *convenience store; depot store; store; superstore.* Synonymous with *superette; vest pocket; supermarket.*

bar code:
(1) *general:* a series of vertical or horizontal parallel lines forming a code that is optically read and interpreted by a bar code scanner. Used on enveloped and form for rapid entry of data and for sorting.
(2) *merchandising:* package bar codes identify items, their prices, and manufacturers. Electronic cash registers scan the code to register price and prepare inventory figures. See *electronic marketing; Universal Product Code.*

bargain:
(1) *general:* an item bought at a low or advantageous price; a good buy.
(2) *retailing:* to arrive at an agreement on the price of goods to be sold.

bargain basement: the below-ground-level floor of a store, where special prices are offered on merchandise. The stock often contains lower price merchandise or items not carried on the upper levels of the store.

bargain counter: an area for the sale of discounted merchandise.

bargain hunter: an individual who seeks out the store that is selling items at the lower possible price.

bargain square: an arrangement tables, traditionally four, to form a square where sale items are arranged.

bargain store: a store that sells merchandise at a submarket price. Assortments and sizes are often limited, and the merchandise frequently is damaged or seconds. See *seconds.*

barn: a discount store where low price is of major importance. Distress merchandise and closeouts are found in much of the stock.

barn-burner wizards: slang for high-powered salespeople who skillfully push to achieve their stated goals or sales.

basement store: historically, the basement of a department store containing bargain items. Today, expanded to any place within the store for items sold at budget prices. Synonymous with *budget store.*

base price: Synonymous with *list price.*

base record: a consumer's file maintained by a store, credit agency, etc., with critical information on the person, beginning with name and address.

basic customer service: See *primary customer service.*

basic item: See *basic stock.*

basic low stock: the predetermined level in inventory below which merchandise is not permitted to drop.

basic stock: merchandise that is in constant demand, thus requiring perpetual inventory throughout the year. See *assortment plan.* Cf. *model stock.*

basic stock list: a method for developing an assortment plan, the basic stock list contains staple goods and is more specific than the model stock plan that is used for evolving assortment plans. Usually included on this list is the name of the item, brand identification, physical description, cost and retail price, and other data that precisely identifies the items. See *assortment plan; model stock plan.*

basic stock method of inventory: a planning method where the value of beginning of month stock can be determined. Used as a tool for planning basic monthly stocks of merchandise.

basing point pricing:

(1) a geographic pricing policy in which the seller designates one or more geographic locations from which the rate that a buyer will be charged is calculated.

(2) to be avoided in the promotion of goods and services, an approach used by an industry whose goal is for all sellers to charge identical prices. The basing point is frequently the location of a plant near the buyer. Such pricing has been declared to be price discrimination in violation of the Clayton Antitrust Act.

battleground map: a map used by the retailer to indicate the geographic location of the flagship and branch stores. Usually includes markings for competitor operations.

battle of the brands: the competitiveness between national brands and private brands in an attempt to split up the market. See *brand.*

BBB: See *Better Business Bureau.*

beat last year's figures: an effort or campaign purporting to exceed the sales figures for the corresponding period one year earlier.

bedding: as defined by the National Association of Bedding Manufacturers; includes mattresses, conventional innerspring bedding, waterbeds, foundations, convertibles, and flotation.

before-after tests: in retail advertising, consumer response to a product measured prior to and following the product being advertised.

beliefs: how consumers feel or think about a product or service that will influence their behavior in making a purchase. Altering beliefs can be a major challenge in promoting a product or service.

bell cow: (slang) a frequently purchased item whose selling price far exceeds its manufacturing cost; a very profitable item. Synonymous with *blue chip.*

bellwether department: in a departmentalized store, effectively presents the store's fashion image or may in other ways establish the nature of the store as perceived by the customer.

belly-to-belly selling: a form of selling where the salesperson confronts the prospect or customer. Synonymous with *nose-to-nose selling.*

below par: at a discount; less than face amount.

below the market strategy: pricing by the retailer according to a plan of offering items below usual levels. See *discount house.*

benchmarking: when a retailer goes to another company's operation, probably a noncompetitive area, and learns by example.

benefit:

(1) *general:* a gain or advantage received by an individual.

(2) *retailing:* that which fulfills a customer's need.

benefit strategy: a method of salespeople in the opening minutes of contact with a prospect. The salesperson attempts to focus on the rewards and benefits of the product. The benefit is usually specific and concrete, such as the savings of money.

best buy: an item of high quality that is also competitively priced in relation to other retailers. A lower than normal markup can be taken in order to achieve an advantage in price.

best seller: merchandise that consistently sells quickly through a season or year at full price. See *key items.*

best selling price lines: lines of items, usually few in number, that yield a large proportion of sales.

Better Business Bureau (BBB): a voluntary agency of business executives created to improve business practices and to define fair standards and ethics in the conduct of business activity. Today, there are in excess of 150 local Better Business Bureaus in the United States.

better offer complaint: a customer's complaint who has found a special offer of a lower price that he or she already paid for the same item or service. Many retailers honor this complaint with a refund or store credit, although they are not legally required to do so. Offer of a lower price that he or she already paid for the same item or service. Many retailers honor this complaint with a refund or store credit, although they are not legally required to do so.

bid: See *bidding.*

bidding:
(1) the offering of money as an exchange for an item or service put up for sale.
(2) the making of an offer of price and other details as solicited by a prospective purchaser wishing to, or is required by law to, get competitive offers prior to placing an offer. Synonymous with *competitive bidding.*

bid pricing: when a supplier fixes the price for items or services to be provided which covers all the costs incurred and make a predetermined contribution to profit.

big pencil: applied to purchasers representing large stores who write large orders. Here the purchase is said to have a big pencil.

big ticket items: merchandise that is large in size and high in price (furniture, appliances, etc.).

big ticket selling: Synonymous with *megaselling.*

bill: See *invoice; statement.*

billed cost: the actual price of merchandise as it appears on the seller's invoice; reflects deductions that are made for trade discounts.

billing: the process of submitting invoices or bills.

billing record: See *purchase journal.*

bill me order: Synonymous with *credit order.*

bill of sale: a contract for the sale of goods.

bill to—ship to: instructions to have the invoice sent to a different address than given for the merchandise.

bird dog: (slang) an individual who is paid to obtain business for a high-power salesperson. Cf. *airedale.*

birthday sale: Synonymous with *anniversary sale.*

black market:
(1) *general:* buying or selling products or engaging in the exchange of foreign currencies in violation of government restrictions.
(2) *merchandising:* a situation when goods are priced a high level when scarce or unavailable from normal market channels.

blank-check buying: the practice of a retailer placing an open order with a supplier, with requests to be made throughout the season as needed.

blanket brand: See *private brand.*

blanket order: a preseason order to meet expected buyer demand. See *blanket pricing agreement; systems contracting.* Synonymous with *yearly order.*

blanket pricing agreement: a purchasing agreement where the purchaser's or-

ders or anticipated time-period requirements are placed in advance, the seller
agrees to make shipments as requested
at the contract price throughout the contract's duration. See *blanket order.* Cf.
incremental pricing agreement.

blind check: goods that are received and
checked in by a person who does not
have a copy of the shipper's invoice to
compare with the actual goods on hand.
The checker cannot be influenced by
what he or she expects to find in the
shipment. See *direct check.*

blind goods: unusual items that can
carry a higher-than-normal margin because of unique and only occasionally
appeals to customers who are more interested in filling their requirements
than they are in the price.

blind items: See *blind goods.*

blind products: See *blind goods.*

blind selling: (slang) selling merchandise
without the customer having a chance to
examine the item prior to purchase.

blister package: a type of plastic packaging that permits visual inspection of the
merchandise. Synonymous with *bubble
wrap.*

blue chip: Synonymous with *bell cow.*

bluefingers:
(1) *general:* used when in planning
strategies; people from one family who
attain common goals with efficiency
and team spirit; for example, relatives
who successfully pursue their objectives while receiving pleasure from
their togetherness.
(2) *retailing:* friends who spend considerable shopping time together and
because of common interests and attitudes, purchase similar styles and items
in a particular price range.
(3) Synonymous with *jebble.*

blue law: any state or local law restricting
business activity on Sunday. Blue laws
have been contested as an infringement
of individual and free enterprise rights.

body fashions: See *intimate apparel.*

bogey: in retailing, a standard of performance, such as the volume of sales beyond which a bonus is given.

BOM: beginning of month.

bona fide sale: a transaction where the
seller behaves in good faith as far as the
terms of the sale are concerned. See *bad
faith.*

bonus: cash given in addition to regular
salary and commissions paid to workers
in recognition of special services performed. Other reasons for providing a
bonus include longevity, holidays, etc.

bonus goods: merchandise given without extra charge by a manufacturer to a
retailer who agrees to purchase a minimum quantity of units in a special
deal.

bonus plan: used by continuity marketers
to solicit multiple purchases, for example, the Book of the Month Club, gives
one free book for every three books
bought. Shipping and handling fees are
charged even on the free item.

booking:
(1) orders for merchandise accepted
on hand as at a given time.
(2) accepting an order for goods to be
transported.

book inventory: Synonymous with *perpetual inventory.*

book method of inventory: See *book inventory.*

book value: the original cost of goods
minus the amount of accumulated depreciation, amortization or depletion.

boomerang: a technique for dealing with
objections, where the salesperson uses
the prospect's statement of reasons for
not buying as the basis of the precise
reason for purchasing. Synonymous with
conversion process; positive conversion.

booster: (slang) a shoplifter.

booster box: (slang) a boxlike package
containing a spring-held side panel
through which stolen goods can pass.

bootlegger: a seller of illegal items, such as untaxed cigarettes.

borax: (slang) inexpensive items that are usually poorly designed and constructed.

border tax adjustment: a rebate of sales, value-added, or other indirect taxes paid on merchandise prior to export.

borrow: to receive something from another, with the understanding that the item is to be returned.

bottom-up technique:

(1) *general:* an approach to strategy making whereby the lower levels of the organization push ideas to the top and strategy is then made.

(2) *retailing:* a budget technique where the budgeter begins with an estimate of the spending needed to supply each classification, finally arriving at a total for the department, and eventually for the company. See *top down method.*

boutique: a shop or part of a store that specializes in merchandise that is new and different. Cf. *salon.*

boutique merchandising: a store where related items from a number of departments are gathered together in one store to fulfill special customer requirements.

box store: See *warehouse store.*

boycott: an attempt to prevent the carrying on of a business by urging people not to buy from the firm or store being boycotted; frequently used on the international scene for political or economic reasons; illustrated by appeals, threats, and so on, to secure redress of a grievance.

Boys' and Young Men's Apparel Manufacturers Association (BAMA): headquartered in New York City, an association of manufacturers of boys' clothing and accessories. BAMA holds semi-annual trade shows in New York City and Los Angeles.

branch house: a location away from headquarters that is maintained by a manufacturer and used almost exclusively for purposes of stocking, selling, shipping, and servicing the company's merchandise.

branch office: an office or department of a company at a location away from headquarters. It is a part of the company and not a separate legal entity, as is a subsidiary, an affiliate, or a joint venture.

branch store: a store owned by a parent store. Usually the parent store is located in the center of the city, with branch stores located in suburban areas of the city or other cities. Cf. *regional store.*

branch store manager: the executive responsible for the operation of a retailer's branch store.

brand: a name, sign, or symbol used to identify items or services of the seller(s) and to differentiate them from goods of competitors. A brand aids consumers in differentiating between items of different manufacturers. Cf. *trademark.* See *battle of the brands; manufacturer's brand.*

brand category: a general classification of products and services. Competing items and services that are similar in nature, all are defined within the same brand category.

brand choice: selecting a particular brand of item from the variety of available brands with similar purpose and content.

brand competitor: an organization that competes with others to satisfy consumers' demand for a specific product.

brand development: a means of determining the penetration of an item's sales, traditionally per thousand population. See *brand development index.*

brand development index: the percentage of a brand's sales in an area based on population in that location as contrasted with the sales throughout the country, related to the total U.S. population. See *brand development.*

brand extension: the competitive strategy involving the application of a market-accepted brand to other firm's products provided that doing so will not confuse present customers or detract from the original image of product or brand; traditionally targeted to a particular segment within the parent brand's general market. Cf. *line extension.*

brand familiarity: the customer's ability to recognize and accept a particular brand of products. Brand familiarity can be separated into brand rejection, brand nonrecognition, brand recognition, brand preference, and brand insistence.

brand franchise:

(1) consumer loyalty toward a particular brand. See *brand loyalty.*

(2) an agreement between the wholesaler or retailer and a brand name manufacturer giving the former an exclusive right to sell the brand manufacturer's item in a carefully defined location. Permits the wholesaler or retailer to sell the item in a noncompetitive market and set price limitations as the traffic will permit.

branding: the assignment of a brand name to an item or service, thus achieving product differentiation within the marketplace. See *generic brands.*

brand insistence: the extreme of brand loyalty, where the consumer says he or she will accept no substitute item.

brand label: a label that indicates little more than the brand name of the item, the manufacturer, and other information fulfilling requirements of the law.

brand leader: an item that is considered best in its field or that is marketed with that assumption.

brand loyalty: the strength of a buyer's preference for a particular brand, which

suggests a refusal to purchase a substitute. Brand loyalty is usually measured in terms of repeat sales and is also reflected in purchases of other items produced by the same company.

brand manager: Synonymous with *product manager.*

brand mark: that part of a brand identification that can be recognized, but not verbalized.

brand nonrecognition: the inability of a customer to recognize a brand, even should he or she be able to recognize the product.

brand preference: when the consumer chooses a particular brand over its competitors, usually resulting from a favorable experience with the item. However, if the product proves to be unavailable, the consumer willingly shifts to a substitute.

brand proliferation: the expansion of similar products within a specific line.

brand recognition: the perception by buyers, when confronted with a product, that they have been exposed to that brand name previously.

brand share: Synonymous with *market share; share of the market.*

brand strategy: plans and tactics relating to the use of brand names.

brand switching: when a consumer selects a product or service different from that purchased previously.

brand-switching model: a model that provides a manager with some idea of the behavior of consumers in terms of their loyalty and the likelihood that they will switch from one brand to another.

bread-and-butter assortments: items that have repeat customer demand and therefore is never permitted to fall out of stock. Synonymous with *checklist; staple stock list.* See *never-outs.*

breadth of assortment: See *assortment breadth.*

breadth of merchandising offering: See *assortment breadth.*

break-down method: an approach to salesforce design in which the size of the salesforce is determined by dividing the forecasted annual sales volume by the expected sales volume per salesperson.

break-even model: a model that shows the basic relationships among units produced (output), dollars of sales revenue, and the levels of costs and profits for an entire firm or a product line.

break-even pricing:
(1) pricing at a level that will enable a firm to break even.
(2) an approach to pricing in which the price of a unit of the product is set high enough to cover the variable costs of producing that unit as well as the fixed costs of producing the product.

breaking bulk: splitting a large inventory of items into smaller quantities as the items move toward its target consumers.

bridal registry: in a store, the service or bureau where the bride registers her choice of flatware, china patterns, and other gift preferences so that wedding gifts will not be duplicated.

bridge jewelry department: the department handling items that lie between fine and costume jewelry as measured by the price of the items.

brochure: in merchandising, a booklet that is printed on quality paper and features copy of the manufacturer's product, service, etc.

broken case-lot selling: a wholesaler's activity of selling fewer than full case lots of items in an effort to accommodate retailers.

broken sized lots: an assortment from which some sizes are not to be found.

broker:
(1) *general:* a person who prepares contracts with third parties, as with a freight broker and customs broker, on behalf of a principal.
(2) *merchandising:* a wholesaling intermediary whose primary function is to supply market information and establish contacts in order to facilitate sales for clients.

brood hen-and-chick method: where branch retail stores are looked upon as part of chains, but with tighter merchandising controls. Cf. *brood hen concept.*

brood hen concept: When the retail buyers at the parent store maintains close communications with his or her branches, receiving requests for items and responds at the buyer's discretion. Cf. *brood hen-and-chick method.*

brown goods: what retailers often call television sets and radios. Cf. *orange goods; red goods; white goods; yellow goods.*

BSNA: See *Bureau of Salesmen's National Associations.*

BTA: best times available.

bubble wrap: Synonymous with *blister package.*

budget-book sale: where the customer contracts for a specific amount to be paid back on a regular basis with a small carrying charge. A book with coupons is used as cash within the store.

budgeting: the process of determining and assigning the resources required to reach market and retailing objectives.

budget store: See *basement store.*

buffer stock: Synonymous with *reserve stock.*

build-up method: a method for arriving at national forecasts for individual regions and then aggregating the regional forecasts.

build-up method of space allocation: planning space requirements for departments found in retail stores. It takes into account factors such as volume of sales, quantities on display and in reserve, etc.

built-in sale: a retail store sale held every year; usually involves the same classifications of goods.

bulk checking: checking arriving goods as against invoices without having to open cartons to verify its contents.

bulk delivery: See *bulk merchandise delivery.*

bulk discount: a reduced charge for quantity or multiple purchases. See *discount.* Synonymous with *volume discount.*

bulk freight: unpacked goods such as coal.

bulk mail: second, third, and fourth class mail, including parcel post, ordinary papers, and circulars; increasingly used by retailers. See *bulk merchandise delivery.*

bulk marking: when the price is indicated on large lots in original shipping containers. Single pieces are marked with the retail price sometime in the future.

bulk merchandise delivery: in retailing, the delivery of large items. Such delivery usually requires more than one person, which are beyond the capability of parcel delivery services. See *bulk mail.*

bulk warehouse: See *warehouse, bulk.*

bundled pricing: an offering of a basic product, options, and customer service for one total price.

burden: Synonymous with *overhead.*

Bureau of Salesmen's National Associations (BSNA): the association of wholesale salespersons of women's, men's and children's apparel, accessories, shoes, toys, and related merchandise.

Bureau of Wholesale Sales Representatives (BWSR): based in Atlanta, Georgia, the association of wholesale sales representatives of apparel, accessories, and western wear.

busheling: tailoring and resewing of men's garments following the purchase and fitting of the item.

business associated site: See *business associated stores.*

business associated stores: stores that are associated with each other because of physical closeness.

business cycle: frequently considered during an advertising campaign, any interval embracing alternating periods of economic prosperity and depression.

business domain: that sector of a market which a company targets as its business environment; often defined in terms of a line of products.

business ethics: applied in the preparation of commercials, socially accepted rules of behavior that place pressure on business executives to maintain a high sense of values and to be honest and fair in their dealings with the public.

buy at best: to bid higher and higher prices without any limit until the required quantity is bought.

buy-back agreement: a provision in a sales contract stating that the seller will repurchase items within a specified time period, usually for the selling price, if the purchaser is transferred from the area. Synonymous with *product buy-back agreement.*

buyer:
(1) *general:* an individual who acquires goods for purposes of making a profit, usually as the result of a resale.
(2) *retailing:* an executive responsible for purchasing merchandise to be sold in a store.

buyer behavior: See *consumer behavior.*

buyer's black book: the retail buyer's unit control book.

buyer-seller dyad: the rapport developed between the customer and the salesperson, often based on close and detailed communication.

buyer's market: an economic situation where supplies of items far exceed demand, which favor the retail buyer rather than the manufacturer. Synonymous with *loose market*.

buyer's order: the order blank used by a retail buyer to buy items from a vendor.

buyer's over: when there are more buyers than sellers.

buyer's surplus: the difference between what a buyer pays for an item and the amount more he or she would be willing to pay for it.

buying: in retailing, the purchase of merchandise at the wholesale level for future resale at the retail level. See *procurement*.

buying allowance: a lowering of price on given items offered by a producer to a purchaser as an incentive to buy the goods.

buying by description: the purchase from a verbal and/or visual presentation of the item. Usually, to be satisfactory, the customer has strong feelings of confidence in the business under consideration.

buying by inspection: buying following the examination of the actual items to be purchased.

buying by sample: buying following the examination of a representative sample or portion of the item.

buying by specification: a store submitting specific requests for delivery rather than purchasing standard merchandise available from the manufacturer.

buying calendar: a retail buyer's schedule of merchandising activities over six months or some other period; includes particular promotions and other seasonal events.

buying close to the vest: the practice of purchasing a little at a time and attempting to minimize money outlays.

buying club: an association of retailers, traditionally in the same geographic area, who purchase goods as a single unit to achieve a price advantage.

buying committee: a group of buyers, often chain stores, who decide by committee on the items that will and will not be purchased.

buying criteria: the requirements of a firm evaluating suppliers of a product or service.

buying direct: the purchase of goods from the manufacturer, bypassing any middleperson.

buying error: the failure to match purchases with demand; often leading to a markdown so as to move the merchandise out of the store. Cf. *selling error*.

buying group: noncompeting stores organized to purchase goods.

buying hours: identified store hours when customers will interact with salespeople.

buying incentive: a premium of additional items, a discount, or gift, available to prospects should they purchase an item or service.

buying intent: the measurement of a prospect's intention to buy an item or service.

buying into trends: retail purchasing where an attempt is made to project future trends in fashion early enough so that items can be ordered in time to take advantage of the trend.

buying judgment: a customer's ability to properly choose the correct item for his or her customers.

buying loader: a manufacturer's gift, either a discount, premium, etc., to a retailer as a bonus for buying the manufacturer's item. See *dealer loader*.

buying office: composed of buyers in national or international market centers who daily shop the market so as to offer their member stores information and to choose and purchase items for them. They are either independent (salaried office or commission buying office) or store-owned (private office, cooperative office, and corporate office).

buying off the peg: the purchase of ready-to-wear merchandise, to be taken home or delivered immediately thus involving no adjustments or alterations.

buying on consignment: See *consignment.*

buying period: the total of the review period and the delivery period. The review period is the time it takes to determine whether the order should be placed; the delivery period is elapsed time before goods arrive.

buying plan: the kind and quantity of goods that a buyer expects to purchase for a department over a specific time period.

buying power: See *purchasing power.*

buying quota: planned money expenditure for goods.

buying role: a customer's behavior pattern shown while buying a specific kind of goods.

buying trip: the retail buyer's visit to the market for the exclusive objective of choosing and buying items.

buying with return privileges: goods that are bought from a vendor with the understanding that some of them can be returned for credit should they not be sold.

buy national: a growing appeal to restrain imports from other nations, especially when public procurement practices are at stake. The concept resists the international sales of goods and services because each competing country claims that the other nation(s) discriminates against foreign competition.

BWSR: See *Bureau of Wholesale Sales Representatives.*

C and F: See *cost and freight.*

cable system: a now obsolete means for handling sales transactions with a carrier running along a wire from the selling department to the cashier's desk or credit authorizer.

cable television ordering system: a technique permitting cable television viewers to find, choose and order items seen at home on their television sets.

CAD: See *cash against documents.*

CAF: See *cost and freight.*

CAI: See *Career Apparel Institute.*

callback: the technique used by a sales representative on a second or subsequent effort to induce a potential customer to buy. Cf. *user calls.*

call bird: to increase store traffic, incorporating lower prices on items not usually bought in large quantities that are shown in windows or advertisements of the retailer.

call credit: credit given for the price of an item when merchandise is picked up from a customer and returned to the store.

call frequency: the number of times that a sales representative contacts a potential or real customer throughout the year.

call planning: a telephone sales planning method used by salespeople; involves defining the goal of the call and devising a selling strategy.

call report: a salesperson's record for his or her supervisor identifying calls made to potential or real customers during a stated time period and/or within a specified market. Tells when a meeting occurred, and what was talked about. Synonymous with *conference report; contact report.*

call slip: See *want slip.*

call station: an area at which a pickup and delivery service is available, although there are no warehouse facilities.

call system: in retailing, when the salesperson receives compensation based at least in some aspects on the amount of business he or she finishes.

call tag: informing a delivery driver to pick up an article or parcel at a customer's address and then, once his or her route is completed, return it to the store.

CAM: See *common area maintenance.*

campaign plan: consecutive mailings, to stimulate interest in a forthcoming event, such as the opening of a new branch. Synonymous with *teaser plan.*

canalization: a sales method that builds on the anxieties and associations of a customer to bring about a dramatic shift in behavior.

cancel: a customer's request to cancel an order or stop service. Synonymous with *kill.* See *cancellation.*

cancellation:
(1) a retraction of an order for goods sent from the buyer to a vendor.
(2) surplus items sold by retailers to discount houses, often in broken lots.

cancellation notice: a form for notifying the vendor that the purchaser will not accept the ordered goods that have not as yet been received.

cancellation of markdown: See *markdown cancellation.*

cancellation shoes: out-of-style, or somewhat damaged, shoes.

canned presentation: a prewritten and usually memorized presentation by a sales representative, recited sentence for sentence, with little or no deviation.

canned sales presentation: See *canned presentation.*

cannibalization: See *cannibalizing the market.*

cannibalizing the market: the result of introducing a new product that, instead of creating greater sales, cuts into existing sales of the item it is intended to replace. Cf. *enhancement.*

canvass:
(1) *general:* to count or examine.
(2) *retailing:* to call on prospective customers in person or by telephone to sell merchandise or services, to determine interest, or to gather information. Cf. *cold canvassing.* See *preapproach.* Synonymous with *territory screening.*

canvasser: a salesperson who tries to obtain orders for goods by going from house-to-house or with telephone calls.

capability survey: in purchasing, inspecting a prospective vendor's operation to secure answers to issues dealing with quality control, capacity to finance and manage, quality of technology, etc.

capacity:
(1) *general:* one of the three elements of credit.
(2) *merchandising:* the volume of space within a container or other space, expressed in units.

capital:
(1) the amount invested in a venture.
(2) a long-term debt plus owners' equity.
(3) the net assets of a retailer, partnership, and the like, including the original investment, all gains and profits.

capital account:
(1) an account maintained in the name of the owner or owners of a retail business and indicating the equity in that business usually at the close of the last accounting period.
(2) balance of payment items not included in a current account.

capital consumption allowance: See *depreciation.*

capital goods: items ordinarily treated as long-term investment (capitalized) because of substantial value and life (e.g., industrial machinery). Synonymous with *durable merchandise; hard goods.* Cf. *soft goods.*

capital intensive:
(1) characterized by the need to utilize additional capital to increase productivity or profits.
(2) processes that require a high concentration of capital relative to labor per unit of output and products produced by such processes.

capitalize:
(1) to include in an investment account expenditures for purchase or construction of property.
(2) to divide income by a rate of interest to obtain principal.

capital turnover: a financial ratio used for measuring the number of times the cost of the average inventory investment is converted into sales during a given period.

capital turnover =

$$\frac{\text{dollar retail sales during}}{\text{average inventory dollar value at cost}}$$

captive market: purchasers who have little latitude in choosing the vendor of a product or service. Consumers purchase these items available through vendors in a particular location.

captive product pricing: a pricing technique of product manufacturers who require supplies, accessories, or additional devices for operation. The major product is moderately priced to attract customers while the supplies are given significant markups, i.e., camera film prices are kept low, while processing prices are high.

captive warehouse: See *warehouse, private.*

carbon-copy concept: a theory that the training of new salespeople is best carried out by their emulating and memorizing the methods of proven salespeople.

care label: a tag secured to merchandise describing the care needed by the item. For example, with apparel, this represents washing, ironing, and/or dry cleaning instructions.

career apparel:
(1) apparel suitable to wear at an executive position.
(2) distinctive clothing and accessories made to the specifications of an employer in order that workers will be uniform in their dress for a given position.

Career Apparel Institute (CAI): based in New York City, an association of suppliers, manufacturers, and retailers of career apparel and uniforms. Affiliated with the National Association of Uniform Manufacturers and Distributors; offers an annual Image of the Year award, conducts public relations activities, and compiles industry data.

cargo: freight hauled by ship, airline, truck, etc.

carload (CL): items that fill a freight car, or the equivalent minimum weight of that merchandise that qualifies as a full car in railroad shipping rates.

carload freight rate: a lower shipping rate provided for large shipments of goods resulting from the economies of a large shipment over a partial shipment.

carriage trade: the class of rich customers who expected and received superior services for their willingness to pay higher prices for merchandise and services; a historic term, rarely used today.

carrier: an individual or organization, usually without a permit of public franchise, that is engaged in transporting products or people.

carrying charge: in merchandising, a charge added to the price of merchandise to compensate for deferred payment.

carrying cost: an expense for the storing of inventory from the time of purchase until the time of sale or use; includes inventory devaluation during storage, storage charges, and interest charges on funds tied up in inventory.

carryouts: items bought in a store that are not shipped, but are taken from the store by the customer. Synonymous with *take-withs.*

carryover merchandise: unsold items remaining from an earlier selling season that are retained for a future sale.

cartage: the charge for pickup and delivery of a shipment.

case: a container used for goods sold at wholesale rates, e.g., a case of canned tuna.

case allowance: the discount that a wholesaler or manufacturer gives to a retailer when items are bought by the case. Usually, the larger the number of cases bought, the greater the discount.

case goods: furniture, traditionally constructed of wood and frequently not upholstered, such as chests of drawers, book-cases.

case wrap around: a sales promotion item created to be placed around the case of merchandise.

cash acknowledgment: a notice sent to a cash buyer mentioning the receipt of an order. Often, cash acknowledgments are accompanied with new information about merchandise and prices, substitutes for out-of-stock items. Used primarily when a delivery is delayed.

cash against documents (CAD): the payment for goods on presentation of documents evidencing shipments.

cash-and-carry store: a retail store that sells goods for cash only; rarely makes deliveries.

cash-and-carry wholesaler: a wholesaler who demands that the buyer must pay when he or she picks up merchandise, without credit, or the wholesaler will not make delivery. Cash-and-carry wholesalers frequently deal in fast-moving (e.g., perishable) items, such as bakery goods. See *truck jobber.*

cash before delivery (CBD): a requirement to pay prior to delivery of goods. Synonymous with *cash in advance.*

cash budget: a schedule of expected cash receipts and disbursements.

cash buyer: a customer who pays by forwarding cash, check, or money order, with his or her order.

cash cancellation: canceling a cash order; requiring a refund. Traditionally such cancellations occur because of customer dissatisfaction with the item or service.

cash card: a card given by a retailer or store owner to a customer to guarantee a discount for cash payment. It is a substitute for credit cards.

cash cow: products that enjoy comfortable profits and whose excess earnings are used (milked) to support other divisions, or weaker selling products.

cash dating: See *cash on delivery; cash with order; sight draft/bill of lading.*

cash discount: a percentage deduction from the selling price permitted by the seller for merchandise sold on credit, to encourage prompt payment of the invoice covering the goods or services purchased. Synonymous with *sales discount.*

cash flow: the reported net income of a retailer, plus amounts charged off for depreciation, depletion, amortization, and extraordinary charges to reserves, which are bookkeeping deductions and are not actually paid out in cash. Knowledge of these factors results in a better understanding of a firm's ability to pay dividends.

cashier: the employee whose task it is to collect and record customers' payments.

cashier method: where customers take their selections to a cashier for payment, and possibly for wrapping.

cashier wrapper: the employee whose task it is to wrap merchandise at a given point and receive cash payment for that item.

cash in advance: Synonymous with *cash before delivery.*

cash incentive: any promotional method to encourage customers to pay when they order in return for a free-complementary gift. The gift usually is less expensive than the cost of sending another bill and waiting for payment.

cash on delivery (COD): any purchase made with the expectation that the item(s) will be paid for on delivery. Synonymous with *collection on delivery.*

cash order: an order accompanied by the required payment. See *cash buyer; cash with order; credit order.*

cash receipts report: a form used by salespeople to record money received from cash sales of goods at the end of every business day.

cash refund offer: a rebate offered by the manufacturer of an item to the customer. Once merchandise is bought, the manufacturer returns a portion of the purchase price in exchange for a label or other proof that a purchase has been made. Cash refunds are used for low-cost packaged items as well as for expensive goods such as cars or refrigerators.

cash-register: See *register.*

cash-register bank: an assortment of change made at the close of the day by the salesperson operating the register or by a cashier for use at the start of the following business day.

cash-register tape redemption plan: Synonymous with *tape plan.*

cash sale: the surrender of cash at the time of sale. See *cash-send; cash-take.*

cash-send: a cash sale where the buyer chooses to have the merchandise delivered.

cash-take: a cash sale where the buyer chooses to take the merchandise away at the time of purchase.

cash terms: an agreement to pay cash for bought items, often within a given time period.

cash with order (CWO): payment for goods in which the buyer pays when ordering and in which the transaction is binding on both parties. See *cash order.*

catalog(ue): printed material that identifies items for sale. In most cases, the merchandise is described and prices are given; often, a photograph or drawing accompanies an entry. See *catalog house.*

catalog appliance showrooms: retail outlets that show sample appliances for customers' inspection alongside catalogs listing prices. Orders can be filled from an adjoining stockroom and prices are generally below list price.

catalog buyer: a person who makes a purchase from a particular catalog.

catalog buying: the practice, used by chain store executives, of selecting and ordering merchandise from catalogs provided by a buying office.

catalog house: a person whose business is based primarily on orders deriving from catalogs and mail order solicitation for orders from retailers. Catalog houses presently supply only a very small percentage of the items sold by stores. Synonymous with *mail-order wholesaler.*

catalog merchandising: the promotion of items for sale in a catalog.

catalog plan: Synonymous with *price agreement plan.*

catalog retailing: selling where the retailer provides the consumer with a catalog of goods and the potential buyer submits his or her order by mail, telephone, or in person in a facility maintained by the store.

catalog showroom: a discount store at which customers review catalogs and then place orders and wait for delivery.

catalog wholesaler: See *catalog house.*

category-killer: a retailer who so dominates its retail category both in terms of profitability and growth of market shares. Synonymous with *cult merchant.*

caution fee: an entrance payment required by designer houses from commercial customers during showings. Intended to deter copying, the fee is usually applied to purchases made.

caveat emptor: Latin expression meaning "let the buyer beware." When merchandise is sold without a warranty by the vendor, the purchaser takes the risk of loss due to defects. See *warranty; without recourse.* Cf. *caveat subscriptor.*

caveat subscriptor **(venditor):** Latin expression meaning "let the seller beware." Unless the seller states no responsibility, he or she is liable to the purchaser for any alterations from the written contract. Cf. *caveat emptor.*

caveat venditor: See *caveat subscriptor.*

CBD: See *cash before delivery.*

ceiling price: a maximum price at which merchandise can be sold as established by law.

Center for Retailing Education and Research: founded in 1986 at the University of Florida; purports to attract the best college students to careers in retailing and to prepare them for entry level management trainee positions; and to facilitate research on retailing problems. The Center also places more than 100 undergraduates in internships with retailers and publishes a quarterly newsletter. centers of influence: people of high social or business standing through whom a salesperson seeks to find qualified buyers. Centers of influence are people who exert power or authority over others, for example, bankers, lawyers.

central business district: the area of a city or town that contains a high concentration of retail businesses, offices, theaters, etc., and high traffic flow; the original retailing center of business activity.

central buyer: the person responsible for choosing and purchasing merchandise for a group of similar departments or merchandise classifications in chain stores or branches of a department store.

central buying: a popular approach in chain stores whereby all purchasing is done through a central or main office. Shipments of merchandise, however, are usually made directly to the branch stores of the chain.

central buying office: a purchasing office that serves a chain store operation that has the final responsibility for choosing and buying the merchandise to be sold in these stores. Cf. *corporate buying office.*

centralized adjustment system: a separate office or department, staffed by trained personnel, in which all customer complaints, adjustments, or refunds are handled rather than in the selling department.

centralized buying: See *central buying.*

centralized organization: the concentration of the decision-making authority and activities in the headquarters or flagship store.

centralized purchasing: a system by which a department or unit is authorized to procure, handle, or store all supplies, materials, and equipment required by some or all of the other departments or units of a company.

centralized sales organization: an organization possessing the overall sales function that is concentrated at the highest levels of management.

central market:

(1) the geographical area with a significant concentration of suppliers, where both buyers and sellers can meet to interact more efficiently.

(2) the location where a large number of the major suppliers or manufacturers of a given item or service may be found.

central merchandise plan: purchasing method found in multi-unit organizations where the purchasing functions are controlled by a central authority that selects the items, determines prices, and supervises distribution to the various stores.

central place: a cluster of retail shops serving as a source of merchandise and services for an area larger than itself.

central warehousing and requisition: See *warehouse and requisition plan.*

central wrap: an area where the store's wrapping and packaging services are localized. See *package wrap.*

centralized adjustment system: a separate office, staffed by trained person-

nel, where all customer complaints, refunds, adjustments, etc. are handled
(instead of being handled in the selling
department.)

centralized buying: See *central buying.*

centralized organization: placing the
decision-making authority and activities in the headquarters or flagship
store.

cents-off coupon: a coupon that entitles
the holder to a discount on merchandise
at the time of purchase. The coupon is
received by the retailer from the buyer,
who submits it to the manufacturer,
wholesaler, or a clearing house. As
many at 150 billion coupons are distributed each year in the United States. See
coupon.

CEO: See *chief executive officer.*

certificate: any written or printed document of truth that can be used as proof
of a fact.

certificate of inspection: a document
certifying that merchandise (such as
perishable goods) was in good condition immediately prior to shipment.

certificate of manufacture: of importance retail importers; a statement
signed by an exporter that goods ordered
by the importer have been finished and
set aside for shipment. This document is
used with a letter of credit for the benefit of the exporter.

certificate of origin: of importance to
retail importers; a certificate declaring
that goods purchased from a foreign
country have indeed been produced in
that country and not in another. Under
most trade accords, traders are required
to submit duly completed certificates
of origin to their international counterparts to claim full or partial exemption
from customs duties.

certification: an administrative task that
awards a product a certificate if it satisfies special tests.

CEW: See *Cosmetic Executive Women.*

CFDA: See *Council of Fashion Designers
of America.*

chain: See *chain store system.*

chain buying office: See *corporate buying office.*

chain discount: a series of discounts
based on an earlier discount for the
same item, i.e., a chain discount of 40%,
5%, and 5% is the same as one discount
of 45.85%, from the list price of the
item. See *series discount.*

chain markup pricing: a form of demand-based pricing in which the final
selling price is determined, markups for
each channel member are examined, and
the maximum acceptable costs to each
member are computed.

chain organization: See *chain store
system.*

chain-owned buying office: See *corporate buying office.*

chain prospecting: prospecting by the
salesperson who wants the names of one
or more prospects from each prospects
that has been approached. Cf. *endless
chain.*

chain ratio method: a method of sales
forecasting in which a firm starts with
general market information and then
computes a series of more specific information. These combined data yield
a sales forecast.

chain store:
(1) two or more stores, usually in different locations, being operated by the
same organization.
(2) a retail organization that consists of
two or more units under a single ownership. See *chain store system.*

chain store law: Synonymous with *the
Robinson-Patman Act of 1936.*

chain store system (CSS):
(1) stores, usually a dozen or more,
commonly owned and managed with
merchandise centrally purchased.
(2) large mass merchandising organizations; Franchise chains, specialty

chains, i.e., Sears, Lerner Shops. Cf. *voluntary chain*. See *chain store*.

chain store warehouse: an operation of a chain store system for the collection and distribution of merchandise and for the performance of other wholesale functions for the stores of a multi-unit organization.

channel captain:
(1) a channel member who is able to influence the behavior of the other members of the channel. See *channel members*.
(2) the manufacturer, retailer, or wholesaler who dominates and controls a channel of distribution, usually setting distribution policy that others follow.

channel change: the relationship between channel of distribution members in conflict.

channel fit: the degree to which a newly introduced item can be distributed through a channel of distribution already in use by the manufacturer of the new product.

channel leader: a channel member who dominates the market and may influence or control decisions.

channel members: those participating in the distribution process.

channel of distribution:
(1) the interrelated network of people and firms for delivering goods from the manufacturer to the consumer. Intermediaries assist as merchant middlepeople who take title to goods and then resell it, and as agent middlepeople who do not take title to goods but serve as brokers.
(2) the route a product follows from an original grower, producer, or importer to the last consumer. Often a middleperson is used, e.g., automobile manufacturers sell to car dealers, who then sell to consumers. See *channel fit; distribution*. Synonymous with *market channel; marketing channel; trade channel*.

channel power: the influence of one member of a channel of distribution over another.

channel strategy: distribution of a product through selected channels. For example, a product can be sold directly to the buyer, with an agent or a wholesaler.

channel width: the different outlets or individual companies employed at each level of the channel of distribution, where selling through almost any wholesaler or retailer occurs in a given area.

charge: to purchase for credit without making an immediate payment; usually to pay following billing.

charge account: a means of making sales on credit to retail customers. Various types are:
(a) open (30-day)—an account in which the store accepts the customer's promise to pay for items bought, usually within 30 days of purchase.
(b) revolving—an account in which the store sets the maximum amount of money the customer may owe at any one time. The amount is determined at the time the account is opened and is based on individual income and credit rating.
(c) budget (flexible)—an account in which monthly installment payments are based on the size of the customer's account balance, and interest is charged on the unpaid amount.
(d) coupon credit plan—an account in which the customer is given credit coupons that may be used in the store as cash. Payment for the coupons is made over a period of time, usually six months. This plan eliminates the need for a monthly billing.

charge-a-plate: the copyrighted name of the small card; identifies a charge account customer; is used to imprint the sales check in a charge sale. No longer in use. See *charge plate*.

charge account: a consumer credit arrangement where the store customer is permitted to purchase merchandise or services and to pay for them within a specified period (often up to 90 days) without incurring interest or service charges. Synonymous with *open account.* See *installment credit; revolving credit.*

charge account credit: short-term extension of credit by a store to its customer. The credit is based on the assumption that the buyer will soon be able to meet purchase commitments out of current income. The purchaser is usually permitted 30 days before the bill becomes due and no interest or carrying charges are incurred during this time.

charge account plan: See *charge account credit.*

charge-authorizing phone: the telephone found at the point of sale, in the selling department, connecting the saleperson to the credit files unit; used only to verify the customer's ability to make a charge purchase. See *charge phone system.*

chargebacks: the retailer's invoice for claims against a vendor resulting from items such as damaged merchandise, cooperative advertising costs, adjustments, and the recovery of transportation charges for improperly routed merchandise. Includes nonreceipt of merchandise, unauthorized transaction, nonmatching number, warning bulletin, and duplicate processing. Chargebacks costs retailers nearly $5 billion annually.

charge buyer: a person who makes a purchase on credit to be billed at a later time. Synonymous with *credit buyer.* See *credit order.*

charge customer: a patron or consumer having credit privileges, usually in the form of a charge account.

charge phone system: where the salesperson has specific orders approved and authorized over the telephone. See *charge-authorizing phone.*

charge plate: used to imprint sales checks, this small card identifies a charge account customer by name, identification number, and signature. Originally was called charge-a-plate.

charge sale: a retail transaction where the amount of the purchase is added to a customer's account; usually it is payable at the end of the month or on a revolving basis.

charge-send sale: a transaction where the amount of the sale is charged to the customer's account and the items are sent to the customer.

charges forward: a system whereby the purchaser pays for merchandise and shipping charges only upon receipt of the goods or, following receipt of goods, when a bill arrives.

charge-take sale: a transaction where the amount of the sale is charged to a customer's account and the customer carries the goods with him or her.

charging what the traffic can bear: an expression suggesting that the seller asks the highest price that he or she believes the market will bear (people will pay).

cheap jack: (slang) an individual who sells merchandise rapidly by unorthodox approaches, including using unoccupied stores to set up his or her goods.

checker:
(1) the cashier who rings up a customer's purchases and takes payment.
(2) personnel who compare the merchandise received to the vendor's invoices.

checking: the process where the retailer examines a shipment from a vendor to be certain that the correct merchandise, in correct quantities and of satisfactory quality, has been received. The process includes matching the purchase order to the invoice, opening containers, sorting merchandise, and studying the quality and quantity of the received merchandise.

checklist: Synonymous with *bread-and-butter assortments.*

checkout: in retailing, a fast selling item.

checkout counter: the location where items bought are checked and paid for; frequently used for point-of-sale displays.

check question: in sales, a carefully phrased question that purports to elicit an answer from a potential customer to provide some clue as to the progress being made towards a buying decision.

checkstand: See *checkout counter.*

cherry picker: a piece of warehouse equipment for obtaining items from elevated locations, consisting of an elevator tower fastened to a truck.

cherry picking: buyer selection of only a few items from a vendor's line, rather than buying a complete line or classification of merchandise from any one source. Synonymous with *hi-spotting.*

chic: in the fashion industry, connotes elegance of style and manner as well as originality of appearance; French word meaning stylish.

chief executive officer (CEO): in retailing, the manager in a large retail organization who occupies the top position in the store or firm.

Childrenswear Manufacturers Association (CMA): a New York City-based association of manufacturers of children's apparel which serves as the liaison between the industry, the U.S. government, and retailers.

China eggs: (slang) people who at first appear to be good prospects to purchase an item or service, but who fail to become customers. Cf. *Chinese walls.*

Chinese walls: (slang) imaginary barriers or false walls between a store's departments. Salespeople, in an effort to avoid infringing on another's territory,

are reluctant to cross these invisible lines, such as assisting a customer who has already been serviced by another salesperson. Cf. *China eggs.*

chiseler:
(1) (slang) for a customer who makes an effort to take advantage of retailers in the hopes of securing a lower price.
(2) (slang) for a buyer who tries to force down a vendor's price on merchandise.

choice criteria: critical characteristics used by the store's purchaser when evaluating merchandise offered for sale.

CIA: cash in advance. See *cash before delivery.*

CIES: See *International Association of Chain Stores.*

CIF: See *cost, insurance, and freight.*

CIF pricing: the seller's price includes cost, insurance, and freight expended in getting the shipment to a specified overseas port.

circ: shortened form of *circular.*

circular:
(1) *general:* regular or small sheets of printed paper to be sent in the mail or delivered by hand.
(2) *retailing:* a store promotion printed on one sheet of paper and distributed by third-class mail or by hand. Often contains technical and mechanical information that is important to the consumer. Often shortened to *circ.* Cf. *flier.*

circulation: in retailing, the number of copies of a store's publication that are distributed. Advertising rates for publications are traditionally based on circulation figures.

CL: See *carload.*

claim:
(1) *general:* charges for damages incurred while merchandise is in the possession of a carrier.
(2) *retailing:* a retailer's charge against a vendor.

claim against a carrier: See *claim.*

claims-paid complaint: a customer complaint dealing with a bill, after the payment for the merchandise or service has been sent to the seller.

class-action suit: a law suit filed on behalf of many affected consumers.

classes: See *classification.*

classic: See *classic merchandise.*

classic merchandise: consistently popular styles that are not subject to fluctuations in fashion. These items are often considered fashion basics or investment purchases.

classification: in merchandising, an assortment of items by classes, all of which are substitutable for one another to the customer. They are classified without regard for style, size, color, price, etc., and are developed in direct response to the needs expressed by customers. They are fundamental merchandising units, change little from year to year even though the actual merchandise within each classification will be in a constant state of flux. Provides for a statistical structure to facilitate item control.

classification control: a means of dollar inventory control separating the stock of a department into several homogeneous classifications so that the dollar value of each is smaller than that of the combined department. See *dollar control.*

classification dominance: the assortment of items so broad that it is almost exhaustive, i.e., almost every possible item is included giving the customer the widest possible range of alternatives. Synonymous with *dominant assortment.*

classification merchandising: a system of record keeping that assists inventory control and results in categorization of merchandise.

Clayton Antitrust Act of 1914: Federal legislation intended to delineate and define acts considered unlawful restraints of trade. See *tie-in sales.*

clean bill of lading: a bill of lading accepted by the carrier for goods received in appropriate condition (no damages or missing items).

clear: in retailing, to reduce inventory (e.g., clearing out merchandise.)

clearance:
(1) *general:* an act of clearing.
(2) *retailing:* a reduction on the price of items; a special sale that is often used to clear inventory and/or off-season goods. Cf. *markdown.* See *clearance sale.*

clearance markdown: See *clearance (2).*

clearance sale: an offering of merchandise at lowered prices in order to clear the store (or department) of slow-moving, shop-worn, or other unsold seasonal items. Usually occurs at the end of a season to make room for new merchandise.

clerk: an employee who sells goods to customers, assures the neat display of stock, and tallies up sales. See *salesperson.*

clerking activities: retail store activities where there is direct customer contact.

clerk-wrap: a system of retail sales where the salesperson who waits on the customer also wraps the purchases and arranges for the shipment of "send" items. See *clerk-wrap department.*

clerk-wrap department: any retail selling unit where the salesperson both waits on the customers and wraps the purchases. See *clerk-wrap.*

close: to secure the customer's written or spoken agreement to purchase the item or service being offered. See *gift close.*

closed assortment: an assortment where the structure of items needed by the consumer is present and is complete. Cf. *open assortment.*

closed-back window: a window backed by a wall forming an enclosed, self-contained display area.

closed display: items placed under glass, requiring a salesperson to open a case in order that the customer can see the item closely. Cf. *open display.* See *top stock.*

closed door discount house: See *closed door membership.*

closed door membership: a retail store in which customers belong based on a common employee, such as government employees. Usually discounts are provided. Synonymous with *membership club; wholesale club.*

closed loop layout: the placing of fixtures and aisles as incentives for the customer to move around the outer sections of the store. Synonymous with *racetrack layout.*

closed loop system: a computerized method of inventory control where item information is recorded at the point of sale for use in ordering and reordering. Merchandise is then removed from the inventory memory bank at the time of sale.

closed sales territory: a geographically defined area where the manufacturer allows only one middleperson to handle certain merchandise. See *exclusive distribution.*

closed stock: goods sold only in sets, e.g., glassware, china. Individual items from a set cannot be purchased, and there is no certainty that replacements will be available at a future time. Cf. *open stock.*

closed window: See *closed-back window.*

closeout: an offer by a manufacturer or retailer to clear away his or her inventory. The savings are often passed along to the consumer as a closeout sale, used to generate increased store traffic.

closeout sale: See *closeout.*

close rate: in assessing salespeople, the individual's number of successful closings divided by that salesperson's number of sales calls.

closing: See *close.*

closing book inventory: See *closing inventory at book.*

closing clue: a verbal comment or body language movement that indicates that the potential buyer is on the verge of placing an order.

closing inventory: the value of merchandise on hand at the end of an accounting period; can be at cost or at retail value.

closing inventory at book: remaining inventory found by subtracting the total of retail reductions from the total merchandise handled.

closing physical inventory: the dollar value of stock remaining at the end of the accounting period as found by an actual count of the stock.

closing technique: an approach used by the salesperson to finalize a sale.

closure: See *close.*

clothing alterations: See *alterations.*

clouter: a shoplifter who does not make any attempt to hide his or her activity, takes goods and leaves the store; depends on the element of surprise to give him or her adequate time to get out.

club packs: products in large, institutional size packages.

club plan selling: a means of retail distribution where the selling organization merchandises only to members. Members are awarded prizes for attracting new members who join by making a purchase.

clucking hens: (slang) new or unusual concerns for a store's senior management which demand time and attention.

cluster: a grouping of specialty stores located within a high-density populated area.

clustered demand: a demand pattern in which consumer needs and desires for a good or service category can be classified into two or more identifiable clusters (segments).

CMA: See *Childrenswear Manufacturers Association.*

co-branded card: a dual purpose credit car that combines the features of a private label card and a bank card. The issuer and a retailer or service provider both have their logo on the card. The card program allows merchants to focus on their core business—selling merchandise and services.

COD:

(1) See *cash on delivery.*

(2) See *collection on delivery.*

COD audit: the organized inspection of accounting records relating to cash on delivery transactions. The method involves showing that all COD merchandise has reached the delivery department or common carrier and that all goods handled by the deliverer has been accounted for in cash or returned goods.

code number: the designation for identifying the source from which sales evolve, e.g., used on cents-off coupons to determine where people obtained them.

coding: a means for identifying goods sequentially by alphabetical assignment or numerically on price tickets.

COG: customer-owned goods; for example, suits left at a store after purchase for alterations. Synonymous with *customer's own merchandise (COM).*

cognitive component (of an attitude): utilized by consumer researchers, a person's evaluation of the characteristics of an object.

cognitive dissonance:

(1) *general:* a mental state that occurs when there is a lack of consistency or balance among an individual's various cognitions after a decision has been made. Two cognitions are in a dissonant state if they disagree with each other, e.g., when a commercial indicates that a cigarette is mild, but the consumer finds, through experience, that it is strong and irritating.

(2) *merchandising:* the state of anxiety or uneasiness that follows a purchase decision and creates a need for reassurance that the decision was the best one. See *dissonance reduction.*

cognitive judgment: for the consumer, the result of his or her perceptions, or communications received from others.

cold call: contacting a potential customer without prior notice in order to make a sale or arrange for an appointment. It is used to obtain a meeting or to give a demonstration; a form of prospecting in order to identify qualified prospects for an item or service. Frequently conducted during a down time period when the salesperson has some free time. Cf. *cold canvassing.*

cold canvassing: determining potential customers without assistance from others or from references, e.g., selecting every tenth name in the telephone directory within a given location and having a salesperson call on these persons. Cf. *canvass; cold call.*

cold list: a list of people's names not used before in promoting a service or item to a prospect.

cold mail promotion: a promotion sent by a mailer to prospects who presently are not listed customers.

Colgate Doctrine of 1919: a U.S. Supreme Court decision holding that a seller can unilaterally decide the terms under which merchandise will be sold and can, therefore, refuse to sell to those who do not meet those terms. Intended to curtail the activities of known price-cutting retailers such as discount houses and catalog retailers. Its effects have been reduced over the years by subsequent decisions, but its thrust was incorporated into the Robinson-Patman Act. See *Robinson-Patman Act of 1936.*

collection:
(1) *general:* the presentation for payment of an obligation and the payment thereof.
(2) *retailing:* an organized gathering of related items.

collection agent: an agency chosen by a seller to collect on credit orders that have not been paid in response to the seller's own attempts. The fee can run as high as 30 percent, and therefore these services are used as a means of last resort.

collection on delivery (COD): Synonymous with *cash on delivery.*

collection period: used as an indication of the size of customers' accounts; a ratio comparing the average period of time it takes to collect accounts receivable to the number of days it takes to obtain that volume of sales.

collection system: a method used by retailers to motivate customers to pay their debts, particularly delinquent accounts; includes several levels of increasing intensity, such as impersonal routine billing, impersonal appeals, personalized appeals, and legal action.

college board: a group of college students working with a retail store as a volunteer and advisory capacity with emphasis on new products and new styles. Cf. *fashion board; teen board.*

College of Retailing: In 1994, the National Retail Federation began offering a two-week program of intensive course work dealing with virtually every aspect of retail operations designed for executives at all levels as well as the retail entrepreneur.

College Stores Research and Educational Foundation: See *National Association of College Stores (NACS).*

collusion: a secret agreement to defraud.

colorable imitation: any mark or symbol resembling a registered mark that may confuse the customer; a form of deception.

COM: customer's own merchandise. Synonymous with *customer-owned goods.* See *COG.*

combination drug store: See *combo store.*

combination house: a merchant middleperson acting as the wholesaler in the industrial market in addition to the retail and institutional market.

combination offer: a type of consumer fraud involving the sale of an item at a low price tied to the purchase of a continuing service.

combination pricing: a pricing approach whereby aspects of cost-, demand-, and competition-based pricing methods are integrated.

combination sale: an item of merchandise that is combined with a premium at one price. It lowers the cost of promotion per dollar of revenue.

combination store: See *combo store.*

combination supermarket: See *combo store.*

combo promotion: a promotion that offers two or more items together.

combo store: a store that is an outgrowth of the supermarket. It is (a) a full-line discount store in that drugs and general merchandise has been transplanted into a food environment; or (b) an outgrowth of the large drugstore where general merchandise is combined with drugs and health and beauty care products. Similar to a superstore in size, usually providing approximately a quarter of the floor space to nonfood items. Synonymous with *combination store.* Cf. *convenience store; express store; superstore.*

command headline: a headline which encourages a reader to use or purchase a product or service.

commercial: the advertiser's message to use or purchase merchandise or a service; presented on any radio or television program. A commercial is produced on film or videotape, then duplicated with copies going to subscribing networks for future airing. Commercials are filmed or taped and copies are then distributed. Cf. *advertisement.*

commercial set: in overseas merchandising; the four major documents covering a shipment—the invoice, the bill of lading, the certificate of insurance, and the bill of exchange or draft.

commissary store: a small retail store that usually sells to the workers of the retailer who own it. Synonymous with *company store; industrial store.*

commission: the amount paid to an agent, which may be an individual, a broker, or agency, for consummating a transaction involving the sale or purchase of merchandise or services. Salespeople receive salaries based on straight commission (compensation solely based on commission income) or a combination compensation plan that offers a fixed-based salary plus a commission or incentives. Most salespeople prefer the latter as it provides immediate income. See *salary plus commission.*

commission agent: a functional middleperson who receives the shipment of goods, mainly perishables, to sell for a principal. See *commission house.*

commissionaire: French, for a foreign-based buying agency that serves as a store's representative overseas. The commissionaire assists in bringing the buyer into contact with vendors, handling foreign exchange rates, and arranges shipping from overseas ports. Compensation is usually a percentage of the store's purchases.

commission buyer of farm products: a wholesaler who buys farm products for others; usually receives a commission.

commission buying office: an independent resident buying department

receiving its compensation from producers as a percentage of orders placed with retailers. Usually deals with small retailers providing little or no services other than the procurement of merchandise. The office can represent many manufacturers and gives the retailer the advantage of choosing from a large assortment of items without paying a fee. Synonymous with *merchandise broker.* See *broker; commission house; manufacturer's agent.*

commission department: a department within the store where the salespeople are paid traditionally through the receipt of commissions on sales.

commissioner: See *commissionaire.*

commission house: an agent who negotiates the sales of merchandise that he or she handles, with control over prices and terms of sale. See *commission agent.*

commission merchant: an agent who performs selling functions for manufacturers, normally on a one-time basis.

commission office: See *commission buying office.*

commission rebating: income earned by advertising agencies on the value of the orders they place with media owners, rather than being paid a fee by their clients.

commitment: items ordered where the purchaser has committed the store to accept, but which has not yet been approved by the merchandise manager.

committee buying: See *committee purchasing.*

committee purchasing: the decision to buy by a group of people within a company who are charged with the responsibility of study and recommending products.

commission with draw: a form of compensation for salespeople where payments are based on a percentage of sales in which regular payments are made from an account set aside for that purpose.

commodity: anything that is bought or sold in commerce. In the plural, refers to agricultural and other staple items.

commodity products: Synonymous with *staple stock.*

commodity rate: in overseas retailing, an allowable deviation from the class rate charged by shippers to customers.

commodity warehouse: See *warehouse, commodity.*

common area maintenance (CAM): upkeep of areas in a shopping center shared by the tenants (walkways, parking lots, etc.) the cost of which is shared by the retailers.

common carrier:

(1) *general:* a transportation company that transports products on a specified schedule and according to regulations and standards established by government regulatory agencies.

(2) *retailing:* used by retailers to set consumer prices; a carrier that moves merchandise for a price and without partiality.

communication overload: a customer's confusion caused by having excessive information furnished by the salesperson.

community market: See *public market.*

community relations: interaction between the retailer and the surrounding trading area. It is usually cultivated to generate good feeling toward the store.

community room: made available by a retailer or a shopping center for meeting civic and other organizations in its trading area as part of a community relations commitment.

community shopping center: a medium-sized shopping center of 100,000 to 300,000 square feet of total floor space. The center sells both convenience and shopping merchandise. Usually consists of a variety or junior department store as an anchor tenant, smaller branch stores, and many specialty stores. The trading area will not usually extend beyond the community in which the center is found.

companion goods: See *related merchandise.*

company-owned buying office: See *cooperative buying office; corporate buying office; private buying office.*

company store: See *commissary store.*

company warehouse: See *warehouse, private.*

comparative messages: implicitly or explicitly contrast a store's offerings with those of competitors.

comparative prices: promotional prices or displays indicating current price as well as a generally higher earlier price, a suggested retail price, or the estimated price.

comparison department: a unit within a retail operation responsible for comparing the store's quality, service, prices, etc., with competitors.

comparison shopper:

(1) an individual sent to competitors' outlets to determine goods carried and relative prices charged as part of information-gathering activity.

(2) an industrial purchasing executive's review of competitors' marketing strategies such as new products offered, competitors' pricing concepts, and promotional initiatives. Cf. *service shopper.*

comparison shopping: See *comparison shopper.*

compatibility: the degree that a consumer perceives that a new item is consistent with his or her current requirements, self-image, and attitude. See *compatibility of product assortments.*

compatibility of product assortments: awareness of how well a store's item lines complement each other and correspond to the needs and wants of the store's customers.

compensating product: an input or product secured by a manufacturer in a domestic market to substitute for an imported input or product used to produce items for export.

compensation:

(1) *general:* payment for any services or items. See *compensation.*

(2) *retailing:* an attempt to disguise an undesirable characteristic by exaggerating a desirable one.

compensation deal: a semibarter arrangement in which goods are bought partially for cash and partially with other goods; a common practice in merchandising worldwide.

competing against all comers: an determined store policy showing a desire to meet all competition on quality, quantity, price line, and services.

competition:

(1) any rivalry; a retailer's rival or rivals.

(2) the situation in which a large number of manufacturers serve a large number of consumers, when no manufacturer can demand or offer a quantity sufficiently large to affect the market price. There are three forms of marketing competition: (a) brand competition—competition by producers offering a similar item; (b) generic competition—when items in totally separate categories perform the identical function; and (c) form competition—merchandise that perform the same function, but are structured differently.

competition-based pricing: a pricing strategy approach whereby a firm uses competitors' prices rather than demand or cost considerations as its primary pricing guideposts. A firm can set prices below the market, at the market, or above the market.

competitive bidding: Synonymous with *bidding.*

competitive-oriented pricing: the policy of a retailer to base prices on those of competing stores instead of on cost or demand factors.

competitive parity: the budget allocation for the promotion of merchandise based on expenditures of competitors; based on the concept that one should defend against competition by spending at least as much (or as little) as one's competitor spends on advertising. Synonymous with *defensive budgeting; defensive spending.* See *competitive parity technique.*

competitive parity technique: a method for setting a budget wherein a retailer determines advertising money to be spent on the basis of the spending by a competitor. Since objectives differ this method can be a poor predictor. See *competitive parity.*

competitive position: the place within the market which allows an item or service to compete on a level with other competitive items or services. At the time the item or service reaches a noticeable percentage share of the entire market, it is declared to be in a competitive position.

competitive price: the price determined in the market by the bargaining of a number of buyers and sellers, each acting separately and without sufficient power to manipulate the market.

competitive segmentation analysis: used by retailers to help choose the target market for their establishments; includes five steps—(a) identifying the potential market segment; (b) identifying the competition; (c) studying the competition; (d) reviewing the environment; and (e) choosing the target market.

competitive variables: activities of competitors that can affect a retailer's own sales.

competitor:

(1) *general:* the seller or maker of an item or service that is sold in the same market as that of other producers.

(2) *retailing:* the provider of merchandise whose item fulfills a consumer need in the market where others offer item and services that may also fulfill the same need.

complaint management: providing quality customer service by quickly requesting and responding to customer complaints; involves securing information on how best to provide customer services and how to resolve existing customer problems. See *customer relations.*

complementary products: items that tend to round out a line of products, e.g., shoes and shoelaces. See *accessories; allied products; suggestive selling.*

complement of markup percentage: See *complement of the cumulative markup percentage.*

complement of the cumulative markup percentage: the difference between the total retail price (100%) and the percentage of markup at retail. The result is usually the cost of the merchandise. For example, if an item is sold at retail for $100.00 and the markup is 40%, the complement of the cumulative markup percentage if 60%. Multiplying the retail price by the cumulative markup percentage gives the cost of the goods: $100.00 x .60 = $60.00.

completed cancel: a consumer who fulfills his or her commitment to the seller prior to cancellation.

completion date: the date on a purchase order identifying the last day on which a manufacturer can ship merchandise to a specific retailer without the threat of cancellation by the purchaser.

compliance bureau: an administrative unit of the store that is responsible for satisfying government regulations, es-

pecially as it relates to merchandising and personnel practices.

comptroller: See *controller.*

computerized-checkout (electronic point of sale) system: a system in which a retailer's cashier manually rings up a sale or passes an item over or past an optical scanner; then a computerized register instantly records and displays a sale.

computerized retail system: using computers to collect, analyze, and retain information of importance to the retailer.

concealed damage: as it affects profits; damage to the contents of a package that is in good order externally.

concealed discount: where items, whether price fixed or not, are identified on the same purchase order at a common discount, which is subsequently shown on the invoice.

concealed loss and damage claims: a claim against a carrier for loss or damage to goods while goods were in the possession of the carrier. At delivery, the loss or damage was not apparent because (a) the shipping container was not opened, or (b) the items were reshipped from a distribution point for delivery to an ultimate consignee and were not inspected.

concentric diversification: a retailer's strategy for expansion by acquiring another firm that provides new product lines that are similar to theirs, which hopefully will appeal to a different set of consumers. See *conglomerate diversification.*

concession:

(1) *general:* any deviation from regular terms or previous conditions.

(2) *merchandising:* a right granted to a company to sell its product or services, e.g., to rent chairs at an outdoor party, to check coats and hats in a theater. See *leased department.*

condition: a contractual clause, implied or expressed, that has the effect of investing or divesting with rights and duties for members of the contract.

conditional sale: See *conditional sales contract.*

conditional sales contract: a sales contract in which ownership of sold items remains with the seller until the goods are paid for in full or until other conditions are met. Should the repossessed merchandise be resold, the resale price is credited to the customer's balance, but the customer is liable for the remainder of the balance due. Cf. *absolute sale; approval sale.*

conference report: See *call report.*

confined goods: merchandise sold by a producer or distributor to a limited number of stores so that each retailer can claim exclusive resale rights in his or her trading area.

confined label: See *private brand.*

confined merchandise: See *confined goods.*

confinement: See *confined goods.*

confirmation of an order: in retailing, a statement from a supplier that he or she will accept a buyer's purchase request. From the vendor's perspective, it notes the receipt of the order and, thus of its legal acceptance.

confirmed order: See *confirmation of an order.*

confusion of items: the intermingling of the items of two or more different owners where once combined the items are difficult or even impossible again to separate.

conglomerate: in retailing, often mentioned in advertising to suggest profitability and/or competitiveness; the result of a merging of retailers that produce different items and services to secure a large economic base, to acquire sounder management, and to gain greater potential profit.

conglomerate diversification: in retailing, a store's strategy for expansion where new acquisitions have no direct relationship to theirs. The store then proceeds to set up this additional service. Cf. *concentric diversification.*

conglomerate market competition: the sale of the identical item by different dealers and distributors; leads to multiplying channels of distribution.

conglomerchant: See *merchandising conglomerate.*

congruent innovation: one of a four-way classification of new items as to degrees of newness. It does not result in any shift to established consumption patterns. The other three are continuous, discontinuous, and dynamically continuous.

congruent production diversification: more items or lines of items which are added to a store's offering based on management decisions. Synonymous with *production-oriented diversification.*

conjoint analysis: a method for presenting the framework of consumer preferences, and predicting consumer's attitudes towards new stimuli.

conmanship: persuading consumers to part with their purchasing power for something which will not provide benefits, or even for nothing. The opposite of salesmanship.

conscious parallel action: deliberating setting identical pricing behavior among competing organizations. It has been declared illegal by the courts in antitrust cases. See *price fixing.*

consign: the act or ordering, via a bill of lading, a carrier to deliver a lot of merchandise from a given point to a given destination.

consignee: the ultimate recipient of goods.

consignee marks: a symbol placed on packages for export, generally consisting of a square, triangle, diamond, circle, cross, etc., with designed letters and/or numbers for the purpose of identification.

consignment: the act of entrusting merchandising to a dealer for sale but retaining ownership of them until sold. The dealer pays only when and if the goods are sold. Merchandise can be consigned by manufacturers to wholesalers or by wholesalers to retailers. See *on consignment.*

consignment buying: See *consignment purchase.*

consignment note: an instrument given when merchandise is dispatched, providing details of the item, the sender, and the individual to whom they are sent. The latter signs it upon arrival, providing proof of delivery.

consignment purchase: an agreement where the retailer takes possession of goods. However, title remains with the manufacturer or vendor. Unsold items can be returned to the vendor following an elapsed time period.

consignment sale: See *consignment purchase.*

consignor: the originator of a shipment, a person who delivers merchandise to an agent.

consistency: the repeated degree to which merchandise in an assortment of items are compatible with each other and with other items located in the store.

consolidated buying: See *central buying.*

consolidated delivery system: run by a private organization whose purpose it is to deliver packages for retailers, i.e., United Parcel Service.

consolidator: an individual or organization who brings together goods from a number of sources into one order for shipment.

conspicuous consumption: the purchase and use of items and services primarily for improving an individual's social prestige rather than for the satisfaction of material needs.

consultative selling: a sales method where the seller positions him- or herself as a customer's consultant; applies low-pressure sales hoping to fulfill the prospect's particular needs.

consumer: any person who uses or consumes goods and services. A consumer need not be the purchaser of an item or service, e.g., the consumer would be the child who eats the baby food purchased by the mother. Synonymous with *end-user.* See *ultimate consumer.*

consumer behavior: based on behavioral science research, manifestations of the decision processes and the search activities in purchasing and using merchandise and services.

consumer behavior research: a technique used to determine what satisfaction people want out of life, how they use products and services to achieve these satisfactions, how they perceive items and various brands, what forms of promotional activities will lead to successful retailing, and how to access the effects of these activities.

Consumer Bill of Rights: See *consumerism.*

consumer buying: purchasing at the level of the ultimate consumer—the person seeking merchandise and services.

consumer convenience goods: low-priced, frequently bought consumer items.

consumer cooperative: a group of consumers who band together to gain buying power; user-owned retail outlets. Such organizations act for the benefit of their consumer owners.

consumer credit: the ability of people to either borrow money or to obtain merchandise on time for the purpose of obtaining consumer items.

Consumer Credit Protection Act of 1968: See *Truth in Lending Act of 1968.*

consumer deal: a price reduction to a consumer. See *retail deal.*

consumer demand: the characteristics and needs of final consumers, industrial consumers, wholesalers and retailers, government institutions, international markets, and nonprofit institutions.

consumer demographic profile: a composite description of a consumer group based on the most important demographics.

consumer demographics: objective and quantifiable population characteristics that are relatively easy to identify, collect, measure, and analyze.

consumer durables: See *consumer goods.*

consumer education: the formalized teaching efforts to provide consumers with the skills and knowledge to allocate their resources wisely in the marketplace.

consumer goods: items bought and used by the final consumer for personal or household purposes, such as automobiles, food, and clothing. Synonymous with *consumer products.*

Consumer Goods Pricing Act of 1975: federal legislation that stopped all interstate usage of resale price maintenance agreements. This law phased out many of the so-called "fair trade" agreements.

consumerism: the organized demand that businesses increase their concern for the public in both manufacture and sale of merchandise. Consumerism grew in importance when President Kennedy signed the Consumer Bill of Rights legislation in 1962 stating that consumers have the right to be safe (from faulty merchandise), to be informed (of a product's negative attributes or inherent dangers), to choose (sustaining market competition absent of monopolies), and to be heard (to be able to make complaints and have legitimate grievances acted upon.) See *consumer protection legislation; Naderism.*

consumerist: an individual or representative who takes a leading position to protect the interests and needs of the consumer. See *consumerism; Naderism.*

consumer jury: pretesting items or advertisements by seeking the reactions of potential buyers or users.

consumer list: people on a list who have inquired about or actually bought items or services that can be contacted in the future.

consumer market:
(1) buyers who purchase for personal needs or family consumption.
(2) a market in which goods and services are actually used up. Synonymous with *product market.* Cf. *organizational market.*

consumer motivation: the major force in a person that compels him or her to act in the marketplace.

consumer obsolescence: the turning away from presently owned items by consumers in favor of something new or in fashion, despite the continuing utility of the original item.

consumer panel: a group of selected people who serve over a period of time as a sample group for marketing research studies.

Consumer Price Index (CPI): used by marketers and advertisers in planning their strategies; a measurement of the cost of living, determined by the Bureau of Labor Statistics; also indicates price trends of more than 400 different items and services. Synonymous with *Cost-of-Living Index.*

consumer products: See with *consumer goods.*

Consumer Product Safety Act (CPSA) of 1972: legislation providing for control of the processing, manufacturing, and distribution of products that may cause unreasonable risk of personal injury. Stipulates that manufacturers must notify the Commission within 24 hours of discovering that they have produced and sold a product that represents a substantial hazard to consumers. A recall procedure must be instituted to correct the defect. Amended in 1976 to provide standards, enforceability, litigation procedures, and funding.

consumer profile: a description of the personal, demographic and psychological characteristics of a specific item or service user, includes age, sex, marital status, income, education, occupation, home location, previous buying patterns, credit ratings.

consumer promotion: sales promotion methods purporting to offer short-term incentives to prospects to stimulate product sales.

consumer protection legislation: a variety of federal, state and local laws to protect the rights of consumers. See *consumerism; Consumer Product Safety Act; deceptive advertising; Federal Trade Commission; product liability.*

consumer research: marketing research to predict the behavior of the consumer in the market; provides data about a consumer's needs, motivation, perceptions and attitudes regarding advertising, reasons for purchasing a service or product, and what influences their choices. Consumer research is of value in determining the target market and setting strategy for advertising campaigns and other promotions.

consumer-sale disclosure statement: a form presented by a dealer giving essential details on financing charges relative to a purchase on an installment plan. This is required under the Consumer Credit Protection (Truth in Lending) Act.

consumer's cooperative: a voluntary association of consumers, organized to help fulfill members needs for goods and services, i.e., a credit union.

consumer's decision process: stages experienced by a consumer when choosing whether or not to purchase an item, includes stimulus, problem awareness, the search for information, evaluation of alternatives, purchase and post-purchase behavior. The process can be impacted by the demographic and psychographic profile of the individual consumer.

consumer's income expectation: income that a person hopes to receive sometime in the future. It impacts on present buying behavior. Expected income affects the purchase of big ticket items.

consumer sovereignty: that the consumer is supreme in the market.

consumer stimulants: promotions and incentives that purport to attract consumers and to stimulate interest and demand for a product or service.

consumer surplus: the difference, as perceived by a customer, between the price he or she pays for the item, and the value of the purchase.

consumption patterns: the patterns of whether consumers use, or do not use, merchandise or a service.

contact report: Synonymous with *call report.*

container: in merchandising, a nonspecific term for a receptacle capable of closure.

containerizing: shipping with large, standardized boxes or crates that each contain a number of packages. The container is sealed at point of origin and opened only at a destination point.

container premium: packaging for merchandise that is reusable for another purpose. It serves as an added inducement for the consumer to purchase the items.

contemporary styling: a sophisticated, updated, fashion-conscious style classification intended originally for the age group that had outgrown junior sizes, but was still interested in fashion and reluctant to adopt a matronly style of dress. The existence of this classification is an acknowledgment of the continued aging of the baby-boom generation.

content label: a tag attached to goods identifying materials used in its production.

content motivation theories: consumer buying theories that focus on the factors within the person that start, arouse, energize, or stop behavior.

contest: a sales promotion technique in which consumers are offered prizes for performing a task, such as making up a slogan. Cf. *sweepstake.*

contingency pricing: where a service organization does not receive payment for services performed until the consumer's satisfaction is assured.

contingent: a store employee, unassigned to any specific department, who is called upon on a daily basis to fill in wherever required. Such employees are usually on a store's regular payroll and can be either part-or full-time workers. See *contingent force.*

contingent force: the collective name for the store workers who move from department to department as required to replace absent employees or cover particularly heavy sales traffic. Synonymous with *flying squad.* See *contingent.*

contra account: a retailer's customer with whom there is agreement that periodic payments will be made on the basis of a fixed percent of the amount owing as shown by a statement issued regularly.

contraband: merchandise that is forbidden by law to be imported or exported, but which is sometimes smuggled and unlawfully sold.

contract account: any credit arrangement requiring customers to pay in periodic installments as stipulated in a contract. See *installment credit.*

contract buying: See *specification buying.*

contract buying office: See *salaried buying office.*

contract carrier: used by marketers to determine added costs; a transportation firm that contracts with shippers to transport their goods. The price is negotiated between the carrier and the shipper. The contract carrier cannot accept shipments from the general public.

contract department: the unit within a department store that is responsible for the sale of large quantities of merchandise at special prices to institutions and other large buyers.

contract price: in merchandising, the sale price negotiated between a U.S. exporter of merchandise and the foreign buyer payable in the United States for the export of U.S. goods and services. This price may include, among other things, freight and marine insurance, but it excludes any charges payable for non-U.S. goods and services unless otherwise permitted, certain engineering services, import duties or levies of a similar nature, charges for local costs, and any other charges not legally payable in the United States.

contract purchasing: a form of purchasing defined in a contract for orders and deliveries, covering a specific time period, usually one year.

contract-type buying office: See *salaried buying office.*

contract wholesaler: a wholesaler servicing a retail cooperative.

contractor: See *apparel contractor.*

contracyclical pricing: a pricing technique that runs counter to traditional economic policy. During periods of prosperity, the company increases output and lowers prices; during economic downturn, lowers production and raises prices.

contribution margin technique: an approach to cost analysis that ignores nontraceable common costs.

contribution plan: an approach for allocating expenses in a retail store where departments are assigned only those expenses that are controllable and can be charged directly to the department. Indirect expenses are not allocated.

contribution plan of expense allocation: See *contribution plan.*

control account: the documentation of financial data summarizing entries and balances appearing in a subsidiary ledger.

control division: a functional division of a retail operation, headed by a controller or treasurer, who is responsible for maintaining accounting records, credit management, inventory management, financial analysis, merchandise budgeting, etc. Usually headed by the controller or the treasurer.

controlled brand: a brand of merchandise owned by its manufacturer whose distribution is restricted to a small number of distributors.

controlled label: See *controlled brand; private brand.*

controller: in retailing, the store's executive whose primary responsibilities include all of the store's fiscal and accounting operations. Administers the store's finances, credits, collections, and accounting records. Synonymous with *comptroller.*

controller's division: See *control division.*

controlling account: See *control account.*

convenience food store: See *convenience store.*

convenience goods: products that the public wishes to purchase with a minimum of effort or time (toothpaste, sodas, paper, etc.) Cf. *bantam store; shopping goods.*

convenience services: See *accommodation services.*

convenience store: a small retail outlet that carries a limited line of high-turnover convenience goods, such as candy, milk, beer, and at times take-out foods; operates for extended hours. Usually offers locational convenience

as well; traditionally designed for motorists with approximately 2,000 square feet of space. Cf. *bantam store; combo store; express store.*

conventional supermarket: provides an average 25,000 square feet with a broad variety of canned and frozen foods, produce, and the like. Most do not have specialized service departments. Synonymous with *traditional supermarket.* Cf. *supercenter; superstore.*

conversion process: See *boomerang.*

cooling-off laws: See *cooling-off period.*

cooling-off period: to protect consumers, there are laws permitting them to reconsider a purchase, and if they so desire, to cancel any commitment. Three days is the typical time-frame used.

co-op advertising: See *cooperative advertising.*

cooperative: an outlet owned and run by the final consumers for purposes of buying and selling items to the members.

cooperative advertising:
(1) *general:* advertising paid for jointly by the advertiser and its wholesalers or retailers. At times shortened to co-op advertising.
(2) *retailing:* an arrangement between the manufacturer and retailer where the producer reimburses the retailer in part or in full for advertising costs. Synonymous with *manufacturer's cooperative advertising; vertical cooperative advertising.*

cooperative buying: consolidation of orders by several stores, in order to take advantage of quantity discounts, etc. The cooperating stores may be independent or members of a consolidated group, includes groups, committee and central buying, buying clubs, cooperative wholesalers, wholesaler-retailer cooperative groups, and manufacturers' cooperative retail groups. Synonymous with *affiliated buying.*

cooperative buying office: a resident buying office controlled and financed cooperatively by a group of noncompeting, independent stores. The office carries out a purchasing function for the member stores in a central market, with each store contributing a prorated share of expenses. Synonymous with *associated buying office.*

cooperative chain: See *retail cooperative.*

cooperative delivery: the joint ownership and management of a delivery system by a group of retailers, all of whom are served by the system.

cooperative display fund: the allocation of monies, given by the vendor, which is usually matched by a retailer for the development, construction, and installation of visual merchandising materials and devices to promote the vendor's products.

cooperative group: See *retail cooperative.*

cooperatively owned resident buying office: See *cooperative buying office.*

cooperative marketing: independent manufacturers, wholesalers, retailers, or any combination of them working collectively to buy and/or sell.

cooperative money: See *co-op money.*

cooperative organization: a retail organization that consists of a set of independent retailers that combine their resources to maintain their own wholesaling operation.

cooperative promotion: See *co-op promotion.*

cooperative resident buying office: See *cooperative buying office.*

cooperative retailing: See *consumer cooperative.*

cooperative store: See *consumer cooperative.*

cooperative wholesaler: See *retail cooperative.*

co-op money: funds that a vendor contributes to the retailer for the promotion of a vendor's merchandise. See *co-op promotion.*

co-op promotion: an effort to promote a product or products where the retailer joins with the manufacturer and/or vendor, with costs usually shared. See *co-op money; promotional discount.*

coordinates: apparel separates, such as blouses, skirts, jackets and slacks, calculated to mix and match harmoniously with regard to color and fabric content. See *ensemble display.*

copy:
(1) *general:* all components to be included in a completed advertisement or direct-mailing piece.
(2) *retailing:* in the apparel trade, the imitation of an original design; often selling at a lower price.

copyright: an exclusive right, guaranteed by federal statute, to reproduce, publish, and sell the matter and form of literary, musical, or artistic works. Any attempt by another person or group to deprive the copyright holder of his or her property is cause for the latter to seek damages. See *Copyright Act of 1976.*

Copyright Act of 1976: federal legislation revising the copyright laws for the first time in 67 years. The Act extends the length of copyright protection to the duration of the creator's life plus 50 years. Previously the protection ran 28 years from the date of publication and was renewable for another 28 years. The Act also sets standards for fair use and reproduction of copyrighted material and a new system of compulsory licensing for cable television and jukeboxes. It also preempts state laws governing copyrighted materials that come within the scope of the federal Act. See *copyright.*

core product: the central benefit or purpose for which a consumer buys a product. Varies from purchaser to purchaser.

The core product or core benefit may come either from the physical good or service performance, or it may come from the augmented dimensions of the product. Cf. *augmented product.*

core services: the basic services that companies should provide to their customers to remain competitive.

corporate buying office: a resident purchasing office that is operated and usually owned by a department store ownership group or by a chain store organization. Purchasers perform many of the functions found in an associated buying office, but their recommendations carry considerable weight as member stores share a common ownership. The corporate buying office, which is not a central buying office, has the responsibility for choosing and purchasing items for individual stores in a chain operation. Synonymous with *chain-owned buying office; syndicated buying office.* Cf. *central buying office; cooperative buying office.*

corrective advertising: Federal Trade Commission law requires that an advertiser, including a retailer, found guilty of placing a deceptive advertisement devote space or time in future announcements with disclosure of the earlier deception.

cosmetic: a preparation that is applied to the face, skin, hair, etc., for improving the appearance of the user. Purports to remove, cover up, or correct blemishes; does not include soap.

Cosmetic Executive Women (CEW): an association of women executives in the cosmetic and related industries. Presents an annual Cosmetic Executive Women Achiever Award.

Cosmetic, Toiletry and Fragrance Association (CTFA): based in Washington, DC, an association of manufacturers and distributors of finished cosmetics, fragrances, and toilet preparations. Conducts safety research and testing.

cost:
(1) *general:* the value given up by an entity in order to receive goods or services.
(2) *general:* the value given up to obtain an item in the volume needed, shipped to the desired location. All expenses are costs, but not all costs are expenses.
(3) *retailing:* the price that a vendor will charge a retailer for goods.
(4) *retailing:* any money expended to bring merchandise into the store including wholesale price of merchandise, freight charges, etc.

cost allowance: the lowering of the invoice cost made by a vendor resulting from an incorrect shipment, damaged items in transit, delay in delivery, etc.

cost analysis: a sales manager's measurement of the cost of sales activities; measures the levels of profitability of individual items and types of customers. Cf. *sales analysis.*

cost and freight (CAF) (C and F): when the seller covers the freight charges to the destination but not the insurance or other charges.

cost-based pricing: a pricing strategy approach whereby a store determines prices by computing merchandise, service, and overhead costs and then adding an amount to cover the store's profit goal. Demand is not analyzed.

cost center: See *expense center.*

cost code: symbols employed to show the cost of goods on price tickets while concealing that information from the customer.

cost complement: the average relationship existing between the cost of merchandise and the retail value of the items handled during an accounting period. The dollar value of the inventory

52   cost department

at cost is divided by the dollar value of the inventory at retail.

$$\text{cost complement} = \frac{\$ \text{ cost of goods}}{\$ \text{ retail value of goods}}$$

Synonymous with *cost multiplier; cost percent.*

cost department:
(1) an operation, such as a beauty salon or fur vault in a retail store, that maintains no inventory at retail. It functions on the cost method of accounting rather than the retail method of inventory for determining profits and losses.
(2) a manufacturing or processing department within a retail store that is operated on the cost method of accounting.

cost, insurance, and freight (CIF): when the vendor pays all expenses for shipping merchandise to a foreign port and assumes the risk of fluctuating freight rates. The vendor is not responsible for the condition of the items once they have been delivered to the shipping company.

cost inventory: the price paid or market value of inventory on hand at a given moment. It represents the present depreciated worth rather than the original price that is paid. The lower of the two figures is always used.

cost method of accounting: an accounting system in which all percentages relate to the cost of the goods to the merchant. Cf. *retail method of accounting.*

cost method of inventory: a method for finding the cost of inventory on hand as a variable of the cost price of the merchandise. The actual cost of the items is noted on each price ticket in code. Inventory is taken by actual physical count and recorded at cost prices, with an allowance made for depreciation. This technique is usually used in small stores and for high-priced goods. The ending inventory at cost becomes the

beginning inventory at cost for the next accounting period. Items bought are recorded at cost. This technique can be used to determine the cost of items sold and the gross margin of the store. Cf. *retail method of inventory.*

cost multiplier: See *cost complement.*

cost of credit: the cost, in addition to the cash price, for the opportunity of purchasing something with an obligation to pay in the future.

cost of goods handled: the total cost of items found in inventory plus the cost of new purchases; represents the cost of goods available for sale during the accounting period.

cost of goods purchased: the net price paid for goods by a retailer, plus the price paid for transportation and delivery to a retail store.

cost of goods sold: the purchase price of goods sold during a specified period, including transportation costs. See *total cost.*

cost of living: the average of the retail prices of all goods and services required for a reasonable living standard.

Cost of Living Index: See *Consumer Price Index.*

cost percent: See *cost complement.*

cost per order: a statistical determination of the costs incurred in selling merchandise divided by the number of orders that are received.

cost per sale: in direct mailing, the cost of making one sale as compared to the cost of mailing.

cost plus pricing: the practice of adding a percentage of the costs of goods to the cost before the selling price is established.

cost price: the dollar amount at which merchandise are billed to a store exclusive of cash discounts.

cost recovery fee: the amount of money charged to a customer in order to cover the cost of certain sales-supporting services, such as delivery of merchandise, alterations, installment credit accounts, etc.

costume jewelry: jewelry made from inexpensive materials such as glass, plastic or wood, or set with imitation gems. Synonymous with *fashion jewelry; junk jewelry.*

Council of Fashion Designers of America (CFDA): an association of designers of fashion apparel, fabrics, accessories, jewelry, and related products. The emphasis of the organization is on the artistic merits of fashion, and in promoting fashion as an art form in the United States.

count and recount: a means of identifying the results of a sale—count the merchandise, run the sale, then recount the merchandise.

count certificate: a document confirming the count of merchandise at the time of shipment or delivery.

counter: a table or top of a cabinet within the store that is used for the display and sale of items; and in a restaurant, the area for the servicing, preparation, and display of foods.

counter card: a sign placed on a counter to advertise and promote an article for sale at that location.

counterfeiting: the illegal use of a well-known manufacturer's brand name on copies of the firm's merchandise.

countermand: to cancel an order that has not yet been carried out.

counterpurchasing: placing an order with a manufacturer in one country with the expectation that merchandise of equal value and/or quantity will be sold in the opposite direction to the other nation.

country club billing: credit billing where the store sends a copy of each sales ticket along with the monthly billing statement to a customer.

coupling: the joining of efforts between the store innovating on new merchandise and other stores or persons; can be upstream (with vendors), downstream (with customers), or sideways (with competitors).

coupon: a certificate that entitles a consumer to a price reduction or a cash refund. Can come from a manufacturer or vendor, in which case the coupon is redeemable at a wide variety of retailers; or from a retailer, in which case they may be used only in that store. See *cents-off coupon; premium.*

coupon account: where the customer purchases coupons for cash and exchanges them for merchandise in the store.

coupon credit plan: See *charge account.*

couponing: with the use of a coupon, offering consumers a special, but temporary price reduction on merchandise without actual changing the regular market price. May be mailed or placed in a package of another item, or published in an advertisement. See *cross-couponing.*

courtesy counter: a store's area, particularly a supermarket, in which such services as verifying or cashing checks, accepting returned goods, etc., are carried out.

courtesy day: the day identified by a store so that its credit customers can avail themselves of reduced price merchandise prior to sale to the public.

courtesy period: an extended period of time, beyond the nominal terms of sale, when a customer can make credit purchases without paying his or her account or arranging to do so. Synonymous with *grace period.*

couture: French for apparel that is both expensive and produced in limited quantities, often by well-known designers.

couturier: the designer of women's fashion apparel, especially one in the business of making and selling the clothes he or she has designed. See *couturiere; designer.*

couturiere: the feminine form of *couturier.* See *couturier.*

CPI: See *Consumer Price Index.*

CPSA: See *Consumer Product Safety Act.*

craze: a current fashion or fad defined by enthusiastic customer responses.

creaming a list:
(1) choosing from a list only key prospects, those who are most likely to purchase an item or service, based on a variety of selection criteria.
(2) an offer that can't be turned down. It usually is made at a loss by the store. Cf. *skimming price.*

creative demarketing: See *demarketing.*

creative packaging: packaging created in order to communicate a message as well as being attractive, appealing, and protective.

creative selling: applying techniques and strategies that elicit consumer demand, by proving the benefits of an offering to those who have never purchased the merchandise from that salesperson before.

credit: sales or purchases that are accompanied by a promise to pay later.

credit bureau: an agency that holds central files of data on consumers in a given trade area. These bureaus collect personal data, data on paying habits, and so on, and make impartial reports for credit grants. Some national credit bureaus have been accused of invading personal privacy. See *Fair Credit Reporting Act of 1971.*

credit buyer: Synonymous with *charge buyer.*

credit cancellation: the cancellation of an unpaid credit order. Synonymous with *kill; kill bad pay.*

credit card: a card issued by an organization that entitles the bearer to credit at its establishments, restaurants, stores, etc.

credit card order: paying for merchandise by using a credit card.

credit interchange: a network of information sources that can be contacted by retailers wishing credit information about potential customers; can include other merchants, trade associations, or credit bureau.

credit limit: the maximum amount a customer may have outstanding on a charge or other credit account.

credit line: See *line of credit.*

credit order: an order received without any payment and that which requires billing at a future time. See *cash order; charge buyer.* Synonymous with *bill me order.*

credit rating: the amount, type, and form of credit, if any, that a bank estimated can be extended to an applicant for credit.

credit-record analysis: See *store credit-record analysis.*

credit slip: See *due bill.*

credit suspension: placing the names of people with unpaid credit accounts on an inactive status list so that they will not receive merchandise or services. At the same time, these people continue receiving bills.

credit terms: See *terms of credit.*

credit union: a cooperative financial organization established within and listed to a specific group of people.

credit voucher: See *due bill.*

crisscross directory: a reverse telephone directory arranged by street addresses; provides the names and telephone numbers of residents. Used by retailers who attempt to delineate a trading area or try to identify the store's target customer.

cross-couponing: a coupon given with merchandise. It carries the price reduction offer of another item and may involve more than one seller. See *couponing.*

cross merchandising: placing displays of complementary items in positions facing each other, with the hope that customers when they see the displays will cross over from one product to another. Synonymous with *related item display.*

cross promote: promoting merchandise to purchasers of another item sold by the same store. See *tie-in promotion.*

cross-promotion: See *tie-in promotion.*

cross-reference book: See *crisscross directory.*

cross-selling: where the salesperson is allowed to work in more than one department within the store, helping the customers with a variety of purchases. See *interselling.*

CSS: See *chain store system.*

CTFA: See *Cosmetic, Toiletry and Fragrance Association.*

cues: weak stimuli that are not powerful enough to arouse consumer action, but capable of providing direction to motivated behavior.

cull: goods that are rejected because they are not up to the standard of quality or are otherwise imperfect.

cult merchant: Synonymous with *category-killer.*

culture: in retailing, the way in which consumers behave in the marketplace.

cumulative audience: See *reach.*

cumulative initial markon: See *cumulative markon.*

cumulative markon: the difference between total delivered cost and total original retail value of merchandise handled within a stated time frame, inclusive of the accumulated inventory. See *initial markup.* Synonymous with *cumulative markup.*

cumulative markon percent: the difference between the cost price of items and the highest retail price at which it is offered for sale expressed as a percentage rather than in dollars.

cumulative markup: Synonymous with *cumulative markon.*

cumulative quantity discount: a type of rebate given to a store when the total price of all goods purchased is identified. The objective is to encourage the dealer to give the seller all his or her business in that line of trade.

current gross margin: See *operating margin.*

current margin: See *operating margin.*

cushion: adding inventory to a basic amount to provide for unexpected increases in demand, delays of delivery, a purchase in great quantity, etc. See *reserve stock.* Synonymous with *safety stock.*

customer: an individual or organization that makes a purchase.

customer accepted trend: See *product life cycle.*

customer convenience: See *accommodation services.*

customer demand: the dollar value of items bought by customers in a specified time.

customer franchise: a loyal item following by a group of consumers with repeat sales anticipated.

customer interchange: the degree to which the customers of one store are also the customers of neighboring stores.

customer market focus: the decision of a store, acknowledging that purchasers can accept or reject the store's merchandise.

customer orientation: See *customer oriented.*

customer oriented: the effort to comprehend the reasons, desires, and problems of the customer with the intent to use this information in fulfilling the customer's needs, at the same time increasing sales and profits.

customer-owned goods: See *COG.*

customer-owned merchandise (COM): See *COG.*

customer profile: the demographic breakdown of the consumers who purchase a brand; includes their purchasing behavior; provides salespeople with data on buyer traits and behavior patterns and becomes useful in choosing the best prospects for a given item or for preparing selling strategies.

customer relations: a salesperson's activities that attempt to ensure that consumers' needs are not neglected. Complaints are to be handled swiftly and courteously. See *customer service.*

customer returns: See *returns and allowances.*

customer satisfaction: the measure of the degree to which a customer's expectations of an item or service matches the item or service's actual usefulness to the customer.

customer service: the department or special unit of an organization that responds to inquiries and consumer/customer complaints about their product or service; either by telephone or mail. Quality customer service usually leads to increased sales and customer attitudes. See *customer relations; query.*

customer service desk: a service area in a department store where customers check parcels, have packages wrapped, purchase stamps, or have parking tickets validated, etc.

customer's own merchandise: Synonymous with *customer-owned goods.* See *COG.*

cut carton: in supermarket selling where goods are displayed in their opened original shipping containers rather than unpacked and placed on shelves.

cut case display: See *cut carton.*

CWO: See *cash with order.*

cycle billing: matching of alphabetical breakdowns to specific days to assist in customer billing. Each breakdown is a cycle and occurs on the same day every month.

D

daily best seller report: a list of merchandise that sells in the largest quantities on a day-by-day basis.

damages: items which are available for sale in a damaged state, usually at greatly lowered prices.

data bank: in retailing and merchandising research, a comprehensive collection of information on a principal subject and related areas.

database: a collection of factual information specific to a issue, group, retail market, etc., that is available for quick retrieval, usually on a computer.

database marketing: takes large files of names, addresses, and attributes and picks out those people who are more likely to respond to direct mail or telemarketing. Retailers are increasingly using database marketing to identify target markets for promotion. In most cases, the best data comes from internal sales records. Whether internal or external, the problem the retailer then faces is finding the programming resources to deal with manipulating, sorting, and preparing the database for marketing purposes. Synonymous with *one-to-one marketing; relationship marketing.*

data marketing: See *database marketing.*

data reduction: the process of transforming large masses of retailing and merchandising data into useful, condensed, or simplified intelligence.

date of invoice (DOI): a form of dating denoting that the discount period commences with the date of the invoice. The cash discount period runs a specified number of days from the date of the invoice.

date for value determination: critical in setting duties for merchandise shipped overseas; the date when imported goods were exported from their country of origin. The value of the merchandise in effect on that date is used in setting duties.

dating: a technique of extending credit beyond the time it was originally given; often used as an inducement to dealers to place orders far in advance of the coming retailing season.

days of average inventory on hand: the financial ratio which results from dividing the number of days in a year (365) by the stock turnover; used as one means of examining the store's performance during the accounting period.

days per outstanding: the ratio of accounts receivable to credit sales per day.

DCA: See *Diamond Council of America.*

dead area: See *dead corner.*

deadbeat:

(1) *general:* a person who tries to avoid paying for things.

(2) *retailing:* a customer who fails to pay his or her entire charge every billing period, thus incurring revolving credit charges. Often their names are ultimately purged from lists for future promotional items or services.

dead corner: the area in a retail store that is either empty or is used for nonretailing activities in order to increase the drawing power of the area for retailing purposes, or tends to stop the flow of shopper traffic between multiple shopping areas. Synonymous with *dead area.*

deadline: the time, day, or other period on which something is due.

dead stock: merchandise that cannot be sold.

deal:

(1) *general:* (slang) a large transaction involving a change in ownership.

(2) *retailing:* (slang) a sales promotion enabling a customer to save money on the purchase of a product or service, often with special discounts. By law, such arrangements must be offered on an equal basis to all dealers or retailers having business with a particular manufacturer. Synonymous with *trade deal.* See *deep discounting; retail deal.*

dealer:

(1) a retailer of goods.

(2) an individual or firm that divides quantity goods or services into smaller units for resale to customers.

dealer brand: See *private brand.*

dealer display: in retail stores, posters, placards, signs, etc. that are used for promotional activities. They are given by manufacturers or distributors and are often shown at point-of-sale. Items are at times used in the display.

dealer helps: given to the retailer by the wholesaler or manufacturer; nonpersonal services, such as reading merchandise for resale through packaging, price ticketing, etc.

dealer imprint: a local retailer's name, address, or other identification, put on material created by an advertiser, indicating where goods are bought. Synonymous with *hooker.*

dealer listing: a list of local retailers appearing on a nationally presented advertisement in a local or regional magazine. The advertisement remains the same in all regional issues, but the dealer list changes by region.

dealer loader: a retail point-of-purchase fixture provided by the manufacturer or supplier; usually placed next to a cash register or checkout counter to display items. Synonymous with *display loader.* See *buying loader; trade promotion.*

dealership: an authorized sales agency, often a franchise for an exclusive territory or region.

deal pack: an item of merchandise with an attached premium. Usually handlers (wholesalers or retailers) expect payment for handling these because regular items must be withdrawn during the promotional period.

debit transfer system: an arrangement in which, when a purchase is made, the amount is immediately charged against the buyer's account; no delayed billing is permitted without an interest charge.

debt: money, services, or materials owed to another person as the result of a previous agreement.

debtee: a creditor.

debtor: one who owes money to another.

DECA: See *Distributive Education Clubs of America.*

deceit: conduct in business whereby one person, through fraudulent representations, misleads another person who has the right to rely on such representations as the truth or is unable to detect the fraud.

decentralization:
(1) placing the decision-making point at the lowest managerial level, involving delegation of decision-making authority.
(2) the redistribution of population and business from a city to its suburban areas.

decentralized adjustment system: a system where customers' complaints are dealt with at the department level by salespeople, managers, and/or buyers.

deceptive advertising: advertising that gives false claims or misleading information, in addition to creating a false impression. Should retailers, on a regular basis, advertise goods and services at low prices to lure people into their outlets and then fail to have the merchandise or services, they are guilty of deceptive advertising. Jurisdiction for regulating and enforcing laws in this area is with the Federal Trade Commission. See *consumer protection legislation.*

deceptive packaging: utilizing packages of differing sizes and shapes that may give the impression that they contain more of the item than it actually enclosed, or that the item is significantly bigger than it actually is. See *deceptive advertising; Fair Packaging and Labeling Act of 1966.*

deceptive pricing: pricing methods that are determined to deceive or confuse consumers, includes misrepresentation of credit procedures. See *deceptive advertising.*

declared value: the value of merchandise stated by the owner when the goods are delivered to a carrier.

decorative stone: a natural gemstone that is less rare and less costly than a precious stone or a semi-precious stone. Cf. *precious stone.*

deep discount drugstore: a drugstore where the major attraction is low price; appeals to that segment of the consuming public that make buying decisions strictly on the basis of low cost. In these stores, practically nothing is sold at regular retail prices and selection is frequently limited to items on which the store operator can find an arrangement. See *deep discounting.*

deep discounting: usually found in drug chains; an off-price retailing activity where the item is bought from the retailer on a "deal" basis from the manufacturer (price reductions may be as high as 20%). The store than passes the savings on to the customer by selling at 25 to 40% off suggested retail price resulting in gross margins in the 15 to 20% range. See *deal.*

deep stock: frequently used merchandise kept in large quantities and in many sizes and colors.

defensive budgeting: See *competitive parity.*

defensive pricing: a firm's strategy where its products are priced so as to protect or defend well-known items or market share. For example, introducing a new product at a higher price than other items of the firm so as not to upset their success.

defensive spending: See *competitive parity.*

deferred billing: delaying invoicing of a credit order buyer at the request of the seller. Traditionally used to promote a product to send it without obligation to pay.

deferred discount: See *patronage discount.*

deferred marking: See *bulk marking.*

deferred payment sale:
(1) buying on installment. See *layaway plan.*
(2) a sale that is extended beyond a customary credit period.

delay card: a postcard with information that is sent to a customer advising of an expected delay in the delivery of ordered merchandise.

delayed marking: See *bulk marking*.

delicatessen buying: a type of item purchasing where numerous lines are sampled, but in which none are bought in depth.

delinquent: See *deadbeat*.

deliverability: the extent to which an organization is viewed as being capable of actually delivering to the customer and adequately servicing a particular new product concept. The measure is an attribute of the concept, much as manufacturability is.

delivered cost: the price at which goods are billed to a store, including transportation charges.

delivered duty exempt: in global retailing, an obligation of the seller to pay the costs of the goods, insurance against loss, the freight charges to get them to the named port of destination, and any duties or surcharges or taxes levied on the items by the importing nation.

delivered at frontier: in global retailing; when the seller is required to supply items that conform with the contract, as his or her own risk and expense; the seller must place the items at the disposal of the purchaser at the named place of delivery at the border at the specified time. The purchaser is responsible for complying with import formalities and duty payments.

delivered price: the price to the purchaser's store, which also includes transportation costs.

delivery: the transfer of possession of an item from one person to another. The three major types of delivery system used by retailers are: store owned delivery services; an independent delivery services; and parcel post and express delivery services.

delivery date:
(1) *general:* the date by which a vendor must ship purchases to a store in order to comply with the agreed-upon terms. Failure by the store to meet this deadline is considered reason for cancellation of the order.
(2) *retailing:* the date on which a customer is promised delivery of purchased merchandise.

delivery period: the passage of time between the placing of an order and the receipt of the item.

deluxe items: higher priced, unique goods maintained for sale to customers who are not price conscious.

demand:
(1) a request to call for payment or for the carrying out of an obligation.
(2) the willingness and capability to purchase goods or services.
(3) the composite desire for particular products and services as measured by how consumers choose to allocate their resources among different products and services in a given market.

demand-backward prices: See *market-minus prices*.

demand-based pricing: a pricing technique based on determining consumers' or distributors' attitudes toward the fair cost of goods and services. Ultimately, the prices are determined by market analysis that provides consumer needs and the range of prices that are acceptable to them.

demand creation: See *sales promotion*.

demand cross-elasticity: a statistic of how much the change in price of one item effects the demand for another item.

demand curve:
(1) the graphic representation of the quantity of goods demanded in relation to price. On each point of the curve, the consumer is in equilibrium and the value of the item equals its price.

(2) the amounts of the goods or services buyers are prepared to purchase at different prices during a specified time period.

demand elasticity: See *elasticity of demand.*

demand inelasticity: See *inelastic demand.*

demand merchandise: goods for which the customer is specifically shopping.

demand-oriented pricing: determining the price of an item taking into account the nature and quality of market demand for the offering.

demand patterns: indicates the uniformity or diversity of consumer needs and desires for particular categories of goods and services.

demand price: the maximum price a purchaser is willing to pay for a stated quantity of a commodity or service.

demand-pulled innovation: innovation caused or at least stimulated by the needs, wants, or desires of customers.

demand rigidity: See *rigidity of demand.*

demand sensitivity: the speed of movement for merchandise in a retail store. See *turnover.*

demand state: See *unwholesome demand state.*

demand stimulation: See *sales promotion.*

demarketing: term coined by Philip Kotler and Sidney J. Levy for the concept that part of marketing attempts to discourage customers, either individually or collectively, from desiring a good or service. Synonymous with *creative demarketing.*

demo: short for *demonstration.* See *sales demonstration.*

demographics:
(1) the statistical breakdown of the population within a given area.
(2) a market containing characteristics that can be used for making retailer-consumer predictions.

demonstration: See *sales demonstration.*

demonstrator: an individual hired by either a retail store or a specific manufacturer to promote merchandise by demonstrating it or simply encouraging customers to purchase the item.

demurrage: in transportation, the fee payable to the vessel's owner, or truck for failure to unload freight in time allowed under an agreement.

denying method: See *direct denial method.*

department: the major subdivision within a store, either selling or nonselling, having a specialized function.

departmental control: retail dollar control applied at the individual department level. See *dollar control.*

departmentalization: the manner in which a store is structurally divided, for example, by function, territory, product, customer, or task.

departmentize: See *departmentalization.*

departmentized specialty store: a specialty shop that has grown in size and now contains a variety of items carried which account separately for profit knowledge and for general decision making by its executives.

department manager: an executive charged with the operation of a selling department of a store. Often this individual is the buyer, but he or she may also be involved with stock and sales.

department operating statement (DOS): a monthly report detailing a store department's sales, inventory, markdowns, expenses, etc.

department store: a retail organization that employs 25 or more people and sells merchandise in the following categories: home furnishings, apparel for men, women, and children; and home linens and dry goods. See *chain store system; department store ownership* group; junior department store; specialty stores; store; traditional department store.

department store group: See depart-ment store ownership group.

department store ownership group: a collection of retailers where which member stores (usually once-independent department stores) are centrally owned and controlled in terms of broad policy-making, but which are operated and merchandised autonomously. The individual stores retail their own names and the general public is not aware of their affiliation with the group.

department wrap: the space in each selling department of a store where customer's purchases can be wrapped. See package wrap.

deposit plan: See layaway plan.

depot store: a store carrying popular items that customers purchase because of the store's convenient location. In most cases, the customer is charged higher prices for the items than in supermarkets, discount stores, and other outlets. Cf. bantam store; convenience store; store.

depreciation: charges against earnings to write off the cost, less salvage value, of an asset over its estimated useful life. It is a bookkeeping entry and does not represent any cash outlay, nor are any funds earmarked for the purpose. Synonymous with capital consumption allowance.

depth: the number of distinct items within a product line. See assortment; assortment depth.

derived demand: the demand for an item that grows out of the wish to fulfill the demand for another item (e.g., when a demand for community tennis courts is filled, it leads to increased sales of supplies for the courts and tennis equipment). Cf. suggestive selling.

descriptive billing: a billing system in which an account statement is not accompanied by copies of original invoices. Instead, the statement contains sufficient detail to permit the customer to identify the nature, date, and amount of each transaction processed during the statement period.

descriptive labeling:
(1) labeling that explains the important characteristics or benefits of a product.
(2) the labeling of merchandise by characteristic, but without considering grades or accepted standards. Cf. grade labeling.

descriptive billing: a charge account statement on which each credit transaction is listed showing the name of the department selling the item and its cost. Individual sales checks are not returned to the customer.

design: the arrangement of the visual elements of an object, including such considerations as color, texture, material, shape, etc. The design itself is a combination of details and other features, e.g., in apparel, design is the total concept, silhouette, detailing, and trim. A particular design is usually referred to as a number. In retailing, many lines of merchandise have significant design components such as clothing, housewares, home furnishings, fabrics, china, and glassware, etc.

designer: the individual who makes original sketches and patterns for apparel, scenery, automobiles, packaging, and a wide variety of other products. Fashion or apparel designers create ideas for new styles of clothing and accessories. See couturier.

designer merchandise: items created by a designer, or which carry the approval of the designer whose name appears on the product, typically under a licensing arrangement. See original.

desk jobber: a merchant wholesaler who usually becomes a middleperson and rarely takes possession of merchandise. Instead, he or she sends items directly to the customer from the manufacturer. The desk jobber traditionally is responsible for billing the customer he or she services.

detailer: a salesperson who places vendor displays and insures that they are stocked with merchandise.

detail person:
(1) a salesperson who visits a manufacturer's customs and is responsible for most of the service details that encourages future sales.
(2) a salesperson whose major task is to increase business from existing and future customers by offering them current product information and other personal selling assistance. Synonymous with *missionary salesperson.*

detention time: the time period trucks and railroad cars are detained at unloading facilities beyond agreed upon limits. The consignee can be billed by the carrier for any excessive detention time.

DGRA: See *Diamond and Gemstone Remarketing Association.*

Diamond and Gemstone Remarketing Association (DGRA): located in Frederick, Maryland, an association of retail jewelers and others who sell investment diamonds and gems. DGRA maintains a database on the price history of diamonds and gems.

Diamond Council of America (DCA): located in Kansas City, Missouri, an association of retail jewelry firms and suppliers of gemstones. Offers gemology and diamontology courses to employees of member firms. Supplies members with advertising and education materials, sales tools, displays, etc.

diary method: a technique used to determine brand purchases and the frequency of buying from stores. The user makes arrangements with households to keep a continuous log of brands purchased day by day over a specified period; also used to follow consumers' product buying.

diary study: See *diary method.*

differential: See *differential advantages.*

differential advantages: selling characteristics that provide an advantage over competitors. These include price, product features, location, method of delivery, advertising skills, packaging, and brand name. Synonymous with *differential.*

differentiation:
(1) a method used by the manufacturer to create close identity in a particular market. The manufacturer will introduce different varieties of the same basic merchandise under the same name into a particular item category and thereby cover the range of items available in that category.
(2) positioning a brand in order to differentiate it from its competition and thereby create a unique image. Synonymous with *product differentiation; segmentation strategy.*

differentiation strategy: See *differentiation.*

diffused demand: a demand pattern in which consumer needs and desires for a good or service category are so diverse that clear clusters (segments) cannot be identified.

diffusion: See *diffusion process.*

diffusion of innovation: See *innovation diffusion.*

diffusion process: the manner in which a new concept evolves in a product or service, going from idea to consumer usage.

dime store: See *variety store.*

diminishing returns: may occur in a store with high sales penetration if the store attempts to attract nonconsumers because the costs of attracting additional consumers may outweigh the revenues. Cf. *point of indifference.*

direct authorization: credit approval secured from a store's credit department before goods are released to the customer, either as a take transaction or for delivery.

direct buying: in retailing, by passing the middleperson, the process of buying directly from the manufacturer. See *direct channel.*

direct channel: a channel of distribution free of a middleperson. The manufacturer sells directly to the consumer. See *direct buying.*

direct check: upon the receipt of merchandise, an incoming order is compared to the invoice to see whether quantity billed tallies with the quantity received. See *blind check.*

direct close: frequently employed after the seller receives positive buying signals from a prospect; a closing method of the salesperson where the seller just asks the prospect for a favorable purchase decision free of persuasive manipulations.

direct competitor: a store or chain running competitively with another, offering possible customers similar or identical items or services.

direct cost: the cost of any good or service that contributes to the production of an item or service, e.g., labor, material. Cf. *indirect costs.* Synonymous with *direct expense.*

direct denial method: where the salesperson, to offset resistance to merchandise or service, presents reasons why the consumer is incorrect. Synonymous with *denying method.*

direct expense: See *direct cost.*

direct inventory: See *inventory.*

direct mail: mailers, store catalogs, bill enclosures, etc., which are mailed directly to customers in an effort to sell merchandise.

direct marketing:
(1) a more personal type of promotion than advertising, the process of selling to consumers, personal or industrial, free of a middleperson. The direct marketer chooses the people who will receive his or her promotion, and is the direct recipient of the response, if any.
(2) similar to retail mail-order, but in addition the advertisement is usually delivered by multiple media instead of only a local advertisement or direct mail piece.
(3) Synonymous with *direct selling.*

Direct Marketing Association (DMA): located in New York City, an association of manufacturers, retailers, etc. Surveys consumer attitudes and collects information for the industry; serves as liaison in the United States with our governments.

direct merchandise check: See *direct check.*

director of stores: in department and specialty stores that have national branches the individual with a strong merchandising background who is the executive responsible for the total look and character of the branches.

direct premium: merchandise given without cost with the purchase at the time of the purchase. A form of premium-giving. See *account opener; premium.*

direct product profitability (DPP): by taking into account all allowances and expenses related to the sale of an item, as well as the item's gross margin, DPP gives a detailed financial picture of an item's profitability.

direct retailing: selling items to consumer without the involvement of middlepersons.

direct selling: See *direct marketing.*

direct selling organizations: firms that sell their merchandise on a house-by-house basis rather than in a retail operation.

direct shipment: See *drop shipment.*

direct store delivery: See *drop shipment.*

direct-to-the-home selling: See *door-to-door retailing.*

director of stores: in department and specialty stores that have national branches, the individual who is the executive responsible for the total look and character of the branches.

discount:

(1) *general:* a reduction from the list price in the form of cash or something else of value. Often used as a strategy to counter competitors' initiatives.

(2) *retailing:* the selling of merchandise or a service at a price below the normal list price. Discounts are often given in reaction to competitive advertising; other discounts are given when customers pay for their services or products in cash instead of using credit cards. See *bulk discount; suggested retail price.* Cf. *rebate.*

discount chain: See *series discount.*

discount department store: See *discount house.*

discount house: a retail operation, usually a no-frills store, in which prices are lower than at other stores selling the same merchandise. Synonymous with *discount store.* See *below-the-market strategy.*

discounting: See *discount merchandising.*

discount loading: in retailing, where all inventory and purchase figures are compared on a comparable basis by predetermining all invoice prices to reflect the assumed desirable cash discount percent. Should a purchaser be unable to secure that size discount from a supplier, the item is costed in as though he or she has been successful. The higher cost base figure traditionally results in setting higher retail prices on the item.

discount merchandising: retailing at less than "manufacturer's list" price with few customer services provided.

discount sale: a price reduction permitted workers and members of other special groups.

discount store: See *discount house.*

discrepancy of assortment: the difference between the extent of choice among goods that are usually interchangeable that is expected by the purchaser and the choice that is available from a given source.

discrepancy of quantity: the difference between the quantity a seller should purchase at a specific time from the manufacturer and the quantity a purchaser chooses to purchase at one time from the store.

discrepancy of variety: the difference between the number of distinct types of merchandise that the purchaser would like a given store to have available and the number actually in stock.

discretionary income: the amount of disposable income that is left over after spending on essentials such as food, shelter, and clothing. Marketers of items compete with these essentials to obtain purchases. During a weak economy, people concentrate on necessities and often have less for advertised goods and services. Cf. *disposable income.*

discretionary spending power: money available to consumers after necessities have been purchased. Cf. *disposable income.*

discriminatory pricing: the sale of merchandise at different prices to different customers, thus giving one party an advantage over another. See *Robinson-Patman Act of 1936.*

disguised retail audit: an audit carried on without any awareness by the store's workers.

dispatcher: an agent responsible for efficiently routing and sending merchandise to its destined location.

display: a visual presentation of data or merchandise. Displays differ based on their placement and type, e.g., window displays, floor displays, point-of-purchase advertising displays.

display allowance: See *retail display allowance.*

display card: a tear-off card containing an advertisement that is affixed to a store display.

display case: a carrying case used by salespeople for displaying their merchandise contained, as with a door-to-door costume jewelry salesperson.

display loader: See *dealer loader.*

disposable income: of particular interest to retailers; personal income minus income taxes and other taxes paid by an individual, the balance being available for consumption or savings. Cf. *discretionary income.* Synonymous with *disposable personal income; personal disposable income.*

disposable personal income: See *disposable income.*

dissection: See *classification.*

dissonance reduction: a postpurchase behavior occurring when the customers become agitated in thinking that he or she has made the wrong purchase decision; often compensated by seeking new reinforcing information on the item or service, or ultimately by returning the item or service. Marketers in anticipation of dissonance-reduction suggest using thank-you letters to purchasers, forwarding additional information on the product. See *cognitive dissonance; perceived risk.*

distress merchandise: goods that must be sold, often for some financial exigency, at reduced prices.

distribution:
(1) the separation of merchandise into different categories and group levels.
(2) the process of making sure that a product is available when and where it is desired. Different forms are:
(a) intensive distribution—where the retailer makes the item available in as many stores as possible.
(b) exclusive distribution—where one store carries the item in a given market.
(c) selective distribution—where the item is available in a select few stores in a market area. See *channel of distribution; physical distribution.*

distribution center:
(1) a warehouse in which the emphasis is on processing and moving goods rather than on simple storage.
(2) a storage facility that takes orders and delivers products.

distribution cost analysis: when marketing an item in a particular location, the breaking down of all direct and indirect costs.

distribution intensity: the measure of the exposure a product receives at the wholesale or retail level. With more outlets, the more intense the distribution.

distribution intermediaries: wholesalers, retailers, and marketing specialists, such as transportation firms, that are acting in their roles as facilitators between manufacturers/ service providers and their consumers.

distribution model: a statistical model used to assist management in choosing and assessing the values of various distribution channels; can also help in determining store and warehouse locations and logistics for inventory purposes.

distribution planning: the systematic decision making regarding the physical movement of goods and services from producer to consumer, as well as the related transfer of ownership (or rental) of them. It encompasses transportation, inventory management, and customers transactions.

distributive education: training, primary at the secondary and junior college level, for careers in retailing, wholesaling, merchandising, and allied trades.

Distributive Education Clubs of America (DECA): located in Reston, Virginia, an organization for high school and junior college students interested in the distributive trades of retailing and wholesaling.

distributor: See *wholesaler.*

distributor brand: See *private brand.*

diversionary pricing: in order to give the impression that all prices are low within a store, some of the items are priced very low. This is considered a deceptive practice when most of the merchandise is found to be higher than the usual pricing for the items.

diversion in transit: in the distribution process, a service of rail carriers that permits a shipper to reroute merchandise to a destination other than the original while the items are in transit.

divest-and-exit strategy: when an item or service fails to sell well and their overall market growth rate is slowing, in order to avoid or minimize losses, efforts designed to eliminate a product or service line by selling or discontinuing it. See *product life cycle.*

divest strategy: See *divest-and-exit strategy.*

division: in a large store, an administrative unit in which certain retail functions have been grouped. There are frequently divided into four divisions: merchandising, control, operations, and publicity.

divisional merchandise manager (dmm): the retail executive responsible for the merchandising activities of a related group of selling departments or divisions.

DMA: See *Direct Marketing Association.*

dmm: See *divisional merchandise manager.*

dock: an area, usually on the side or in the back of a store, where goods are unloaded from trucks and moved into the receiving department.

dock warrant: when items are imported but immediate delivery is not required; may be deposited in a warehouse, owned either by the dock authority or by the public warehouse people.

DOI: See *date of invoice.*

dollar control: an inventory information system where planning is based on the number of dollars invested in merchandise rather than on the number of units in stock. See *classification control.*

dollar inventory control: See *dollar control.*

dollar margin method: a retail price-setting technique where merchandise classifications are given a markup percentage on the basis of estimated volume disregarding the profitability individual items. For example, a store can mark up an item a lesser amount if it anticipates very heavy demand thus increasing the gross margin significantly. Cf. *dollar merchandise plan.*

dollar markup: See *markup.*

dollar merchandise plan: an estimate of anticipated store sales, frequently over a six-month period, integrated with inventory estimates and purchases in harmony with sales and profit goals. See *sales plan.* Cf. *dollar margin method.*

dollar open-to-buy: See *open-to-buy.*

dollar store: a store selling damaged or irregular goods or manufacturers' closeouts at prices that are about half regular retail.

dollars returned: See *net profit.*

domestic-only orientation: an approach that excludes all foreign sales, both imports and exports.

domestics: yard goods from which sheets, linens, towels, and so on, are cut. Today, the term is more popularly identified with finished products.

dominant assortment: Synonymous with *classification dominance.*

dominant store: a store that commands the largest share of the available business in a retail trading neighborhood.

don't wants: (slang) COD packages refused by the customer.

door-to-door retailing: selling of a product or service directly from the manufacturer by the manufacturer's employee to potential customers in their homes or offices. This process eliminates the middleperson, with the expectation of cutting costs. See *Green River ordinance.*

doors: in the cosmetics industry, the number of stores where the firm's product(s) are offered for sale. If a firm has 20 doors, it has 20 outlets at the retail level.

dormant account: See *inactive account.*

DOS: See *department operating statement.*

double top: in the merchandising of goods; when a price twice reaches a high point, only to fall back. In such a situation, the likelihood is that the price will continue to fall.

downstairs store: See *bargain basement.*

downtown: a central business district or the center-city section where a large number of stores function. Frequently, the older commercial portion of the city and at times housing the flagship store of a retail chain, along with numerous specialty stores.

downtown store: See *downtown; flagship store.*

DPP: See *direct product profitability.*

dramatic strategy: a sales approach in the opening minutes of consumer contact where the store's salesperson demonstrates how the product functions. Frequently the item or service is shown in the context of a real-life highly emotional situation, e.g., replacing a tire on a wintry night because the tire was defective.

draw: See *drawing account.*

drawing account: a regular allowance made available to salespeople employed on a straight commission basis. The commission earned is balanced against the drawing account at various intervals. Synonymous with *draw.*

dress code: See *dress regulations.*

dress regulations: rules that set forth what is seen by management as appropriate dress for store workers.

drive: See *drive stimulus.*

drive-in market: See *convenience store.*

drive stimulus: a sales promotion offered in the form of a deal to retailers, sales prospects, and consumers to stimulate sales for the duration of the campaign, when the item or service is being actively advertised.

drop: See *drop shipment.*

drop shipment: items that are shipped directly from manufacturer to retailer, usually involving large items, such as ovens and refrigerators that are considered expensive to retain in inventory. Suppliers of drop shipments charge a premium to retailers, who, in turn, charge such costs to consumers. The wholesaler receives only the invoice and then bills the retailer. See *drop shipper.*

drop shipper: a wholesaler who performs most wholesaling activities except storage and handling. He or she sends requests to the manufacturer, who ships directly to the customer. The customer pays the drop shipper, who has already paid the bill to the manufacturer. See *desk jobber; drop shipment; jobber; shipment.*

drugstore: See *pharmacy.*

drumming: a salesperson who calls on retailers of soft goods or meets them at buying centers.

dry goods: specifically, fabrics made from cotton, wool, rayon, silk, and other textile materials; includes ready-to-wear clothing, bed linens, and so on. Cf. *soft goods.*

dual billing and posting: posting a customer's purchases to ledger independently from the preparation of a bill for the customer.

dual distribution: the sale of a product through more than one distributive system; a common technique found in the men's clothing and in the shoe industry.

dual marketing: See *dual merchandising.*

dual merchandising: offering for sale by a particular company items made by other firms as well as itself.

dual offer: a "either-or" promotional method; increases response because store customers can select from two items, and because the offer enhances the perceived value of the items.

dual pricing: See *unit pricing (2).*

dud: (slang) an item of merchandise which is slow selling.

due bill: issued by the store, a certificate that can be redeemed for goods of a specified dollar value; often issued to customers in lieu of cash refunds for merchandise returned. Synonymous with *credit voucher; merchandise certificate; scrip coupon; store credit; store money.*

dummy invoice: a statement prepared by a retailer as a temporary replacement for a vendor's invoice if the latter is not available when the goods are to be received, marked, and put in inventory.

dump bin: a container to hold items as they are dumped into it from the shipping case. Only the one item is displayed in it. See *jumble basket.*

dump display: goods that are casually tossed on a table or into a box, often to project a bargain image to customers.

dumping:

(1) the selling of goods abroad at prices below those which the exporter charges for comparable sales in his or her own country, often involving a subsidy.

(2) in the United States, selling imported items at prices less than the cost of manufacture.

(3) selling merchandise to other countries below cost for purposes of eliminating surplus or to hurt foreign competition. See *unloading.*

dun: to repeatedly demand payment on a delinquent account.

dunnage: loose material, often lumber, that is packed around cargo on trucks, rail cars, ships, to protect goods from damage in transit.

durability: the lasting quality of an item.

durable merchandise: See *capital goods; hard goods.*

Dutch auction: an auction sale in which the prices on items are continuously lowered until a bidder responds favorably and buys.

duty-free: merchandise brought into the country that are not affected by any customs duty.

E

early acceptors: See *innovators.*

early adopters: See *early acceptors.*

early followers: See *early majority.*

early majority: consumers who wait and watch others before adopting a new product. A new product or concept is considered after numerous early adopters have used it and found it fulfilling. Consequently the time required between trial and adoption may be long. Synonymous with *early followers.*

early markdown: a reduction in the selling price of merchandise taken at the beginning of the season while demand is still strong.

earmuff problem: a condition when a salesperson becomes so involved in monopolizing the customer's interest that incoming communications from the prospective consumer are frustrated, thus destroying the value of listening.

EAS: See *electronic article surveillance.*

economic lot technique: an approach that describes the amount of an item that should be made or sold at one time to reduce the total costs involved.

economic man theory: in consumer behavior, where price is the primary motivating variable in consumer buying decisions.

economic ordering quantity: See *economic order quantity model.*

economic order quantity (EOQ) model:

(1) the optimum quantity of a product to order at a given time; used by retailers in setting strategies.

(2) an inventory decision-making approach used to create a formula for determining when to order supplies for the store and in what quantity.

economic shoppers: one of a four-way sociological classification of consumers who are interested primarily in price, quality, variety, and ease in forming conclusions. They are the largest group of the four, which also include apathetic shoppers, ethical shoppers, and personalizing shoppers. See *apathetic shoppers; ethical shoppers; personalizing shoppers.*

economies of scale:

(1) the savings that result when fixed costs are spread over more units of a product; applied in setting retailing strategies.

(2) the result of production functions showing that an equal percentage increase in all inputs leads output to increase by a large percentage. Cf. *economies of scope.*

economies of scope: the ability of a manufacturer to offer a wide product variety at the same time significantly limiting the costs for manufacturing and then distributing. Cf. *economies of scale.*

economy pack: in merchandising, its appeal derives from the savings when several items are included in one wrapping; a form of repackaging. "Two for the price of one," is an example of a *price pack,* or when featured as two related items packaged together and priced at a reasonable rate, e.g., a toothbrush and toothpaste, it is a *banded pack.* See *banded pack; pack; price pack.*

economy size: a large quantity of an item, sold in a single, very large package to provide the customer with a lower per unit price.

eco-retailing: the evolution of specialty stores with an environmental mission.

edge of downtown site: a store location in an unplanned business-associated cluster of stores found at the outer perimeter of a downtown area.

editorial credit: identification of a specific retail operation as a source for a fashion item features editorially (i.e., not in an advertisement) in a consumer magazine or newspaper.

EDM: See *electronic direct marketing.*

Educational Foundation for the Fashion Industries (EFFI): an association of labor and management representatives of the fashion industries. Serves as an advisory body to the Fashion Institute of Technology, provides funds for scholarships and development, and advises on the placement of graduates according to their aptitudes and interests.

effective demand:
(1) the combination of the desire to buy and the ability to buy.
(2) the demand by a particular market to purchase, combined with the capacity to pay.

effective rate of protection: the annual percentage of domestic prices of items that are attributed to tariffs that raise costs to consumers, in order to dissuade them from buying imported merchandise.

EFFI: See *Educational Foundation for the Fashion Industries.*

effort scale: a system for charting the amount of effort a buyer will expend to purchase a specified item.

ego-involved items: merchandise that consumers feel has an emotional or psychological stake.

800-number (eight-hundred number): a toll-free telephone number created for a company who pays for this service, enabling a consumer to order merchandise and services.

eighty-twenty (80-20) principle: the concept that a retailer gets 80% of its activity from 20% of its product line, while spending 80% of its energy to get the remaining 20% of volume.

elastic demand: used in setting retailing goals; demand that changes in relatively large volume as prices increase or decrease. When a small change in price results in a greater change in the quantity people buy, the demand for the items is said to be elastic. The demand for jewelry, furs, and second homes is considered to be elastic. See *elasticity; price elasticity.*

elasticity: used in setting retailing goals; the impact on the demand for an item created by changes in prices, promotion, or other factors affecting demand. See *elastic demand.*

elasticity of demand: a theory relating quantities of merchandise sold to changes in price. Usually, the demand for merchandise varies inversely to price with other factors remaining constant. Synonymous with *demand elasticity.*

elasticity of expectations: the ratio of the future expected percent change in price to the recent percent change of the price.

elastic supply: supply that changes in relatively large volume with a minor change in price.

electronic article surveillance (EAS): to combat the shoplifting problem, retailers use EAS which strikes a balance between the security trade-off that retailers face. Electronic tags are affixed to merchandise and removed or deactivated by a salesperson after purchase. If the tag is not removed, sensors near the store exit trigger an audible or silent alarm.

electronic banking network: See *electronic funds transfer system.*

electronic catalog: a relatively new means of retailing; electronically showing goods to consumers on a television screen on a preset basis. Can be scattered throughout, in public buildings, shopping malls, or via a consumer's own television set. Some electronic catalogs are now interactive, permitting viewers to respond electronically. Most remain noninteractive, requiring the use of another means to respond, such as calling in on the telephone. See *electronic direct marketing.* Cf. *electronic retailing.*

electronic data interchange: a network by which retailers are linked by computer with manufacturers, and ultimately, with every part of the retail distribution pipeline.

electronic detection device: an electronic tag that is affixed to an item which, if not properly removed at the point of sale, will trigger an alarm as the customer walks out of the store.

electronic direct marketing (EDM): an interactive unit, where the ideas of direct marketing are united with television, radio, and/or the telephone; purports to secure a direct response on the part of potential customers.

See *electronic catalog.* Cf. *electronic marketing.*

electronic funds transfer: utilizing automated electronic equipment, such as computer terminals, to move money directly from the customer's account to the retailer's account at the point of sale or service. Can also be used to speedily obtain credit authorization, verify checks, approve credit card transactions, etc. See *electronic funds transfer system.*

electronic funds transfer system: a computerizing banking network that brings branch banking to the customer within the retail store and permits money to be transferred from the customer's account to the retailer's account automatically. Synonymous with *electronic banking network.* See *electronic funds transfer.*

electronic marketing: utilizing electronically generated consumer purchase information in marketing, retailing and sales promotion activities; used in supermarkets and other stores where information is received by having customers use computer-readable cards, such as bar codes, that log data on their product purchases. See *bar code; electronic retailing.* Cf. *electronic direct marketing.*

electronic point-of-sale system: See *computerized-checkout system.*

electronic retailing: utilizing electronically transmitted data to facilitate customer shopping without having to enter the grounds of the store. A form of direct marketing with telephones hooked directly to home computers, television screens, etc. The manufacturer usually bypasses the retailer and sells directly to the consumer. See *electronic marketing.* Cf. *electronic catalog.*

electronic shopping: See *electronic marketing; electronic retailing.*

embourgeoisement: considered obsolete, the theory that affluent workers adopt middle-class standards, lifestyles, and purchasing patterns as the result of their higher earnings.

emergency items:
(1) goods which numerous consumers do not purchase until needed, e.g., tires for their car, plumbing repairs.
(2) goods that are needed to solve an immediate crisis.

emergency products: See *emergency items.*

emotional buying motives: subjective, irrational motivation that affects consumer purchasing in stores.

emotional buying trigger: a drive or emotion, such as self-assertion, sex, acquisitiveness, or curiosity, that motivates a consumer to purchase a particular item.

empathy: the ability to perceive how potential customers feel and what their attitudes, needs, and expectations are.

empirical credit system: a means for learning about the credit-worthiness of store applicants determined by the creditors' experience with borrowers and which attributes points to traits describing the applicant such as previous credit history, whether the applicant owns or rents a dwelling, length of employment, salary.

empirical method of trading area delineation: a means for determining the size and boundaries of a retailer's trading area based on observation and/or experimentation.

employee: any person hired by a store or other retail operation or another person to work for wages (salary or commission).

employee discount: a reduction in the retail price given to a store's own workers (and sometimes their dependents) when buying items at the store.

employee handbook: a manual of facts and instructions provided for the workers of the store or other business.

Often includes the history and philosophy of the store, regulations, policies, procedures, benefits, dress code, etc. Often used in the orientation of new employees.

employer: the person, store, or firm that hires others to work for wages (salary or commission).

emporium: a major place of trade; a large store. Rarely used today.

empowering employees: when companies give their store workers broad latitude to satisfy customer requests. Employees are encouraged and rewarded for showing initiative and imagination.

emulative product: a new offering by a competitor of a similar product.

enclosed mall: a shopping center where the stores all face an internal central promenade. The mall is usually air conditioned throughout the year.

end-aisle display: a point-of-purchase display of goods, that is placed at the end of a row of shelving. Found most frequently in discount stores and supermarkets, they are created to attract the consumer's attention in order to increase sales of the featured item.

end display: a display with a considerable amount of goods set up at the end of a store aisle. It can be readily dismantled.

ending inventory: merchandise on hand at the end of a given accounting period expressed either in dollar value or number of units.

endless chain: a prospecting method where sellers solicit referrals from consumers, and then obtain other names from the people to whom they were originally referred. Each individual contact is encouraged to offer additional names, thus evolving a chain of referrals, going on and on. Cf. *chain prospecting.* See *lead generation.*

end of aisle: See *end-aisle display.*

end of month: See *end-of-month terms.*

end-of-month dating: See *end-of-month terms.*

end-of-month, receipt-of-goods dating: an invoice agreement specifying that the time permitted for payment is calculated from the end of the month in which shipment was made and the cash discount period begins upon the retailer's receipt of the goods.

end-of-month (EOM) terms: in the dating of invoices, an agreement providing that the cash discount and net credit periods beginning at the end of the month the goods were shipped. Invoices dated on the 25th of the month or later are generally treated as if dated on the first day of the next month.

end run: the competitive strategy where a store determines a new approach to securing sales that avoids a direct collision with a market leader who is well known and established with consumers.

end sizes: the large and small sizes that set the range in the line carried by stores. Synonymous with *fringe sizes; outsizes.*

end-user: See *consumer.*

energy management: in retailing, the development and implementation of energy conservation policies and procedures by a store.

engrossing: purchasing and holding away from the market large quantities of merchandise until the time arrives when it is believed they can be sold at a higher price.

enhancement: when new merchandise is introduced to the public, it tends to increase the sales rates of one or more other items in the store's line. Opposite of cannibalizing the market.

ensemble: a costume of matching, complementary, or harmonious items of apparel that create a coordinated look.

ensemble display: in retailing, an interior display for showing all items that it suggests be used simultaneously. These articles are referred to as coordinates. Cf. *coordinates.*

entrepreneur: in retailing, one who assumes the financial risk of the initiation, operation, and management of a given store, business, or undertaking.

environmental forecasting: projecting future events by marketers and retailers, in order to prepare strategy programs by adjusting existing strategies to the altering environment.

environmental scanning: a set of procedures for monitoring the organization's external environment; of particular importance to retailers.

environmental selling: displaying items for sale in a setting that simulates a buyer's home. Purports to aid the customer to visualize the overall effect while generating additional sales of coordinated merchandise.

environmental variables: any factor, such as the weather, the global economy, elections, fuel shortages, and unemployment, that can have a significant effect on a retailer's sales but that is not directly related to retailing functions.

EOM: See *end-of-month terms.*

EOM dating: See *end-of-month terms.*

EOM inventory: See *end-of-month terms.*

EOM, ROG dating: See *end-of-month terms; ROG dating.*

EOM terms: See *end-of-month terms.*

EOQ: See *economic order quantity model.*

Equal Credit Opportunity Act: federal legislation prohibiting creditors from discriminating against credit applicants on the basis of sex or marital status. After March 1977, discrimination on the basis of race, color, religion, national origin, age, and receipt of public assistance was prohibited. Compliance with the law comes under the jurisdiction of the Federal Trade Commission.

equal-store concept: a growing trend in retailing; a multistore retailing agreement where instead of a flagship store and branch stores, all downtown and suburban outlets are given equal status. Synonymous with *sister-store concept.*

equal-store operation: See *equal-store concept.*

equation price: a store price attained by the adjusting action of competition in any market in any time, or a unit of time, such that the demand and supply become equal at that price.

equilibrium price:
(1) the quantity that maximizes a store's profitability.
(2) the quantity of goods determined in the market by the intersection of a supply and demand curve.

equipment: in a store, includes the heating, plumbing, and lighting systems as well as the elevators, cleaning machinery, etc.

erratic demand: the desire for goods and services that is unstable and unpredictable over a given time period. Cf. *seasonality.*

erratic fluctuations: short-term changes that are difficult to measure and predict because they tend to be unexpected; of critical importance to retailers who Seek ways of saving money.

escalator clause: in purchasing, a clause permitting adjustments of price or profit in a purchase contract under specified conditions.

escort shopper: a salesperson who accompanies individual shoppers throughout the store assisting them with advice in making purchase decisions.

essential customer service: See *primary customer service.*

established trends: patterns of increased demand for particular items by color, style, price, etc., as shown by consumer preference reflected in either sales or consumer research.

establishment:
(1) a factory, store, or other place of business, under the ownership of one management, usually located in one geographic area, and producing related goods.
(2) more recently, those in power, and the system under which such power is exercised, maintained, and extended.

ethical advertising: advertising that is determined to meet standards of fairness, honesty, and equitable content.

ethical drug: See *prescription drug.*

ethical pricing: consciously holding back from charging all that the traffic will bear; not overcharging customers.

ethical shoppers: one of a four-way classification of consumers who feel obligated to support local and small retainers because they desire their availability and because it ensures viability to the community. See *apathetic shoppers; economic shoppers; personalizing shoppers.*

ethnic buying habits: the ways a particular ethnic group conducts its buying activities. Retailing strategies are often targeted to fulfill needs of differing ethnic groups.

ethnicity: a retailing and marketing approach to attracting buyers by emphasizing the satisfactions and fulfillment of needs in acquiring ethnic goods or services.

ethno-centers: a retailing operation, for example, bookstore, that appeals to a specific ethnic customers, such as an African-American.

evaluation of merchandise: the inspection and sampling of purchases made by a retailer to determine their quality and assortment.

even-ending prices: See *even-line pricing.*

even exchange: a transaction where the purchaser returns an item for a variety of reasons, then obtains another item with the same selling price rather than a cash refund.

even-line pricing: a strategy of giving whole number selling prices to goods to give the impression of high-end retailing. For example, a retailer using even-line pricing would charge $10.00 for an item rather than $9.95. Cf. *odd pricing*. See *price ending*.

even pricing: See *even-line pricing*.

evoked set: a specific group of brands to which a consumer limits the considerations of choice for purchase. See *span of recall*.

ex-: the point from which merchandise is shipped, not necessarily its point of origin. For example, a machine made in New York and exported through the port of Elizabeth, New Jersey, is said to have been shipped "ex-Elizabeth."

exception report: a statement or accounting showing any deviation from the normal pattern as established by the store's buyer.

exception reporting: See *exception report*.

exchange:
(1) *general:* an exchange occurs when two or more individuals, groups, or organizations give to each other something of value in order to receive something else of value. Each party to the exchange must want to exchange, must believe that what is received is more valuable than what is given up, and must be able to communicate with the other parties.
(2) *retailing:* to return an item to a store to substitute another item.

exchange desk: a space in the store where buyers can return items for exchange, credit, or refund depending on the store's exchange policy.

exchange functions: the buying and selling activities in the market process resulting in the exchange of title to merchandise or services.

exclusive:
(1) goods obtainable from a limited number of stores or dealers.
(2) sales of merchandise limited to a single retailer in a given location. See *exclusive outlet selling*.

exclusive agency method of distribution: See *exclusive distribution*.

exclusive agency selling: that form of selective selling whereby sales of an article or service or brand of an article to any one type of buyer are confined to one dealer or distributor in each area, usually on a contractual basis.

exclusive dealing: See *exclusive dealing contract*.

exclusive dealing contract:
(1) an agreement that a buyer will make all purchases of a specific item from only one seller and will refrain from carrying competing goods.
(2) a method of control over distribution in which the manufacturer forbids dealers to carry competitors' products.

exclusive distribution:
(1) a manufacturer's protection of a dealer against the location of the dealers in the same area, often giving the right to sell an item to the exclusion of other sellers.
(2) an approach to distribution in which the number of intermediaries is limited to one for each geographic territory. Cf. *intensive distribution; open distribution; selective distribution*. See *closed sales territory*.

exclusive merchandise: items not available in other retail outlets in a particular market. See *confined merchandise; exclusive outlet selling*. Synonymous with *exclusives*.

exclusive outlet selling: one retailer or wholesaler in a location having exclusive control over the sale or an article or service, usually determined by contract. See *exclusive merchandise*.

exclusives: See *exclusive merchandise*.

exclusive selling: where a supplier or manufacturer agree with a wholesaler or retailer not to sell to other whole-salers or retailers within the same market. Can be illegal if found to be in restraint of trade.

executive:
(1) *general:* a person whose responsibilities are to administer or manage the affairs of a business or other organization.
(2) *retailing:* managers and assistant managers of divisions and departments who administer the affairs of a retail operation.

executive development manager: the store executive who is responsible for identifying, employing, and training potential new managers.

exempt commodity: merchandise shipped in interstate commerce to which published rates do not apply.

expectation: the benefits or satisfaction that the customer anticipates following the purchase of goods and services.

expectation impact: rising prices can increase the demand for merchandise as purchasers rush to secure the item before the price rises further. The opposite may also take place when buyers put off purchasing in a falling price situation.

expected customer service: any product-related customer service assumed by purchasers that may be available. For example, delivery of major appliances, free alteration of men's clothing, dressing rooms in apparel departments, etc.

expected income: See *consumer's income expectation.*

expected price: the level at which a customer expects an item or service to be priced.

expected service: See *expected customer service.*

expenditure multiplier: the amount resulting from an increase in store sales because of the induced spending created thereby.

expense:
(1) *general:* the cost of resources used to create revenue.
(2) *general:* the amount shown on the income statement as a deduction from revenue. Should not be confused with cost. All expenses are costs, but not all costs are expenses.
(3) *retailing:* involves the money paid out to get the merchandise out of the store and into the hands of the customers and includes such items as wages, rent, utilities, delivery, alterations, and promotions. Excludes the cost of the goods themselves.

expense center: the location within the store where specific, controllable costs can be assigned and which becomes responsible for those costs. Cf. *profit center.*

expense management: a procedure for learning whether the spending needs of a store have been properly allocated.

expense manager: the store executive responsible for analyzing and checking up on expenses.

experience items: merchandise that a consumer tries to be able to assess the claims made for the item. See *search goods.*

expert channel: where independent experts offer statements regarding specific items or services to target customers.

expiration date: in food retailing, the last date on which perishable merchandise should be sold.

expire file: a list of the store's expired customer records used primarily for promotional activities. Retailers use these files for a few years and then the names and addresses are purged because they are no longer considered useful.

explosive: (slang) describing a very successful item, a best seller in the store.

exponential diffusion: See *exponential growth.*

exponential growth: following the introduction of a new product, the slow, initial growth of store sales as the item becomes better known and accepted. It then slows down as the market becomes saturated and the purchase becomes a repeat or replacement decision.

export:

(1) to ship an item away from a country for sale to another country (verb).

(2) to send an item or service out of one sovereign domain to another for purposes of sale (verb).

(3) an item or service sent from one sovereign domain to another for purposes of sale (noun).

exporting: selling merchandise and/or services to other nations.

export license: a government document that permits the licensee to engage in the export of designated merchandise to certain destinations.

exports: a general principle in global retailing; merchandise produced in one country and sold to another.

export tariff: a tax or duty on merchandise exported from a country.

exposure area: the area in a store that is actually visible to customers. More specifically, areas of shelving on which products are exposed to view by buyers.

express store: an exclusive convenience store of approximately 7,000 square feet, with many items of a large supermarket, but with a limited assortment. Cf. *combo store; convenience store; superstore.*

express warranty:

(1) *general:* a statement that specifies the exact conditions under which a manufacturer is responsible for a product's performance.

(2) *retailing:* a seller's position statement concerning the quality, benefit, or value to a consumer of his or her goods, intended to convince an individual to make a purchase. The consumer has the right to expect the store seller to back up these statements. Cf. *implied warranty.* See *warranty.*

extended item: elements which are both tangible and intangible that follow merchandise or service, such as warranties, service contracts, ownership prestige.

extended product: the item of merchandise in addition to all accompanying services, such as warranty and repairs.

extended terms:

(1) *general:* a contractual obligation that has been prolonged beyond the originally stated date of maturity or termination.

(2) *retailing:* where a customer has been given an additional period in which to pay for merchandise.

extensible market: a market with room for growth, either by securing more new customers, or by increasing per capita consumption.

extensive distribution: the sale of an item through the broadest possible number of outlets giving it increased exposure.

exterior visibility: the degree to which a storefront, marquee, or window display can be Seen by a passing pedestrian or a person riding in a vehicle.

external credit: consumer credit at the retail level financed by a lending institution.

external site: a store location found along a highway between major cities; requires the retailer to depend on intercity automobile traffic for its clientele.

external traffic management: the control and direction of goods between the vendor or other supplier and the receiving division of the store.

extra dating: adding days beyond the regular date for invoice payment. Extensions are usually for 30- or 60-day periods.

extraneous items: charges for gift wrapping, special mailing, and so on, that must be subtracted when auditing sales to arrive at true net sales totals.

extras: part-time salesforce hired on an irregular basis.

extrinsic cues: cues that can influence a consumer's perception of a product or service, as factors separate from the item or service itself. Cf. *intrinsic cues.*

eyeball control: the visual examination of store inventory to determine whether there is sufficient stock on hand until requested by the wholesaler, retailer, or consumer. See *inventory control.*

facade: See *storefront.*

face-out: a display fixture where goods, usually apparel, are hung so that they face the customer.

facing: the appearance of a display on shelves. Each unit of an item is one facing wide, because its face occupies one space. The overall shelf display in measured by the number of facings per item.

factor:
(1) *general:* an individual who carries on business transactions for another.
(2) *merchandising:* an agent for the sale of goods who is authorized to sell and receive payment for the merchandise.

factoring:
(1) *general:* selling accounts before their due date, usually at a discount.
(2) *retailing:* the selling of a retailer's accounts receivable to another party, or factor. The factor assumes the loss resulting from any uncollected accounts and receives a relatively high commission from the retailer. Also used in the apparel manufacturing industry.

factor's lien: a factor's right to retain the merchandise consigned to him or her as reimbursement for all advances previously made to the consignor.

factory outlet: historically, a manufacturer-owned store located at the factory where merchandise is sold at greatly reduced prices. Today, also includes the selling of top graded merchandise, often of more than one manufacturer. Synonymous with *outlet store.*

factory outlet mall: a shopping center that focuses on quality, name brand items offered at lower than usual prices.

factory pack: See with *banded pack.*

factory position warehouse: a facility where merchandise is stored, usually close to the manufacturer.

fact sheet: an informational document included in a package of sales material, providing data on the firm manufacturing the item, and the item itself.

factual approach: a copy approach where technical information about merchandise or a service are emphasized to indicate the logic of the benefits for which the market should purchase the merchandise or service. Synonymous with *reason-why approach.*

fad item:
(1) a short-lived fashion, usually limited to a small portion of the population.
(2) a demand pattern for merchandise or services that rapidly achieves considerable popularity but loses it just as

quickly. Such goods or services have extremely short product life cycles as they rarely satisfy major consumer needs.

fad product: See *fad item.*

Fair Credit Billing Act: an amendment to the Federal Truth in Lending Act that protects charge account customers against billing errors by permitting credit card customers to use the same legal defenses against banks or other third-party credit card companies that they previously could use against merchants. See *Truth in Lending Act of 1968.*

Fair Credit Reporting Act of 1971: federal legislation giving the user of credit, the buyer of insurance, or the job applicant the right to learn the contents of his or her file at any credit bureau. See *credit bureau.*

Fair Debt Collection Practices Act of 1978: federal legislation prohibiting the use of abusive, deceptive, and unfair debt collection practices.

Fair Labor Standards Act of 1938: as amended in 1966, this Act sets the current minimum wage rate, the maximum number of hours that may be worked, and makes provisions for overtime pay. Also governs equal pay, child labor, and working conditions for covered employees. Retail stores were exempt before 1964, and small retailers can request exclusion from this Act.

fair market value: the value an imported item would command, under similar circumstances of sale, were the goods sold in the country of origin.

Fair Packaging and Labeling Act of 1966: Federal legislation requiring manufacturers of many consumer items to state clearly the net quantity of contents on the principal display panel of a package. That Act is of importance to manufacturers since they are required to meet all government labeling requirements prior to introducing any new product. Synonymous with *Truth in Packaging Act.* See *deceptive packaging.*

fair price hypothesis: a retail price strategy theory claiming that buyers respond to prices by making mental reference to what they believe is a fair price. Purchasing decisions are less influenced by price comparisons to other similar goods.

fair trade: Consumer Goods Pricing Act of 1975, fair trade acts, resale price maintenance.

fair trade acts: laws passed by various states by which retailers are obliged to maintain specified prices on select goods. In recent years, fair trade pricing has been withdrawn by a great number of retailers and manufacturers. The Consumer Goods Pricing Act of 1975 is federal legislation prohibiting the use of resale price maintenance laws in interstate commerce, resulting in the near elimination of fair trade arrangements. See *Miller-Tydings Act of 1937.* Cf. *unfair practices acts.*

fair trade laws: See *fair trade acts.*

fair trade price: the retail price fixed by the manufacturer of a branded item below which the retailer is prohibited by law from making sales. Increasingly, states are removing this form of pricing. See *price control; resale price maintenance; retail price maintenance.* Cf. *list price.*

family brands: brands that appear on two or more products of a company (e.g., Hershey Company using the Hershey name for both candy bars and cocoa; Lipton Corporation using its name for both soups and teas). Synonymous with *family packaging; umbrella brands.* Cf. *individual brands.*

family life cycle: of considerable importance to retailers and merchandisers, the identified consumer stages:
(a) bachelor stage—young, single person;

(b) newly married couples—young married couple with no children;

(c) full nest I—married people where the youngest child is under age 6;

(d) full nest II—married people where the youngest child is over age 6;

(e) full nest III—older married couples with dependent children;

(f) empty nest I—older married couples with no children at home and the head of the household still earns income at work;

(g) empty nest II—older married couples with no children at home and the head of the household is retired; and

(h) solitary survivors—older people living alone, either retired or still working.

family packaging: See *family brands.*

FAS: See *free alongside ship.*

fashion: the style that is popular within a major part of the market at any given time period. As styles constantly change in response to consumer demands fashion reflects change and is an evolving process.

fashion appeal: the intangible quality of a design making it attractive to the buyer.

fashion board: consumers, frequently high school or college students, hired by retailers to test consumer acceptance of new items and styles. See *college board; teen board.*

fashion clinic: found in the form of a seminar within the store, which may or may not include a fashion show. The fashion clinic includes reports on aspects of fashion, such as color, fabric, silhouette, and is presented for the benefit of store personnel from top management down to salespeople, or for the customers of the store. Usually the clinic is instigated by the fashion director.

fashion consultant: the person or firm that provides professional fashion advice to groups, businesses, or people.

fashion coordination: the continuous monitoring of fashion trends to assure that store items are in keeping with updated style, quality, and appeal.

fashion coordinator: the person responsible for organizing in-store fashion promotions, doing trend research for various fashion departments, etc. These people rarely have direct merchandising responsibilities and in large organizations they often work for the fashion director.

fashion cycle: a variation of the product life cycle reflecting the sales history of the prevailing style of consumer items, such as clothing, car design. Its cycles are: (a) distinctiveness—when the fashion is first sought; (b) emulation—where followers seek it out; and (c) economic stage—when the style enters the mass market. Synonymous with *arc of fashion.*

fashion designer: See *designer.*

fashion director: the person with primary responsibility to promote the store's fashion merchandise by researching trends in fashion, by developing plans for the coming season, and by communicating information to store personnel and customers.

fashion fakes: the low end of the fashion jewelry business.

fashion forecasting: predicting future trends in fashion regarding color, fabric, styles, etc.

fashion goods: distinctive items with a great deal of current customer appeal; characterized by a short product life span, unpredictable level of sales, the need for broad assortments to create a favorable store image, and the importance placed by consumers on style and color. Purchases of fashion items is often done on impulse, or minimally as the result of emotionally based, subjective buying decisions.

Fashion Group, The (TFG): located in New York City and having affiliated chapters in 26 states and 9 countries; members are women executives in fashion and allied fields. TFG provides career counseling and courses, community service, and management training services.

fashion image: a public perception and encouraged by retailers of the store's fashion expertise, leadership, and place within the fashion cycle.

fashion influential: a person whose advice is sought after by associates and others as to apparel styles and trends and whose adoption of a new style promotes its acceptance by a peer group.

fashion innovator: the individual who tends to be in the forefront of accepting and adopting a new fashion style.

fashion jewelry: See *costume jewelry.*

fashion life cycle: See *fashion cycle.*

fashion merchandise policy: a guide to the long-range merchandising strategy of a store, including fashion aims, quality standards, price ranges, and competition. See *fashion merchandising.*

fashion merchandising: the planning, advertising, promotion, and selling of apparel and other fashion-related merchandise to meet the needs of prospective customers as to price, quantity, quality, and style. See *fashion merchandise policy.*

fashion piracy: See *knockoff.*

fashion plate:
(1) an individual who is dressed according to the latest mode of attire.
(2) a picture showing a current style of attire.

fashion product: See *fashion goods.*

fashion sense: being skilled at noticing what captures the public's aesthetic attention and what can potentially develop into a profitable seller.

fashion show: a formal presentation of new apparel styles by an apparel manufacturer or designer to buyers and the press, or by retailers to consumers. The display is frequently held in advance of, or at the beginning of a new fashion season. Live models are often used to display the apparel.

fashion stylist: the person responsible for the presentation of merchandise in a store under the direction of the fashion director or coordinator. The stylist often draws together a variety of garments and accessories for a fashion show or for the display unit where creative judgment is required.

fashion theme: the primary motif around which the merchandise assortment in fashion departments is coordinated.

fashion trend: the movement of fashion from limited to wide acceptance.

FAS pricing: See *free-alongside-ship pricing.*

fast food outlet: a food retailer with a limited menu of prepared food, usually a take out capability, a high turnover of customers, and self-service counters.

fast mover: a high-demand item that sells rapidly.

fast seller: See *fast mover.*

fast-selling stock report: a statement charting the rate of sale of high-demand, fast-selling goods as a safeguard against stock shortages.

fat budget items: merchandise approved by buyers in the hope that the goods will substantially increase sales potential.

FC:
(1) See *fixed cost.*
(2) See *Footwear Council.*

FCC: See *Federal Communications Commission.*

feature:
(1) *general:* a characteristic of a product or service.

(2) *general:* the components of an item or service that yields a benefit.

(3) *merchandising:* a product given special sales promotion.

(4) *retailing:* giving a dominant display and space to an item.

featured items: goods that are given special attention in a display or advertisement.

features/benefits approach: where the retail salesperson assumes that a product's characteristics mean little to the consumer unless he or she can be convinced that it is a benefit to them. It results in the salesperson seeking a way to incorporate this message into his or her presentation.

Federal Communications Commission (FCC): a federal agency established in 1934 to regulate interstate and foreign commerce in communications by both wire and radio activity. Its jurisdiction now includes radio, television, wire, cable, microwave, and satellite. The FCC consults with other government agencies on matters involving radio communications and with state regulatory commissions on telegraph and telephone matters; it also reviews applications for construction permits and relevant licenses.

Federal Equal Credit Opportunity Act of 1977: federal legislation prohibiting discrimination, when responding to credit requests, on the basis of race, color, religion, national origin, sex, marital status, or age; because all or part of a person's income derives from any public assistance program; or because a person has exercised in good faith any right under the Truth in Lending Law. It gives married persons the right to have credit information included in credit reports in the name of both the wife and the husband if both use or are responsible for the account. This right was created, in part, to ensure that credit histories will be available to women who are later divorced or widowed.

Federal Hazardous Substances Labeling Act of 1960: federal law establishing a list of hazardous household substances subject to stringent labeling standards. As a result, the words "danger," "warning," and "caution" now appear more often in labeling.

Federal Trade Commission (FTC): a federal agency established in 1914 to enforce antitrust laws by seeking voluntary compliance or civil remedies. The enabling legislation, which also declared unfair methods of competition illegal, was amended by the Wheeler-Lea Act of 1930. The FTC is empowered to investigate interstate and foreign commerce as well as to take legal action to enforce the laws that fall under its jurisdiction. In the advertising industry, the FTC attempts to prevent fraudulent or deceptive advertising and unfair trade practices. See *consumer protection legislation; grade labeling.*

field: in retailing, the geographic location where goods or services are sold. Consumer research is carried out, via interviews with people; accomplished by sending interviewers into the field.

field salespeople: a saleperson who travels about and visits prospects and customers in their office, factory, or residence. Cf. *inside salespeople.*

FIFO (first in-first out): relating to inventory valuations where the balance sheet figures for inventory should be qualified accordingly. That means that the cost shown for the first shipment of an item is used for valuations. This could inflate or deflate profits.

fifth season:

(1) a slow, mid-winter period when sales must be encouraged by clearance sales, white sales, etc.

(2) a time of the year, characterized by some demand for cruisewear.

figure-eight layout: See *link traffic pattern layout.*

fill-ins: merchandise secured during a period of demand to replace those already sold to avoid lost sales of merchandise that is moving well. See *running.*

final consumer: See *ultimate consumer.*

final consumer's decision process: the procedure by which consumers collect and analyze information and make choices among alternative goods, services, organizations, people, places, and ideas. It consists of six basic stages: stimulus, problem awareness, information search, evaluation of alternatives, purchase, and postpurchase behavior. Demographics, social factors, and psychological factors affect this process.

final sales: the total of net sales to consumers, governments, and foreigners. Final sales exclude sales made to producers, except sales of durable plant and machinery.

financial ratios: the relationship that exist between various items appearing in balance sheets, income accounts, and occasionally other items. These ratios are used to measure and evaluate the economic condition and operating effectiveness of a firm.

financial risk: a consumer-perceived risk that merchandise may not be worth its purchase price.

financial statement: any statement made by an individual, a proprietorship, a partnership, a corporation, an organization, or an association regarding the financial status of the legal entity.

financing: a retailing and marketing activity that includes the management of money and credit needed to obtain the goods and services desired by consumers. It excludes manufacturing activities.

fine jewelry: highest quality jewelry made of precious metals; often set with precious or semi-precious stones.

fines: a consumer-protection legal concept in which dollar penalties are levied on a store for deceptive promotion.

finished goods: completed products awaiting sale.

finished-goods inventory: all items a manufacturer has made for sale to customers.

fire sale: merchandise sold at greatly reduced prices because they have been damaged or water-soiled in a fire.

firm:
(1) describing the full acceptance of an obligation to perform, deliver, or accept (e.g., a firm bid, a firm offer).
(2) any business, corporation, proprietorship, or partnership.
(3) an unincorporated business or a partnership. Unlike a corporation, a firm is not a separate person apart from those managing it (i.e., not an entity).

firm bidding: a policy as requesting bids for merchandise in which prospective vendors are informed that original bids are to be final, that changes cannot be accepted under any circumstances.

firm market: a condition of stable prices.

firm order: a definite order that cannot be canceled. It may be written or oral.

firm price: an obligation to the maker of a stated price that must be met if accepted within a specified time period.

first cost: the wholesale price for items in a foreign market, exclusive of shipping costs and customs duties.

first in-first out: See *FIFO.*

first in, still here (FISH): describes ending inventory. See *ending inventory.*

first quality: merchandise without imperfections.

first-time buyer: a customer who purchased an item or service from a seller for the very first time. They are considered sound future prospects and are often recipients of promotional materials.

fiscal year: twelve consecutive months selected by a business; used as an accounting period for annual reports.

FISH: See *first in, still here.*

five-and-ten store: See *variety store.*

fix: setting the cost of an item or service.

fixed assets: permanent assets required for the normal conduct of a business, which usually are not converted into cash during the period after they were declared fixed (e.g., furniture, land, buildings).

fixed-based budgeting: a means of determining a retailer's budget by permitting an estimated amount of disbursement for each of the store's expenses. At the close of the period, the actual expenditure is placed alongside the estimate. Variations are traditionally indicated in dollar amounts and/or percentages.

fixed charges: in retailing, business expenses that are not related to the level of store operations.

fixed cost (FC): a cost for a fixed period and range of activity that does not change in total but becomes progressively smaller per unit as the volume increases. Synonymous with *fixed expenses; period cost.* Cf. *variable cost.*

fixed cost contribution: the portion of a selling price that is left over after variable costs have been accounted for.

fixed expenses: See *fixed cost.*

fixed-fee buying office: See *salaried buying office.*

fixed-order period model: a method for determining the number of items to be ordered at fixed time intervals up to a predetermined maximum level.

fixed-order quantity model: a method for determining the standard number of merchandise to be ordered when the inventory reaches a predetermined level.

fixed period system: a method of reordering goods where orders are submitted to the vendor when stock levels reach a predetermined low level or cushion regardless of when the last order was submitted.

fixed routing: calling on customers on a regular basis.

fixtures: items used by a store to stock and display its goods, including tables, racks, etc.

fixturing: choosing and arranging store fixtures, such as racks and counters, for the purpose of display and customer convenience, especially in the case of self-service stores.

flagship division: See *flagship store.*

flagship store: a downtown or home office store where executive, merchandising, and sales personnel are located. To qualify the store must have one or more branches. See *parent store.*

Flammable Fabrics Act of 1953: federal legislation banning the sale of certain items of clothes and household furnishings that present an "unreasonable risk of death, personal injury or significant property damage" due to fire.

flanker brand: See *flanker product.*

flanker product:
(1) a new product similar to an already existing companion product, with the same brand name.
(2) a new product introduced into a product category by a firm that already markets an existing brand in that category. The flanker can be of a different shape, size, but basically the same product.

flanking: See *flanker product.*

flash in the pan: popular merchandise that is successful for a brief time period, but for which there are no expectations of producing long-lasting interest. See *fad item.*

flash report: See *flash sales report.*

flash sales report: an unaudited report of a previous day's sales.

flat: with no interest.

flat rate: a uniformly charged rate for each unit of goods and services, irrespective of quantity, frequency of purchase, and so on. Cf. *variable pricing.*

flea market: historically, an outdoor bazaar where vendors offered cheap, secondhand merchandise for sale to the public. Today, may also include the indoors and merchandise may also be new, though still inexpensive compared to the prices paid in stores.

flexible approach to pricing: a price setting policy that considers several variables. Full costs are computed to set a minimum price at which the items can be sold. The merchant works from this point with flexible markups which can be adjusted to meet changes in consumer demand, competition, etc.

flexible charge account: Synonymous with *all-purpose revolving account.*

flexible markup pricing: See *flexible approach to pricing.*

flexible price policy: See *variable pricing.*

flexible pricing: a pricing strategy based on the study by the manufacturer of all market forces, as contrasted to an approach of a rigid adherence to a set ratio of profit to sales. Synonymous with *variable pricing.*

flier: a handout used to promote an idea, product, or person (e.g., a political candidate). Synonymous with *flyer.* Cf. *circular.*

float:

(1) *general:* the amount of funds in the process of collection.

(2) *retailing:* variations in the placement of a label on a form.

floation (flotation): a method of interior packaging to protect a packed item from shock and vibration by wrapping it in a cushioning substance thick enough that the wrapped shape of the item conforms to the dimensions of the container.

floating display: a display that is taken to different spaces within the store or between branch stores.

floodlight: the high-intensity artificial light that reflects a broad beam in order to provide uniform illumination over a large area; used in parking lots, storefronts, display windows, etc.

floor allowance: a discount permitted the buyers in the selling department or at the point of sale when purchasing a damaged or otherwise defective item.

floor audit: utilizing the selling floor cash register to obtain total cash and credit sales for each salesperson, department, and form of sale.

floor limit: the largest amount for which a merchant may accept noncash payment (check or credit card) without obtaining an authorization. A zero-floor limit calls for authorization for every transaction, and this is becoming more feasible as the time and cost of obtaining authorization decline. See *authorization line; negative authorization.*

floor plan: the scale drawing of the layout of rooms and facilities on a floor of a store or other structure.

floor plan financing: short-term financing of big ticket items, where the retailer borrows funds and pays the vendor for the goods at time of receipt. The lending institution that has loaned the money retains title to the items as collateral and is repaid by the retailer once the merchandise is sold.

floor planning: See *floor plan financing.*

floor price: in the marketing of goods and services; the minimum price which normally cannot be further reduced, due to economic, political, or trade reasons.

floor pyramid: in retailing, a point-of-purchase advertising display where products for sale are piled in the shape of a step pyramid, usually within arm's reach.

floor-ready merchandise (FRM): a means of receiving merchandise quickly, overcoming slowness resulting from ticketing with retail prices, and proper hanging of items. New industry-wide guidelines for FRM are a top priority, and department store retailers are using technology investments to assist in this effort. Retailers want to move merchandise shipments, once received, in no more than one hour prior to displaying the items. Bar codes, preticketing, and pre-hanging of goods is required.

floor stand: a rack, frame, or mounting used by retailers for goods in a point-of-purchase advertising display.

floor stock: items accessible to customers within the store. See *back up merchandise*. Cf. *shelf stock*.

floor value factor: a means of equating productivity to the location of the selling department:

floor value factor =

$$\frac{\text{distance from entrance to back}}{\text{distance from entrance to department}}$$

floorwalker: a person who moves about a store through various selling departments and assists customers in ways not handled by sales personnel.

fluctuating demand: in retailing, the haphazard demand for goods and services; usually less stable than demand for consumer goods and services.

flyer: See *flier*.

flying squad: See *contingent force*.

FOB: free (freight) on board. Identifying the point from which a store is to pay transportation on incoming shipments. When the terms are FOB shipping point, the store must pay all charges from the vendor's shipping point. When the terms are FOB store, the vendor must pay all charges up to the store's receiving dock. See *FOB pricing*.

FOB pricing: a geographic pricing policy in which buyers pay transportation

costs from the point at which they take title to the product. See *FOB*.

focused market unit: a market-oriented division that services potential customers regardless of their location.

fold-over statement: the bill to be sent to a charge customer which comes prefolded so that the name and address of the store or other creditor will appear when inserted in the transparent window of an envelope that is provided.

follow-up letter: a letter that is never mass mailed; a sales communication sent to someone who has made an inquiry inviting the prospect to make a purchase; generally reserved for expensive store merchandise.

Food and Drug Administration: a U.S. agency established in 1930 by federal legislation (now part of the Department of Health and Human Services) to develop standards and conduct research with respect to reliability and safety of drugs. It evaluates new drug applications and claims for drugs, conducts clinical studies on the safety of drugs, operates an adverse drug reaction reporting program, maintains a nationwide network of poison control centers, and advises the Justice Department on the results of its research. See *Food, Drug, and Cosmetic Act of 1938*.

food brokers: people who introduce buyers and sellers of foods and related general-merchandise items to one another and bring them together to complete a sale.

Food, Drug, and Cosmetic Act of 1938: federal legislation that strengthened food labeling requirements and extended strict requirements to advertising and labeling of cosmetics. The Act requires that drug advertising and labels include "all material facts" about a drug. See *Food and Drug Administration*.

Food Marketing Institute: located in Washington, DC, an organization comprised of food retailers and wholesalers. Publishes annual operating results for the industry and supports the Food Marketing Institute Political Action Committee.

football item: goods used as an incentive to attract customers to a retail store as the retailer raises and lowers the price of this item daily.

Footwear Council (FC): the public relations unit of the shoes industry; represents manufacturers, retailers, tanners, suppliers, importers, and road salespersons. The FC purports to increase retail sales of shoes in all categories and improve the image of the shoe industry.

forced distribution: promotional activities, including advertisements, which encourage consumers to ask for (and at times demand) merchandise not handled by some retailers. Its purpose is to compel retailers to order the requested product(s). Synonymous with *pull distribution strategy.*

forced sale: selling an item below market price usually to enable the merchant to liquidate merchandise and meet demands of creditors.

forced saving: the situation that occurs when consumers are prevented from spending a portion of their income on consumption.

forcing method: a motivator hoping to stimulate a customer to make an immediate purchase of an item.

ford: See *ford item.*

ford item: a popular, mass-produced item or style selling in large quantities. The item may be widely copied at a variety of price levels, comes from the Ford automobile which achieved wide popularity before other brands of cars could be developed.

forecast: the prediction of future sales potential or customer acceptance of a new style or product. See *forecasting.*

forecasting: of critical importance to market researchers for goal setting; projecting events of the future utilizing current data. See *forecast; sales forecast.* Synonymous with *projection.*

forecasting model: a model for predicting the sale of goods or services, market share levels, and other related variables.

foreign buying office: a facility located overseas to assist in purchasing goods from foreign vendors.

foreign national pricing: local pricing in another nation.

foreign sales agent (FSA): an individual or firm that services the foreign representative of a domestic supplier and seeks sales abroad for the supplier.

foreign trade zone (FTZ): See *free trade zone.*

foreign valuation: the value of imported merchandise; expressed in terms of the currency of the country of origin for the purpose of customs duty.

forfeiting: the purchase, without recourse, of receivables from the export sales of items.

former purchaser: a customer who has not bought additional goods within a specified time period, traditionally one year. In general, they represent future potential sales in that they have shown an ability to buy merchandise.

formula pricing: a pricing technique where the final price is set using a formula.

form utility: the characteristic of merchandise that makes it possible to fulfill a consumer's needs when processing is altered to put it into a more useful form. See *utility.*

fortnight: a store-wide promotional effort with goods of a specific country set on display for a two-week period.

These are often annual events and may include tie-ins with the community.

forward buying: committing bought items to provide for needs during a time period longer than is needed for immediate gratification.

forward dating: a strategy for encouraging present purchases by moving the billing date ahead to a future time.

forwarder: See *freight forwarder.*

forward integration: a technique where the producer owns or controls the distribution channels through which his or her goods pass as it approaches prospects.

forward invention: the development of new goods for overseas markets.

forward order: a commitment to accept merchandise to be delivered at a later time.

forward stock: stock that is brought into the selling department. The merchandise, which may be hidden from people, is usually stored on the selling floor rather than in a stockroom. See *inventory.* Cf. *shelf stock.*

forward stock room: See *stock room.*

foul-weather pricing: selling an item without profit, at times not even covering costs of production and advertising; used to keep a store or firm in operation during recession.

foundation: in the apparel industry, describing any supporting undergarment used by women. For example, bras, girdles, and corsets.

4-5-4 calendar: See *retail calendar.*

four-way rack: a store fixture having four extended arms. Used for hanging items; permits 360-degree accessibility to merchandise. Synonymous with *quad rack.*

fragmentation: when marketers and retailers identify and then divide the total market into units with common characteristics, interests, and needs. Cf. *segmentation.*

frame of reference: a sociological-psychological interpretation of how a person perceives his or her external environment. A significant portion of consumer behavior and store purchasing is based on an individual's frame of reference.

franchise:

(1) a privilege granted to a dealer for distribution of a manufacturer's product.

(2) a legal contractual relationship between a supplier and one or more independent retailers. The franchisee gains an established brand name and operating assistance, while the franchisor gains financial remuneration as well as some control over how the business is run. See *franchiser; franchisor.*

(3) specific territory or outlet involved in such a right. See *refusal to sell.*

franchise cooperative: a voluntary association of retailers who form a franchise organization by establishing a retail cooperation chain or a wholesale operation for their mutual benefit.

franchised dealer: a retail dealer who, under terms of a franchise agreement, carries a supplier's products.

franchise department: See *leased department.*

franchisee: a retail outlet that purchases the right to market the goods or services of a franchisor in exchange for the use of the latter's name, product line or service, marketing and management expertise, etc. See *franchise; franchisor.*

franchise extension: a new product that capitalizes on a firm's market strength. A franchise has a relationship with customers that may be based on brand, a salesforce, a favorable trade relationship, etc. The new item is often not unique but sells based on the favorable franchise.

franchise lease agreement: See *leased department.*

franchiser: an individual or company that licenses others to sell its products or services.

franchise store: an independently owned store that sells branded items produced by a franchise holder. The store pays the franchiser a percentage of sales for the use of the name.

franchise wholesaling: a full-service merchant wholesaling format whereby independent retailers affiliates with an existing wholesaler to use a standardized storefront design, business format, name, and purchase system.

franchising: See *franchise.*

franchisor: a manufacturer, wholesaler, or service distributor that sells the right to use its name, advertising, management and marketing expertise, etc., to retail outlets for a fee. Provides assistance, guidelines, and established business patterns to the franchisee. See *franchise; franchisee.*

fraud: intentional misrepresentation of the truth in order to deceive another person. Aspects of fraud include the false representation of facts, with the intent that the deceived person act thereon; knowledge that the statement would deceive; and knowledge that the person deceived acted, leading to his or her injury. See *bad faith; deceit; pyramid selling.*

fraudulent purchase:
(1) an order written by a store buyer to a vendor which is paid for by the store but never delivered.
(2) stolen merchandise returned to a store for credit.

free alongside ship (FAS): where the seller or other shipper will pay transportation charges to the ship's side. The expense of loading the merchandise onto the vessel, the shipping charges, and all concomitant risks are the purchaser's responsibility.

free-alongside-ship (FAS) pricing: in billing, indicating that the seller's price includes the cost of getting the merchandise alongside the ship being used to transport the items. It does not include the actual cost of shipping goods to the buyer.

free carrier: similar to free on board, except that the seller fulfills his or her obligations when the merchandise is delivered into the custody of the carrier at the named point. Cf. *FOB.*

free deal: See *free goods.*

free examination offer: See *trial offer.*

free-flow pattern: the physical assortment of a store's fixtures using a series of circular, octagonal, oval, or U-shaped patterns to create an atmosphere of informality, considerable open space, and the ability of the customer to select different directions.

free-flow pattern layout: See *free-flow pattern.*

free-flow traffic: See *free-flow pattern.*

free-form layout: See *free-flow pattern.*

free-form retail organization: See *merchandising conglomerate.*

free goods: items that are so abundant that it is not profitable to attempt to charge for them (e.g., sunlight). Free items are treated as price concessions by the Federal Trade Commission.

free goods offer: merchandise received by a buyer at no cost for having purchased some unit of goods. Cf. *traffic builder.*

freely offered: the concept where merchandise will be offered in the normal course of trade to all buying on essentially the same basis.

free mat: advertising copy made in advance, that is provided to a retailer who has only to fill in the name and location of the store.

free on board: See *FOB.*

free on rail: the price of merchandise that includes the cost of moving them to a railhead for shipment and loading into a rail wagon.

free on truck: the price of merchandise that includes the cost of moving them to a truck for shipment and loading onto a truck.

free-standing location: a store location not physically connected to other stores in the vicinity. The store may be large with its own parking facilities (as in highway retailing), or it may be a neighborhood retailer, such as a small corner grocery store.

free-standing neighborhood store: See *neighborhood store.*

free-standing store: See *free-standing location.*

free trade agreement (FTA): a means for lowering tariffs of exported merchandise; a comprehensive agreement design to remove barriers to substantially expand all trade through eliminating tariffs and quotas, enhancing market access, improving standards for treatment of investors, etc. FTAs cover virtually every aspect of trade between signatories. They purport to remove all significant barriers to trade in goods and services. Under free trade agreements, firms will be able to make decisions based on their market advantage, rather than on arbitrary tariff and nontariff barriers. See *free trade zone.*

free trade zone: a port designated by the government of a country for duty-free entry of any nonprohibited goods. Merchandise may be stored, displayed, used for manufacturing, and so on, within the zone and reexported without duties being paid. Duties are imposed on the merchandise (or items manufactured from the merchandise) only when the goods pass from the zone into an area of the country subject to the customs authority. Synonymous with *foreign trade zone.*

free trial offer: See *trial offer.*

freight: all merchandise, goods, products, or commodities shipped by rail, air, road, or water, other than baggage, express mail, or regular mail.

freight absorption:
(1) where the seller is not charging a customer for freight outward.
(2) a geographic pricing policy in which the seller charges the same freight rate as the competitor located nearest to the buyer.

freight allowance: See *freight allowed.*

freight allowed: an agreement whereby a store pays the transportation charges on incoming goods, but is permitted to charge back all or part of that cost to the vendor; may be based on the cost of the merchandise, the weight of the merchandise, or the quantity of the merchandise ordered. Synonymous with *postage stamp pricing.*

freight equalization: See *unsystematic freight equalization.*

freight forwarder:
(1) a transportation company that pools many small shipments to take advantage of lower rates, passing some of the savings on to the shippers.
(2) an organization that consolidates the less-than-carload or less-than-truckload shipments of manufacturers into carload or truckload shipments. Synonymous with *make bulk center; package consolidating agency; packing house.*

freight-in: shipping charges on bought merchandise.

freight inward: freight paid on shipments received.

freight on board: See *FOB.*

freight outward: freight paid by a seller on outgoing customer shipments. See *freight absorption.*

freight paid to: where a seller must forward the goods at his or her own expense to the agreed destination and is responsible for all risks of the goods until they are delivered to the first carrier.

freight pool: a cooperative shipping arrangement where manufacturers often ship in less-than-carload lots. By combining their small shipments into one carload lot, they reduce expenses and thus their costs.

friend-of-a-friend promotion: a promotional method where established customers are presented with incentives (e.g., a free gift) for referring to the seller names of people who might be interested in securing the product or service. Cf. *member-get-member promotion.* See *referral leads.*

fringe assortment: items that generate only marginal customer interest and, therefore, having a slow turnover rate.

fringe market: the segment of a store's clients who are outside the store's core market; i.e., who frequent the store on an occasional basis.

fringe sizes: See *end sizes.*

fringe stock: goods that generate only a small percentage of a store's sales. See *fringe assortment.*

fringe trade area: See *fringe trading area.*

fringe trading area: the area outside a store's primary and secondary trading areas that provides some of the store's customers, even though they are widely dispersed. See *primary trading area.*

FRM: See *floor-ready merchandise.*

front: in retailing, the selling area of the store.

front end: in retailing, where store buyers pay for their merchandise.

front end checkout: a store layout with checkstands and registers at or near the store's entrance rather than throughout the store.

FSA: See *foreign sales agent.*

FTA: See *free trade agreement.*

FTC: See *Federal Trade Commission.*

FTZ (foreign trade zone): See *free trade zone.*

fulfillment: processes for receiving, servicing, and tracking orders sold via direct marketing. They include subscriptions, book club orders, catalog items, fund raising. Fulfillment systems purport to fill order rapidly, maintain customer files, sent invoices and record payments, react to customer complaints and other inquiries, and to produce purchase and payment information to be used in future marketing programs. See *customer service.*

fulfillment system: See *fulfillment.*

full cost approach to pricing: a method of setting prices of items that are to be sold at retail. The price of each item sold in the store covers all the costs of that particular item. Each aspect of selling cost is taken into account, including rent, utilities, salaries, delivery costs, and returns. Added to these considerations are the cost of the merchandise itself and a percentage high enough to provide a reasonable profit.

full-cost pricing: See *full-cost approach to pricing.*

full demand: where buyers want and are willing to pay for all the items that are being manufactured.

full disclosure: providing total information to consumers regarding merchandise and services. In products, found on labels and in advertisements.

full-function wholesaler: See *full-service wholesaler.*

full-line: goods found in a store having all styles, sizes, colors, etc., that a customer can expect to find.

full-line discount store: a department store with lower prices, a broad merchandise assortment, a lower rent location, more emphasis on self-service, brand-name merchandise, wide aisles, shopping carts, and more merchandise displayed on the selling floor. Synonymous with *promotional department store.*

full-line forcing: urging the customer to purchase the least desirable item of a seller's line in order to secure the more desirable goods. See *cherry picking.*

full-line retailer: See *full-line store.*

full-line store: a retailer who carries all of the goods that are anticipated by customers for that type of store.

full-line wholesaler: See *general line wholesaler.*

full-mark: a 100 percent markup in goods.

full-service merchandiser: a vendor who provides promotional assistance, accounting systems, training programs, and other services to the retailer in addition to merchandise. The retailer, in turn, agrees to buy a significant order from the vendor.

full-service store: a retail store that is adequately staffed with sales and support personnel so as to provide a full range of services. These services include individual sales assistance, credit, delivery, gift wrap, installation, repair, etc.

full-service wholesaler: a wholesaling middleperson who takes title to goods that are resold, frequently takes physical possession of the items. Such people often operate warehouses, extend credit, assist customers with accounting and marketing data. Synonymous with *regular wholesaler; service wholesaler.* Cf. *limited-service wholesaler.* See *wholesaler.*

full-time worker: an employee in a store or other business who is employed on a year-round basis and who works a full work week, usually 35 to 40 hours per week. Cf. *part-time employee.*

full-warranty: See *Magnuson-Moss Warranty Act of 1975.*

functional classification: a means of separating positions and responsibilities among specialized functional areas such as sales promotion, buying, and store operations.

functional costing: classifying costs by allocating them to the various functions performed (warehousing, delivery, billing, etc).

functional departmentalization: placing of similar activities involving similar expertise in the same department of the store or other business.

functional discount: See *trade discount.*

functional expense: See *functional expense classification.*

functional expense classification: a system of identifying the reason for an expenditure by assigning it to a specific retail activity.

functional manager: a manager who is responsible for a specialized area of operations, such as retailing.

functional middleperson: an independent business which purports to assist in the passing of title to merchandise without taking title to the items in the process. Synonymous with *agent middleperson.*

functional need: the need of a buyers that is met by the practical application and use of a product or service without referring to style, image, etc.

functional product grouping: arranging and displaying goods according to usage.

functional risk: the consumer-perceived risk that a product, if purchased, may not perform as it was promoted or advertised.

functional satisfaction: the satisfaction received from the tangible or functional features of a product.

functions of physical supply: the function of distribution, transportation, and warehousing.

furnishings:

(1) items in a store that are not regarded as equipment or fixtures, e.g., carpeting, furniture, office appointments, etc.

(2) in men's wear, includes ties, shirts, socks, underwear, sleepwear, robes, and accessories.

Fur Products Labeling Act of 1951: federal legislation protecting the public against false labeling and advertising of furs.

future dating: a sales agreement setting the beginning of the discount and net periods for some time in the future rather than at the time the merchandise is shipped.

G

GAA: See *Gift Association of America.*

GAFF (GAFFO): abbreviations for a store category including general merchandise, apparel and accessory, furniture and home furnishings, and appliances stores.

garment center: the section to the east and west of Seventh Avenue in New York City, running from the low 30s to 40th Street, where some of the nation's women's ready-to-wear industry is located. In recent years, there has been a shift to other parts of the city and elsewhere across the United States. See *Seventh Avenue.*

gemstone: a mineral found in nature that is appropriate for use in jewelry because of factors such as beauty, clarity, rarity, etc. Some stones are far more valuable than others, dividing them into precious and semi-precious categories.

general credit contract: a retail installment contract providing no right of repossession to the merchant or other creditor. The merchant can sue the purchaser if the terms of the contract are not met. At times, merchants use wage assignments to secure credit. In these cases, a default allows the retailer to garnishee the wages of the debtor.

general line distributor: an industrial distributor called a general line wholesaler. Synonymous with *general line house.* See *general line wholesaler.*

general line house: See *general line distributor.*

general line retailer: a retailer who carries a wide range of products.

general line wholesaler:
(1) a merchant wholesaler who carries merchandise in a host of unrelated lines.
(2) a full-service wholesaler that carries a wide variety of product lines.

general merchandise retailer: See *general line retailer.*

general merchandise store: a retail operation with a wide variety of items.

general merchandise wholesaler: See *general line wholesaler.*

general sales manager: the sales executive responsible for complete coordination of the store or division's salesforce. Although he or she will not traditionally set policy, developing strategies and methods to fulfill the store's plan is a major responsibility along with supervisory involvement.

general sales tax: a tax on most items, collected at the time of purchase. In many states, purchases of food and medicine are excluded from this tax.

general-specific-general theory: See *retail accordion theory.*

general store: a small retailing operation, not departmentalized, often found in country areas, where a wide variety of items can be bought, including food, clothing, and supplies.

general trading area: a geographical area from which most of the store's customers are drawn.

generative business: that part of the store's sales that are generated through its own efforts, such as promotions, high quality merchandise, competitive prices.

generator store: See *anchor store.*

generic brands: unadvertised, plain label grocery items that often sell for 30 to 40 percent less than advertised brands. Packaging tends to be sparse, with only the generic product name and required governmental labeling information given. See *branding; generic product.* Synonymous with *noname brands.*

generic competitor: an organization that competes with others to satisfy consumers' wants or needs within a general category of products or services.

generic market: a market where vendors offer substitute items that are different perceptually and physically.

generic name: a brand name that has become associated with a product category rather than with a particular brand.

generic product:
(1) an item sold under a common name rather than a brand name.
(2) not the product itself, but a concept that incorporates the hopes the purchaser has with regard to the item.
(3) a set of tangible or intangible attributes that are assembled into an identifiable form. See *generic brands.*

geodemography: a retailer's tool that links households with geographic locations to identify regional lifestyles that impact directly on consumer attitudes, behavior, and buying patterns.

geographical market segmentation: the subdivision of the population of possible buyers that is based on where they live; provides the retailer with a plan for differences in regional preferences as well as differences in product requirements; includes segmentation based on region of the nation, degree of urbanization, city size, and population density. See *market segmentation.*

geographic segmentation: See *geographical market segmentation.*

Giffen good: See *inferior goods.*

Gift Association of America (GAA): located in New York City, an association of retailers and wholesalers of gifts, china, glass, and decorative accessories. Formerly the Gift and Decorative Accessories Association.

gift certificate: a purchased certificate written in any dollar amount; given as a gift that is redeemable in goods at the store of purchase.

gift close: a salesperson's closing method purporting to provide the prospect with an added incentive to buy the item or service immediately. Usually a service is rendered, such as shipping the same day, and not a "gift" as suggested in the term, since no hard item is involved. See *close.*

gift and decorative accessories association: See *Gift Association of America.*

gift transaction: a sales transaction where the item is to be the gift. Instructions for the removal of price tags and wrapping are included on sales check.

gift wrap: providing decorative boxes and wrapping paper for goods bought in the store at the customer's request. Some stores have special gift wrapping departments, although smaller stores often combine this function with salesperson wrap. Two kinds of gift wrapping services are provided—regular gift wrapping that is free of charge in boxes and paper bearing the store name and/or logo, and special gift wrapping—provided for a fee and consists of artistically wrapped pages in decorative paper with ribbons. Cf. *package wrap.*

gift wrapping: See *gift wrap.*

giveaway: See *traffic builder.*

GLA: See *gross leasable area.*

globalization: the tendency for retailers and others to expand across national boundaries, leading to increasing competition among firms from different nations and a growing dependence on diverse, multinational, and multicultural customer bases.

global marketing: where a multinational firm seeks to achieve long-run, large-scale production efficiencies by producing standardized products of sound value and long-term reliability in every segment of the market.

global quotas: explicit limits set by one country on the value or quantity of merchandise that may be imported or exported through its borders during a given period on a global basis.

glut: to oversupply.

GMROI: See *gross margin return on inventory investment.*

goal: an objective or something specific to be achieved.

going-rate pricing: applying the average price level charged by the industry to determine the price charge by the firm, in part so that markup cannot be used effectively in price setting. Synonymous with *imitative pricing.*

golden circle: a group of brands in a particular product field, all of which are equally acceptable to consumers.

gondola: in retailing, a merchandise display stand; a bank of freestanding shelves open on all sides. Its primary function is to display goods and provide space for back-up stock.

Good Housekeeping Seal: a seal of approval of a product that meets the standards of the Good Housekeeping Magazine. The magazine, to protect consumers, will license use of the seal by an advertiser, but will set limits for the ways the seal can be used. Since the public recognizes and trusts this Seal, its use provides a seemingly independent endorsement of a product's safety and quality, leading to the belief that using the seal in advertising will enhance sales of the product.

goods:

(1) the result of industrial work, equaling the gross national product for one year.

(2) any movable personal property, excluding livestock and excluding intangible property such as leases. Cf. *merchandise.*

goods in free circulation: merchandise not subject to customs restrictions.

goods on approval: items obtained when a potential buyer requests and receives from a retailer the right to examine them for a stated time period before deciding whether to purchase the goods.

goods-services continuum: visualizing the distribution between objectives and services. The continuum is shown graphically as a spectrum with pure goods at one extreme, for example, a bottle of hair conditioner, and a pure service at the other extreme, for example, a haircut. The continuum shifts gradually from the tangible to the intangible.

good 'til canceled order (GTC): an order to buy or sell that remains in affect until it is either executed or canceled. Cf. *open order.*

good will: the intangible possession that enables a business to continue to earn a profit in excess of the normal or basic rate of profit earned by other businesses of similar type.

gouge: (slang) to acquire an excessive profit by either overcharging or defrauding.

gourmet shop: an independent store or an area in a larger store specializing in fancy groceries and other food items, such as pasta, baked goods, delicatessen, cheeses.

grace period: See *courtesy period.*

grade label:
(1) the merchandise's label indicating its quality.
(2) a label that identifies the quality of a product by a letter, number, or word.

grade labeling: as authorized by government agencies, the labeling of certain consumer items as specified by standards (e.g., the grading of meat). See *Federal Trade Commission; Food and Drug Administration.* Cf. *descriptive labeling.*

grading:
(1) the classification of major goods into well-defined grades.
(2) the standardization of quality differences of staple goods for purposes of identification during trading periods.

graduated lease: as provided in a graduated lease, store rent is increased in stages over a period of time. The rent increases are not related to gross sales or any other measure of the retailer's activity.

graphics: all visual elements of communication affiliated with the presentation of an item or service to the market. It includes art, color effects, photographs, copy, etc. In retail stores, graphics is often concerned with department identification and merchandise presentation.

grass-roots method: a sales forecasting method that relies on input from salespeople in the field.

gray market:
(1) sources of supply from which scarce items are bought for quick delivery at a premium well above the usual market price.

(2) goods that are either mimics or counterfeits of genuine items.

Green River ordinance: a municipal law regulating house-to- house selling, unless the resident has invited the salesperson. See *door-to-door retailing.*

greige goods: unfinished fabric as it comes from the loom before bleaching, dyeing, printing, or the application of particular finishes.

grid layout: the placement of fixtures and aisles within the store; based on rectangles, squares, and other right angle patterns. Traditionally found in supermarkets and discount stores.

gridiron pattern: See *grid layout.*

Grocer's Political Action Committee: See *National Grocers' Association.*

gross: in merchandising, twelve dozen.

gross amount: the total before deductions. The gross amount minus deductions equals the net amount. See *gross profit.*

gross cost of goods handled: See *cost of goods handled.*

gross cost of merchandise sold: See *cost of goods sold.*

gross floor space: the total store area, including selling and nonselling departments.

gross leasable area (GLA): popularly employed in the shopping center industry, a standard unit of measure of the total floor area designed for tenant occupancy and exclusive use, including basements, mezzanines, and upper floors. It is measured from the center line of joint partitions and from outside wall faces. Tenants pay rent based on the total GLA.

gross margin:
(1) *general:* the amount, determined by subtracting the cost of goods sold from net sales, that covers operating and financial expenses and provides net income.
(2) *retailing:* the dollar difference between net sales and the net cost of goods

sold during a stated time frame. Gross margin percentage is calculated by dividing net sales into this figure. Gross margin is usually found in merchandising and retailing. Cf. *gross profit.*

gross margin of profit: See *gross margin.*

gross margin per dollar of cost inventory: See *gross margin return on inventory investment.*

gross margin pricing: a system for setting prices based on wholesale costs rather than the full cost. Applying this technique, retailers add a percentage of the wholesale cost or a percentage of the retail price to the wholesale cost to arrive at a price.

gross margin return on inventory investment (GMROI): an approach based on the store's gross margin to the cost of merchandise inventory required to generate the profit. Although not a true measure of the return on investment, it purports to measure the return on one of a retailer's most significant investments, his inventory. The concept of gross margin return on inventory investment is regarded as a standard used in effective merchandise management. Synonymous with *gross margin per dollar of cost inventory.*

gross profit: the total receipts minus the cost of merchandise sold, but before selling and other operating expenses have been deducted and before income taxes have been deducted; used primarily in manufacturing. Cf. *gross margin.*

gross profit on merchandise investment: The total profit realized on the amount invested in the average inventory of an item or line expressed as a percentage.

$$\frac{\text{gross profit of line}}{\$ \text{ invested in average inventory of line}} =$$

gross profit on merchandise
investment (%)

gross response: See *gross amount.*

gross revenue: See *gross sales.*

gross sales: total sales over a specified period, before the customer returns and allowances have been deducted.

gross weight: the full weight of a shipment, including goods and packaging. See *tare.*

groupage: a service that consolidates small shipments into containers for movement.

group buying: purchasing where several noncompeting stores consolidate orders for merchandise, usually staple goods such as trade books, to secure a lower price through volume purchasing.

group discounting: a special discount for the purchase of large quantities of an item or service (e.g., group discounts on air fares).

group plan: See *party selling.*

group purchase plan: a selling where the retailer offers purchase incentives to a group. An identity card is frequently distributed to users.

group purchasing: See *group buying; group purchase plan.*

group selling: the presentation for sale of goods or services to two or more people simultaneously.

growth strategy: the strategy used by a store that wants to expand its product's market share at the expense of a short-term profit, either by targeting users of a competitor's item to get them to switch, or by targeting people who have never used the item before.

GTC: See *good 'til canceled order.*

guarantee: a written statement assuring that something is of stated quantity, quality, content, or benefit, or that it will perform as advertised for a stated period. In some cases, all or part of the purchaser's money will be refunded if the item fails to meet the terms of a guarantee. See *guaranty; product reliability.* Cf. *warranty.*

guarantee against price decline: See *price guaranty.*

guaranteed draw: a means of compensating salespeople by permitting them a draw that is not repayable if the commissions earned in a stated time period is less than the draw.

guarantor: See *guaranty.*

guaranty: a contract, agreement, or undertaking involving three parties. The first party (the guarantor) agrees to see that the performance of a second party (the guarantee) is fulfilled according to the terms of the contract, agreement, or undertaking. The third party is the creditor, or the party to benefit by the performance. See *guarantee.* Cf. *warranty.*

guaranty against price decline: See *price guaranty.*

guerilla warfare: a technique used by small firms in trying to compete with large stores. A tightly bounded or well-defined small market is chosen to defend, and let the remaining portion go to the larger store. Two additional concepts are:

(a) guerillas do not accept the marketing or organizational practices of brand leaders, no matter how successful the former become;

(b) guerilla firms respond firmly and quickly to market changes by exiting the market when situations call for it.

HABA: See *health and beauty aids*.

habitual purchasing: a person's repeated buying of an item or service, done out of habit as contrasted with brand loyalty, especially when the consumer concludes there is little difference between products or services. See *brand loyalty*.

haggling: See *higgling*.

half sizes: the range of apparel sizes from 10½ to 26½ for women approximately 5'2" to 5'4" having a fuller figure than younger misses.

handling allowance:
(1) a special price or discount given by the manufacturer to a wholesaler, distributor, or retailer when a manufacturer's goods demand special handling.
(2) an incentive given to the retailer for handling a particular promotional program that demands extra effort on the retailer's part.

hand marking: goods labeled or tagged by hand with price and other information written out in pen, pencil, or by mechanical means.

hand-to-mouth buying: small quantities of retail purchasing purporting to gratify immediate needs.

hanger appeal: the degree that apparel motivates customers to look at goods while still on the hanger.

hard goods: Synonymous with *capital goods; durable merchandise; major appliances*. Cf. *soft goods*.

hard lines: See *major appliances*.

hard offer: a promotion, that requests payment at the time an order is placed, which includes an option to review the merchandise first and then pay or return the items as desired by the customer. No matter what the offer, the right of the purchaser to return unwanted items for a refund or prior to payment will be honored by most retailers.

hard sell: a dynamic, determined, and insistent approach to sales, where the seller attempts to control the sales situation by creating a level of tension. Cf. *soft sell*. Synonymous with *high-pressure selling*.

hardship point: the territory of a prospective customer who lives in a difficult area to reach or in a part of the community that is isolated.

hard-to-wrap: because of its shape, fragility, perishability, etc., goods that are difficult to prepare for shipment and therefore, frequently at added cost, require special handling.

haute couture: French for high fashion; clothing in original design from a French fashion house produced in limited quantities for the fashion-conscious innovator. See *couture; high fashion.*

Hazardous Substances Labeling Act of 1960: See *Federal Hazardous Substances Labeling Act of 1960.*

HBA: See *health and beauty aids.*

HCI: See *Home Center Institute.*

header: a sign or marking at the top of a display, merchandiser or exhibit.

head of stock: in a large retail store, a major sales key clerk or other specialist responsible for maintaining front stocks and for advising the buyer of shortfalls and other related problems.

health and beauty aids (HABA) (HBA): includes:

(a) merchandise of over-the-counter medicines and remedies.

(b) personal care products, e.g., toothpastes, mouthwashes.

(c) hair care products, e.g., shampoos, setting lotions.

(d) body care products, e.g., body lotion, skin moisturizers.

(e) cosmetic products, e.g., perfume, face make-ups.

heartland: See *primary market area.*

heavy buyers: people in the market for an item who account for more than half of the total volume of sales of the merchandise. They represent less than half of the number of users of the item. Synonymous with *heavy-half users; heavy users.*

heavy-half users: See *heavy buyers.*

heavy market: a declining market created when buying exceeds the demand for store orders.

heavy users: See *heavy buyers.*

hedonic items: consumer products whose attractiveness is that they offer the user considerable pleasure.

heterogeneity: the concept that the consumer market is composed of diverse or dissimilar elements.

heterogeneous shopping items: merchandise perceived by the customer as different in quality and suitability.

heterogeneous staples: items retained in stock at all times because of constant demand. Such goods while not being identical, relate closely to each other.

hidden service sector: encompasses the delivery, installation, maintenance, training, repair, and other services provided by stores that emphasize goods sales.

higgling: the procedure whereby, when the buyer offers a low price and the seller asks a high price, a third price is arrived at through bargaining to satisfy both parties. Synonymous with *haggling.*

high-end:

(1) *general:* the most expensive items in a classification.

(2) *retailing:* the price range at retail, i.e., the highest priced items found in the catalog or store.

high fashion: haute couture (French). In the United States, usually refers to high-priced, innovative apparel from well-known designers or design houses targets at fashion-conscious, trendy people.

high-pressure selling: See *hard sell.*

highway site: a free standing store that is separate from other businesses and is located on a highway or major road interchange.

hire purchase: purchasing by installment payment where title does not pass to the buyer until final payment is made.

hi-spotting: See *cherry-picking.*

hitlist: a salesperson's list of prospective customers he or she plans to pursue; includes both weak and strong prospects, with the stronger ones receiving the greatest attention. See *prospecting.*

hoarding:
(1) collecting for the sake of accumu-
lating.
(2) a planned effort by persons to accu-
mulate items beyond normal need (e.g.,
purchasing dozens of cartons of socks
in anticipation of a price hike).

Holder in Due Court Act of 1976: Federal credit law; purports to insure
the rights of consumers to raise claims
and defenses based on misconduct
by sellers, including breach of contract, misrepresentation, and fraud.
Any third-party contract holder, such
as a finance company, is now subject
to all claims and defenses that the purchaser would otherwise have claimed
against the retailer.

hold slip: the form used for identifying
goods that people wish to buy at a later
time.

home and hearth: a retailer's term for
sales of domestics and housewares.

Home Center Institute (HCI): based in
Indianapolis, Indiana, an association of
chain and independent home center retailers; a division of the National Retail
Hardware Association.

home centers: stores, or departments in
stores, which specialize in hardware,
lumber, tools, and other building materials for the home improvement
buyer.

homogeneous demand: a demand pattern in which consumers have relatively uniform needs and desires for a
good or service category.

homogeneous staples: goods, kept in
stock, that are so much alike as to be in-
distinguishable from one another even
though they may have been manufactured by different firms.

hook: in retailing, a free offer given
along with the purchase of a product.

hooker: See *dealer imprint.*

horizontal competition: in retailing,
competition between stores of similar

purpose, e.g., discount store in head-
to-head competition with another discount store.

horizontal fashion trend: See *horizontal
flow theory.*

horizontal flow theory: a concept of
fashion adoption where new styles are
seen as gaining acceptance at the same
time across socioeconomic strata at a
number of levels. Every level of society
contains influential people serving as
innovators who transmit new styles lat-
erally. The horizontal movement in this
concept runs counter to the downward
movement assumed in the trickle-down
theory. Synonymous with *mass market
theory; trickle-across theory.*

horizontal price fixing:
(1) an agreement on price among competitors at similar levels of distribution.
(2) a form of price fixing in which marketers at the same level of the distribution system get together and decide the
price at which all of them will sell the
product; an illegal practice.

horizontal sales company: a salesforce
company employing both company and
external salespeople who are assigned
sales responsibility on a geographic
basis, form of merchandise, type of
customer, or specific selling activity.

horizontal saturation: See *saturation.*

hot items: (slang) any goods that show
quick salability.

house brand: See *private brand.*

house charge: worker purchases charged
to their store account.

house list: a mailing list of existing customers and people who are not yet customers, but have made inquiries about
the store product or service.

house-to-house retailing: See *door-to-
door retailing; house-to-house salesperson; in-home retailing.*

house-to-house salesperson: a sales representative who visits homes in an attempt to make direct sales; made with

or without an appointment. See *door-to-door selling.*

house-to-house sampling: the distribution of a product sample to homes in a market location as a way of introducing people to the merchandise; a strategy to stimulate word-of-mouth promotion.

housekeeping: involves stockkeeping (keeping stock on the floor, and in reserve, neat, clean, and accessible) as well as the physical maintenance of the store (collecting trash, sweeping floors, changing light bulbs, etc.).

huckster: a peddler or petty retailer who will attempt to sell anything that is profit making.

huckstering: See *huckster.*

Huff's model: a concept of consumer shopping behavior developed by David L. Huff where the travel time from a shopping center is seen as directly affecting the probability of consumers shopping there.

HVAC: initials for heating, ventilation, and air-conditioning.

hypermarche: first developed in France, a large retail operation, combining the features of a supermarket and a discount house. Traditionally brings food and general merchandise together in a warehouse atmosphere. Such stores include elements of the traditional discount operation as well as those of the supermarket and may be as large as 200,000 square feet. Merchandise carried is almost always high volume sellers as the operation depends on moving very large quantities of goods to turn a profit. See *superstore.* Synonymous with *hypermarket.*

hypermarket: See *hypermarche.*

iceberg principle: the concept that 10 percent of required data are apparent and the other 90 percent are not seen. Used in store sales predictions to indicate that gross numbers can hide the bulk of the critical data that would be determined upon closer examination.

ICMAD: See *Independent Cosmetic Manufacturers and Distributors.*

ICSC: See *International Council of Shopping Centers.*

IDEA: See *International Downtown Executives Association.*

ideal other: the concept of how a person wishes others to perceive him or her; impacts on retail buying behavior and spending on promotions. Cf. *ideal self-image.*

ideal points: the combination of attributes that consumers would like products to possess.

ideal self-image: the way an individual would like to be. Cf. *ideal other.* See *self-image.*

ideal stock: See *balance stock.*

illegal merchandise: the unlawful sale of items, e.g. stolen goods.

image:

(1) *general:* what people believe to be true about something.

(2) *general:* a buyer's mental picture of himself or herself; how and individual sees a product.

(3) *retailing:* the feelings of customers toward a store. See *store image.*

image advertising: See *institutional advertising.*

image builder pricing: in retailing, where one item within the line is offered at a significantly higher price than the other line products so as to upgrade their image in the consumer's perception.

Image of the Year Award: See *Career Apparel Institute.*

imitative pricing: See *going-rate pricing.*

imperfects: See *seconds.*

implicit costs:

(1) *general:* costs originating within the business that are the responsibility of the owner (e.g., time, money).

(2) *retailing:* those expenses which are, unlike explicit costs, less obvious and accountable, but which may affect the overall profitability of the store.

implied warranty: a legal promise that a product will serve the purpose for which it is intended, whether stated by the manufacturer or not. The implication is that, written or not, there is a promise implied when items are offered for sale. Cf. *express warranty.* See *warranty.*

import:
(1) to receive goods and services from abroad (verb).
(2) an imported item (noun).
(3) to bring goods and services from abroad (verb).

import fair: a promotion by a retailer where imported items of a specific country or area are given greater attention.

import goods: items made in one nation and offered for sale to another country.

import quota: a protective ruling establishing limits on the quantity of a particular merchandise that can be imported.

impulse buying: purchasing by the customer without any prior planning; usually determined by a rapid appeal of the item or service; a spontaneous purchase made in response to an unexpected urge or external stimulus. Synonymous with *impulse purchasing.* See *impulse merchandise; planned impulse buying.*

impulse merchandise: items susceptible to spontaneous rather than purposeful purchasing. These goods benefit from display in store locations that have a considerable flow of customers; they are a specific category of convenience goods and tend to be low cost items, e.g., candies, candles. See *impulse buying.*

impulse products: convenience items that the consumer does not plan to buy on a specific trip to a store.

impulse purchasing: See *impulse buying.*

inactive account: a credit account which has not been used by a store's customer over a lengthy time period. Synonymous with *dormant account.*

in arrears: See *arrears.*

in bond: items shipped by a producer several months before a store's usual selling season. The items are held in the store's warehouse until the selling season.

incentive: a motivational force that stimulates people to greater activity or increased efficiency. Customers sales promotions often involve incentives such as coupons, rebates, and discounts.

incentive buying: when a retail buyer places orders at the beginning of a season, encouraged by discounts offered from manufacturers for the early orders.

incentive pay: available fund on top of straight salary paid to salespeople as a reward for greater sales levels.

income expectation: See *consumer's income expectation.*

income-producing services: retail store services, such as travel agencies, equipment rentals, beauty salons, fur storage, wrapping of gifts, jewelry-watch repair, etc.

income statement: the profit and loss statement of a given concern for a particular period of time. See *profit and loss statement.*

incremental pricing agreement: the pricing arrangement between a buyer and seller utilizing a schedule of price which shifts with the cumulative increment purchased. Cf. *blanket pricing agreement.*

indebtedness: a debt that is owed; any form of liability.

independent:
(1) *general:* an individual whose behavior is self-determined.
(2) *retailing:* a store that does not belong to an association of companies or chains.

independent buying office: See *commission buying office; salaried buying office.*

Independent Cosmetic Manufacturers and Distributors (ICMAD): an association of small cosmetic manufacturers, distributors, and retailers; represents the cosmetic industry to Congress and the Federal Drug Administration.

independent delivery service: a firm organized specifically to provide delivery service to other firms structured on a contractual basis. Parcels are picked up from the retailer, sorted, and warehoused, and later delivered to the customer; the firm provides the personnel, warehousing, and equipment and assumes responsibility for lost merchandise. The service also makes COD deliveries and picks up customer returns. The retailer is charged on the basis of size, weight, and the number of items to be delivered. Charges are traditionally passed along to the customers by the retailer.

independent display: a display that does not relate, either by theme or goods, to adjoining display windows.

independently owned delivery service: See *independent delivery service.*

independent retailer: a retailer that owns a single outlet that is not affiliated with any other retail outlet.

independent store: a retail operation that is controlled by individual ownership or management, not by outside management. Such a store may be a member of a voluntary chain.

index: the symbol or number used to identify a particular quantity in an array of similar quantities.

index of retail saturation: See *index of saturation.*

index of sales activity: a relative measure of a store's sales record within a given market.

index of saturation: the number of stores a retail trading area can accommodate. Three factors are taken into account: total dollars spent on specific goods or services, the number of retail stores, and the size of population.

$$\text{index of saturation} = \frac{(C)\ (RE)}{RF}$$

where C = the number of prospective customers; RE = the average expenditure for the proposed product line for a selected period of time; and RF = the number of competing and planned retail outlets in the trading area measured in square feet of space devoted to the proposed lines of merchandise.

indirect costs: in measuring store profits; costs not usually identifiable with or incurred as the result of the manufacture of goods or services but applicable to a productive activity generally. Included are costs from manufacturing operations (wages, maintenance, overhead, etc.). Cf. *direct cost.* Synonymous with *indirect expenses.*

indirect expenses: See *indirect costs.*

indirect exposure: a consumer purchase of a good or service resulting from the influence of another person who has been exposed to an advertisement.

indirect inventory: See *inventory.*

indirect promotion: sales promotion that is impersonal as contrasted with personal selling. Advertising and packaging are examples. Purports to make a service or item known to the market and to present it in the most favorable light.

indirect retail outlet: a retailer that purchases items via a wholesaler.

individual brand: a name applied to one product only (e.g., Kleenex, Xerox, Tide). Cf. *family brands.*

individual resident buying office: See *private buying office.*

induced consumption: additional consumer buying caused by new capital formation.

induced investment: new capital formation caused by an upturn in consumer buying.

industrial goods: merchandise purchased for commercial reasons, instead of for personal or domestic needs.

industrial store: See *commissary store.*

inelastic demand: the condition that exists when a price increase leads to a higher total sales revenue, or a price decrease leads to a lower sales revenue. A perfectly inelastic demand occurs when the demand for an item does not change with changes in price. Cf. *price out of the market.* See *price elasticity.* Synonymous with *demand inelasticity.*

inelasticity: See *inelastic demand.*

inelasticity of demand: See *inelastic demand.*

inept set: in consumer behavior, those particular brands that a potential customer refuses to consider when seeking an item within the product category. Cf. *inert set.*

inert set: in consumer behavior, those particular brands that a potential customer remains indifferent towards when seeking an item within the product category. Cf. *inept set.*

inferior goods: any item for which demand decreases as income increases.

informal buying group: See *pooled buying.*

informal organization: a rather complicated and nebulous network of communication and interaction patters of groups, or cliques within the formal organizational structure. Such a phenomenon usually arises spontaneously in order: (a) to augment, interpret, speed up, or change the formal communication system (or the lack of it); (b) to regulate the flow, extent, manner, and enforcement of formal authority; (c) to humanize the formal organization by trying to maintain a feeling of individuality among the members, while providing some security, unity, integrity, and feelings of belonging; (d) to meet related psychological and social needs to such an extent as to give the impression of being the organization.

information superhighway: in retailing, applying computers in the promotion and sales of merchandise. See *interactive television.*

informative institutional advertising: See *institutional advertising.*

informative label:
(1) a message or affix to merchandise providing data about the item.
(2) a label that advised consumers about the care, use, or preparation of a merchandise.

infringement:
(1) *general:* the production of a machine that yields the same results by the same action as a patented machine. This is a patent infringement.
(2) *merchandising:* the reproduction of a registered trademark and its use on merchandise to mislead the public into believing that the items bearing the reproduced trademark are the product of the true owner of the trademark. This is a trademark infringement.

in-home retailing: retailing where the sale occurs within the purchaser's house. See *house-to-house retailing.*

initial contact: when a store customer and a salesperson have their first interaction.

initial markon: the difference between the retail value of goods and the delivered costs when they are first priced and placed on display. See *markon.*

initial markup: See *initial markon.*

initial mark-up percent: the difference between the cost of goods and the price at which it sells converted to a percentage figure and expressed on a storewide basis.

initial purchase: the first-time store purchase of an item or service by a consumer.

initial retail price: the cost of merchandise plus the amount of initial mark-up.

inner fashions: See *intimate apparel.*

inner wear: See *intimate apparel.*

innovation diffusion: the concept that anything introduced into the market as new is quickly purchased for use by a group of people. See *diffusion process.*

innovativeness:
(1) when applied to the seller; the degree to which the firm has the capability of, and follows the practice of, being innovative.
(2) when applied to a buyer; the extent to which that person or firm is willing to accept the risks of early purchase on an innovation.

innovators: these are the people who are among the first to try or adopt an idea, service, or product. Synonymous with *early acceptors.*

INP: information-need-product; a traditional method of selling in which the sales presentation is made step-by-step.

inplacement: in retailing, shifting employees around the store.

inquiry conversion: the conversion of an inquirer to a customer.

inside buying organization: the retail purchasing function performed by store employees as contrasted with an arrangement where goods are bought through a purchasing office.

inside salespeople: salespeople, usually involved in wholesaling who take calls from customers within an office. Cf. *field salespeople.*

inspection purchasing: buying an item only after each item has been thoroughly studied for imperfections.

installment: See *installment buying.*

installment buying: acquiring goods or services with no down payment or a small down payment, to be followed by payments at regular intervals.

installment credit: a form of consumer credit involving regular payments, permitting the seller to reacquire the purchased item if the buyer fails to meet the payment schedule. Cf. *revolving credit.*

Institute of Store Planners (ISP): based in Chicago, Illinois, an association of store planners, designers, and decorators that seeks to establish store planning as a profession; maintains a code of operating ethics and professional standards, conducts a placement service, works to establish legal and contractual standards, sponsors a Store Design Awards Competition, and sponsors reviews of technical subjects relating to store planning.

institutional advertising: an attempt to sell the image of a store, other retailer or other firm—its quality, services, role in community activities, merchandise, and so on—rather than specific items. Goodwill and position are foremost in the development of institutional advertising. Synonymous with *image advertising; informative institutional advertising.*

institutional sales: sales of items to not-for-profit agencies, such as schools, hospitals.

institutional store: See *nonpromotional store.*

in stock: merchandise on hand, available for shipment or sale.

in-store demonstration: to increase store sales, an item is demonstrated.

in-store lighting: lighting used not only to make merchandise easily seen and used for reducing accidents, studies have shown that customers tend to examine and handle more merchandise when the lighting is bright than when it is soft.

instrumented store: a retail outlet designed and organized based on computer analysis in the setting of efficiency, layout, and shelf space, inventory control, ordering, etc.

integrated retailing: a situation where the retailer has consolidated its activities to include functions such as production, wholesaling, distribution, and transportation.

integration: See *forward integration.*

intensive distribution:
(1) placement of an item in all available outlets. Its shortcoming is that retailers have little commitment for promoting the item as their competitors will also be offering the merchandise.
(2) an approach to distribution that seeks the largest possible number of outlets in a given territory. Cf. *exclusive distribution; open distribution; selective distribution.*

interaction: the impact or relationship that exists between a salesperson and his or her potential customer.

interactive retailing: See *electronic catalog; electronic direct marketing; electronic retailing; interactive television.*

interactive television: a relatively new concept, where consumers shop without leaving their home. Merchandise is displayed on a television screen and can be ordered by pressing keys on a special keyboard or on a touch-tone telephone dial that is connected directly to the seller. See *electronic catalog; electronic direct marketing; electronic retailing; information superhighway.*

intercepting sites: retail locations between two crucial areas—the area where people live and the area to which people are drawn to shop.

interdepartmental merchandise: See *transfers.*

interior display: goods shown in the store in such a way that the customer is encouraged to try the item. Interior displays are intended to stimulate unplanned purchases and to enhance the ambiance within the store.

intermediary: See *middleperson.*

intermediate customer: a buyer who is not a consumer.

intermediate markdown: a lowering of the retail price, made prior to the current, and usually final reduction that is advertised. Current retail price are

often attained in stages, i.e., via several intermediate markdowns.

intermediate market: a set of wholesalers and retailers that buy goods from others and resell them.

internal audit: a review of the retailer's files, records, reports, financial statements, etc., to verify their accuracy and conformity to the organization's policies. The internal audit is conducted by employees instead of using an outside company as with an external audit. See *audit.*

internal credit: consumer credit financed by a retailer.

International Association of Chain Stores (CIES): located in Alexandria, Virginia, an association of food industry chain stores and suppliers that provide articles and services to chain food stores. CIES purports to promote greater cooperation between chain stores and their suppliers and among chain store organizations in different nations.

International Council of Shopping Centers (ICSC): a global agency that includes owners, developers, retailers, and managers of shopping centers, architects, engineers, contractors, leasing brokers, promotion agencies, and others who provide services and products for shopping centers. ICSC encourages higher standards of performance in the development and operation of shopping centers throughout the world. Also conducts research and gathers data on all aspects of the shopping center industry and compiles statistics; gives the Maxi Award for excellence in shopping center promotions.

International Downtown Executives Association (IDEA): located in Washington, DC, an association of individuals and organizations involved in downtown and central city improvement and revitalization. Provides consultation services and conducts conferences on downtown revitalization in urban areas.

international forwarding agent: See *freight forwarder.*

international freight forwarder: See *freight forwarder.*

international marketing:

(1) operations within the home nation, to produce merchandise and services for export, to be marketed overseas.

(2) activities in foreign nations that manufacture merchandise in that nation for sale there. Some overseas operations are wholly-owned subsidiaries of the parent firm while others may be joint or licensed ventures (franchises) or contract manufacturing operations.

international retailing: activities of retailing on a global range. See *international marketing; retailing.*

interselling: assigning sales personnel so that each is able to work in two or more related departments rather than being limited to one. See *cross-selling.*

intertype competition:

(1) *general:* competing for business using differing methods of distribution.

(2) *retailing:* where stores of different types sell the same merchandise, e.g., magazines sold in pharmacies as well as in supermarkets and variety stores. See *scrambled merchandise.*

intimate apparel: women's apparel including: (a) foundations (bras, girdles, corsets, etc.); (b) lingerie (daywear, slips, panties, sleepwear, etc.); and (c) loungewear (robes, house coats, and other casual apparel) for at-home entertaining. Synonymous with *inner fashion; inner wear.*

intrabrand competition: competition, usually among resellers or between resellers and the direct salesforce, for sales of same-brand products. Cf. *intratype competition.*

intrastore transfer: the purchase of goods from one selling department for use by another selling department.

intratype competition: competition between retailers using the same selling concepts, e.g., head-to-head competition between two specialty stores. Cf. *intrabrand competition.*

intrinsic cues: reasons for a buyer's feelings toward a product or service, as physical characteristics of the item itself. Cf. *extrinsic cues.*

introductory offer: an offer, such as a free gift, premium, or discount given to prospects of a new product, or a reintroduced item that has been altered or improved upon.

introductory price dealing: when prices are temporarily lowered during the introduction phase of an item and raised at the end of the introductory period.

introductory technique: See *introductory price dealing.*

inventory: the name given to an asset of a business. Inventories are of two general types, direct and indirect. (a) Direct inventories in an industrial concern consist of raw materials, work in process, and finished goods; represent various stages of fabrication; in commercial and retail businesses, they are inventories purchased for resale; (b) indirect inventories, in general, are all supplies used to carry on the business and not purchased for resale; are usually considered deferred assets. See *forward stock; perpetual inventory.*

inventory at end of period: See *closing inventory.*

inventory audit: See *stock count.*

inventory carrying costs: costs for conducting business related directly to the merchandise found in inventory, along with warehouse and insurance costs.

inventory change: the amount of increase or decrease in business inventories during a specified period.

inventory control: the control of merchandise on hand by accounting and physical methods. See *eyeball control; periodic stock control.* Synonymous with *stock control.*

inventory cutoff: the determination of which inventory items are to be included in the year-end inventory balance.

inventory management:

(1) *general:* involved with providing a continuous flow of goods and matching the quantity of goods in inventory with sales demand.

(2) *retailing:* activities which assure the flow of goods from vendors into warehouses and stockrooms and, finally, to the selling floor resulting in stock levels that are consistent with consumer need.

inventory overage: See *stock overage.*

inventory policy: the relationship desired between the quantity of stock on order and the quantity available, and the rate of usage.

inventory profit: the profit accrued on merchandise held in inventory during a period when the value of the items increased.

inventory risk: the financial risk of carrying items in inventory as their value may decrease or because of reduced demand.

inventory shortage: inventory reduced by theft, internal or external fraud, waste, sabotage, or careless operation. Synonymous with *inventory shrinkage.* See *pilferage; shrinkage; stock shortage.*

inventory shrinkage: See *inventory shortage.*

inventory turnover: the number of times, on the average, that inventory is replaced during a period. It is calculated by dividing cost of goods sold by average inventory. Cf. *stock turnover.*

invisible shrinkage: stock shortages due to shoplifting, employee theft, losses due to clerical error, etc., which are undiscovered until a physical inventory is made. Cf. *visible shrinkage.*

invisible supply: uncounted stocks in the hands of middlepeople, manufacturers, and consumers. Cf. *visible supply.*

invoice: an instrument prepared by a seller of goods or services and rendered to the buyer. The instrument usually lists all items making up the bill for the convenience of the buyer; to prevent disagreements, the amount is stated on the instrument.

invoice apron: affixed to an invoice form prepared by the shipper of merchandise or by the receiving party on which relevant notations are made. For example, on the receiving end, an apron may be prepared on which quantities received are noted so that items can be passed to the selling floor before the seller's invoice arrives. Cf. *receiving apron.*

invoice cut-off: when preparing a physical inventory invoiced goods will not be added into the total count following a particular date.

involvement: the importance made by a consumer to the purchase of a specific service or item; varies based on the degree of relevant the item or service has to the purchaser, for example, a high-involvement item is one that has a significant degree of emotional importance to the consumer.

inward freight: charges accrued in transporting goods from a vendor to a retailer.

irregular: items containing some imperfection, but which is not apparent to the naked eye. An irregular is closer to being perfect than a second.

island display: merchandise shown in a store's aisle or open space. Items are readily accessible from all sides and the display is often freestanding.

isolated location: a store located alone within a residential area; usually a convenience store.

isolated store: See *isolated location.*

ISP: See *Institute of Store Planners.*

item: singular for good or merchandise.

item merchandising: the attempt to take advantage of sales opportunities presented by merchandise that is in the greatest demand by customers. Lost revenue is created when such demand cannot be filled because stock is not available.

item price removal: a practice whereby prices are marked only on store shelves or aisle signs and not on individual items. Cf. *item pricing.*

item pricing: establishing prices which permit for deviations from the standard markon percentage. The retailer takes into consideration factors such as whether an item is a fast or slow mover, personal experience, the amount of risk involved, etc., to alter the selling price. Cf. *item price removal.*

JA: See *Jewelers of America.*

jam auction: (slang) a store that sells inexpensive jewelry, souvenirs, and the like. Synonymous with *jam pitch.*

jam pitch: See *jam auction.*

jebble: See *bluefingers.*

Jewelers of America (JA): based in New York City, an association of retailers of jewelry, watches, silver, and related items. Carries out surveys, collects relevant industry data and provides workshops for members.

jewelry: items, such as necklaces, earrings, pins, rings, that are worn on the body and are made from either precious or nonprecious materials.

JIT purchasing: See *just-in-time purchasing.*

JND: See *just noticeable difference.*

job: in merchandising, to purchase or sell merchandise in quantity, not in selected categories.

jobber:
(1) a middleperson who buys from a manufacturer and sells to a wholesaler.
(2) a middleperson who handles merchandise in odd or job lots. Some jobbers take possession of the title to the goods, which they resell to another jobber, to a retailer, or directly to the consumer. Others have a buying agreement with the manufacturer to drop-ship the merchandise on orders obtained by the jobber. See *drop shipper; premium jobber; rack jobber; truck jobber.* Cf. *wholesaler.* Synonymous with *reseller.*

job lot: in merchandising, a miscellaneous grouping of items of various styles, sizes, colors, and so on, bought at a reduced price by a store or an individual middleperson. Synonymous with *odd lot.*

job ticket: a tag affixed to an order that provides details about the pertinent data about work to be done as well as the information about the person or firm for whom the job is being done. For advertising agencies, the job ticket gives the date, name of agency, name of client, and printing instructions to be carried out.

joint decision making: the process whereby two or more consumers have input into purchases.

joint demand:
(1) demand for two or more items that are usually used together because of necessity or consumer preference. Used primarily with industrial goods.
(2) demand for two items that are complementary.

joint promotion: where a group of stores sponsor a sale.

judgment forecasting: utilizing judgment in forecasting sales of both present and future store merchandise.

jumble basket: the merchandiser having a jumble display of a number of different items. See *dump bin; jumble display.*

jumble display: a collection of items tossed together in a container or on a table counter. It is an open display that is primarily used in retail operations where customers can rummage through to find different items. See *jumble basket.*

junior: a size range in women's clothing in odd numbers 3 to 15, with height range from 5′2″ to 5′5″.

junior department store: a retail operation smaller than a traditional department store that carries a wide variety of merchandise. Often large appliances, such as washing machines, television sets, are not sold in this store.

junk jewelry: See *costume jewelry.*

junk mail: promotional mail containing unsolicited material. Many store customers complain that they receive too many store promotions.

just-in-time (JIT) purchasing: an approach to inventory management in which products are bought in small quantities to reduce store inventory carrying costs and obtain delivery just in time for use.

just noticeable difference (JND): the small difference in an item that is apparent to consumers when the item's characteristics are modified, either to face competition or to save money. See *Weber's Law.*

Kanban: in Japanese, visible record. When applied to the vendor-carrier-retailer relationship, it facilitates the movement of goods from manufacturer through the transportation system thus making it easier for the retailer to regulate inventory levels. Cooperation by all parties is central to its efficiency.

KBI: See *key buying influence.*

KD: knocked down; applies to sales or shipment of equipment that are to be assembled by the receiver. Cf. *knocked down price.*

Kefauver-Harris Drug Amendment to the Food and Drug Act of 1962: Federal legislation requiring the manufacturer to test for both the safety and effectiveness of drug items before marketing them to the public. Also, the generic name of the item had to appear on the label of the product. See *Food and Drug Administration.*

key buying influence (KBI): the person in a store who is the central figure in making buying decisions of specific merchandise or services.

key items:

(1) those in greatest consumer acceptance.

(2) merchandise which determine the acceptance of a line of products. See *best seller.*

key resource: a vendor whose former activities with a specific retailer has been outstanding and from whom the retailer has consistently purchased a significant portion of its goods. Cf. *preferred resource.*

key selling price: the price that is almost midway between the prices a retailer's customers regard as low and high. When a bell curve is made representing the store's price range, the key selling prices will be at the top of the curve.

keystone markup: See *keystoning.*

keystoning: the doubling of the maker's prices to determine retail prices. Synonymous with *keystone markup.*

key vendor: See *key resource.*

kickback:

(1) *general:* an illegal rebate given secretly by a seller for granting an order or contract (e.g., a payoff).

(2) *retailing:* a type of money payment to a retail buyer by the vendor as a type of reward, or means of thanks, for the purchaser's patronage.

kill: See *cancel; credit cancellation.*

kill bad pay: See *credit cancellation.*

Kimball tags: prepunched tags affixed to goods, containing the size and style data that speed up inventory control. See *marking*.

kiosk: originated in European cities, a freestanding display used to provide merchandise information. They are located on streets, in shopping malls and in stores.

knocked down: See *KD*.

knocked down price: in retailing, a seller's asking price that has been lowered for purposes of making the sale. Cf. *knocked down*.

knocker: (slang) a door-to-door salesperson.

knockoff:

(1) *general:* (slang) to cease working, take a break, generally for lunch or at the end of a working day.

(2) *retailing:* (slang) the imitation of a design of clothing or of a textile item, usually done so to sell at a lower price than the original; reproduction by another manufacturer.

known loss: a loss discovered before or at the time of delivery of a shipment.

label:

(1) *general:* an identification record.

(2) *retailing:* the portion of an item that provides information about the item to the buyer. A tag that may be attached to the item or inserted with the package.

(3) *merchandising:* the brand name of a clothing manufacturer, retailer, fashion house, or recording company. See *labeling.*

labeling: all labels and other written, printed, or graphic matter appearing on any article or any of its containers or wrappers. See *label.*

landed cost: the cost of an item including the cost of loading, transporting, and unloading at a specified destination.

Lanham Act of 1947: the Trademark Act; officially the Lanham Trademark Act; federal legislation governing trademarks and other symbols for identifying merchandise sold in interstate commerce. As amended, it allows a manufacturer to protect his or her brand or trademark in the United States by having it recorded on a government register in the U.S. Patent Office, and provides for the legal right to register any distinctive mark. See *trademark.*

last-in, first-out: See *LIFO.*

late night only (LNO): an employee who works when the store is open during the evening.

latent defect:

(1) a defect in goods that is not visible to the naked eye.

(2) a deficiency in merchandise offered for shipment not discernible by careful inspection.

law of demand: where the quantity demanded in a time period is negatively related to price; based on the assumption that the average potential customer is aware of alternative goods, has limited purchasing power, and a determination to maximize the utility accruing to him or her. See *bandwagon impact.*

law of retail gravitation: See *Reilly's Law of Retail Gravitation.*

law of threes: enjoins the retailer to limit choices in each line to good, better, and best; purporting to reduce the potential confusion to customers.

lawyer: (slang) in retailing, a friend who advises another in a store regarding whether or not to purchase an item, frequently resulting in the customer's not buying the item.

layaway plan: a method of deferring payments whereby goods are retained by the store until the customer has completed payments for them. See *deferred payment sale.* Synonymous with *deposit plan.*

layout: in retail stores, the interior arrangement of departments and merchandise within departments, as well as space allocation for aisles, counters, fixtures, etc.

L/C: See *letter of credit.*

LCL: See *less-than-carload lot.*

lead: the name and address of a potential customer, either an individual or organization. See *referral leads.*

leader: a dealer offer conditioned by a unit volume-purchase. See *leader pricing; loss leader.*

leader brand: a specific well-known item, that is priced below regular retail to attract customers to the store. See *leader pricing.*

leader merchandising: See *leader pricing.*

leader price: a special low price placed on an item to attract customers. See *leader pricing.*

leader pricing: a method where prices of specific merchandise are set at levels so low that they yield minimal or no profit. Its purpose is to increase consumer traffic and to give the impression that the establishment offers items at low prices. See *loss leader.* Synonymous with *bait pricing.*

lead generation: a salesperson's identification of the best possible prospects (leads) that he or she can approach using sales calls or personal visits, by either asking known customers for names of others believed to be candidates; joining associations; speaking before professional or community groups, etc. See *endless chain.*

lead-in: that part of the interaction that permits a sales representative to move toward a summing up or to close with a customer.

leads: See *lead.*

lead tenants: larger anchor retailers who provide most of the attraction in bringing customers to shopping centers.

lead time: the elapsed time between placement of an order and the arrival of the merchandise. See *order cycle.*

leaseback: a seller who remains in possession as a tenant after completing the sale and delivering the deed.

leased dealership: where a firm leases a retail establishment to an operator and where the operator purchases supplies from the leasing firm.

leased department: a department in a retail store, usually a department, discount, or specialty store, that is rented to an outside party. Shoes, jewelry repair, photo services, etc., are leased departments frequently found in department or discount stores. See *concession.*

leave behind: See *leave piece.*

leave piece: printed information that the salesperson uses and leaves with a prospect. This piece usually has the name and telephone number of the salesperson so the prospect, upon making a decision, will contact the salesperson and no one else. Synonymous with *leave behind.*

leaving paper: writing an order for goods and giving it to the vendor.

legal lexicography: See *nationally advertised brand.*

legitimization: with new merchandise, where early users serve as examples for future consumers who may be somewhat more conservative.

lender: See *note.*

less-than-carload lot (LCL): a freight shipment that does not fill a rail freight car and does not qualify for full car rates.

less-than-truckload lot (LTL): goods in amounts that do not make a truckload and that do not qualify for full-load rates.

letter of credit (L/C): an instrument or document issued on behalf of a buyer by a bank on another bank or banks or on itself. It gives the buyer the prestige and the financial backing of the issuing bank. The acceptance by the bank of drafts drawn under the letter of credit satisfies the seller and the seller's bank in the handling of the transaction. The buyer and the accepting bank also have an agreement as to payment for the drafts as they are presented.

letter of indemnity: a document issued by a merchandise shipper to a steamship company as an inducement for the carrier to issue a clean bill of lading, where it might not otherwise do so; serves as a form of guarantee whereby the shipper agrees to settle a claim against the line by a holder of the bill of lading arising from the issuance of a clean bill.

level of saturation: See *saturated area.*

liability: an obligation an individual has by virtue of law, e.g., a debt, a responsibility.

liberal return policy: the practice of a store to accept goods returned for refund or exchange with a minimum of difficulty to the customer.

license plate analysis: the noting and filing of license plate numbers of cars parked in the parking lot of a store or shopping center. When the license plates are correlated to addresses, this procedure may help to define the retailer's trading area.

licensed department: See *leased department.*

licensee: the person or organization who is granted a license by a licensor.

licensing: a business arrangement in which the manufacturer of a product (or a firm with proprietary rights over technology or trademarks) grants permission to a group or an individual to manufacture that product in return for specified royalties or other payments.

Licensing Industry Merchandiser's Association (LIMA): identifies some of the key licensed categories and their volume. LIMA maintains thousands of licensed names, and hundreds of thousands of licensed products.

licensor: the person or organization who grants a license to a licensee.

lien: a legal claim upon goods for the satisfaction of some debt or duty. See *seller's lien.*

life span of merchandise: See *retail life cycle.*

lifestyle: a way of living centered around certain activities, interests, opinions, and demographic characteristics, especially as these characteristics differentiate one group from another group.

lifestyle merchandising: where the retailer repeatedly changes the merchandise mix to what the customer wants and will purchase; recognizes that people are conscious of value, newness, and quality and that the customer's lifestyle, demographics, value system, and buying habits all play a role in his or her buying behavior.

LIFO (last in-first out): in valuation of inventories, the system whereby the price shown on the last incoming shipment of a particular item is the one used for current valuations and cost.

lighting: See *in-store lighting.*

LIMA: See *Licensing Industry Merchandiser's Association.*

limited assortment store: a convenience store carrying up to 1,000 food items, usually private labels or packer labels. Usually the customer does his or her own packing of purchased items.

limited distribution: See *selective distribution.*

limited-function wholesaler: See *limited service wholesaler.*

limited-line grocery store: a store that falls between the supermarket and the convenience store; specializes in nonperishable staples sold at a discount.

limited-line stores: smaller retail operations that carry most goods in a narrow line of items (e.g., a women's apparel shop that carries casual and formal ladies' garments, sportswear, and lingerie, but not baby clothes).

limited-line wholesalers: See *specialty-merchandise wholesalers.*

limited order: an order in which the customer has set restrictions with respect to price.

limited-service store: a retail outlet where the traditional store services (such as check cashing, delivery, credit, sales help) are lacking.

limited-service wholesaler: a wholesale middleperson who, takes title to merchandise he or she resells, but provides fewer services in an effort to lower costs. Synonymous with *limited-function wholesaler.* See *jobber; wholesaler.*

line:
(1) *merchandising:* the silhouette and description of any apparel style.
(2) *retailing:* items carried by a merchant. Cf. *product line.*

linear system: a marketing system that is directly linked to a plant. Should the merchandise not be correct for a market, they pile up at the factory.

line extension:
(1) a new variety of a basic product.
(2) adding of another variety of an item to an already established brand line of goods. Cf. *brand extension.*

line-for-line copy: in apparel, copying the original design, often of foreign origin. Some copies are made with the permission of the designer, others do not receive authorization.

line haul: the movement of cargo between cities and towns, as distinguished from pickup and delivery activities.

line of business: the general goods/service category, functions, geographic coverage, type of ownership, and specific business of a firm.

line of credit: money that a borrower, such as a retailer, may have outstanding from a lending institution at any one time. The borrower may use available funds up to the specified amount over a period of time without additional approval from the lender. Synonymous with *credit line.*

lingeries: See *intimate apparel.*

linking phrase: in retail sales, the words that connect a feature with a benefit in a smooth, logical fashion. See *objection.*

link traffic pattern layout: the placement of fixtures and aisles in a store forming a figure-eight or chain-link pattern providing greater flexibility in the retailer structure.

liquid assets: assets that are easily converted into cash.

liquidity: the solvency of a business, with special reference to the speed with which assets can be converted into cash without loss.

list price:
(1) *general:* the price of an item, subject to sale and cash discounts; any quoted price in excess of that obtained in the actual sale. Synonymous with *base price.* See *phony list price.*
(2) *retailing:* the retail price suggested for fixed by the manufacturer rather than the retailer. Cf. *fair trade price.* See *unchanging list price.*

live goods: displayed items that are for sale that are in great demand.

LNO: See *late night only.*

loader: a dealer offer tied to a single, volume purchase. A form of dealer premium.

loading: the amount added to an installment agreement to cover selling and administrative overhead, interest, risk, and so on.

loading of cash discount: in retailing, when the vendor's invoice amount is increased (loaded) to compensate for a lower than expected cash discount.

The increased amount is charged to the department purchasing the goods; thus, on paper, creating the illusion that the items cost more than they really did. The objective of this practice is to induce buyers to gain the largest discount possible to avoid the penalty of increased invoice prices, and to gain a higher markup for the items.

loading dock: See *receiving dock.*

loading the invoice: See *loading of cash discount.*

loan slips: a buyer's receipt from the selling department, when goods are borrowed for use in window displays, etc.

local brand: a brand found in a limited geographic territory.

local costs: expenses incurred for goods or services purchased from suppliers in the buyer's country. The goods or services purchased must be needed to execute the exporter's contract or to complete the project of which the exporter's contract is a part.

local market: the area where the first steps are taken in assembling items from a number of farmers. Synonymous with *primary market.*

local wholesaler: a wholesaler who operates within a small circle from his or her operation, usually less than one-hundred miles. Cf. *sectional wholesaler.*

location habit: the buyer's idea as to the type of marketing establishment he should use as a source of supply for certain goods.

long-run planning capacity: the rate of activity needed to meet average store sales demand over a period long enough to include seasonal and cyclical fluctuations.

long-term sales: sales of goods and services on terms of five years or more.

loose market: See *buyer's market.*

loss leader:

(1) merchandise generally sold at a loss to attract customers.

(2) a retail merchandising strategy of advertising an item at a price below cost, to attract customers to the store in the expectation that they will purchase other items at full profit margins. See *leader pricing; merchandising leader; price lining.*

loss leader pricing: See *leader pricing.*

loungewear: See *intimate apparel.*

low-ball price: the promotion, usually by telephone, of a product to lure the customer into the store, where the customer finds the salesperson unwilling to sell him or her the item at the previously announced price and attempts to pressure the customer to purchase a more expensive item.

low-cost merchandising: See *low-end merchandising.*

low-end merchandise: cheap, low quality goods.

low-end merchandising: in retailing, where retailers are located in low rent areas and their goods are shown with limited amenities. Items are often displayed on dump tables or in cartons and bins and little sales help is available. Low-end merchandisers depend largely on low prices to attract customers and to generate the high volume necessary to make a profit. These retailers are commonly referred to as low-margin/high-turnover stores.

low-end strategy: See *low-end merchandising.*

low involvement merchandise: items that are bought routinely by the consumer without much thought, search, or purchase time. These consumers are usually indifferent to particular brands since there is minimal personal consequence to the purchase decision, nor does it relate to major objectives or values of the consumer.

low-margin/high-turnover store: See *low-end merchandising.*

low-margin retailing: discount selling or mass merchandising.

low-pressure selling: a strategy used by a relatively new salesperson where the potential buyer is led to make the purchase by skillful questioning and apparent hesitation and reluctance on the part of the salesperson. Purports to give the customer the impression that he or she has throughout the conversation been in full control of the situation.

LTL: See *less-than-truckload lot.*

LULU Awards: annual awards presented by the Men's Fashion Association of America for excellence in the editorial coverage of men's fashion.

luxuries: comforts and amenities of life that are in excess of what is needed for normal or standard living. See *optional consumption.*

luxury goods: the top-of-the line goods of the finest quality.

macrosales model: a way of illustrating the sales process by permitting sales to be presented by one variable consisting of units or dollars, and then examining this in relation to other pertinent variables. Cf. *microanalytic sales model.*

MADA (money, authority, desire, access): used in setting retailer's strategy; an acronym for a method of predicting sales and measuring market potential. MADA attributes are assigned to differing populations to quantify consumers who have the money to buy a product, the power to make the buying decision, the interest in making a purchase, and the actual ability to obtain it.

made-to-measure: items that are custom made, e.g, clothing that is cut and fitted to the dimensions of a specific person or slip covers made for a particular piece of furniture.

Magnuson-Moss Improvements Act of 1975: federal legislation designed to broaden the powers of the Federal Trade Commission with respect to eliminating misleading packaging and advertising of toys. Fines can result when violations are determined. Cf. *Magnuson-Moss Warranty Act of 1975.*

Magnuson-Moss Warranty Act of 1975: federal legislation requiring that all consumer items distributed in interstate commerce and sold with a written warranty must have the warranty designated as "full" or "limited," as the only permitted designations. To be known as a "full warranty," it must promise to remedy any defect or malfunction within a given and reasonable time period, by refund or free repair or replacement with an equivalent or very similar product. The consumer need not do anything more than give notice of the defect or malfunction. Cf. *Magnuson-Moss Improvements Act of 1975.*

mail-in premium: a gift given as a special promotion by a manufacturer in exchange for appropriate representation of purchase of goods that is mailed to the manufacturer or sometimes directly in a store.

mail order: activities that use the mail as the primary means for promoting and delivery goods and services, and to communicate with customers. Mail order is different from other forms of direct marketing in that the purchaser and seller do not have any direct contract with each other.

Mail Order Association of America (MOAA): based in Schaumburg, Illinois, an association of retail firms selling items by mail order. MOAA focuses on catalogs, packaging, and sizing.

mail-order house: a retailing organization that receives orders and makes sales by mail, thereby avoiding the need for a physical store. Some types of retail stores conduct a mail-order business, usually through departments set up for that purpose, but this does not make them mail-order houses.

mail-order retailer: a reseller that enters and fulfills customer orders through the mail.

mail-order wholesaler: an individual who sells by mail and usually advertises goods and services in a catalog. See *catalog.*

main-floor retailing: the ground floor merchandising activities found within the department store. The main floor often includes women's purses and other leather items, a cosmetic department, jewelry, hats, misses sportswear and separates, and often men's clothing.

main store: See *parent store.*

main stream: See *traditional merchandise.*

maintained mark-on: the difference between the cost for delivering goods and the price at which they are sold. The maintained markup figures, expressed as a percentage of net sales, does not reflect deductions for cash discounts and workroom costs. It does represent the actual markup that was achieved for the selling period. See *gross margin.*

maintained prices: See *resale price maintenance.*

maintenance marketing: the monitoring of the market for shifts in customer demand.

MAJAPS: See *major appliances.*

major appliances (MAJAPS): large in size and price, electrical housewares, such as refrigerators, freezers, television sets. Synonymous with *hard goods; hard lines; white goods.*

make bulk: the process of placing together large shipments from multiple or smaller shipments to take advantage of large-volume discounts from carriers.

make bulk center: See *freight forwarder.*

make good: to discharge an obligation or debt.

maker:
(1) a manufacturer, processor, or producer of merchandise or products.
(2) an individual, firm, or other legal entity that signs a note, check, or other negotiable form as a responsible party.

make the cash: to decide whether the funds on hand, following receipts and payments, balance with the record of sales and payments of obligations.

making the plan: the daily contrasting of sales from those of the previous year. Should current figures exceed those of last year, the buyer is said to be making his or her plan.

mall:
(1) a shopping center of a few or numerous blocks closed off to car traffic.
(2) a public promenade or concourse open only to pedestrian traffic. Synonymous with *shopping mall; shopping plaza.*

mall intercept interview: an interview conducted by a researcher in a shopping mall. The interviewer randomly chooses people walking around the mall, thus introducing a potential bias in how they are chosen.

managed obsolescence: See *planned obsolescence*

manifest: a statement itemizing the contents, value, point of origin, destination, and so on, of cargo that is shipped.

manikin: See *mannequin.*

mannequin:
(1) French for human model, the person who wears and models clothing in a fashion show.

(2) in United States, lifelike figures used for displaying clothing on the selling floor or in store windows.

manufacture: to produce, make, or fabricate something.

manufacturer-owned chain: a chain of stores that promotes and sells items of the firm that manufactures them, e.g., the majority of shoes sales are made through such retail outlets.

manufacturers:

(1) *general:* products for resale to other consumers.

(2) *retailing:* synonymous with *supplier; vendor.*

manufacturer's agent: an agent (wholesale or middleperson) who takes neither title to nor possession of the merchandise he or she sells. The agent represents several noncompeting producers of goods that are purchased by one type of trade (e.g., a manufacturer's agent in women's apparel might sell dresses, blouses, belts, coats, stockings, and so on, for different manufacturers). Synonymous with *manufacturer's representative.*

manufacturer's brand:

(1) *general:* items licensed for sale by other firms outside the manufacturer's product category. For example, a clothing manufacturer licenses its name to firms who use the name on jewelry. See *brand.*

(2) *merchandising:* a brand name owned by the item's maker (e.g., Hershey's chocolate kisses). The primary goals of having such a brand is to attract people loyal to the manufacturer's name. Synonymous with *national brand.*

manufacturer's cooperative advertising: See *cooperative advertising.*

manufacturer's coupon: See *coupon.*

manufacturer/service provider wholesaling: occurs when a producer undertakes all wholesaling functions itself. It

may be carried out via sales offices and/or branch offices.

manufacturer's marking: See *vendor premarking.*

manufacturer's representative: Synonymous with *manufacturer's agent; sales representative.*

manufacturer's sales branch: an operation owned and controlled by a manufacturer separate from his or her factories out of which salespeople may work, and which contains stocks from which deliveries can be made to customers. Cf. *manufacturer's sales office.*

manufacturer's sales office: Synonymous with *manufacturer's sales branch,* except no stock is housed within the office.

manufacturer's sales representative: See *manufacturer's agent.*

manufacturers'/service providers' agents: agents who work for several manufacturers/service providers and carry noncompetitive, complementary products in exclusive territories. A manufacturer/service provider may employ many agents, each with a unique product-territorial mix.

manufacturer's/service provider's branch office: a form of manufacturer/service provider wholesaling. It includes facilities for warehousing goods, as well as for selling them.

manufacturer's/service provider's sales office: a form of manufacturer/service provider wholesaler. Located at a company's production facilities or a site close to the market, no inventory is carried there.

manufacturing: converting raw materials into a completed product by a mechanical, electrical, or chemical (i.e., not manual) process. See *production.*

manufacturing-driven firm: a company that gives major emphasis on manufacturing requirements in lieu of marketing considerations.

margin:

(1) the difference between the market value of collateral pledged to secure a loan and the face value of the loan itself. See *gross margin; markup.*

(2) the difference between the cost of sold items and the total net sales income.

marginal analysis:

(1) *general:* analysis of economic information by examining the results of the value added when one variable is increased by a single unit of another variable. See *direct cost.*

(2) *retailing:* a budgeting method used to determine how much each marketing expenditure increases the store's profits.

marginal buyer: a buyer who will refuse to buy if the price is increased.

marginal cost:

(1) *general:* the increase in the total cost of production that results from manufacturing one more unit of output.

(2) *retailing:* the amount of money expended to produce one further unit of merchandise or service.

marginal cost pricing: the rule enforced by competitive markets that price should be equal to the cost of producing the final (marginal) unit of merchandise.

marginal customer: a purchaser judged by the seller to be at the edge between providing a profit large enough to be continued as a customer by the seller and a profit, so small, that he or she may be dropped as a customer.

marginal product: the additional product derived by increasing a given factor of production by one further unit of merchandise or service.

marginal profits: the increase in total profits that is obtained by producing

an additional unit of merchandise or service.

marginal revenue: the quantity of money accruing from the sale of one further unit of merchandise or service.

marginal seller: a seller who refuses to sell if the price is lowered.

margin of profit: operating income divided by sales. Income taxes are usually excluded and depreciation is usually included in the operating expenses.

margin of safety:

(1) *general:* the balance of income left after payment of fixed charges.

(2) *retailing:* the amount by which sales exceeds the break-even point, thus providing a cushion against a drop in store sales or other unforeseeable forces. See *break-even model.*

mark: See *trademark.*

MARK: a research project of the Center for Retailing Education at the University of Florida; an implementable model-based approach and interactive pc-based program that can assist retail store buyers to make optimal markdown and related inventory decisions with respect to single items of fashion merchandise (e.g., sweaters, swimwear, shoes). The model is useful to a buyer who must procure a quantity of the item in advance of the season and then has the opportunity to reprice the merchandise one or more times at regular intervals of the season. Typically, a buyer can sell an item at either the initial price or at one of a few off-price levels allowed by store policy.

markdown: a reduction of an originally established selling or previous retail price; popular with domestic goods sold in overseas markets where incomes tend to be lower, where wholesalers require a large piece of the revenue, and/or where surplus items are discarded. Cf. *clearance; markup.* See *price verification procedure.*

markdown cancellation: the increase in the retail price of an item that has been reduced. The increase can be up to the retail price at which the item was originally placed for sale, but not higher. This upward change often comes at the end of a sale when merchandise is returned to the former retail price. See *retail method of inventory.*

markdown control: a method for analyzing reductions in retail price (markdowns) in order to determine their cause and, if excessive, to take corrective action.

markdown money: the payment of money by a vendor to a retailer compensating the retailer for the losses incurred resulting from lowering the selling price of the vendor's items.

markdown percentage: the amount of a price reduction expressed as a percentage rather than as a dollar amount. There are two approaches for making such a computation: (a) markdown expressed as a percentage of the new reduced price:

$$\frac{\text{amount of markdown}}{\text{new reduced price}} =$$

markdown percentage

(b) markdown expressed as a percentage of the original retail price:

$$\frac{\text{original retail price} - \text{new reduced price}}{\text{original retail price}} =$$

markdown percentage

markdown threshold: in the merchandising of fashion goods, a concept asserting that a style that is two weeks behind what was originally estimated to be a reasonable rate of sale is not going to sell out during its fashion life. The purpose is to spot slow-movers early, mark them down quickly, and hope to sell out the style at the marked down price. See *markdown timing.*

markdown timing: the setting of planned price reductions so as to minimize lost profits.

market:

(1) *general:* people who possess the ability and desire to purchase, or prospects for a product or service.

(2) *general:* a geographical area that includes a significant number of potential customers.

(3) *retailing:* a store's market is the retail trading area, i.e., a geographical entity containing potential customers.

(4) *retailing:* a meeting place where representatives of manufacturers present their lines for the inspection of retail buyers.

marketable: that which can be sold.

market appeal: the attractiveness of a market based on its size or annual rate of which is growing. This appeal is influenced by economic and technological forces, to competitive variables and environmental considerations.

market attractiveness: See *market appeal.*

market-basket pricing: setting prices applicable to a situation where the sale of one item encourages a buyer to purchase other items in the store. Specials and tie-in sales are often used.

market channel: See *channel of distribution.*

marketcide: self-inflicted and avoidable harm caused to a store due to a lack of attention to and poor implementation of marketing concepts and principles.

market cleavage: See *segmentation.*

market concentration:

(1) *general:* a form of market segmentation where the firm's efforts

are concentrated on one segment of the potential population.

(2) *retailing:* that portion of an item's sales volume that is determined by a small number of large stores, expressed in dollars, units sold, etc.

market delineation: determining who will be the customers and prospects for a product and what their particular characteristics are. See *market segmentation.*

market demand: the total amount of merchandise that is wanted at a specified price at a specific time. Market demand is measured by: (a) product levels—determined by product type, form, sales (national, industry wide, etc.); (b) space levels—determined by territory (region, nation, global); and (c) time levels—determined by whether it is for a short, medium, or long-term period.

market development: an approach where a firm develops new markets for its merchandise or services; the store creates alternate uses for the same items to increase sales.

marketer: those involved in the activity of attempting to sell something to someone.

market expansion promotion: attempts to find new customers with the introduction of new items or by presenting new means for showing items.

market fit: the likelihood that new merchandise will be purchased by the same people who buy a store's other goods.

marketing: activities that accelerate the movement of goods or services from the manufacturer to the consumer, including everything connected with advertising, distribution, merchandising, product planning, promotion, publicity, research and development, sales, transportation, and warehousing of goods or services. Cf. *merchandising.*

marketing audit: a careful study of the marketing system within a company to determine the value of the system's parts and how well the parts are performing their given tasks. To be successful these audits should be comprehensive—examining all critical components of the marketing program—and systematic—including appropriate diagnostic steps that deal with the marketing environment, resources, and existing marketing initiatives.

marketing budget: a financial plan, based on projected sales of merchandise or services, that is used for allocating store funds to cover marketing costs over a time period.

marketing channel: See *channel of distribution.*

marketing concept:

(1) a strategy or idea for marketing products or services.

(2) a business philosophy consisting of the notions that marketing strategy should be developed based on customer needs and desires and that all marketing functions should be structured within the firm, with one person having overall responsibility. See *consumer behavior research; marketing management; market research.* Synonymous with *marketing philosophy.*

marketing director: the individual who is responsible for overseeing all marketing activities with the store or retail operation.

marketing function: an activity, such as buying, selling, shipping, warehousing, grading and standardization, financing, assuming responsibility for taking the risk, and data accumulation.

marketing information system (MIS): the entire system employed by a store to gather, analyze, store, and disseminate relevant marketing information to those who require these data.

marketing institutions: includes manufacturers and producers, wholesalers, retailers, transporting firms, advertising agencies, etc.

marketing management: planning, directing, and controlling the total marketing operation within the store or retail operation, including formulation of marketing goals, policies, programs, and strategy, and often embracing product development, organizing and staffing to discharge plans, supervising marketing operations, and monitoring performance. See *product manager.*

marketing mix:

(1) *general:* the concept developed by Neil Borden that market strategy is based on the product, price, promotion, and channels in an integrated marketing program.

(2) *retailing:* the combination of activities involving product, price, place, and promotion that a store undertakes in order to provide satisfaction to consumers in a given market.

marketing performers: includes manufacturers and service providers, wholesalers, retailers, marketing specialists, and organizational and final consumers.

marketing philosophy: See *marketing concept.*

marketing plan: a carefully designed outline providing the store's self-image, its objectives, all marketing programs to fulfill goals, and the means for assessing the effectiveness of such efforts. Also indicates responsibilities for discharging the plan, the strategies involved in the suggested development of the items, the definition of its target market(s), and the types of media and sales promotions to be incorporated. Synonymous with *action program; marketing strategy.*

marketing research:

(1) a systematic, objective approach to the development and provision of information for decision making regarding a specific marketing problem. Its results provide facts required to make marketing decisions and will determine the extent and location of the market for a product or service.

(2) the process of gathering, recording, and analyzing information pertaining to the marketing of goods and services. Cf. *market research.*

marketing risks: possible losses of the marketer, including waste, obsolescence, damage, physical deterioration, stealing of items, credit, discontinuity of supply, shifts in demand affecting pricing, and acts of God.

marketing strategy: See *marketing plan.*

market leader: the store that controls the market share of merchandise or services.

market minimum: the rate of store sales for merchandise that would be accomplished without any demand-stimulating costs, such as promotional campaigns or advertisements.

market-minus prices: in retailing, trying to price similar items for less than the competition. See *at-the-market prices; market-plus pricing; variable pricing.* Synonymous with *demand-backward prices.*

market niche: usually a strategy used by small stores; a narrow market segment that a store targets because the segment lacks competitors, yet offers a sizeable sales potential.

market-oriented pricing: in establishing retail prices, the price at which the item or similar items are selling in the marketplace; employed as a standard rather than the cost of the items.

market penetration:

(1) *general:* the degree to which a product captures a percentage of the total market for that item. This includes the absence of competition for the item.

(2) *retailing:* the extent to which a store dominates a trading area, either

in terms of total business or in a single classification or department.

market period: the period from when merchandise is manufactured until the moment it has been purchased.

market place: See *market.*

market-plus pricing: the price at which merchandise is exchanged in the market from day to day. Synonymous with *above-the-market strategy.* See *variable pricing.*

market-positioned warehouse: a storage facility where merchandise is kept that is owned by the manufacturer, distributor, or retailer and is used to consolidate shipments and position items near their ultimate destinations.

market positioning: See *positioning.*

market potential: the maximum sales potential for all sellers of a product or service over a fixed period. See *sales potential.*

market power: the ability of a purchaser or seller to control price and quantity of an item.

market price:
(1) the price established in the market where buyers and sellers meet to buy and sell similar products.
(2) a price determined by factors of supply and demand rather than by management decisions.

market representative (MR): the executive of a store's buying office who gives his or her time and effort to a particular grouping of goods and makes data about it available to buyers of owned or operated stores.

market research: the part of marketing research that deals with the pattern of a market, measuring the extent and nature of the market and identifying its characteristics. Market research precedes marketing research. See *product planning.* Cf. *marketing research.*

market segment: a subdivision of the population, the people sharing similar characteristics. The store often develops different marketing programs for each segment of its target market. Cf. *market segmentation.*

market segmentation: separating the market for an item into categories of location, personality, or other characteristics for each division; evolves as a result of the observations that all potential users of merchandise or services are different and that what appeals to some will not appeal to all prospects. Once the market has been segmented by a store, it then engages in one of the following marketing strategies: differentiated marketing, undifferentiated marketing, or concentrated marketing. See *geographical market segmentation; market target; segmentation; whole market approach; zoning price.* Cf. *market segment.*

market share:
(1) a firm's percentage of its industry's total sales.
(2) the total number of units of a product (or their dollar value) expressed as a percentage of the total number of units sold by all competitors in a given market. Synonymous with *brand share; share of the market.*

market share analysis: a forecasting technique in which it is assumed that the store's market share will remain constant and sales forecasts for the store are based on forecasts for the industry.

market share goal: a benchmark representing that portion of a market a store wishes to capture.

market skimming: an introductory pricing strategy of charging a high price in order to recover investment quickly. See *skimming price.*

market target: the people or groups for whom an item and its program or marketing are intended. A strategy and a meaningful approach to fulfilling a stated goal must be established with respect to a market target. See *positioning*. Cf. *target customers; target market*.

market testing: See *test marketing*.

market trip: when the retail buyer visits the wholesale market in order to write orders for future merchandise.

marking: placing the correct tag on new goods, usually containing price, size, and style data. See *Kimball tags*.

markon: the difference between the billed-cost price and the original retail price of an item. Markon is:

$$\frac{\text{retail price} - \text{cost price}}{\text{cost price}} = \text{markon percentage}$$

Markon usually refers to the total amount added to the cost of all the merchandise in a department; most frequently found at the manufacturing level. See *initial markon; markon goal*. Cf. *markup*.

markon goal: the desired results of the markon applied to each line of store goods including covering expenses, covering transportation costs of merchandise coming into the store, providing for expected markdowns, providing for net profits, and inspiring appropriate turnover.

markup:

(1) the difference between cost price of goods and their retail price. Markup can be expressed in dollars or as a percentage. If stated as a percentage it may be based on either cost price or retail price. Markup is sometimes used synonymously with the term markon, but certain distinctions exist. Markup is:

$$\frac{\text{retail price} - \text{cost price}}{\text{retail price}} = \text{markup percentage}$$

(2) amount added to cost to reach a retail price for individual items; used at the merchandising/retail level of the distribution chain. Cf. *markon*.

markup cancellation: price lowering on an item once it has been subject to additional markup. Markup cancellation never exceeds the amount of additional markup applied to an item.

markup on cost: See *markon*.

markup on retail: See *markup*.

markup percent: calculated as a percentage of retail price. Some retailers use cost price as the basis for comparison. See *markup*.

markup percentage: See *markup percent*.

markup table: a chart indicating markup percentages on both cost price and retail price.

marquee: a rooflike construction, such as a canopy, that is constructed over the entrance to a store to shelter customers as well as to provide a place for the retailer's name and logo.

mass display: in retailing, a large additional display of merchandise already on the shelf, positioned in a separate prominent place where the majority of store traffic will walk past it.

massed promotion: communication concentrated in peak periods, like holidays.

mass fashion: styles with broad appeal, moderate prices, and a high degree of fashion acceptance, especially among lower income people. Synonymous with *volume fashion*.

mass marketing: the approach used to sell large volumes of merchandise to everyone. This usually requires distribution in discount stores and supermarkets.

mass market theory: See *horizontal flow theory*.

mass merchandise: consumer goods with broad appeal that sell to large numbers of customers at relatively low prices.

mass merchandiser: an outlet with a discount image and following; requires the handling of at least three merchandise lines within a floor space of 10,000 or more square feet. See *mass merchandising.*

mass merchandising: retailing on a large scale, of staple items at prices lower than those commonly found in department and specialty stores; characterized by (a) emphasis on products whose market is not highly segmented, (b) customers who are willing to sacrifice sales assistance and store services in return for lower prices, (c) high volume and rapid stock turnover rate, and (d) a very highly competitive marketplace. See *mass merchandiser.*

Mass Merchandising Distributors' Association (MMDA): located in St. Joseph, Missouri, an organization of mass merchandising distributors who sell and service hardline products to mass merchandising retailers. MMDA assists in stocking, merchandising, demonstrations, marketing data, and planning.

Mass Retailer's Merchandising Report: See *National Mass Retailing Institute.*

mass promotion: sales promotion activities of retailers concentrated at a specific time, such as summer.

maturity stage: the beginning of the demise of a product. The merchandise's life cycle conclusion is measured by the leveling off of demand, a decline in profit, and increasing competition. Small and financially insecure retailers tend to drop out of the market in the maturity stage.

MAXI Award: See *International Council of Shopping Centers.*

maximum distribution: the number, usually given as a percentage, of outlets that have stocked the item at any time since an earlier retail audit.

McGuire Act: See *Miller-Tydings Act of 1937.*

media coverage: See *reach.*

meeting competition: See *pricing at the market.*

megaselling: selling orders of large quantities, or for significant sums of money. Synonymous with *big ticket selling.*

"me" generation: a consumer lifestyle that stresses being good to oneself.

member-get-member promotion: a sales promotion method used in getting new customers by providing an incentive to current customers who then make referrals. As contrasted with friend-of-a-friend promotion, this form of promotion provides incentives only to people who are existing customers. Cf. *friend-of-a-friend promotion.*

membership club: Synonymous with *closed door membership.*

membership group: a reference unit to which a person belongs and participates in, such as clubs, unions, or religious organizations.

membership warehouse club: a retailing format in which final consumers and businesses pay small yearly dues for the right to shop in a huge, austere warehouse. Consumers buy merchandise at deep discounts.

memorandum sale: the sale in a retail operation of consigned goods whose title rests with the vendor for a stated period. At the end of the period, unsold items are eligible for return to the vendor, and the sold or held goods are billed to the merchant. Cf. *on consignment.*

Men's Fashion Association of America (MFA): based in New York City, an association that includes representatives of the textile, men's apparel, yarn suppliers, and retail industries; serves as the consumer education bureau of the menswear industry. Engages in public relations programs to increase the sales of men's and boys' wear. Presents the annual LULA awards and Adam Awards.

Menswear Retailers of America (MRA): located in Washington, DC, an association of retailers of men's and boys' apparel; serves as a government liaison and conducts training programs for members.

mercantile credit: deferring payment between a buyer and the seller, both of whom are merchant middlepeople.

mercantile customer: any merchant middleperson.

merchandise:
(1) *noun:* purchased articles and merchandise of business held for sale.
(2) *verb:* to plan or promote the sale of goods. Cf. goods.
(3) Cf. *merchandising.*
(4) See *backup merchandise; carryover merchandise; classic merchandise; confined merchandise; customer's own merchandise; demand merchandise; designer merchandise; distress merchandise; durable merchandise; evaluation of merchandise; impulse merchandise; low-end merchandise; mass merchandise; off-price merchandise; popularly price merchandise; presold merchandise; prestige merchandise; promotional merchandise; related merchandise; sale merchandise; merchandise; scrambled merchandise; seasonal merchandise; second line goods; short merchandise; special merchandise; specialty merchandise; tabletop items; traditional merchandise; transition merchandise; unbranded merchandise; visual merchandise.*

merchandise acceptance curve: See *product life cycle.*

merchandise adjustment: See *adjustment.*

merchandise agent: See *broker.*

merchandise allowance: See *returns and allowances.*

merchandise assortment: See *assortment.*

merchandise broker: Synonymous with *commission buying office.* See *broker.*

merchandise budget: in retailing, a dollar plan of identified efforts involving merchandise for a given time period; includes sales projections, inventories, markdowns, discounts, expenses, returns, and controllable net profits. Used for assessing current practices as well as for projecting future activities.

merchandise certificate: See *due bill.*

merchandise charge: extraneous costs (including shipping, insurance, demurrage, etc.) added to the cost of goods prior to markon.

merchandise classification: See *classification.*

merchandise control: the collection and analysis of data on purchases and sales items, either by unit or by dollars. See *dollar control; unit control.*

merchandise cost: See *cost of goods sold.*

merchandise coverage: items that should be retained in inventory to fulfill basic customer demand.

merchandise dissection: See *classification.*

merchandise handled: the amount of goods handled in a given period; determined by adding purchases for the period to the inventory at the beginning of the period. It can be calculated at either cost price or retail price.

merchandise inventory: products held by an entity for resale to customers.

merchandise islands: tables or areas stacked with merchandise as a selling floor promotion.

merchandise life cycle: See *product life cycle.*

merchandise line consistency: See *assortment consistency.*

merchandise line depth: See *assortment depth.*

merchandise line width: See *assortment breadth.*

merchandise loan book: the book or file where goods that are loaned to other departments is recorded.

merchandise loans: merchandise temporarily transferred to another department to be used in a display or for some other reason.

merchandise management: deals with inventory balance and composition, although buying, pricing, and selling are important components. See *merchandise manager; merchandising.*

merchandise manager: an executive who is responsible for supervising the purchasing, selling, and inventory control activities in a store.

merchandise mart: a building that contains manufacturers' showrooms where retailers can examine the goods and place orders. Cf. *resident buyer; sales office.*

merchandise mix: See *assortment breadth.*

merchandise plan: See *sales plan.*

merchandise planning: the evolution a strategy at the management level to conclude what items are to be stocked. Considerations given are of consumer demand, budget limitations, and the formulation of precise buying plans.

merchandiser: a display unit that holds items to be sold on the floor of the store.

merchandise resource: the source of supply from which salable and reliable goods are purchased on a recurring basis with few complications, if any, over an extended time period. See *resource.*

merchandise scrambling: See *scrambled merchandise.*

merchandise source: See *vendor.*

merchandise space: locations within a store where goods are to be stored, i.e., stock room, behind counters.

merchandise transfer: the transfer of goods from one accounting unit of a store to another. Merchandise can be transferred from department to department, from one branch store to another branch, or from home office to branch store.

merchandise turnover: See *stock turnover.*

merchandise vending machine operator: See *vending machine.*

merchandising:
(1) all activities connected with buying and selling of merchandise, including displays, promotions, pricing, and buying.
(2) the activities required in the attempt to make a product interesting to buyers (packaging, promotion, pricing arrangements, etc.). Cf. *marketing.*
(3) activities undertaken to ensure a product is available to its target consumers and prominently visible in the stores in which it is sold; related to product and product line decisions.
(4) See *automatic merchandising; bait-and-switch merchandising; boutique merchandising; catalog merchandising; classification merchandising; cross merchandising; discount merchandising; dual merchandising; item merchandising; lifestyle merchandising; low-cost merchandising; low-end merchandising; mass merchandising; program merchandising; remerchandising; retail merchandising; segmented merchandising; trend merchandising.*

merchandising allowance: the lowering of the wholesale price as an incentive to middlepeople and to wholesalers by compensating the retailer for expenditures made to promote the merchandise.

merchandising and operating results (MOR): issued by the National Retail Merchants Association, an annual statistical study containing detailed data on the performance of the retail industry. Information is given voluntarily by members of the NRMA and is presented by store type and size, then by department and merchandise classification. Individual store results are not identified, only averages for all stores in a particular store category.

merchandising conglomerate: a corporation made up of a number of diversified retailing organizations under a single management. Their stores may be of various types. Synonymous with *conglomerchant.*

merchandising division: a location within a large store organization that is responsible for the planning, buying and selling of goods, the supervision of sales people, etc., and is considered the most essential division.

merchandising group: several members of a cooperative chain that join forces under a common name to facilitate their advertising and promotion.

merchandising leader: a store that promotes several items at attractive prices for the purpose of inducing customers into the store. See *loss leader.*

merchandising life cycle: See *product life cycle.*

merchandising service: merchandising assistance provided by one of the communications media for the placing of copy, advertising, commercials, layouts, etc. Traditionally, this type of service is provided without charge to advertisers.

merchant: an individual who takes title to goods by buying them for the purpose of resale.

merchantism: the responsibility of the merchant to his or her customers; deals with appropriate customer service, emphasizing merchandise awareness and knowledge of the goods.

merchant middleperson: an intermediary that takes title to the products it distributes.

merchant wholesaler: a middleperson who receives title to merchandise purchases for resale to firms that plan to resell the goods or process them in some fashion. See *wholesaler.*

merit goods: items for which the government determines or heavily influences levels of consumption because individuals are not qualified to make the choices (e.g., education, automobile safety equipment).

metroarea: See *metromarket.*

metromarket: the area, usually the inner city and its suburbs, from which a retail store draws most of its customers.

MFA: See *Men's Fashion Association of America.*

MFN: See *most-favored nation.*

microanalytic sales model: identifying the sales process by having all sales be the item of the number of purchasers within the market, the percentage who purchase from the company, and the average rate of buying. Cf. *macrosales model; microbehavioral sales model; microcomponent sales model.*

microbehavioral sales model: identifying the sales process by having awareness of the individual customer's knowledge, attitudes, actions toward products, and environmental variables affecting him or her so that the probability of a purchase can be determined. Cf. *macrosales model; microanalytic sales model; microcomponent sales model.*

microcomponent sales model: identifying the sales process by displaying sales as composed of additive components, each subject to separate analysis. These variables can be sales by item, by customer, or by salesperson, etc. Cf. *macrosales model; microanalytic sales model; microbehavioral sales model.*

micromarketing: identifying the wants and needs of the local marketplace as well as the ability to customize strategies at the store level, allowing the retailer and manufacturer to exploit trading area differences in consumers and with the competition.

middleman: See *middleperson.*

middle-of-month dating (MOM): the 15th and the last day of the month are used as cut-off dates, where all invoices dated before the 15th are considered dated the 15th; for invoices dated on and after the 15th, the credit period begins with the last day of the month. Discount and due dates are counted as from one of the two cut-off dates.

middle-of-month terms: See *middle-of-month dating.*

middleperson: an individual who buys merchandise with the expectation of reselling it for profit. At times, a middleperson may arrange for such transactions without actually having possession of the goods. Synonymous with *intermediary; middleman.*

midget market: See *convenience store.*

milking: (slang) management's attempt to squeeze the last remaining profits from the store without leaving sufficient reserves for improvements or for a downturn period.

Miller-Tydings Act of 1937: federal legislation enabling manufacturers to take advantage of state fair trade laws without being prosecuted for violation of the federal antitrust laws. Full name is Miller-Tydings Resale Price Maintenance Act. See *fair trade acts; nonsigner's clause.*

Miller-Tydings Resale Price Maintenance Act of 1937: See *Miller-Tydings Act of 1937.*

milling in transit: See *transit privileges.*

mill store: a retail establishment that is opened in an unoccupied factory building, started in New England during the 1940s.

mill supply house:
(1) a general-merchandise wholesaler that operates in an industrial setting.

(2) the industrial equivalent of a general line, full-service merchant wholesaler, often focusing on supplying one industry.

minimarket test: a type of controlled-sale market testing whereby the outlets used are a small, nonrepresentative sampling of the market. Product is usually placed into the outlets (not sold), and promotion is much less than planned ultimately. Primarily tests just the willingness to spend some money for a product trial.

minimum: See *caution fee.*

minimum markup laws: See *unfair practices acts.*

minimum stock: the level of goods found in inventory that represents the absolute low point that can be reached before there is a likelihood of letting items go out of stock.

minimum system of stock control: See *automatic reorder.*

minimum wage law: See *Fair Labor Standards Act of 1938.*

miniwarehouse mall: a type of shopping center in which a large warehouse offers space to a variety of sellers, including both retailers and wholesalers.

mirror principle: a marketing approach suggesting that customers will respond in the same fashion as they are treated. Cf. *mirror response technique.*

mirror response technique: when the salesperson responds to a customer's objections to a product or service by repeating what the prospect is understood to have said. It attempts to have the customer reconsider the statement. Synonymous with *repeating technique.*

MIS: See *marketing information system.*

misredemption: the incidence of error and fraud in redemption to the manufacturer coupons given to or secured by retailers as the result of a couponing effort.

missionary sales: the activity of personnel from a manufacturer who work closely with various firms and middlepeople to increase the product sales. See *detail person.*

missionary salesperson: See *detail person (2).*

mix:

(1) *retailing:* combining merchandise in a retail package or the complete variety of inventory of a retailer, wholesaler, or distributor.

(2) *merchandising:* the combination of goods, including various sizes of the same item, for a specific brand in a particular store. See *product mix; promotional mix.*

mixed brand method: a strategy where a manufacturer produces a number of similar items under differing brand names, or where the retailer or middleperson sells items under differing brand names, or where a retailer or middleperson sells items under a dealer or generic name as well as under the manufacturer's name.

mixed-use center: a grouping of retail stores, offices, hotels, etc., combined with reactional and other facilities serving the area

MMDA: See *Mass Merchandising Distributors' Association.*

MOAA: See *Mail Order Association of America.*

mobile franchise: a conventional franchise except that the franchisee dispenses his or her merchandise from a vehicle that is taken from place to place.

model:

(1) *general:* a theory used to analyze various forms of behavior. The closer the model is to the real world, the more useful it is for analysis.

(2) *merchandising:* an individual who wears clothes for the purpose of displaying them to others.

modeling:

(1) *general:* the changes in human behavior, either on the part of people or groups, as the result of the influence of leadership.

(2) *retailing:* showing clothing on live persons at fashion shows, in showrooms, etc.

model stock: the ideal sales situation of having the right goods at the right time in the right quantities at the right price. See *assortment plan; balanced stock.* Cf. *basic stock.*

model stock list: See *basic stock list; model stock plan.*

model stock method: See *model stock plan.*

model stock plan: a means for developing the assortment plan; includes some staples; largely composed of shopping and specialty items. Because of this, the model stock plan is less specific than the basic stock list despite the fact that it includes certain information, such as classification, cost, price, color, size, retail selling price. The inclusion of fashion and seasonal merchandise in the model stock plan adds to its lack of predictability. See *basic stock list.*

modification:

(1) any adjustment of an existing product's style, color, or model.

(2) any product improvement; or a brand change.

MOM: See *middle-of-month dating.*

mom-and-pop outlets: an affectionate term for small stores, generally operated by members of a family with limited capital. See *bluefingers.*

money, authority, desire, access: See *MADA.*

monitoring results: involves comparing the actual performance of a store, business unit, or product against planned performance for a specified period.

monthly sales index: the measure of variations in sales volume from month-to-month based on the index number 100 representing sales for an average month. Changes are reflected as deviations from 100.

MOR: See *merchandising and operating results.*

most-favored nation (MFN): in international trade, a provision against tariff discrimination between two or more nations. It provides that each participant will automatically extend to other signatories all tariff reductions that are offered to nonmember nations. U.S. retailers favor continued MFA status because without it goods purchased from nations, such as China, would not be affordable for most, if not all, consumers. Retailers rely on foreign-made footwear, toys, apparel, small electronics, and household items to stock the shelves of stores for quality merchandise at competitive prices that low- to moderate-income consumers can afford.

motivation: an important component of store buying; a stimulus that differentially energizes certain responses within a person. See *rational buying motives; self-concept theory; trio of needs.*

motivational needs: psychological forces that affect thinking and behavior (e.g., needs for self-actualization, belonging, feelings of security). A theory developed by A. Maslow details an individual's motivational needs.

motive: a need or want that is activated by a particular stimulus and initiates behavior toward some goal.

moving average: a perpetual inventory cost-flow assumption whereby the cost of goods sold and the ending inventory are determined to be a weighted-average cost of all merchandise on hand after each purchase.

MR: See *market representative.*

MRA: See *Menswear Retailers of America.*

MSA: See *Museum Store Association.*

multibrand strategy: a product strategy based on the expectation that a store that markets two brands in the same market will, with all else constant, hold a greater brand share than one brand will obtain on its own, and with the right circumstances, three brands can also achieve greater share than two, etc.

multipack: a container holding two or more separately packaged items.

multiple brand entries: several brand names used by a manufacturer on essentially the same product to open up new market segments. See *emulative product.*

multiple buying influence: any purchase decision that is shared among several people, usually at differing levels of management.

multiple packaging: including more than one item in a single container (e.g., the six-pack approach to beverage packaging).

multiple pricing: a price reduction offered if more than one item is purchased.

multiple retailers: See *chain store.*

multiple sales: the result of selection by customers of multiple rather than single items to purchase.

multiple source purchasing: purchasing goods from more than one supplier.

multiple unit packaging: combining a variety of units of an item into one wrapping or container with the expectation that the purchaser will take the number as a unit item. (e.g., beer six-packs.)

multiple-unit pricing: pricing goods by "so many for a price" (e.g., 5 for $1.00). Cf. *unit pricing.*

multiprice store: a store where goods are not price marked. Salespeople vary prices quoted on the basis of what they believe the customer may be able and willing to pay.

multi-unit operation: a retail unit with various branches that are of relatively equal importance and in which there is no main or flagship store. All units are managed by centrally located administrative executives.

municipal market: See *public market.*

Museum Store Association (MSA): located in Doylestown, Pennsylvania, an association of sales departments in museums of fine arts, history, ethnography, and science.

mystery technique: the method used by salespeople in the first few minutes of customer contact. A dangling statement is used to attract the prospect's attention.

NACDS: See *National Association of Chain Drug Stores.*

NACS:
(1) See *National Association of College Stores.*
(2) See *National Association of Computer Stores.*
(3) See *National Association of Convenience Stores.*

NACSM: See *National Association of Catalog Showroom Merchandisers.*

Naderism: used synonymously with *consumerism,* after advocate Ralph Nader. See *consumerist.*

NADI: See *National Association of Display Industries.*

NAFTA: See *North American Free Trade Agreement.*

NAGMR: See *National Association General Merchandise Representatives.*

nailed down: furniture or appliances displayed in a store that are advertised as for sale, but which the merchant has no intention of selling at the marked price. This unethical practice is often the first stage of a bait-and-switch strategy.

NAM: See *National Association of Manufacturers.*

NAMSB: See *National Association of Men's Sportswear Buyers.*

NARD: See *National Association of Retail Druggists.*

NARDA: See *National Association of Retail Dealers of America.*

narrow market: a condition that exists when the demand for merchandise or service is so limited that small alterations in supply or demand will create major fluctuations in price.

NAS-RAE: See *National Association of State Retail Association Executives.*

NATAD: See *National Association of Textile and Apparel Distributors.*

National Association General Merchandise Representatives (NAGMR): located in Chicago, Illinois, an association of manufacturers' agents selling drug, health, beauty, and other nonfood items to food chains. NAGMR also sells grocery items to the nonfood market.

National Association of Catalog Showroom Merchandisers (NACSM): located in New York City, an association of catalog showroom operators, catalog coordinators, manufacturers, and buying representatives. NACSM compiles data on the industry, provides specialized training courses for members, and conducts research.

National Association of Chain Drug Stores (NACDS): based in Alexandria,

Virginia, an association of chain drug retailers that includes manufacturers, publishers, and advertising agencies. NACDS serves as a liaison with government agencies regulating pharmaceuticals, and interprets government decisions for members.

National Association of College Stores (NACS): located in Oberlin, Ohio, an association of institutional, private, and cooperative college stores selling books, supplies, etc. to college students and faculty. NACS conducts store accreditation, placement, and research; maintains the College Stores Research and Educational Foundation.

National Association of Computer Stores (NACS): located in Stamford, Connecticut, an association of firms engaged in the retail selling of personal and small business computer systems.

National Association of Convenience Stores (NACS): located in Falls Church, Virginia, an association of retail food stores that carry a more limited selection than supermarkets and usually do business during extended hours for the shopping convenience of their customers.

National Association of Display Industries (NADI): based in New York City, an association of manufacturers, distributors, and importers of visual merchandise materials and equipment used by stores and retailers. NADI conducts research and maintains statistics on the industry.

National Association of Food Chains: See *Food Marketing Institute.*

National Association of Manufacturers (NAM): a major organization of employers, founded in 1895, and structured with departments of trade, law, industrial relations, and publicity.

National Association of Men's Sportswear Buyers (NAMSB): located in New York City, an association that holds trade shows for buyers of clothes for mens' wear stores three times a year, in January, March, and October.

National Association of Retail Dealers of America (NARDA): located in Chicago, Illinois, an association of retailers and distributors of consumer electronics and household appliances. NARDA is geared to encouraging more profitable dealerships and provides management consulting, sales training, advertising workshops, etc., for its members.

National Association of Retail Druggists (NARD): located in Alexandria, Virginia, an association of owners of independent drugstores and pharmacists employed in retail drugstores which offer pharmacy services.

National Association of Retail Grocers of the United States: See *National Grocers' Association.*

National Association of State Retail Association Executives (NAS-RAE): a parent organization of state retail associations (SRAs) throughout the United States. Assists state associations in providing the first, and often only, line of defense as the primary pro-active vehicles for providing the retailing agenda in state capitals.

National Association of Textile and Apparel Distributors (NATAD): formerly the National Association of Textile and Apparel Wholesalers and the National Wholesale Dry Good Association, an association of wholesale distributors of textile and apparel products. NATAD compiles industry statistics, conducts educational programs, and holds an annual trade show.

National Association of Textile and Apparel Wholesalers: See *National Association of Textile and Apparel Distributors.*

National Association of Truck Stop Operators (NATSO): located in Alexandria, Virginia, an association of owners and operators of truck stops serving professional truckers. NATSO attempts to set standards of excellence.

National Association of Variety Stores (NAVS): located in Chicago, Illinois, an association of independent variety store operators. Membership is restricted to one store per town. NAVS develops lists of resources for merchandise, offers standardized office systems and forms, and conducts retail market tests for product development.

National Beauty Salon Chain Association (NBSCA): based in High Point, North Carolina, an association of beauty salons and beauty school chains.

national brand: See *manufacturer's brand.*

National Fashion Accessories Salesperson's (Salesmen's) Guild (NFASG): an association of salespeople in the handbag, jewelry, and belt industry. NFASG serves as a bargaining and negotiating unit for its membership.

National Grocers' Association (NGA): based in Reston, Virginia, an association of independent retailers and retailer-owned cooperatives. NGA was formed by the merger of the National Association of Retail Grocers of the United States and the Cooperative Food Distributors of America.

National Home Furnishings Association (NHFA): based in Chicago, Illinois, an association of retailers of furniture, carpeting, and related home furnishings. NHFA conducts institutes, workshops, and seminars for members.

National Independent Nursery Furniture Retailers Association (NINFRA): based in Kansas City, Missouri, an association of retailers of juvenile furniture, baby carriages, and nursery furnishings. NINFRA was formed to improve communications between member and to improve the national image of the industry.

National Liquor Stores Association (NLSA): located in Bethesda, Maryland, a federation of associations of liquor stores, including 30 state groups.

National Luggage Dealers Association (NLDA): located in New York City, retailers of luggage, leather goods, gifts, and handbags.

nationally advertised brand: the basis for legal lexicography; evolves from a case before the New Jersey's Alcoholic Beverage Commission where Seagrams attempted to disenfranchise liquor distributors based on the statute permitting this action if the liquor or wine sold was not appropriately a "nationally advertised brand." Applying definitions from English dictionaries going from the 17th century to the present, J. M. Rosenberg helped to convince the Commission that Seagrams had improperly disenfranchised the distributors since their products were indeed national advertised brands.

National Mass Retailing Institute (NMRI): located in New York City, an association of mass retailing chains. Associate members include manufacturers, accounting firms, banks, and service organizations. NMRI conducts research and educational programs on self-service general merchandising; maintains a public affairs program for liaison with local, state, and national government. NMRI is active in consumerism, and maintains links with government agencies as well as consumer groups.

National Retail Federation (NRF): based in New York City, formed by the merger on January 17, 1990, of the American Retail Federation and the National Retail Merchants Association, NRF represents employers of nearly 20 million Americans, employing 1 in 5 workers in the country, generating almost $2 trillion in sales in 1992.

National Retail Hardware Association (NRHA): located in Indianapolis, Indiana, a federation of U.S. and Canadian hardware associations.

National Retail Merchants Association (NRMA): located in New York City, an association composed of department, chain, and mass merchandise and specialty stores retailing men's, women's and children's apparel and home furnishings. NRMA provides materials and advisory services to its members including financial planning, shortage control credit, EDP, buying, etc. NRMA presents the annual Gold Medal and Independent and International Retailer of the Year Awards. Merged with the American Retail Federation to form the National Retail Federation.

National Retail Pet Store and Groomers' Association (NRPSGA): an association of owners of retail firms relating to the pet industry; includes groomers, manufacturers, distributors, wholesalers, and other supplying goods and services to the pet care industry.

National Shoe Retailers' Association (NSRA): located in New York City, an association of chain stores, specialty stores, department stores, and independent retailers of shoes.

National Shoes Traveler's Association (NSTA): an association of traveling salespeople of shoes and related merchandise on both the wholesale and retail levels.

National Wholesale Dry Goods Association: See *National Association of Textile and Apparel Distributors.*

national wholesaler: a wholesaler whose activities can reach most or the entire nation. Cf. *sectional wholesaler.*

NATSO: See *National Association of Truck Stop Operators.*

natural: a specific item of merchandise that stimulates customer interest.

natural brands: Synonymous with *producer-controlled brands.*

natural business year: a 12-month period, usually selected to end when inventory or business activity is at a low point.

natural classification of expenses: an accounting method used by small retail stores where expenses are grouped into classes based on the kinds of expenses involved (e.g., salaries, rent, supplies, taxes) rather than on the function of the expenditure (e.g., the cost of operating a particular department).

natural selection theory: See *adaptive behavior concept.*

natural trading area: the geographic boundaries containing customers that use a particular store or company. In most studies, customers become fewer as the distance increases from the store or company.

NAVS: See *National Association of Variety Stores.*

NBSCA: See *National Beauty Salon Chain Association.*

near-pack premium: discounted merchandise or gifts that are too large to include inside or to affix to the item being promoted. Such premiums are placed near the product display so as to visually and physically connect the item and the premium.

need awareness: the degree to which customers become aware of their needs and are prepared to talk about them with others.

needle trades: apparel-producing industries.

need-satisfaction approach: a selling method based on the principle that each customer has different characteristics and wants. The sales presentation is adapted to each individual customer.

negative authorization: credit approval where a list is maintained of delinquent payments. Should a customer's name not appear on the list, his or her request for credit is then approved. See *floor limit*.

negative demand: where a major segment of a market dislikes merchandise so much that it will take proper action to avoid the item.

negative option selling: where the consumer informs the salesperson by a given date not to forward the items that he or she does not want. Used extensively by book clubs and record clubs.

negotiated contract: a contract to buy goods or service where the buyer and seller negotiate specific terms for agreement. Often used when there is only one supplier and therefore no competition in the market.

negotiated price: the result obtained by a purchaser who desires something different from what is available or is powerful enough to force the seller to accept prices lower than those usually charged. See *variable pricing*.

negotiation:
(1) *general:* the act by which a negotiable instrument is placed in circulation by being physically passed from the original holder to another person.
(2) *retailing:* that stage in the buying process at which the vendor and retail buyer negotiate price, terms, delivery dates, etc.

neighborhood business district: See *neighborhood cluster*.

neighborhood cluster: the centralization of several stores surrounded by a residential community. Most are convenience stores with the majority of its customers living in the area.

neighborhood shopping center: See *strip center*.

neighborhood shopping district: See *neighborhood cluster*.

neighborhood site: See *neighborhood store*.

neighborhood store: a free-standing retail outlet that serves the requirements of a small part of a community.

nested: packaged one within another.

net: in retailing, a vendor's billing concept indicating that no cash or trade discount is allowed.

net alteration and workroom cost: the difference between what it costs to provide the services and what the customer pays for them.

net back: the sale of an item less out-of-pocket expenses to move it from the factory to its point of sale. Such costs include freight expenses, agents' commissions, etc.

net cash flow: the net cash consumed or produced in a period by an activity or product during a unit of time, including all revenue and expenses except non-cash items, such as depreciation.

net cost: the true cost of an item; determined by subtracting all income or financial gain from the gross cost. See *cost of goods purchased*.

net income: Synonymous with *net profit*.

net lease: the retailer assumes such expenses as heating, maintenance, insurance, etc., as well as basic rent charges.

net loss: See *net profit*.

net markdown: the price reduction on goods found in stock because of a lowering of the value of the merchandise.

net markdown: the increase over cost price at which an item is sold after markup cancellations have been made.

net-net: a retail purchasing technique where all advertising allowances and terms of payment are eliminated from the cost of merchandise (especially in the case of branded merchandise) so that a competitive edge is gained over other retailers.

net operating income: See *net profit*.

net operating profit: See *net profit*.

net period: See *dating.*

net price: the price after deductions, allowances, and discounts have been made. See *cost of goods purchased.*

net profit: the excess of all revenues over all costs and expenses incurred to obtain the income in a given enterprise during a given period of time. If the total expenses exceed the income, the amount is known as *net loss.* Synonymous with *net income; net operating income; net operating profit; net revenue.*

net profit method: See *net profit plan.*

net profit plan: a means of allocating expenses in large retail organizations where each department is treated as a separate entity and charged with both direct and indirect expenses. See *direct cost; indirect costs.*

net purchases: the invoice cost of merchandise purchased plus the transportation charges for the items, minus the sum of returns, allowances, and cash discounts taken.

net realizable value: the selling price of an item less reasonable selling costs.

net revenue: See *net profit.*

net sales: gross sales, minus returns and allowances, over a stated period. See *sales.*

net sales to inventory level ratio: the ratio resulting when the annual net sales figure is divided by merchandise inventory as it appears on the balance sheet. Not a measure of actual physical turnover, it is used instead to compare stock-to-sales ratios of one store with those of another or with the stock-to-sales ratios of the industry as a whole.

net space yield: a scheme for determining the profitability of specific items available in the store in which handling costs and space costs are computed along with the cost of the merchandise to produce a gross margin figure for each item. These gross margin figures can

then be compared to determine which merchandise yields the greatest profit.

net terms: conditions called for the billed amount of an invoice to be paid in full, with no cash discounts permitted.

net weight: See *tare.*

network room cost: the total cost of operating a workroom, including payroll and supplies.

net worth:

(1) *general:* the owner's equity in a business, represented by the excess of the total assets over the total amounts owed to outside creditors at a given time.

(2) *retailing:* as to the owner's equity in a store, the excess value of total assets over total liabilities.

neural computing: See *neural networks.*

neural networks:

(1) *general:* a statistical technique for getting a close approximation to a solution for a particular problem. Synonymous with *neural computing.*

(2) *retailing:* allows retailers to track forecasts vs. what is happening. For example, permits retailers to answer the question: What is the optimal mix of markdowns and advertising to maximize gross profit? For direct marketing, neural networks can cluster the various characteristics in different segments of the population.

never-outs: store merchandise that should never run out of stock during a season because of continuous demand. See *bread-and-butter assortments.*

new customer gift: a small, free gift given to new customers the first time they patronize the retailer. Serves as a premium.

new product:

(1) any item perceived by prospective customers as significantly different from other available items.

(2) for manufacturers and retailers, an item never before produced, either

unique or significantly different from earlier products.

news technique: a sales approach used within the first few minutes of communication with a prospect. The salesperson pulls news items for discussion (e.g., a neighborhood fire is mentioned to promote the sale of fire extinguishers).

new unsought items: items offering new concepts and uses of which the consumer is unaware of; requires promotion to inform the customer of its potential. Cf. *regularly unsought items.*

NFASG: See *National Fashion Accessories Salesperson's (Salesmen's) Guild.*

NGA: See *National Grocers' Association.*

NHFA: See *National Home Furnishings Association.*

niche marketing: a marketing approach, usually undertaken by small firms or by divisions of larger companies; where a manufacturer or supplier defines a narrow market segment that he or she feels best equipped to compete in. Often items or services are especially created or made for a niche market.

Nielsen Drug (Food) Index: developed by A.C. Nielsen, statements on the market change of products, by type and brand, issued through panels of experts from drugstores and other stores.

NINFRA: See *National Independent Nursery Furniture Retailers Association.*

NLDA: See *National Luggage Dealers Association.*

NLSA: See *National Liquor Stores Association.*

NMRI: See *National Mass Retailing Institute.*

no-back window: a display window with no wall in back thereby opening up the store to be seen from the street.

no frills product: See *generic product.*

nonadopters: consumers who may try an item, but fail to become regular users.

noname brands: See *generic brands.*

noncabled point-of-sale (POS): wireless capabilities that permit stores to move cash registers wherever they are needed. They are either existing terminals that are adopted to run in a wireless network or specially designed portable, hand-held devices. The elimination of cabling not only makes the installation faster and easier, but provides store management the flexibility to move registers on demand or when required by remodeling. See *point-of-sale (POS).*

noncompeting retailers: although though they carry similar merchandise, stores that do not compete with each other because they function in different markets.

noncumulative quantity discount:
(1) a price reduction that is given based on the size of the individual order placed.
(2) a quantity discount that is offered on each sale made to a particular buyer.

nondisguised retail audit: an audit made with the full knowledge by the store's employees.

nondumping certificate: a seller's certificate indicating that the items described are being sold at a price no lower than that applicable to like sales in the country of origin.

nondurable goods: See *soft goods.*

nongoods service: where no tangible item is offered for sale or rental, e.g., medical services. Often an individual performs some function for the customer, e.g., a personal shopper, baby sitter, doorman, etc., in return for a fee.

noninstallment credit: See *charge account credit.*

nonmarking: offering merchandise for sale in a store without marking each item with the price.

nonmerchandise services: See *store services.*

nonmerchant middleperson: See *auction company; broker (2); manufacturer's agent; selling agent.*

nonoperating expense:

(1) *general:* any expense resulting from transactions incidental to a firm's main line of business, i.e., outside daily activities.

(2) *retailing:* in a store, expenses not directly connected with the buying and selling of merchandise.

nonoperating revenue: revenue that is not directly related to the sale of products and services. For example, interest is considered nonoperating revenue, in contrast to operating revenue that is derived from the sale of goods and services in the ordinary operation of the store.

nonperpetual inventory: an inventory control system where a physical count is made to find out how much stock is on hand. Cf. *perpetual inventory.*

nonpersonal retailing: where the prospect makes a purchase without entering a store. This is done using a catalog, mail-order house, vending machine, or electronic interphase.

nonprice competition: competitive activity between stores that have comparable prices. These retailers usually have different services, project different images, or otherwise attempt to distinguish themselves from their competitors. Cf. *price competition.*

nonproduct: an item or service prepared for a specific segment of the market only to discover that the segment did not really exist. Should the item or service be offered, it almost always fails.

nonpromotional store: a retail operation providing minimal emphasis on price. Instead attention is paid to quality, uniqueness, good taste, distinctiveness, convenience, or services. Synonymous with *institutional store.*

nonsalable: because of their condition or some other variable, goods that are not offered for sale to the public.

nonselling area: retail space that is devoted to activities not directly related to the selling of merchandise (e.g., loading docks, executive offices, stock rooms, dressing rooms, elevators and escalators).

nonsigner's clause: a feature of many state resale price maintenance laws evolving from the Miller-Tydings Act of 1937. It permits a manufacturer to impose resale price agreements in a state should one retailer sign a contract agreeing to resale price maintenance. See *Miller-Tydings Act of 1937.*

nonstore retailer: See *nonstore retailing; retailer.*

nonstore retailing: a form of retailing, where the traditional store building is not involved. The retailer and customer transact their business via activities of vending, mail-order, two-way television, and house-to-house salespeople. See *retailer.*

nonvariable price policy: See *one-price policy.*

NoRMA awards: presented each year by the former NRMA (now the NRF) and the Newspaper Advertising Bureau for 10 different categories of retail newspaper advertising.

normal goods: Synonymous with *superette; superior goods.*

normal margin retailer: offers items at prices similar to those found at other stores at the same market level. The normal margin retailer chooses not to compete by attempting to undersell the competition.

normal price: the price to which the market price tends to return following fluctuations up or down. When the purchase price does not reflect all consideration given by the buyer to the seller, the value of the goods will be adjusted for customs purposes.

normal sale: the transaction that pleases both the buyer and the seller of an item and in which no unforeseen or abnormal situations surface.

North American Free Trade Agreement (NAFTA): effective January 1, 1994, a trade accord that can create challenges and opportunities for overseas retailing and merchandising of United States sales and promotion of goods and services. NAFTA is the name given to economic links formed by the United States, Canada, and Mexico. Of particular importance to retailers, United States exports of textiles and apparel to Mexico will be eliminated immediately and another $700 million freed from restriction within six years under NAFTA. All North American trade restrictions will be eliminated within 10 years.

nose-to-nose selling: See *belly-to-belly selling.*

note: an instrument, such as a promissory note, which is the recognized legal evidence of a debt. A note is signed by the marker, called the borrower, promising to pay a certain sum of money on a specified date at a certain place of business, to a certain business, individual, or bank, called the lender.

notions: small sundry items such as needles and thread, ribbon, buttons, etc. Some large department stores have a notions departments.

NRF: See *National Retail Federation.*

NRHA: See *National Retail Hardware Association.*

NRMA: See *National Retail Merchants Association.*

NRPSGA: See *National Retail Pet Store and Groomers' Association.*

NSRA: See *National Shoe Retailers' Association.*

NSTA: See *National Shoe Traveler's Association.*

nutritional labeling:

(1) a form of labeling that informs consumers of the amounts of protein, fat, carbohydrates, and calories in a processed food product.

(2) showing on packaged foods the nutritional value of an item, especially the United States recommended daily allowances supplied by a particular quantity of the item, and the specific ingredients contained.

number: See *design.*

number of stock turns: See *stock turnover.*

O

objection: in sales, the reason provided by a prospect for rejecting a salesperson's offer for a product or service. See *linking phrase.*

objective: in retailing, the short- or long-term goal that the retailer hopes to attain; may include sales, profit, image, etc. The objectives of a retail establishment are periodically reevaluated. See *retail audit.*

objective-and-task method of promotional budgeting: See *objective-and-task technique.*

objective-and-task technique: a promotional budget method in which a store outlines its promotional goals, determines the activities needed to satisfy those goals, and then establishes the appropriate budget.

objectives: See *objective.*

objective value: the price an item can command in terms of other items in the market.

obligee: a creditor or promisee.

obligor: a debtor or promisor.

observation: See *observational technique.*

observational technique:
(1) a research method that entails observing consumer behavior.
(2) a research method in which a researcher observes people's behavior and records what they see, but avoids direct interaction.

obsolescence:
(1) *general:* the state of being out of date and therefore of little use to society.
(2) *retailing:* a stage in the fashion cycle when the style ceases to be seen positively and is therefore no longer saleable.

obsolete material: inventory items that have little or no possibility of being used in the near future. Often found with merchandise that has undergone structural design changes or products that have been discarded for new ones.

oddball pricing: in the selling of an assortment or a group of related products at the same price that does not relate to cost, desired markup or margin, or customary price of any of the separate products.

odd-cent pricing: See *odd pricing.*

odd-ending pricing: See *odd pricing.*

odd-even pricing: a means of pricing purporting to make the cost of an item or service psychologically attractive to prospects without markedly lessening the desired profit margin.

odd-line pricing: See *odd pricing.*

odd lot: See *job lot.*

151

odd-number pricing: See *odd pricing.*

odd pricing:

(1) a form of pricing in which the price is an odd number or a number just below a round number.

(2) pricing at odd amounts (e.g., at 99 cents instead of at a dollar). Synonymous with *odd-ending pricing; odd-number pricing; off-even pricing; psychological pricing.* Cf. *even-line pricing; persuasive pricing.*

odds and ends: assorted leftover goods, incomplete sets of style, color, and size.

off-brand: a brand that is not considered acceptable to a consumer.

offer:

(1) to present for acceptance or refusal.

(2) a contractual agreement made by a seller pending acceptance by a purchaser.

offer test: a promotion test that assesses responses to differing prices and/or terms of quantities. For example, usually the price of $9.95 results in greater purchases than $10.00.

off-even pricing: See *odd pricing.*

off factor: a chain discount brought to a single percent. This is the complement of the on factor. Cf. *on-factor.*

off-price: See *off-price merchandise; off-price retailing; off-price store.*

off-price merchandise: merchandise that carries prestige or premium labels, offered at lower than "regular" prices. These items, which are often manufacturer's surplus in the form of end-of-season liquidations, are in perfect condition and are sold at prices somewhat lower than those found in traditional retail establishments. Increasingly, in-season merchandise is becoming available to off-price retailers by vendors. See *off-price retailing; off-price store.*

off-price retailing: the selling at retail of goods, which frequently carry prestige or premium labels, at less than "regular" prices. In contrast to discount retailing (where the discounter pays the same price for merchandise as everyone else and sells it for less than traditional retailers), off-price retailers buy merchandise at cut-rate prices and pass the savings along to their customers. In addition, expenses are lowered by limited advertising, turning stock over quickly, and other cost cutting methods. See *off-price merchandise; off-price store.*

off-price store: a discount store that buys manufacturer's overruns and end-of-season goods at below-wholesale prices and resells them at prices significantly lower than the regular department store price. See *off-price merchandise; off-price retailing.*

offer response method of research: a technique for testing the effectiveness of an advertisement where the customer presents proof of having read the advertisement, such as a coupon, at the time of purchase.

off-retail: markdowns from the original retail price.

off-retail markdown percentage: See *markdown percentage.*

off-retail percentage: See *markdown percentage.*

off-season pricing: a markdown offered during a slow period to move items; occurs traditionally during a pre-season or post-season periods; reaches a different market segment than regular season customers.

off-the-rack: ready made clothing. See *ready-to-wear.*

omnibus cooperative advertisement: for wholesaler agreements, a full-page advertisement from a retailer carrying his or her own name. The retailer bills each manufacturer a pro rata share of the cost of the entire advertisement based on earlier cooperative advertisement agreement with the manufacturers.

on account:
(1) a payment made toward the settlement of an account.
(2) a purchase or sale made on open account.

on-approval offer: a proposition made to a consumer whereby he or she is permitted to see, feel, taste, use, or otherwise experience the nature of a product without first paying for it and without being placed under the obligation to buy. Usually a time limit is given for such an offer, at the expiration of which the consumer is expected to return the product or to pay for it. See *approval sale.*

on consignment: items turned over by an owner (the consignor) to someone else (the consignee) with the expectation that the items (the consignment) will be sold by the consignee. If all the items are not sold, the owner is entitled to the return of the items. Cf. *memorandum sale; purchase allowance.* See *consignment.*

one-cent sale: a sale's offer where two products are sold with each other for the price of one of the items, plus one additional penny. Often used to introduce a new product. The general practice of manufacturers is to indicate in advertisements that the offer is restricted to a specific market area and good for a limited time.

100-percent location: the location within a given shopping area that is the best possible place for a specific type of store.

one-more-yes close: a salesperson's closing method based on the concept that people are creatures of habit and tend to say "yes." Consequently, the seller raises questions about the prospect's feelings toward the merchandise, with the final question suggestive of a positive reply from the prospect.

one-price policy:
(1) a situation in which the price of goods is firm and cannot be negotiated.
(2) a pricing policy in which the marketer assigns a price to the product and sells it at that price to all customers who purchase the same quantity of the product under the same conditions. Synonymous with *nonvariable price policy.* Cf. *single-price policy.*

one-price store: See *single-price policy.*

one-shot deal: goods that cannot be re-ordered, but are frequently bought for a specific promotional event.

one-shot promotion: See *one-shot deal.*

one-stop shopping: a retail outlet that attempts to contain everything that a customer would need for everyday life.

one-time purchaser: a customer found on a list who has made only one purchase since an initial order.

one-to-one marketing: See *database marketing.*

on-factor: the difference between 100 percent and the single discount representing a chain discount. For example, a chain discount of 40 percent and 10 percent equals single discount of 46 percent. The on-factor is 100 percent less 46 percent or 54 percent. Cf. *off-factor.*

on hand: the number of items available in stock, at a given place and time period.

on memorandum: See *memorandum sale.*

on order: goods paid for, but not yet received.

on-pack: a package with a display card used by hanging on hooks, to which an item has been attached without using any cover. Synonymous with *banded premium; package-band.*

on-pack premium: See *on-pack.*

on percentage: the product resulting from multiplying together the complements of a series of discount percentages.

on the books: See *charge account.*

on the floor: time spent by a buyer in the selling department; gives the buyer with customer and salesperson contact as well as information about what is being requested, what sells, and what should be reordered.

open account: See *charge account.*

open assortment: an assortment where the consumer does not have at hand all the items usually needed. Cf. *closed assortment.*

open-book credit: See *unsecured credit.*

open bid: the offer to perform a service or provide merchandise to a buyer with an adequate public communication in order that all interested bidders are aware of the price submitted.

open charge account: See *charge account.*

open-code dating: See *open date labeling.*

open credit: credit that is allowed without immediate proof of a customer's credit-worthiness. See *charge account; open-credit account.*

open-credit account: a credit arrangement in which a buyer receives a monthly bill for goods and services bought during the preceding month. The account must be paid in full each month.

open-date labeling: clearly printed, the date marked on merchandise with limited shelf life, usually an item that can spoil, identifying the last date that the item can safely be sold to the public without danger of deterioration or spoilage. Synonymous with *open-code dating.*

open dating: See *open-date labeling.*

open display: products placed where they can be handled and studied by prospects, in fact, the entire store can become a display. Cf. *closed display.* See *top stock.*

open distribution: the distribution of the same merchandise by a given area or region, by differing dealers. The dealers carry competitive lines and there are no barriers regarding the number of items a deal sells, offers, or delivers to a retailer. Cf. *exclusive distribution; intensive distribution; selective distribution.*

open-end contract: an agreement whereby a supplier contracts to meet the buyer's requirements for a specific item during a stated period, whatever those requirements may be. The agreement is open-ended because all the terms are left indefinite.

open-end discount store: a discount store that is open to the general public as compared to a closed-door discount house.

open front: frequently found in an interior retail, the entrance to a store that has no physical barriers such as doors and windows. This design encourages customers to enter the store for browsing and shopping.

opening: the first showing of a new season's line of items by a manufacturer or an entire industry.

opening inventory: the value of merchandise available at the beginning of an accounting period, given at either cost or retail value.

opening price point: the lowest price line of a particular item, such as the least costly of several brands of toothpaste.

open money: the portion of the open-to-buy a store buyer allows a resident buyer to commit without receiving prior approval during a specified time period.

open order:

(1) an order made without price or delivery stipulation.

(2) an order shipped to a market representative without specifying the vendor. Cf. *good 'til canceled order.*

open pricing: marking merchandise with shelf-life expiration dates clearly shown in acceptable symbols. See *open-date labeling.*

open stock: replacement items or additions of goods carried in quantity and retained in a warehouse for several years. Found most frequently with china, glassware, and flatware sales. Cf. *closed stock.*

open the kimono: (slang) to reveal to prospective customers company plans regarding future products, to impress upon the buyer that the firm is ahead of its competitors in developing new or superior items.

open-to-buy (OTB): the quantity of goods that a store can receive in stock over a stated time without exceeding its planned inventory levels. See *open-to-buy by classification; open-to-buy report.* Cf. *open-to-receive; open-to-spend.*

open-to-buy by classification: the open-to-buy a buyer is allowed for a specific time period. The classification is broken down for each category or classification of goods.

open-to-buy report: a study that is used for calculating the open-to-buy summarizing the existing or projected relationship between inventory and sales. It is usually prepared on a weekly basis for the department buyer; indicates the amount of merchandise on hand at the beginning of the period, the amount received, the amount sold, markdowns, current inventory, and merchandise on order. See *open-to-buy.*

open-to-receive (OTR): the amount of items that are received (regardless of what is on order) during the period if the planned stock is to be achieved. Cf. *open-to-ship.*

open-to-reduce: the dollar amount of markdowns that is taken in a department during a specified time period.

open-to-ship: the amount of merchandise a vendor is allowed to send to a retailer, regardless of what is on order, during the specified period if the planned stock is to be achieved. Similar, but not synonymous with open-to-receive except given from the vendor's point of view. Cf. *open-to-receive.*

open-to-spend: expense commitments made by the buyer during a given period of time, as contrasted with the planned expenditures of open-to-buy. This information is periodically summarized in a report which is used to determine the remaining money to be spent for the fiscal period. See *open-to-buy.*

open window: See *open display.*

operating division: a division of the retail store that is responsible for such matters as merchandise receiving, store maintenance and housekeeping, security, and certain special services such as a restaurants.

operating expenses:

(1) *general:* any expense incurred in the normal operation of a business. See *margin of profit.*

(2) *retailing:* direct expenses (those paid out for the benefit of a specific department) and the indirect expenses (those paid out for the benefit of the entire store). Expenses of financing the store are not included nor are merchandise costs.

operating income: in retailing, income derived from the sale of goods and/or services.

operating leverage: the distribution of fixed costs over sales. As more items are sold, the fixed costs may be spread over the larger sales volume, thus lowering the costs per item.

operating losses: losses incurred in the normal (i.e., nonnegligent) operation of a store.

operating margin: the difference between the revenues from sales and the current replacement costs of goods sold. Used as a measure of operating efficiency.

$$\text{revenues from sales} - \text{operating margin} = \begin{array}{c}\text{current replacement cost}\\\text{of good sold}\end{array}$$

Synonymous with *current gross margin; current margin.*

operating profit ratio: the ratio of a store's operating profit to its net sales. See *net profit.*

operating ratio based upon net sales: the financial ratio that results when a store's total expenses are divided by its net sales. A means of examining the store's performance over the accounting period.

$$\frac{\text{operating ratio based}}{\text{upon net sales}} = \frac{\text{total expenses}}{\text{net sales}}$$

operating ratio based upon revenues: the financial ratio that results when a store's total expenses are divided by its total revenues.

$$\frac{\text{operating ratio based}}{\text{upon revenues}} = \frac{\text{total expenses}}{\text{total revenues}}$$

operating results of self-service discount department stores: See *National Mass Retailing Institute.*

operating revenue: revenue derived from the sale of merchandise and/or services in the normal operation of the store, in contrast to nonoperating revenue, which includes dividends, interest, rents, etc.

operating statement: a statement for a store's management, providing net sales, costs, expenses, and the net operating profit or loss for a fixed period. See *profit and loss statement.*

operating stock level: where the retailer maintains an adequate quantity of stock, in addition to the reserve stock, to carry the store or department through the buying period.

operational buying motives: consumer motives based on how the item being considered for purchase works or performs.

operational satisfaction: gratification experienced by the buyer of merchandise when a recently purchased item performs properly.

operations budgeting: the setting of immediate goals for sales, production, expenses, costs, and the availability of cash. Synonymous with *revenue-and-expense budget.*

opinion leader: a member of an organization who, because of ability, power, access to information, or prestige, can influence the attitudes, opinions, or behavior of those around him or her. See *membership group.*

opinion strategy: a method of salespeople who display the item under consideration to the prospect and invite opinions. The prospect is directly involved in the conversation.

optimal lot size: See *economic order quantity model.*

optional consumption: the buying of items and services that are not required for daily fulfillment and well-being. See *luxuries.*

optional customer service: any customer service provided by the retailer beyond the primary and expected services (e.g., a children's playroom staffed by attendants).

optional product pricing: a pricing method for items offered to the public with several options (e.g., refrigerators with a host of options). Decisions have to be made as to which options are included and those not included in the base price, or those requiring additional costs to the consumer.

optional service: See *optional customer service.*

orange goods: in merchandising, consumer goods, such as clothing, that will eventually have to be replaced as they wear out, at a rate, or at the consumer's discretion. Cf. *brown goods; red goods; white goods; yellow goods.*

order: a request to deliver, sell, receive, or purchase goods or services.

order blank: See *order form.*

order checking: See *checking*.

order cycle: includes the activities of the vendor. Divided into four parts:

(a) *order transmittal*—what happens and how long it will take to get the order to the vendor from the moment of initiation;

(b) *order processing*—what the vendor does and how long it takes from the time of receipt of the order to notification of the proper warehouse to get the order prepared for shipping;

(c) *order picking*—what occurs at the warehouse and how long it takes to prepare the order for pickup and to place the shipment into the hands of the chosen carrier; and

(d) *order delivery*—what occurs and how long it takes during the process of pickup and final delivery to the customer. See *lead time*.

order delivery: See *order cycle*.

order entry: approaches used in entering customer orders into an order-processing system, to provide an efficient and accurate means to ensure that customers receive their merchandise quickly and as ordered.

order-filling cost: a store's cost incurred in storing, packing, shipping, billing, credit and collection, and other similar aspects of selling merchandise.

order follow-up: a method of reviewing ordered goods so as to insure prompt delivery to the retailer. Orders are arranged by their due date and vendors are contacted when the due date comes up.

order form: a form for requesting goods or services, from a wholesaler, manufacturer, or direct mail retailer; often included in such direct-marketing materials as catalogs. See *preprinted order form*.

order getter: a salesperson, using highly developed approaches in dealing with prospects in a creative fashion.

order-getting cost: a marketing cost incurred in an effort to attain a desired sales volume and mix.

order handler: a salesperson who closes the sale of goods that have already been chosen by the customer. For example, a department store cashier is an order handler.

order picking: See *order cycle*.

order processing: See *order cycle*.

order-processing costs: expenses associated with recording and handling orders, such as order entry, computer-information handling, and merchandise handling.

order register: the retailer's official record of orders placed with vendors; includes the date of the order, vendor's name, amount of order, month shipment is due, etc.

orders: requests made for the delivery of goods or services.

order size: the appropriate amount of merchandise, parts, and other items to purchase at one time. It depends on the availability of quantity discounts, the resources of the firm, the inventory turnover rate, the costs of processing each order, and the costs of maintaining goods in inventory.

order taker: a salesperson whose function is primarily to receive calls and who accepts orders for items and services.

order transmittal: See *order cycle*.

ordinary course of trade: a principle that places the dutiable value of merchandise at the price at which it would normally sell if customary channels of distribution were observed.

ordinary dating: See *ordinary terms*.

ordinary interest: interest that is calculated based on 360 days to the year.

ordinary terms: as found in invoices, where a cash discount is deducted should the bill be paid within the discount period. If not, the full payment is due at the end of the cycle shown. The cash discount and the net credit periods are both counted from the date of the invoice, which is traditionally the date of shipment. See *regular dating.*

organizational buying objectives: includes the availability of items, reliability of sellers, consistency of quality, delivery, price, and customer service.

organizational climate: a set of properties of the work environment perceived by consumers and assumed to be a major factor in influencing their behavior.

organizational consumer: includes manufacturers, wholesalers, distributors, retailers and government units, and not-for-profit organizations. Usually these institutions use the items they receive to make other products, or to maintain their operations, or to be offered for resale.

organizational consumer expectations: the perceived potential of alternative suppliers and brands to satisfy a number of explicit and implicit objectives.

organizational consumer's decision process: consists of expectations, the buying process, conflict resolution, and situational factors.

organizational market: the market segment made up of people and firms that buy merchandise and services for reasons other than for individual consumption, such as goods to be used in the manufacturing of other goods. Its purchasers engage in large-volume, highly professional, and detail-oriented purchasing efforts. Cf. *consumer market.*

original: merchandise designed and made by a designer and his or her staff. This is different from copies or reproductions. See *designer merchandise.*

original cost: the initial price paid to a vendor for merchandise, exclusive of discounts, shipping charges, etc.

original markup: See *initial markup percent.*

original order: the first order received from a specific customer; important to maintain records of sources of original orders so that first-time purchasers can be concentrated on the best sources.

original price: the initial price quoted by a vendor for merchandise, exclusive of discounts, shipping charges, etc.

original retail: in the retail accounting method, the sales price of items that is a total of the cost plus the original markon.

original source: See *original order.*

OS&D: See *over, short, and damaged.*

OTB: See *open-to-buy.*

OTC (over-the-counter): See *proprietary drug.*

other income: income not derived from the sale of goods, i.e., interest and dividend income. OTR: See *open-to-receive.*

outbound telemarketing: a direct-marketing approach of seeking out customers and prospect using the telephone; involves sales representatives calling individuals to both generate and qualify leads. See *telemarketing.*

outer belt: See *outer loop.*

outer-directed: a consumer purchase that is based on how the consumer perceives his or her actions. Such purchase behavior is affected by the person's wish to conform to peer group pressures.

outer envelope: the envelope, in direct-mail, that includes the package's promotional materials.

outer loop: a ring of urban growth formed where a radial artery intersects with other roads. Examining the outer loop is helpful in identifying future sites for retail operations. Synonymous with *outer belt.*

outlay: any expenditure.

outlet retailing: See *factory outlet.*

outlet store: See *factory outlet.*

out of stock:

(1) lack of merchandise in a store in certain styles, sizes, and colors.

(2) goods that are not in the store when requested by a customer. See *periodic stock control; stockout.*

out-of-stock cost: estimated profits that are never realized because of insufficient inventory available to fulfill the demands of customers. Customers and sales are lost through a stockout.

out-post: See *out-post display.*

out-post display: items placed with signs at well crossed points within a store away from the traditional selling department of the merchandise. At times the goods are sold directly from the out-post.

outshopper: an individual who travels outside of his or her usual community or local area to obtain products or services. See *outshopping.*

outshopping:
(1) the number of shopping trips made outside a buyer's usual community over a given time period.
(2) the proportion of money spent made away from the buyer's usual community or traditional shopping area. See *outshopper.*

outside auditor: an independent accounting firm used by the retailer or other firm to check and attest to the accuracy, fairness, and conformity to generally accepted accounting standards of the records and statements of the firm.

outside buying organization: See *salaried buying office.*

outside merchandise source: See *vendor.*

outside shop: See *apparel contractor.*

outsizes: See *end sizes.*

outstanding: any unpaid or uncollected debt.

outstanding order: goods on order from the vendor but not yet received by the retailer. See *partial shipment.*

over: See *stock overage.*

overage: See *stock overage.*

overall expenses technique: a method for determining the cost of goods sold by dividing the seller's total expense over time by the number of products sold during that time; prevents the seller from failing to include relevant expenses in the calculation and is a helpful measure of the change in expense realized relative to a change in the number of sold units.

overbought:
(1) reflecting an opinion about price levels of an item that has had a sharp rise or of the market as a whole after a period of vigorous buying, which some argue has left prices too high.
(2) when some element in the planning process has not evolved as anticipated, leading to a zero open-to-buy.
(3) where the store finds that it is overstocked with merchandise in excess of its demand. Synonymous with *overordered.*

overcarriage: the transportation of goods, beyond the initially intended destination, usually resulting from the goods being refused at the destination.

overcut: manufacturing merchandise, usually apparel, in excess of demand.

overdue: a payment that has not been made at the time it was due.

overhead: costs of materials and services not directly adding to or readily identifiable with the product or service of the entity. Synonymous with *burden.* See *fixed cost.*

overheating: excessive price or money activity that some economists believe will lead to inflation.

overkill: an expensive promotional effort that yields diminishing returns because it repels rather than attracts prospect interest.

over (or short): the difference between established store sales statements and the actual audited figure. This discrepancy is often a result of errors in making change or missing sales checks.

overorder: goods ordered by a buyer in excess of demand.

overordered: See *overbought.*

overproduction: producing more than can be sold at any price or at a profitable price.

over ring: a cash register error in which a higher price than the actual price of the goods is recorded on the store's register.

over, short, and damaged (OS&D): used in international merchandising; the discrepancy between the amount and/or condition of cargo on hand and that shown on the bill. Cf. *clean bill of lading.* See *short merchandise.*

overstock: See *remainder.*

overstored area: See *overstored conditions.*

overstored conditions: where retail operations are opened longer than the need for extended hours suggest. It leads to an extra expense and overinvestment.

over-the-counter (OTC): See *proprietary drug.*

over-the-counter drug: See *proprietary drug.*

over-the-counter selling: the sale of particular stock retained in display cases, drawers, or on shelves. A salesperson shows the stock to customers and completes the sale.

owe: to be obliged to pay something to someone for something received; indebtedness results.

own brand: an item bearing the name or brand of the store selling the item rather than the name of the producer.

owned department: a department that is an integral part of the store organization, i.e., not a licensed or leased department.

owned-goods service: provides a customer with a service that had previously been used (e.g., plant maintenance). Frequently these stores or departments also sell auxiliary goods at retail such as shoes polish, upholstery sprays, etc.

ownership: possession of a legal title with the rights to enjoy the benefits derived from any assets accompanying or accruing from such title.

ownership franchise: a form of franchise where the franchisor maintains a partial ownership in the individual outlets.

owner's equity: See *equity.*

pack:

(1) to add to the total cost of merchandise charges for items not included or inflated charges.

(2) to give an undeserved discount without lowering the actual price. See *banded pack; economy pack; price pack.*

package: any container or wrapping in which goods are placed for shipping or carrying.

package-band: See *on pack.*

package-band premium: a gift shown on a strip wrapped around the package of the item being promoted. The gift can be free or offered at a reduced price to buyers of the item.

package consolidating agency: See *freight forwarder.*

package delivery: See *delivery.*

packaged goods: consumer items packaged by producers and sold through retail stores, e.g., food, tobacco, beauty aids, household cleaners.

package engineering: a discipline of scientific and engineering principles applied to solving problems of functional design, formation, filling, closing, and/or preparation for shipment of containers, regardless of the type of product enclosed.

package goods: items found within a container designed for display and handled by the retailer, e.g., detergents, paper goods, cereals.

package insert: printed material found with the item to explain its operation. Synonymous with *package stuffer.*

package store: a retail store that displays and sells alcoholic beverages to be consumed off the premises.

package stuffer: See *package insert.*

package wrap: the placing of goods in a box, bag, or paper at the customer's request or as a routine function of the store. It can serve either as a useful container or a decorative one; includes gift wrap, wrapping for the purpose of mailing, and the wrapping of carryouts. The wrapping material is often distinctive and helps to identify the retailer. See *central wrap; department wrap; gift wrap; salesperson wrap.*

packaging:

(1) the preparation of merchandise for shipping and marketing. The package must provide protection, ease of carrying and handling, convenience, and information.

(2) all activities that are related to designing and producing the container or wrapper for a product.

packaways: items that are purchased before the selling season and stored until the appropriate time for sale.

pack date: the month, day, and year that food was packed, canned, or boxed. It appears on a package to indicate possible loss of freshness.

packing house: See *freight forwarder.*

packing list: a list showing the number and kinds of items being shipped, as well as other information needed for transportation purposes.

packing slip: the form used for listing items to be shipped and to identify the recipient of the shipment. The slip goes with the shipment and, upon arrival at its destination, is used for confirming that the shipment is sound and complete.

paid buying office: See *salaried buying office.*

paid money: See *co-op money.*

painting the bus: (slang) altering the appearance of a presentation, proposal, or idea without changing any of the basics.

pantry check:
(1) the physical examination of items possessed by respondents.
(2) a study of consumer product usage based on an actual checking and listing of items in the homes of the study group. Synonymous with *pantry inventory.*

pantry inventory: See *pantry check.*

paper: See *order form.*

parasalesperson: usually a sales trainee who rarely completes the closing with a customer, but is assisted in this task by a more experienced salesperson.

parasite store: a store depending on the flow of customers emanating from events external to those generated by the store itself, which is usually negligible compared to the total traffic flow.

parcel delivery: See *delivery.*

parcel post (PP): a unit of the U.S. Postal Service that delivers small packages up to 50 pounds and fourth-class literature; often used by retailers when sending small packages to customers outside the normal delivery area.

parcel shipment: a small package restricted as to value; generally samples of goods or advertising matter.

parent store: a controlling organization that owns or manages store properties. See *flagship store; regional store.* Synonymous with *main store.*

parlor shipper: See *drop shipper.*

partial payment: a payment that is not equal to the full amount owed and is not intended to constitute the full payment to the retailer.

partial shipment: an incomplete order shipped to a retailer by the vendor. Remaining items can be back ordered and shipped at a later time. See *outstanding order.*

particular average: damage or loss less than the total value; partial loss.

partnership: a contractual relationship between two or more people in a joint enterprise who agree to share, not necessarily equally, in the profits and losses of the organization.

part-time employee: in retailing, a worker in a store who does not work a full 35- to 40-hour work week. Part-time employees are usually hired for additional coverage during peak sales hours of the day or during peak selling periods, such as the pre-Christmas rush. Cf. *full-time worker.*

part-timer: See *part-time employee.*

party plan selling: See *party selling.*

party selling: door-to-door selling where a hostess is convinced to invite friends to a mid-day event for a salesperson to demonstrate items. Usually, a free gift is given to the hostess for her participation, as in a Tupperware party. Synonymous with *group plan; party plan selling.*

pass-along deal: an arrangement to induce the retailer to lower the price of merchandise, thus increasing the volume and perhaps share of the market for the manufacturer.

past-due order: goods distributed by the vendor to the retailer on the given date.

past-due statement: a reminder sent to the customer by the store or other creditor when credit payment has remained unpaid for a given time period; usually includes a request for payment.

patent:

(1) a government grant to an inventor to protect the results of an invention.

(2) the legal right of exclusive use and licensing granted by a government to the person who invents something. An invention is patentable if it is a useful, novel, and nonobvious process, machine, manufacture, or composition of matter.

patent medicine: See *proprietary drug.*

patron: See *customer.*

patronage buying motive: See *patronage motives.*

patronage discount: a discount permitted on the basis of the amount of business carried out with the retailer. Synonymous with *deferred discount; quantity discount; volume discount.* See *cumulative quantity discount.*

patronage dividend and rebate: wholesaler vouchers given to retailers to be used as incentive builders by wholesalers to generate increased retailer sales and goodwill. The patronage dividend occurs when the wholesaler offers the retailer a pro rata share of earnings from one or many of the wholesaler's goods. A patronage rebate, occurs when the wholesaler refunds part of the retailer's original payment for merchandise. In both cases, payment is issued to retailers in the form of a merchandise credit voucher or a bank check. See *rebate.*

patronage motives: the reasons that customers shop in a particular retail outlet.

patronize:

(1) to frequent a store.

(2) to be a regular customer.

payee: the person or organization to whom a check, draft, or note is made payable. The payee's name follows the expression "pay to the order of."

payer: a person who gives a sum of money in the form of cash, check, or note in exchange for goods and/or services.

payment guarantee: a guarantee to the supplier of merchandise that if he or she performs his or her obligations, payment will follow.

peak: an exceptionally busy period in a business.

peak inventory: bringing stocks to the highest level of the season, typically prior to the height of when selling begins.

peak season:

(1) the period of days or months in which an item is in customer demand (e.g., charcoal for barbecuing during the summer months).

(2) the time of the year when a retail store does its greatest volume of sales, such as the weeks before Christmas.

peak selling: See *peak season.*

peddler: (slang) a person who travels and sells small quantities of merchandise.

pedestrian mall: a downtown area (usually having undergone extensive renovation and enhancement), including the closing of its streets to cars and other moving traffic. This purports to facilitate foot traffic and to attract customers back to the downtown stores, away from suburban shopping areas.

penetration price: See *penetration pricing.*

penetration pricing:

(1) an approach in which the price of an item is set low in order to enter the market quickly.

(2) a pricing strategy in which the initial price is set at a low level in order to

generate the greatest possible demand for the product. See *skimming price.*

penetration strategies: there are two forms of pricing and promotional strategies used when merchandise is first introduced: (a) rapid penetration—setting a low product price and placing aside a large amount of money for promotion to get the fastest market penetration and the largest market share. This method is used where there is a low level of product awareness and the market is large; and (b) slow penetration—setting a low product price and allocating little money for promotion, thereby suggesting a rapid market acceptance of the item, because of its low price, and keeping costs down; used when the market is large and when product awareness is quite high. See *market penetration; skimming price.*

pennysaver: See *shopper.*

per annum: by the year.

perceived risk: the hazards a customer believes to be related to the buying of a specific term (e.g, difficulty of obtaining servicing, cost of servicing, lifetime of the item, obsolescence of the item). Perceived risk can be socially based. Marketers try to understand reasons for perceived risk and therefore they provide product information to assist people in their buying decisions. See *dissonance reduction.*

perceived-value pricing: a method where the price of an item or service is based on the purchaser's perception of its value and not on the seller's cost of production.

percentage cost markup: See *markup.*

percentage deviation method: See *percentage variation method.*

percentage markdown: See *markdown percentage.*

percentage markup system: a retail price-setting method where goods are marked up to a level, when taken together, yield a specific average markup percentage for the entire store. A single markup percentage cannot be applied to each item because different goods sell at different rates and generate different selling costs.

percentage of gross profit: the ratio resulting from dividing the store's profit for the accounting period by the sales for that period. Expressed as

$$\frac{\text{percentage of}}{\text{gross profit}} = \frac{\text{profit}}{\text{sales}}$$

percentage of sales method: a method of setting a marketing budget based on a forecast of sales. A budget allocation approach for advertisers that is both simple and can relate advertising costs directly to sales. Two shortcomings of this technique include a failure to recognize that as conditions are altered, advertising costs must change with them; and this approach can falsely lead to excessive spending for large established brands and an inadequate budgeting for items that would profit from further advertising, such as new brands.

percentage variation method: a means of planning stock levels based on the relationship between average stock and average sales, and actual stock and actual sales. The actual stock on hand should deviate from the planned average stock only half as much as the actual sales deviate from the planned average sales. For example, should sales for a given month run 50% ahead of expectations, stock should be increased by 25% over the average monthly stock. This may be used to compute the beginning of month inventory (BOM) as:

$$\text{BOM} = \frac{\text{net \$ sales}}{\text{stock turnover}} \times \frac{1}{2} \times$$

$$\left[1 + \frac{\text{net \$ sales}}{\text{number of months}} \right]$$

percent of sales method: See *percentage of sales method.*

perceptual mapping: creating a graph of brand attributes, one product at a time, as noted by consumers on a scale of low to high. Helps to identify the positioning of all brands in a product category where consumer preferences are not being well provided for. *See product positioning.*

performance analysis: a means to compare the actual performance of a retailing strategy with the expectations for the plan. It is used to upgrade the operations of the program, spot trouble areas, and correct shortcomings.

period cost: See *fixed cost.*

periodic actual count: a method of unit inventory control where goods on hand are counted on a systematic, regular basis.

periodic inventory: an ongoing systematic physical count of items on hand to approximate the dollar value of sales. Opening inventory is added to purchases and the sum of closing inventory and markdowns is subtracted from this total; a system of dollar control:

$$\text{sales} = \begin{array}{l} \text{opening inventory} + \\ \text{purchases} - \text{closing} \\ \text{inventory} + \text{markdowns} \end{array}$$

periodic inventory method of classification control: a method involving frequent counts on goods on hand within each classification to determine sales data for a specific classification.

periodic inventory system: See *periodic inventory.*

periodic stock control: a unit control system in which stock is identified and recorded periodically and sales for intervening time slots are calculated. See *inventory control; out of stock.*

peripheral site: a store local on the edge of a community or on the access roads off the main highways.

perishability:
(1) the rate at which an item's freshness, quality, and sale ability deteriorate over time. This applies primarily to food products.
(2) the rate at which the fashion appeal of a item declines in popularity and sale ability; usually applied to fashion items. See *perishable goods.*

perishability of services: where some services cannot be stored for future sale. The service supplier attempts to manage consumer usage so there is consistent demand throughout various periods of the week, month, and/or year.

perishable distinctiveness: a product having serious competition over the coming years, usually five. At first the item may have an exclusive distinctiveness, but with the passing of time, as others capture a larger share of the market, the product passes into a stage of declining distinctiveness.

perishable goods: items that are subject to rapid decay unless given proper storage (e.g., meat, dairy products).

perpetual actual count: a technique of unit control of inventory relying on a continuing physical count of items on hand.

perpetual budget account: See *revolving credit.*

perpetual control: See *perpetual unit control.*

perpetual inventory: a book inventory identifying the stock on hand by means of a detailed record, enabling the firm to know the composition of its inventory at any point in time. See *inventory; perpetual inventory control.* Synonymous with *book inventory.* Cf. *nonperpetual inventory.*

perpetual inventory control: a unit control system whereby orders, receipts, and sales are identified as they occur and inventory is computed. See *inventory; perpetual inventory.*

perpetual inventory system: keeping a record of the firm's inventory by constantly noting the movement of merchandise into and out of the company. Usually involves the recording of orders and receipt quantities, and requisitions of sale quantities. See *perpetual merchandise control.*

perpetual merchandise control: Synonymous with *perpetual inventory system,* but limited to retailing.

perpetual unit control: a means of unit inventory control where all variables impacting on the number of units on hand (such as purchase orders, receipts of merchandise, and sales for individual styles) are recorded on a continuing basis.

perpetual unit control system: See *perpetual unit control.*

personal care items: hair dryers, electric shavers, toothbrushes, facial cosmetics, and the like.

personal consumption expenditures: the funds spent by households for consumer items. Disposable personal income minus savings equals personal consumption expenditures.

personal disposable income: See *disposable income.*

personal income: national income less various kinds of income not actually received by individuals, not-for-profit institutions, and so on, plus certain receipts that do not arise from production. See *disposable income.*

personal influence: the power of people to sway or influence the purchasing decisions of others. For this reason, retailers attempt to identify those people who exert influence over others. See *bluefingers.*

personality segmentation: See *psychographic market segmentation.*

personalizing shoppers: one of a four-way sociological classification of consumers who seek out retail outlets that they are most secure in; in particular, those with salespeople they feel they can relate best with. See *apathetic shoppers; economic shoppers; ethical shoppers.*

personal selling:
(1) *general:* a promotion method involving interpersonal communication between individuals.
(2) *retailing:* a verbal presentation to a prospective customer for the purpose of making a sale. As contrasted with advertising, personal selling is usually more effective.

personal shopper: a retail store worker whose task it is to choose items for customers in response to mail and/or telephone requests as well as to accompanying shoppers while in the store to help them choose items.

personal trade: the continuing rapport between the customer and salesperson. The same salesperson serves that customer over a long period of time, gets to know the customer's preferences, and the customer comes to trust the salesperson's advice and opinions.

personal trade file: See *resource file.*

personnel division: a retail store functional unit with primary responsibility for hiring and training employees, maintenance of benefit plans, general record-keeping, setting rates of pay, etc.

personnel space: locations of the store reserved for the use of the store's workers (e.g., restrooms, employee cafeterias).

persuasive label: the label, whose primary objective is to attract the consumer to buy the item and not to inform with information.

persuasive pricing: psychological pricing which tends to convey a sense of extra-good value to the consumer. Cf. *odd pricing.*

phantom freight: the difference between estimated shipping cost (as quoted by the vendor to the retailer) and actual shipping cost.

phantom shoppers: sellers' representatives who pose as customers to assess methods used by dealers in selling some items. They may receive
prizes if preferred methods are being
used.

pharmacist: See *pharmacy.*

pharmacy: retail operation, where
drugs and medicines are prepared and
dispensed according to a physician's
written prescription. Today, in their
expansion, include proprietary drugs,
health and beauty aids and related
items. Some department stores, proprietary stores, and supermarkets have
added pharmacy departments in which
licensed pharmacists fulfill the traditional functions of their professions.
The single-owner pharmacy is se-
verely impacted on by these larger
stores that are able to purchase items
at reduced prices. Synonymous with
drugstore.

phony list price: the list price presented to
a prospect to indicate that the price has
been discounted. At times, customers
wind up paying more for the item or service than the actual market price. This
practice is outlawed by the Wheeler-Lea
Amendment. See *list price; Wheeler-Lea
Amendment of 1938.*

physical distribution:
(1) the movement of merchandise from
manufacturer to consumer.
(2) the movement of materials from
sources of supply to producers. See *distribution.*
(3) all the activities that provide for
the efficient flow of raw materials, in-
process inventory, and finished goods
from the point of procurement to the
ultimate consumer.

physical goods: See *goods.*

physical inspection system: a technique for checking the inventory level
by either a periodic actual count or by
an eyeball control.

physical inventory:
(1) *general:* inventory calculation obtained by making an actual listing of
stock on hand.
(2) *retailing:* the dollar value at retail
of goods on hand during inventory, including only the stock actually present
in the department or store; usually includes the unit count, quantity, weight
or measure as well as the dollar value.
See *physical inventory system.*

physical inventory system: a means for
determining net sales over a given time.
The previous physical inventory (opening physical inventory) is added to new
purchases received from vendors. The
ending physical inventory is subtracted
from this total. The resulting figure approximates net sales but does not take
stock shortages into account.

net sales = (opening physical inventory +
                new purchases) − ending physical
                inventory

physical obsolescence: any worn out, broken item resulting from normal wear
and tear.

physical risk: the fear by the consumer
that a purchased item can injure the
user.

physiological motives: motives whose
satisfaction is needed for survival. Cf.
psychological satisfaction.

pick-and-pack: goods shipment methods
where merchandise is chosen from a
warehouse based on what has been ordered by each customer, and then
packed for shipment.

piece goods: fabrics purchased in required lengths for home sewing. Used
most often in relation to apparel manufacturing and the retailing of items for
the house sewer.

piggyback: trailer trucks transported by
railroad cars. This practice eliminates
costly and time-consuming unloading

and reloading of the merchandise being shipped.

piggyback service: See *piggyback.*

pilferage: taking of another's property while such goods are in transit or being stored. See *inventory shortage.* Cf. *shoplifting.*

pin ticket: the price tag affixed to goods by a pin, staple, or another fastener. Can contain additional information such as size, color, and style number that is used by the retailer in inventory control.

pinochle season: (slang) in the garment industry, the off-season.

pioneering stage: the first stage in the product life cycle. Emphasis is placed on achieving a demand for sale of the item. Synonymous with *primary stage.*

pipeline: a manufacturer's inventory purchased by wholesalers and retailers, but not as yet purchased by consumers.

pitch: a presentation to a prospect by the salesperson in order to obtain an order or new business; as in a sales pitch. See *sales pitch.*

planned average monthly stock: a planning figure determined by dividing seasonal planned sales by expected turnover; permits the retailer to estimate the amount of stock that should be on hand for each month of the selling season and to add further stock as required.

planned average monthly stock =

$$\frac{\text{planned sales for season}}{\text{planned turnover}}$$

planned impulse buying: a form of impulse buying where the customer plans to use the store's stock as a shopping list. See *impulse buying.* Cf. *pure impulse buying.*

planned markdown: a markdown anticipated by the retailer's buyer for a specific selling season. As it is expected, it is taken into account in sales projections for that season. Planned markdowns are frequently used to encourage the flow of people in the store.

planned obsolescence: consciously making an item out-of-fashion in the eyes of the consumer by repeatedly bringing out new models or products featuring improvements that are promoted as being superior or beneficial. There is a question of the value to the consumer of these systematic changes. The weakest-link theory claims that the least durable component in a product will determine its useful life. Synonymous with *managed obsolescence.*

planned profit: a retailer's expected profit for a future accounting period.

planned purchases: the means to determine the dollar value of items drawn into stock during a given season or cycle; helps insure having adequate stock on hand to fulfill increased demand.

planned purchases =

$$\text{planned ending inventory} + \text{planned sales} + \\ \text{planned sales} - \text{planned reductions} - \\ \text{beginning inventory}$$

planned reduction: a retail reduction that is expected by the retailer for a stated accounting period; estimate linked to historic performance and taken into account when projecting the retailer's net profit for the period.

planned sales: projected sales over a defined accounting period; useful in formulating projections based on previous sales patterns of comparable periods.

planned shopping center: a retail location that consists of centrally owned or managed facilities. It is planned and operated as an entity, ringed by parking, and based on balanced tenancy. The three types of planned centers are: regional, community, and neighborhood. See *shopping center.*

planned stock: the dollar amount of items a retailer expects to have on hand to meet sales expectations and inventory requirements. Can be determined for a department, merchandise classification, price line, etc. The four basic methods of planning are the basic stock method of inventory, the percentage variation method, the weeks' supply method, and the stock-sales ratio.

planogram: a computerized diagram used in merchandising to design the ideal display of merchandise on retail store shelves.

plateauing:
(1) when salespeople cease expanding their sales efforts because of a variety of variables, including the lack of motivation.
(2) moving sideways, rather than upwards, within the store.

play money: See *due bill.*

PLC: See *product life cycle.*

PLMA: See *Private Label Manufacturers Association.*

plug:
(1) *general:* to work hard and steadily.
(2) *merchandising:* a type of closure made to be inserted into the opening of a container.

plus business: the sale of goods or services that exceed expectations and projections for the time period. See *plus over normal.*

plus over normal (PON): expressed as a percentage of the expected volume of sales for the time period.

p.m. deal: a monetary payment made to retail salesclerks by a manufacturer for every item sold by the clerks under a special incentive plan. In order to induce clerks to push the product and to encourage them to favor his or her item over those of competitors, a manufacturer may offer a special payment or bonus for each unit sold during the life of the offer.

pneumatic tubes: See *tube system.*

point of equal probability: the point between two significant shopping areas where each becomes equally desirable to potential retail customers. See *point of indifference; Reilly's Law of Retail Gravitation.*

$$\frac{\text{point of equal}}{\text{probability}} = \frac{\text{distance (in miles) between site A and site B}}{1 + \sqrt{\text{population/population B}}}$$

point of equilibrium: the point at which supply equals demand.

point of indifference: the point at which the cost of an added increment of land, labor, capital, or management merely equals the money return of the additional item made because of that increase. Cf. *diminishing returns.* See *point of equal probability.*

point or origin: the location at which goods are received for transportation.

point-of-purchase (POP): See *point-of-sale.*

point-of-purchase advertising: See *POP advertising.*

point-of-sale (POS): in retailing, the location within the store where a sale is completed, i.e., the cash register, where merchandise is picked up. See *noncabled point-of-sale.* Synonymous with *point-of-purchase.*

point of sale perpetual inventory control system: an automated retail system where the store cash registers are linked to computer processing systems. Merchandise is ticketed with colored bar code tags which are read with want readers at the checkout counter. The computer accumulates sales transaction information on magnetic tape for daily input into the computer memory bank or storage system.

point-of-sale terminal (POST): a communication and data-capture terminal located where payment is made for goods or services. The terminal issues sales checks, prints transaction records, and feeds information about each transaction into the databank of the computer.

point scoring: a means for assessing the credit application as to the applicant's credit worthiness; given to such factors as home ownership, other credit cards, bank accounts, income, length of time at present position, etc. Usually, a minimum score is established for the granting of credit.

polarity of retail trade: a concept that retailers will in the future be divided into two extreme groups. One group will be the high-volume mass merchandisers, and the other group will be high-yield specialty boutiques.

policy: in retailing, assists in defining procedures and objectives for the store's employees and promotes consistency (e.g., the creation of a return policy).

policy adjustment: any shift away from a standard return and/or adjustment policies of the store. It is intended to retain the customer's good will and continuing participation.

policy allowance: See *policy adjustment.*

policy rights: in purchasing, the authority given managers to set procurement goals.

PON: See *plus over normal.*

pooled buying:
(1) an informal and voluntary consolidation of orders by several independent merchants all dealing with the same vendor.
(2) a number of independent middlepeople who combine their orders to keep costs lower. Synonymous with *informal buying group.*

pooled purchasing: See *pooled buying.*

POP: point-of-purchase. See *point-of-sale.*

POP advertising: promotional material placed at the point of purchase, such as interior displays, printed material at store counters, or window displays. See *aisle advertising; point-of-sale.*

popularly price merchandise: See *popular priced merchandise.*

popular priced merchandise: goods available for sale at prices that are believed to be acceptable to the mass of consumers.

portfolio analysis: a technique by which an organization individually assesses and positions every business unit and/or product. Company efforts and resources are allocated and separate marketing mixes are aimed at their chosen target markets on the basis of these assessments.

Porter-Lawler model: an extension of the expectancy theory that draws together individual, job, and organizational characteristics to describe the motivational process.

POS: See *point-of-sale.*

positioned retailing: the identification of a retailer's target market and the development of a specific merchandising strategy to meet the needs of that market.

positioning:
(1) *general:* the projection of an item as possessing a desired image, to make it attractive to a part of the market for that type of merchandise (e.g., a low-priced sports car that looks like an expensive model). See *market target.*
(2) *retailing:* a process in which a retailer communicates with consumers to establish a distinct place for its product or brand in their minds. Synonymous with *market positioning.* See *product positioning.*

positive conversion: Synonymous with *boomerang.*

POST: See *point-of-sale terminal.*

postage stamp pricing: See *freight allowed.*

post audit: an audit of the day's net sales that are reviewed on the next day.

post dating: See *advance dating.*

post exchange (PX): a nonprofit retail store operated by the U.S. armed forces at a military post or camp; provides a broad selection of items for personal use at low prices to military and diplomatic personnel and for their families.

postpurchase anxiety: a customer's feeling of doubt following his or her purchase commitment. See *postpurchase behavior.*

postpurchase behavior: the final stage in the consumer adoption process, includes the continued evaluation of the item or service, maintenance, and if the item or service should be repurchased. See *postpurchase anxiety.*

postpurchase customer service: See *postpurchase behavior.*

postpurchase doubt: See *postpurchase anxiety.*

postpurchase service: See *postpurchase behavior.*

post test: a procedure to assess an advertisement or advertising campaign. Posttesting by advertisers is used to obtain insight into consumer responses to certain advertising methods and to minimize costly mistakes in the future; measures both the impact of an advertising message as well as its ultimate impact on product sales and store purchases. Cf. *pretest.*

potential customer: See *prospect.*

PP: See *parcel post.*

praise method: using compliments by the salesperson to convince a prospect to purchase an item or service.

preapproach: in selling, the preparation involved before the prospect can effectively be contacted, including analyzing the prospect prior to the interview, developing a sales strategy, planning the sales presentation, and planning the best way to set up the initial contact. See *canvass.*

pre-audit: the examination of a creditor's invoices, payrolls, claims, and expected reimbursements before actual payment, or the verification of sales transactions before delivery.

pre-authorization: credit authorization secured for a charge-send transaction before the merchandise is allowed to leave the department.

prebuying process: planning, budgeting, shopping the competition, and other relevant activities of the purchaser before he or she actually goes into the market to purchase for the store.

precious stone: the most expensive of the three categories of natural gemstones. Stones are regarded as precious largely on the basis of their hardness, brilliance, and rarity (such as the diamond, ruby, and emerald). Cf. *decorative stone; semi-precious stone.*

precustomer contact: the training of a salesperson *before* he or she meets with customers on the selling floor. Includes learning the store stock in addition to the policies and procedures of the store.

predatory pricing: cutting prices with the objective of harming one's competitors. The opposite of umbrella pricing. See *price war; rate war.*

preference item: a consumer's choice of a particular item even when similar items are less costly (e.g., insisting on Coca Cola, although a chain grocery store's cola-type soft drink is less expensive).

preferred discount: See *trade discount.*

preferred resource: a seller chosen by the consumer as his or her first choice source of supply for a particular good or service. Cf. *key resource.*

premarking: See *prepricing.*

premium:
(1) *merchandising:* a product that is offered free or at less than the regular

price in order to induce the consumer to buy another product.

(2) *retailing:* an offer of merchandise, at a minimal cost or at no charge, as an inducement to the customer to purchase a given item. See *coupon; direct premium; referral premium.*

premium center: See *redemption center.*

premium jobber: a wholesaler of incentive items who usually deals with a full range of merchandise. See *jobber.*

premium offers: they are (a) a free gift, (b) the free-, send away premium (a free gift in exchange for proof of purchase), and (c) self-liquidating premium where the consumer sends both money and proof of purchase to obtain the offer.

premium pack: a promotional package used by manufacturers to encourage consumer buying. Two or more of the same product are combined at a special price, or a related premium is attached to or included in the promoted item. See *on pack.*

premium promotion: See *premium.*

premium representative:

(1) a manufacturer's representative working with premium users; offers factory price, support, experience and personal attention.

(2) a commission salesperson serving a host of manufacturers on a direct-factory-price basis.

premium store: See *redemption store.*

prepackaged: See *prepackaging.*

prepackaging:

(1) *merchandising:* packaging of fresh foods (meat, vegetables, cheeses) in consumer units for self-service sales.

(2) *retailing:* to avoid repackaging by the retailer, packaging of merchandise such as chinaware and furniture by the manufacturer so that it may be sold directly to the consumer without opening. Synonymous with *prepak.*

prepaid: indicating that shipping charges have already been paid or are to be paid at the point of delivery.

prepak: See *prepackaging.*

prepay: to pay before or in advance of receipt of goods or services.

prepricing: the manufacturer at times prints the retail or suggested price of an item directly on the packaging of the item. Although its saves the dealer the cost and time of pricing merchandise, it locks him or her into a situation where the items cannot be sold to a customer at a higher price. Synonymous with *premarking; preticketing.* See *vendor premarking.*

preprinted order form: a vendor's order form where items are shown that are carried by the vendor, including check-off spaces for entering quantity desired, unit price, and total price. See *order form.*

prepurchase customer service: a customer service carried out prior to when a purchase is made and which can encourage the purchase. For example, interior and exterior displays, telephone and mail-order services, fitting rooms, shopping hours, fashion shows, and demonstrations.

prepurchase service: See *prepurchase customer service.*

preretail: See *preretailing; retailing the invoice.*

preretailing: assignment by the retailer of retail prices to goods at the time an order is made, thus allowing the determination of retail values of items on order. This practice also speeds up the checking and marking procedures when merchandise arrives. See *retailing the invoice.*

presold market: buyers waiting for the arrival of a new product or service.

presold merchandise: goods for which consumer demand has been stimulated by vendor promotion. Little or no in-store selling is required to move the items.

prestige advertising: advertising to enhance the prestige of a store or its products.

prestige builder: a top of the line item that is also the most expensive. It is meant to add status to the store's image and to attract status-conscious customers.

prestige price zone: See *prestige zone.*

prestige pricing: increasing the price of an item to establish a quality image of the product or the seller. May be used to attract those customers who associate high price with quality.

prestige merchandise: See *prestige builder.*

prestige zone: the price range of a retailer's most costly goods. It is targeted for the customer who is status-conscious and interested in expensive and/or exclusive items. Cf. *price zone; volume zone.*

pretest:

(1) a test given to determine an individual's performance in some area in advance of training, education, or some other condition that is expected to improve performance. Cf. *posttest.*

(2) the measure of the acceptance of a concept, items, or service presented to prospects; usually accomplished with interviews and impacts on selling strategy.

preticketing: See *prepricing.*

previous balance method: a method by which retailers determine the balance in a charge account upon which a service charge is to be assessed. Under the earlier balance methods payments made during the billing period are not subtracted from the outstanding balance before the service charge is assessed. See *adjusted balance procedure; average daily balance method.*

prewrap: to wrap or package merchandise before it is placed on the floor for sale. See *prepackaging.*

prewrapped: See *prewrap.*

price:

(1) that which the buyer gives up in exchange for something that provides satisfaction.

(2) the amount of money a seller receives for goods or services at the factory or place of business. Price is not what the seller asks for the product or service but what is actually received. See *pricing.*

price adjustment: the increase or decrease of the retail price of merchandise; provides the store with a means for altering price, markups, and markdowns, to draw customers into the store as well as to increase profits.

price agreement plan: a central purchasing accord where the purchase for the stores arranges prices, colors, sizes, etc., in addition to the shipping terms. Synonymous with *catalog plan.*

price-based shopping products: products for which consumers believe the attributes of alternatives are relatively similar and look around for the least expensive items or stores.

price bracket: See *price zone.*

price break: the advertised price reduction intending to attract customers into the store.

price change: See *price adjustment.*

price change form: a record used for showing any raising or lowering of the retail price of goods in stock. For example, additional markups, markup cancellations, and markdowns would all be recorded on price change forms.

price code: the symbol found on the price tag and/or bin ticket showing the cost of goods to retail personnel while hiding this information from the retail customer.

price comparison: sale price contrasted with regular or list price, both of which can appear on the price tag or label; permits consumers to recognize the true value of a purchase. In accordance with Federal Trade Commission rulings, the regular price must be accurate and not artificially manipulated.

price competition: competition among firms that purport to differentiate their merchandise based on price alone. Items are marked as being preferred based on how much less they will cost. Cf. *nonprice competition.*

price control:

(1) *general:* regulation of the prices of goods and services with the intent to reduce increases in the cost of living. A government imposed strategy that is rarely used.

(2) *merchandising:* the result of the demand by a manufacturer that the buyer for resale not be able to determine a resale price for the goods. See *fair trade price.*

price cutter: See *price cutting.*

price cutting: used when firms have excess capacity and wish to generate additional business without increasing selling efforts, add to the cost of advertising, or improving the item. Price cutting offers goods or services for sale at a price below that recognized as typical or appropriate by buyers and sellers. Coupons, rebates, larger packages at the same price, or lowering the retail price are approaches used in price cutting. Its negative side is that consumers can perceive that the quality of the item has been reduced. See *underselling.*

price decline guarantee: the guarantee by the manufacturer to a retailer than any decline in price on goods ordered ahead of delivery date will be passed on to the retailer in the form of a credit or refund.

price differential:

(1) a departure from the usual one-price policy granted by a vendor to the store based on significance of the purchase, type of customer, or geographical location; includes quantity discounts, trade discounts, and other reductions in price.

(2) the difference between the base price for merchandise of a given quality or size and the base price for similar goods differing in quality or size, but which are possible substitutes for the original. Can be expressed as a percentage of the base price or as a fixed amount deducted from the base price.

price discretion: reflected in the decision of a sales representative to alter the price of an item for purposes of making a sale.

price discrimination: the practice of charging different prices for the same quality and quantity of merchandise to different buyers. Should this practice result in reducing competition, it is illegal under the antitrust laws. See *resale price maintenance; Robinson-Patman Act of 1936.* Cf. *trade discount.*

priced out of the market: See *price out of the market.*

price elasticity: reflected in a reduction in sales when the price of an item is raised. Cf. *price inelasticity.* See *elastic demand; elasticity.*

price ending: manipulating the final digit of the price to create an attractive psychological effect in the eyes of the consumer. For example, an original retail price may be set in full or whole dollar prices (e.g., $20.00), markdowns may all end in 99 cents (e.g., $8.99) and promotional merchandise may all end in 90 cents (e.g., $8.90). See *even-line pricing; odd pricing.*

price equalization: a competitive pricing policy leading to a company's delivered price to a customer; composed of the price of the item at the factory plus the freight cost to the customer as if the shipment began at the shipping point of the company's competitor nearest to the company's customer.

price escalation: increase in the final price of an item or service because of unanticipated or miscalculated costs of distribution, transportation, tariffs, etc.

price-feature advertising: advertising that emphasizes the reduced price on goods instead of claims of utility, quality, etc.

price file: a computer memory bank used with the universal product code (UPC); matches the store price to the item and is central to effectiveness of UPC operations in the store.

price fixing: an agreement by competing organizations to avoid competitive pricing by charging identical prices or by changing prices at the same time; is in violation of the Sherman Antitrust Act. Cf. *conscious parallel action.* See *price negotiation; resale price maintenance.*

price floor: the lowest price that a company can sell an item or service and still realize a profit.

price-floor pricing: a form of cost-based pricing whereby a firm determines the lowest price at which it is worthwhile to increase the amount of goods or services it makes available for sale.

price guarantee: See *price guaranty.*

price guaranty: a seller's agreement to make a proportionate refund to a customer on all items in the buyer's inventory at the time of a price reduction. Usually has a time limit following purchase. Synonymous with *guarantee against price decline; price protection; price protection rebate; vendor paid markdown.*

price index: a measure to illustrate the changes in the average level of prices. See *purchasing power.*

price inelastic demand: See *inelastic demand; price inelasticity.*

price inelasticity: a change in price that yields a disproportionately small change in demand. Cf. *price elasticity.* See *inelastic demand.*

price inflaters: charges placed on top of the list price of an item or service that thereby increases its true selling price. Would include credit charges, service contracts, handling fees, etc.

price leader: See *price leadership.*

price leadership:
(1) *general:* a situation in which prices can be determined by one major manufacturer in an industry, thus influencing others to accept the prices as determined. See *administered price.*
(2) *retailing:* merchandise whose price has been significantly dropped to enhance store traffic. See *loss leader.*

price level: the value of money in comparison with a specified base period. See *price zone.*

price line: the specific predetermined retail price level that merchandise is offered for sale. Stores using this pricing strategy traditionally limit their price lines to three to five per classification. Merchandise which would normally fall within a particular price zone can be priced identically. The price lines are easily identifiable as "good, better and best" by the customer. See *price lining.*

price line control: a form of dollar control inventory management where accounting is based on price lines, i.e., the particular prices at which the store's items are available for sale.

price lining:
(1) placing several items of varying costs together and selling them all at the same price. This practice is used frequently in retailing. See *loss leader.*
(2) a pricing strategy in which prices are used to sort products into "lines"

based on an attribute such as quality, prestige, or style. See *price line.*

price loco: the price at the place where a purchase occurs.

price maintained line: See *resale price maintenance.*

price maintenance: See *resale price maintenance.*

price-minus pricing: a method for determining the price of an item or service by initially estimating the price that the item or service would find a share of the market, and then developing the item or service to be profitable at that found price.

price mix: a store's strategy of raising and lowering prices in order to meet competition head on.

price negotiation: price fixing based on the belief that the purchaser is a price-maker rather than a price-taker. See *price fixing.*

price-off: a price reduction that is used to induce trial or increase usage of a product. The percentage reduction is traditionally noted on the product package. See *price leadership.*

price out of the market: setting the price of an item so high that it is no longer purchased in its usual market (e.g., vendors of $12 ice cream cones would find themselves priced out of the juvenile market). Cf. *inelastic demand.*

price pack: items available at a lower price to consumers. Two forms of price packs are: (a) reduced-price packs—two single packages sold together at a lowered rate, such as three for the price of two; and (b) banded price packs—two related items, bound together, and sold at a price lower than it would cost if they were bought separately, such as shaving cream and a razor. See *economy pack.*

price planning: the systematic decision making by an organization regarding all aspects of pricing.

price point: the standard retail price used by marketers for some items that vary slightly in wholesale cost, but share a similar level of perceived value to the consumer (e.g., instead of selling five shirts on an absolute profit margin, resulting in prices such as $19.95, $18.75, $18.00, $17.50, and $17.00, the marketer could price all of them at $18.25). Small difference in price tend to have a disproportionate impact on sales.

price policy: the broad guidelines used by a retailer in making pricing decisions. This policy reflects the retailer's position regarding factors such as competing stores, costs, promotional expenditures, etc.

price protection: See *price guaranty.*

price protection rebate: See *price guaranty.*

price quality association: the belief that consumers equate high prices with higher quality and low price with lower quality. See *prestige pricing.*

price range: the range between the highest and lowest possible differences in price.

price reducers: methods for lowering the selling price, i.e., providing free services, rebates, discounts.

price sensitive: the tendency of the demand for an item or service to vary based on the variations in price. Some items or services are more price sensitive than others, impacted on by demand, availability. Retailers and merchandisers of price-sensitive items often test new prices before implementing them, to assess the impact on demand. See *elasticity; elasticity of demand; price elasticity.*

price sensitivity: See *price sensitive.*

price shading: where discounts are available to wholesalers, retailers, and consumers with the expectation that an increased demand will evolve.

price space: the distance between price points in the product line, i.e., the distance from one price to another. This is intended to minimize the products' competing with one another while also minimizing the existence of gaps into which competitors may move and make sales.

price strategy: See *pricing strategy.*

price tag: a tag affixed to goods by the store. Contains the retail price of the merchandise, and data such as style number, vendor number, coded data purchase, coded cost price, size, and other information to be used in inventory. Synonymous with *price ticket.*

price takers: firms that have no market power over price. Therefore, the market dictates price for them.

price ticket: See *price tag.*

price verification procedure: ensures that the price on a ticket, or on the shelf, matches what the customer will see on the register at checkout. See *electronic article surveillance; markdown.*

price war: a combative, competition between stores shown by the lowering of prices in the attempt to undersell each other for sales. Often the result of a price war is the failure of one or more competitors. See *predatory pricing.*

price zone: price lines that appeal to a group of a store's customers. See *price lining.* Cf. *prestige zone; volume zone.*

pricing: the setting and/or changing the cost to the consumer for a service or item. See *price; pricing above the market.*

pricing above the competition: See *pricing above the market.*

pricing above the market: establishing prices lower than those of the competitor so as to maximize the use of price as a competitive factor. Cf. *pricing at the market.*

pricing at the market: a price policy where retailers compete on a nonprice basis establishing prices at approxi-

mately the same level as their competitors. It attempts to reduce the usage of price as a competitive factor. Cf. *pricing above the market.*

pricing below the competition: See *pricing below the market.*

pricing below the market: where retailers set prices lower than that of competition. The retailer chooses this price policy because of an inconvenient location, self-service organization, concentration on volume sales, and/or the stocking of private label merchandise. This strategy can also be an alternative to expensive promotional efforts.

pricing error: the incorrect original price, usually set too high, so that the goods do not sell. At times, the price can be corrected through markdowns.

pricing strategy: long-range planning using price as a means of attracting customers into the store. Can be used as a substitute for a prime location, advertising expenditures, and other promotions.

pricing under the competition: See *pricing below the market.*

primary buying motive: the reason a person purchases a particular class or type of product, no matter what the specific brand. See *primary demand.*

primary customer service: a customer service activity that is primary to retailing operation. These may differ from store to store and from region to region, but the following are usually included: maintaining convenient store hours, having sales personnel available, display, wrapping, adjustments, and parking facilities. See *primary service area.*

primary demand:

(1) *general:* demand for a product type.

(2) *merchandising:* the market demand for a product class rather than a particular brand. See *primary buying motive; selective demand.*

primary demand advertising: advertising purporting to create primary buying motives with consumers.

primary market: See *local market.*

primary market area: the major area of sales and distribution for goods or services (e.g., the primary market for bathing suits would be southern U.S. or other warm climate areas). Synonymous with *heartland.*

primary package: a protective container into which an item is put. For example, glass or plastic jars, cans, tubes are all primary packages. Often this is supplemented by another package, such as a box, for further protection and brand identification.

primary research: gathering market data in the field by a firm or individual to examine a specific retailing or marketing problem or situation.

primary service: See *primary customer service; primary service area.*

primary service area: the geographical area surrounding a radio or television station where the ground waves are not subject to objectionable interference or fading. See *primary customer service.*

primary stage: See *pioneering stage.*

primary supplier: See *local market.*

primary trade area: See *primary trading area.*

primary trading area: the geographic boundary that a marketing organization has dominance, and often control. See *fringe trading area; secondary trading area.*

prime resource: See *key resource.*

principle of massed reserves: a concept of reducing the size of many inventories at the retail level while at the same time increasing the size of inventories carried by wholesalers, with the impact of lowering the total stock carried in the store.

principle of minimum total transactions: the inclusion of an intermediary between buyers and sellers that should reduce the number of transactions.

principle of relative loss: a producer's failure to sell his or her goods to a retailer and thus retain unused capacity, and unrealized profit opportunities.

prior donor file: computer listing of people who have already bought gifts from a retailer or marketer in a completed sale transaction. Prior donors are usually fine prospects for additional gift promotions.

prior source: a source from a previous order from a client who has ordered again. It is important to know who these people are since they tend to become repeat buyers.

prior stock: goods in inventory for the duration of the previous season, usually in excess of six months.

prior stock report: a report prepared by the retailer that summarizes quantitative information about all stock on hand remaining from the earlier season.

Privacy Act of 1974: federal legislation designed to protect citizens from invasion of privacy by the federal government and permitting individuals, for the first time, to inspect information about themselves contained in federal agency files and to challenge, correct, or amend the material. The Act prohibits an agency, including a retailer from selling or renting an individual's name or address for mailing list use.

private brand:

(1) a middleperson-owned brand name or trademark (e.g., Sears Roebuck owns the Kenmore brand).

(2) a brand sponsored by a wholesaler, retailer, dealer, or merchant (e.g., a supermarket item bearing a store label with an item's name), as contrasted with a brand having the name of a manufacturer or producer; usually priced lower than manufactured brands and

appeals primarily to bargain conscious customers.

(3) Synonymous with *confined label; dealer brand; distributor brand; private distributor brand; private label; reseller brand.*

private buying office: a store-owned buying office maintained in a market center by a large retailer. Buyers perform functions that are similar to those in a cooperative buying office.

private cost: the cost of a specific item to an individual.

private distributor brand: See *private brand.*

private label: See *private brand.*

Private Label Manufacturers Association (PLMA): based in New York City, an association of manufacturers, brokers, wholesalers, retailers, and consultants who endeavor to educate consumers on the quality and value of private labels or store brand products and to promote private label products.

private office: See *private buying office.*

private party selling: See *party selling.*

private sale: the sale of items at lower than regular prices to a special group of customers, such as charge customers. The sale is advertised in mailings to those customers, but not to the public-at-large. Can immediately precede a sale of the same items to the general public.

private warehouse: See *warehouse, private.*

prizm: information used in segmenting a market based on a combination of geographic and demographic variables. The data defines areas by zip code, census tract, and block group. Such data is used in developing marketing mix variations and media planning to attempt to reach prospects most likely to purchase the sellers' merchandise.

problem awareness: the stage in the final consumer's decision process during which the consumer recognizes that the merchandise, service, etc., under consideration may solve a shortage problem or unfulfilled desire.

problem child: (slang) a high growth item that can only attract a low market share. If prolonged, the store either must abandon the item or invest more money to alter its appearance or for promotional activities.

problem detection analysis: a study focusing on the complaints or problems that consumers have with the item or service.

processing in transit: See *transit privileges.*

process materials: See *producer goods.*

procurement: the purchase of goods for resale to a store's customers. Synonymous with *purchasing.* See *buying; purchasing agent.*

produce:

(1) *verb:* to make or manufacture.

(2) *noun:* in food retailing, fresh fruits and vegetables and the department where they can be purchased.

produce exchange: a market for perishable agricultural products.

producer:

(1) an individual who manufactures goods and/or services.

(2) creators of goods and services that are made for consumers of a particular target market.

producer-controlled brands: brands owned or controlled by firms that are primarily in the manufacturing business. Synonymous with *natural brands.*

producer cooperative: a member-owned wholesale operation that assembles farm products to sell in local markets.

producer goods: items intended to be used and worn out in the course of producing other items in the future (e.g., ink in newspaper printing).

producer market: a set of buyers who purchase goods and services and use them to make other products.

product: See *goods.*

product adaptation: altering items to fulfill local or regional requirements (e.g., changing the current fixtures for items sold overseas).

product analysis: in retailing, the research carried out by a buyer to determine the performance of a purchased item. The objective of the research is to achieve the desired level of quality at the lowest possible price.

product assortment: the brands and types of items in a product class available to consumers. See *assortment.*

product augmentation: a technique for maintaining sales of items marketed in their mature life cycle stage. The life may be extended by repackaging, reducing selling price, etc.

product buy-back agreement: See *buy-back agreement.*

product characteristics: attributes that buyers and sellers use when deciding if a product or service meets a particular need.

product class: a group of items that are treated as natural substitutes and/or complements by most consumers.

product classification: See *product-line departmentalization.*

product concept: the general belief that consumers are interested in purchasing quality items and fair and reasonable prices, thus the manufacturer concentrates on means to fulfill these characteristics, such as improving the item's performance at minimal cost.

product departmentalization: See *product-line departmentalization.*

product depth: the number of items in each product line that is available for purchase.

product development: the generation of new ideas for new or improved goods to be added to or to replace existing items.

product differentiation: See *differentiation.*

product disfeature: a characteristic of a product that the consumer does not like; frequently, its price.

product fit: the degree to which a product fulfills the needs of the marketplace.

product image: how a prospect or user perceives one or more characteristics of an item. This image may be as important, or more important, to the specific real usage of the item. See *product positioning.*

product improvement: activities for increasing sales by upgrading an item's attributes to attract either new customers or to encourage existing customers to buy the product more often. Product improvement is carried out by: (a) quality improvement—increasing the function of the product, such as making it stronger to last longer; (b) feature improvement—adding new features to introduce versatility or convenience for people, such as the adding of accessories; and (c) style improvement—altering the item to enhance its physical or aesthetic appeal, such as a new design for a television set. Synonymous with *product modification.*

production:

(1) any form of activity that adds value to goods and services, including creation, transportation, and warehousing until used.

(2) a criterion of effectiveness that refers to an organization's ability to provide the outputs demanded of it by the environment.

(3) usually, but not always the same as manufacturing.

production-oriented diversification: See *congruent production diversification.*

product item: a specific model, brand, or size of a product that a company sells.

product liability: liability imposed for damages caused by accident and arising out of goods or products manufactured, sold by a store, handled, or distributed by the insured or by other trading under his or her name. The accident must have occurred after possession of goods had been relinquished to others and away from premises owned, rented, or controlled by the insured, the retailer. In the case of food products, however, the accident does not have to occur away from the premises (e.g., in a restaurant). Cf. *warranty.* See *consumer protection legislation; guarantee.*

product life: See *shelf life.*

product life cycle (PLC):
(1) a sequence of stages in the marketing of a product that begins with commercialization and ends with removal from the market.
(2) the six stages of market acceptance of any goods: pioneering, growth, maturity, saturation, decline, and abandonment. See *divest-and-exit strategy.*

product line: the assortment of items presented by a store or firm, or a group of items that are closely related because they either satisfy a need, are used with each other, are sold to the same consumer, are marketed within the same outlets, or are within similar price ranges. See *line; product mix.*

product-line departmentalization: the organization of the retailer based on the differing categories of goods sold and the division of jobs within the store along the same product or service lines.

product management: the business activities dealing with the evolution of new items or brands, their introduction to the market, and their management through the product life cycle.

product manager: an executive responsible for marketing approaches, such as promotion, pricing, distribution, and establishing product characteristics. The product manager deals more with the planning aspects than with actual

selling to the consumer. Synonymous with *brand manager; program manager; project manager.* See *marketing management.* Cf. *sales manager.*

product market: See *consumer market.*

product mix: the composite of items offered for sale by one company. Some firms have a wide product mix geared for a diverse consumer group, while others maintain a narrow product mix geared toward a particular market segment. See *mix; product line.*

product modification: See *product improvement.*

product motives: why people purchase a particular product.

product-oriented advertising: retail advertising that emphasizes the sale of a particular item or product line rather than the store as a whole.

product planning: the process leading to the identification of goals and procedures as well as the precise nature of the merchandise to be marketed. See *marketing research.*

product positioning: the way in which a product is characterized to attract consumer interest and purchase. A product may be positioned in a variety of ways, such as economical, durable, stylish, safe, convenient, and so forth. See *perceptual mapping; positioning; product image.*

product pretest: See *pretest.*

product publicity: publicity used for promoting a new or existing item.

product reliability: the probability that a product will perform a stated function under specific conditions for a specified period without failure. See *guarantee; reliability.*

product rotation: the practice of placing new items under or behind older goods that lie on the shelf; purports to insure the sale of the older products first.

product spotter: any eye or ear catching device, such as a colored spotlight, for attracting consumer's attention to a product or package. Used most frequently in promoting a new store item.

product value: the sum of all aspects of merchandise that purport to fulfill a customer's needs minus the negative aspects of the item.

professional discount: a reduction from the list of traditional price given to customers in a particular field or profession; used to yield good will and hopefully assure repeat business activity. For example, a hardware store may give professional discounts to builders and contractors who are frequent customers.

profile: See *customer profile.*

profit:
(1) the reward to the entrepreneur for the risks assumed by him or her in the establishment, operation, and management of a given enterprise or undertaking.
(2) the monies remaining after a business has paid all its bills.
(3) the excess of the selling price over all costs and expenses incurred in making a sale.

profitability: a firm's ability to earn a profit and its potential for future earnings.

profitability range: the difference between the most profitable and least profitable lines of merchandise calculated on the basis of profit per square foot of selling space. See *profit per square foot of selling space.*

profit and loss statement: in retailing, the summary listing of a store's total revenues and expenses within a specified time period. See *operating statement.*

profit-based pricing objectives: those that orient a store's pricing strategy toward some type of profit goals; profit maximization, satisfactory profit, re-

turn on investment, and/or early recovery of cash.

profit booster: goods that have an inflated retail price to offset losses derived from loss leaders.

profit center:
(1) *general:* a segment of a business that is responsible for both revenues and expenses.
(2) *retailing:* any area of the store which contributes to the overall profit of the retailer, i.e., the selling areas. In department stores, the profit centers correspond to the departments. In smaller stores, profit centers may be based on product lines. Each center, or unit, is uniquely distinct from other store units in order that its contribution to profits might be measured. Cf. *expense center.*

profit-centered services: retailing activities that are merchandised for a profit. Can be the principal business of the organization, such as shoe repair, or may represent part of the business, for example, a restaurant in a store.

profit margin: sales less all operating expenses divided by the number of sales.

profit mix: variables contributing to a retailer's profit, all of which may be adjusted and altered for a desired profit result. These component variables consist of price, volume, sales, cost of goods sold, operating expenses, etc.

profit per square foot of selling space: the amount of dollar profit generated by an item or line calculated on an annual basis:

$$\frac{\text{gross profit on line (annual)}}{\text{square feet of selling space}} =$$

$$\text{gross profit per square foot}$$

profit sharing: in retailing, a method of compensation in which employees share in the profits of the store; usually made in addition to salary and/or commission.

profit target analysis: determining the volume of sales required to pay for all the costs of operation and still command a predetermined profit for the firm.

pro forma invoice: a preliminary invoice indicating the value of the items listed and informing the recipient that all have been sent. It is not a demand for money. See *receiving apron.*

program manager: See *product manager.*

programmed merchandiser: a resource providing numerous services to a retailer in addition to a product line. These services are performed in exchange for a promise to purchase products. Promotional assistance is one of the services provided by most programmed merchandisers.

program merchandising: combined efforts of a retailer and a key source to make merchandising and promotion plans for a store. A limited number of cautiously selected key resources are involved, with the retailer usually purchasing an entire line of merchandise from these resources for an extended time period, often one year.

prohibited articles: in shipping, merchandise that will not be handled.

projection: See *forecasting.*

project manager: See *product manager.*

promo: See *promotional message.*

promotion:

(1) stimulating the demand for goods by advertising, publicity, and events to attract attention and create interest among consumers. See *advertising; sales promotion.*

(2) any technique that persuasively communicates favorable information about a seller's product to potential buyers, includes advertising, personal selling, sales promotion, and public relations. See *promotional mix; trade promotion.*

promotional advertising:

(1) *general:* advertising purporting to stimulate the rapid buying of a particular merchandise or service.

(2) *retailing:* advertising by a retailer purporting to create sales of a particular item or group of items and to bring customers into the store immediately. Also used to announce special sales and the arrival of new and/or seasonal merchandise, etc., as well as to create a market for the regular stock.

promotional assistance: See *programmed merchandiser.*

promotional department store: See *full-line discount store.*

promotional discount: a discount that is offered to intermediaries as compensation for carrying out promotional activities. See *co-op money; co-op promotion.*

promotional elasticity of demand:

(1) *general:* holding other variables constant, the percent change in quantity requested that may result from a percent shift in promotional activity. Cf. *price elasticity.*

(2) *retailing:* the percent change in customer demand for merchandise that results from a percent change in promotional activity, when all other factors are constant. See *elasticity of demand.*

promotional item: See *promotional stock.*

promotional kit: a vendor's materials given to a retailer for promoting the vendor's goods; can include plans, ideas, suggestions for displaying and selling the merchandise, etc., as well as displays, advertising copy, and consumer information materials. See *promotional package.*

promotional markdown: a lowering of the retail price hoping to encourage greater store traffic. Unlike clearance markdowns, promotional markdowns are regarded as an integral part of the retailer's offensive strategy calculated to increase sales.

promotional merchandise: See *promotional stock*.

promotional message: often shortened to *promo*.

promotional mix: the combined promotional efforts of advertising, publicity, sales promotion, and personal selling as they attempt to communicate with customers to sell a product. See *mix; promotools*.

promotional money: See *co-op money*.

promotional package: materials forwarded to the dealer to assist with the advertising campaign, such as inserts, banners, etc. See *promotional kit*.

promotional price: a lowered price offered on a temporary basis to promote particular merchandise.

promotional stock: merchandise available for sale to the consumer at an unusually low price so as to enhance the sales volume and store traffic. The item is frequently a special purchase from a vendor and can be advertised as such.

promotion mix: See *promotional mix*.

promotion price zone: See *promotion zone*.

promotions: activities either within or out of the store calculated to increase sales or to create a favorable store image. Promotions are typically one-time affairs, such as exhibitions, in-store demonstrations, shows, parades, displays, import fairs, theme events.

promotion zone: the range of prices of low-end items that are sold at low prices; aims at customers with limited financial resources or those who are otherwise budget conscious. See *price zone*.

promotools: a variety of media used in the promotional mix, such as demonstrations, contests, free give-aways, catalogs. See *promotional mix*.

proof of purchase: evidence that merchandise or a service has actually been bought. Programs that request users to retain a collection of multiple proofs of purchase over a time period are continuity programs.

proprietary drug: a medicine or other remedy that is sold without the physician's prescription. Synonymous with *over-the-counter drug*.

proprietary store: a retail store that sells essentially the same items as a drug store, with the exception of prescription drugs.

prospect:
(1) a person that has never purchased the item or service before.
(2) a potential customer of a service or product. See *qualified prospect; prospecting*.

prospecting: the first phase of the selling process; searching for an individual or concern that needs a product or service and possesses the ability to purchase it. Two major methods of prospecting are: (a) endless chain—asking existing customers for the names of people they know who might be interested in the seller's product or service; and (b) centers of influence—asking influential and professional people for the names of potential customers. See *business cycle; hitlist; prospect; qualifying*.

prospect list: names of people who marketers believe are qualified to purchase a product or service; held for promotional purpose in the expectation that they can be reached and will become customers.

protection in transit: in shipping, the purpose of a product's package.

proximo dating: See *proximo terms*.

proximo terms: in invoice dating, an agreement where the cash discount and net credit periods begin on a specified day of the month following delivery. A credit period of 60 days from the first of the month is allowed to those who have not availed themselves of the discount. Full payment must be paid within 60 days of the first of the month following delivery.

pseudo sale: a category of market testing methods wherein the customer does various things to indicate reaction to the product and to its marketing strategy but does not actually spend money.

psychographic market segmentation: choosing people who react in the identical fashion to a particular emotional appeal, or who share common behavioral patterns. Cf. *demographics.*

psychographic segmentation: See *psychographic market segmentation.*

psychographics: psychological profiles of prospects within a given market.

psychological discounting: offering an illusionary lowering of prices by providing artificial comparisons of present price with an earlier price, where the earlier price never even existed. Illegal today. Synonymous with *was-is pricing.*

psychological moment: that point when the salesperson feels he or she is ready to attempt the trial close.

psychological pricing: See *odd pricing.*

psychological product: the physical product along with its warranties, services, and psychological overtones.

psychological risk: the consumer-perceived risk that a product, if purchased, could somehow be damaging to the consumer's ego.

psychological satisfaction: the satisfaction received from the intangible benefits of a product, such as a feeling of self-worth. Cf. *physiological motives.*

publicity:

(1) any message about an organization that is communicated through the mass media, but is not paid for by the organization.

(2) any event or communication, through established media or otherwise, free or paid, solicited or not, that

attracts attention to a product or service. Cf. *advertising; public relations.*

public market: a municipal or community-sponsored market active in the wholesale and/or retail sale of food and related products. Synonymous with *community market; municipal market.*

public relations:

(1) *general:* any communication or activity created or performed primarily to enhance prestige or goodwill for an individual or an organization. Cf. *publicity.*

(2) *retailing:* a promotional activity that aims to communicate a favorable image of a product or its marketer and to promote goodwill. Differs from advertising and sales promotion that disseminate marketing information through paid media.

puff: (slang) a free promotion of a product or service.

puffery:

(1) *general:* a story or news release lacking news value or is perceived to be overly self-serving.

(2) *retailing:* an exaggerated store advertising campaign or promotion, often with words such as "the best," "the greatest," "the longest lasting." Deception can be the next step.

puffing: See *puffery.*

pull: See *push-or-pull distribution strategy.*

pull date: in food retailing, the date stamped on perishable products (e.g., bakery and dairy goods), after which the items should not be sold.

pull distribution strategy: See *forced distribution.*

pulling power:

(1) *general:* the ability to draw an audience.

(2) *retailing:* the power of a retailer or store to attract customers; to draw responses from the advertiser's prospects and customers, usually measured by the

number of orders or inquiries received after publication of the advertisement.

purchase allowance: a lowering of the price of an item when the merchandise as requested does not meet the expectations as identified on the invoice. Cf. *on consignment.* See *returns to vendor.*

purchase contract: an agreement between a buyer and seller that itemizes items and services to be bought and sold, respectively.

purchase discount: a reduction in the price of an order that has been paid promptly. See *cash discount.*

purchase distribution: the percentage of all retail outlets that received a shipment of the product since a previous audit, whether or not they were in stock then or at the current audit.

purchase history: a customer record of purchases over a time period.

purchase invoice: See *invoice.*

purchase journal: prepared on a monthly or semi-monthly basis, a report including the charge to a department or classification for items received, all invoices for the merchandise, transfers of merchandise, returns and claims against vendors, short shipments, lost merchandise, etc.

purchase order: a statement permitting a vendor to deliver merchandise or materials at an agreed-upon price; becomes a contract upon its acceptance by the vendor.

purchase price: the amount for which an item or service is bought.

purchase-privilege offer: See *semi-liquidator; trade cards.*

purchaser:
(1) a buyer.
(2) a person who obtains title to or an interest in property by the act of purchase.

purchase requisition: See *requisition.*

purchase returns and allowances: a contra-purchases account in which the returns or allowances for previously purchased merchandise are recorded.

purchasing: See *procurement.*

purchasing agent: an individual who buys products for store maintenance and daily operation, not for resale to customers. Some purchasing agents are employed as company staff, others are independent middlepeople who work for a company on a contractual basis and are paid on commission. Cf. *procurement.*

purchasing cooperative: See *consumer cooperative.*

purchasing leverage: the impact of effective purchasing on profitability.

purchasing power:
(1) *general:* the value of money measured by the items it can buy. Cf. *real value of money.* Synonymous with *buying power.*
(2) *retailing:* the capacity to purchase possessed by an individual buyer, a group of buyers, or the aggregate of the buyers in an area or market.

Pure Food and Drug Act of 1906: federal legislation prohibiting manufacturers' mislabeling of the contents of food, liquor, and medicine containers.

pure impulse buying: impulse purchasing where the customer purchases because he or she becomes consumed with the uniqueness or worthiness of the offering. Cf. *planned impulse buying.*

push distribution strategy: See *push-or-pull distribution strategy.*

pushing strategy: See *push-or-pull distribution strategy.*

push-or-pull distribution strategy: a strategy for increasing market penetration of an item. Push refers to intense personal selling on the part of sales personnel representing the vendor. Dealers are encouraged to stock and push the product. Pull refers to direct appeals to the ultimate consumers, persuading them to demand that their dealers stock the product.

push-pull strategy: See *push-or-pull distribution strategy.*

push strategy: See *push-or-pull distribution strategy.*

PX: See *post exchange.*

pyramiding: See *pyramid selling.*

pyramid schemes: See *pyramid selling.*

pyramid selling: business opportunity frauds, usually promoted through advertisements for job opportunities guaranteed to yield enormous or quick profits, requiring little education or demanding a minimal personal investment. There are government regulations against certain pyramid schemes. The pyramider induces many people to buy his or her merchandise, which they are to resell at a higher price. For example, if 10 people buy 50 units each, but can sell only 15 each, the pyramider is still ahead, because he or she has sold 500 units. See *fraud; roll-out.* Synonymous with *pyramid schemes.*

Q-system: an inventory control system that holds the reorder quantity constant and shifts the reorder period. Synonymous with *reorder system.* See *reorder point.*

quad rack: See *four-way rack.*

qualified lead:

(1) *retailing:* a person who shows interest, usually by making an inquiry from a retailer, in purchasing an item or service.

(2) *merchandising:* an individual possessing the financial ability to purchase an item or service; a valid potential customer. See *qualifying.*

qualified prospect: a potential store customer who is able to buy a product and has the authority to make a decision to purchase. This conclusion is often arrived at following a check on the individual's credit. See *prospect.*

qualifying: determining whether or not a sales prospect is a serious and potential customer, and therefore, worth following. Attempts are made to minimize lost time and to avoid involvement with people who are not interested in or able to make a purchase. Criteria used are: (a) the seller determines if the prospect has the funds to purchase the item or service; (b) whether the prospect has

the authority for making the decision to buy; and (c) whether the prospect has a need to secure the product or service. See *prospecting.*

quality: a product's or service's characteristic making it appropriate for its intended goal; a product or service that is valid.

quality check: a form of product checking carried out by the receiving department where the condition of the arriving merchandise is determined.

quality creep: a new product that is better than it needs to be to fulfill needs of its target customers.

quality discount: a lowering of price offered by the seller as a way to get the purchaser to buy large quantities of the item.

quality market: a market in which quality is more important than price.

quantity check: a form of merchandise checking done in the receiving department in which correctness of quantity received is verified.

quantity demanded: the amount that would be purchased at a particular price, at a time.

quantity discount: See *patronage discount.*

quasi-chain: independently owned retail outlets that are affiliated with a form of central organization. See *voluntary chain.*

query: a customer or prospective customer's request for information on his or her account or about the item or service involved. See *customer service.*

quick response (QR): a partnership between vendor and retailer through which orders are replenished automatically via computer link up. See *quick response (QR) inventory system.*

quick response (QR) inventory system: a cooperative effort between retailers and their suppliers aimed at reducing retail inventory while providing a merchandise supply that more closely addresses the actual buying patterns of consumers. See *quick response.*

quota:

(1) *general:* the amount of production expected from the average employee in order to receive the specified base pay. See *sales quota.*

(2) *merchandising:* a specific limit on the number of items of a particular kind that may be imported.

quota bonus plan: a sales compensation method where a salesperson is paid a bonus for sales greater than a predetermined amount, or quota.

quotation: an offer to sell goods at a stated price and under specified conditions.

quoted price: the stated price for merchandise or a service.

RAC: See *Retail Advertising Conference.*

racetrack layout: Synonymous with *closed loop layout.*

rack: the floor stand for holding goods on shelves, hooks, or in pockets. See *rack jobber.*

rack display: See *rack.*

rack jobber:
(1) a limited-service wholesaler that supplies nonfood products to supermarkets, grocery stores, and drug retailers. (2) a wholesaler who maintains stocks of convenience-type merchandise, primarily in supermarkets, drugstores, and other related retail operations. He or she delivers merchandise by vehicle, sets up displays and makes frequent visits to stores and refills the inventory of display items. See *jobber; rack.*

rack merchandiser: See *rack jobber.*

Rack Service Association (RSA): located in Dresher, Pennsylvania, an association of manufacturers and retailers of items that are sold off racks. Provides members with access to retail outlets, assistance with display and visual merchandising, restocking and rotation of merchandise in stores on a regular basis.

radial site: a retailer found near major traffic arteries between the central business area and neighboring residential areas.

Radiation Control for Health and Safety Act of 1968: federal legislation establishing performance standards and limits of radiation that may be emitted from consumer items (television sets, microwave oven, etc.)

radiation selling: using a specific sale as a starting point for future related sales, based on the first sale as the example of need (e.g., selling the camera that will lead to sales of film and film processing services).

rag business (trade): (slang) name given to the fashion apparel industry. See *rags.*

rags: (slang) garments made by the apparel industry. See *rag business.*

rag trade: See *rag business.*

rain check: in retailing, a certificate giving the customer the privilege to purchase an out-of-stock advertised special at a later date at the same advertised price.

rate: the movement and handling of goods or persons, the determining factor used in arriving at the charge or fare for services rendered.

rate of sale: for staple stock, calculated as previous inventory plus new merchandise less the amount of merchandise currently on hand. The result is expressed for a specified period (e.g., 250 per week sold).

rate of stock turnover: See *stock turnover.*

rate war: a negative form of competition in which sellers drop their prices below their costs for purposes of putting the competition out of business. See *predatory pricing; underselling.*

rational buying motives: all costs of money, use, labor, and profit that affect a purchaser in buying merchandise. Cf. *motivation.*

rationalized retailing: the application of existing techniques and standards of efficiency to store management; encourages a centralized management control.

ratio of finished goods inventory to the cost of goods sold: a ratio determined by dividing the cost of goods sold by the average finished-goods inventory. The resulting figure is the number of times the investment in the finished-goods inventory has turned over during the period under consideration. The present ratio is compared with a similar ratio for several previous periods, since it portrays the stability and trend of sales, or a possibly overstated, or an expanded inventory.

reach:
(1) the percentage of total prospects that are exposed to a specific retail advertisement in a specified period.
(2) the total potential store audience a medium reaches, without duplication. See *audience; exposure area.* Synonymous with *media coverage.*

reactive selling: when customers seek out a particular vendor.

ready-to-wear (RTW):
(1) any article of apparel that is manufactured for sale in a retail store.
(2) mass-produced ready-made clothing made in factories to standard size

measurements for purchase by customers from racks.

real estate manager: the executive of the store responsible for the land and buildings occupied by the store, a warehouse, or other service facility operated or owned by the store.

real estate subsidiary: a subsidiary of a retail organization that exists to operate and own property. In this situation, the retailer can own an entire shopping center, leasing space to other tenants, and controlling the type of store included in the center as well as the hours of business, parking facilities, etc.

reason-why approach: See *factual approach.*

rebate:
(1) *general:* any refund of a payment.
(2) *retailing:* any deduction made from a payment or charge. In contrast to a discount, a rebate is not deducted in advance but is returned to the consumer following payment of the full amount (e.g., a GE appliance costs $24, with a rebate of $5 after the consumer has mailed in a coupon from the appliance package). Cf. *discount.*
(3) *retailing:* any refund given to a consumer for sending in proof-of-purchase following a sale. See *patronage dividend and rebate; refund offer.*

rebate offer: See *refund offer.*

rebuyer: the individual working in a large retail organization with responsibility for purchasing further merchandise. Traditionally, the buyer will have placed the original order with the rebuyer given the task of ordering items to bring inventories up to their proper level later in the year.

receipt: written acknowledgment of value received.

receipt-of-goods dating: See *regular dating; ROG dating.*

receipt-of-goods terms: a cash discount agreement specifying that the period for the discount allowed by the vendor to the retailer commences when goods reach the retailer instead of the shipment date. It purports to benefit retailers far from their resources.

receivables: bills and payments due to a creditor; can be a customer's charge payments to the store or the amount owed by the store to its vendors.

receivables turnover: the financial ratio resulting from dividing net sales on account (i.e., credit sales) by the average net accounts receivable during the accounting period. A means of examining the company's operations over the accounting period.

receivables turnover =

$$\frac{\text{net sales on account}}{\text{average net accounts receivable during period}}$$

receiving:

(1) accepting and taking physical possession of goods delivered to a store or warehouse.

(2) the department or location within in a store that is responsible for accepting, opening, checking, and often marking merchandise delivered to a store.

receiving apron: a statement used in the receiving department of a store that contains all pertinent data concerning an incoming shipment. The form is used to identify the shipment for purposes of accounting and control. Cf. *invoice apron.* See *pro forma invoice.*

receiving book: the recording, located in the retailer's receiving department where incoming shipments of items are entered. Information recorded include the number of packages, the name of vendors, dates of arrival, etc.

receiving dock: the platform, usually at the rear of the store, where freight cars, trucks, or other deliverers are loaded and unloaded. Synonymous with *loading dock.*

receiving by invoice: checking a shipment of merchandise as it arrives at the store or warehouse against an accompanying invoice.

receiving by purchase order: checking a shipment of goods received by the retailer against the purchase order, a copy of which remains on file in the store.

recency/frequency: the measure of the value of a customer or group of customers based on the number of purchases made and the length of time in between purchases as well as the time passed since the last purchase. The most valued customer has a high degree of recency and frequency. See *recency/frequency/monetary value.*

recency/frequency/monetary   value: the measures for determining the value of a customer or group of customers based on time since the last purchase, the number of actual purchases, and the dollar value of the bought merchandise. See *recency/frequency.*

receptivity to innovation: the extent to which a person or firm is willing to consider and hopefully purchase a new item or process.

recessed front: the store entrance, including the receding space or niche where customers get out of the traffic flow, examine the store's window displays, and through which they can enter the structure.

reciprocity:

(1) in retailing, the purchasing of goods by one retailer from another on a preferential basis, with the expectation that the second retailer will preferentially buy the goods of the first.

(2) in international retailing, a provision of a guarantee of similar or at least nondiscriminatory opportunities for retailers to operate in foreign markets on the same basis as local retailers.

recommended retail price: See *suggested retail price.*

recording delay: the delayed response effect indicating a time lag between the actual buying of merchandise and the manufacturer's knowledge of the purchase in his or her accounting records. Important because it impacts on re-orders, promotional needs, etc.

recovery:

(1) *general:* the period of the business cycle that follows a depression.

(2) *retailing:* the difference between the purchasing price and the selling price of goods or services.

rectangular layout: See *grid layout.*

recruiting: the activity of locating skilled salespeople and inducing them to apply for employment.

redemption: returning, usually to a retailer, coupons or proofs of purchase in order to receive a discount or premium. Firms follow these numbers to measure the effectiveness of a promotion. See *redemption center.*

redemption center: a store or outlet established by a trading stamp firm where holders can redeem filled stamp booklets for goods. See *redemption.* Synonymous with *redemption store.*

redemption store: See *redemption center.*

red goods: food items and other consumer goods that are consumed and replaced at a rapid rate and have a low profit margin. Cf. *brown goods; orange goods; white goods; yellow goods.*

rediscount: to discount for the second time.

red label: a shipping label indicating flammable contents.

reduced-price pack: a package clearly marked with a price that is less than regular retail.

reduced rate: See *allowance; discount.*

reduction: See *retail reduction.*

reduction from retail: See *retail reduction.*

reference group: See *membership group.*

referral: See *referral leads.*

referral gift: See *referral premium.*

referral leads: names of potential customers given to a sales representative, usually by satisfied customers. Referrals respond to promotions at a much higher rate than other prospects. See *friend-of-a-friend promotion; lead.*

referral premium: a reward offered to a satisfied customer when a prospect recommended by the customer purchases a product or service. See *premium.*

refund: dollar returned by a seller of merchandise or services in exchange for the return of some part of merchandise or service; can be in the form of store credit, cash, or check.

refund check: a statement for a customer's purchase that is returned.

refund offer:

(1) a sales-promotion technique guaranteeing the purchaser a refund if not completely satisfied. See *rebate; trial offer.*

(2) a sales-promotion or manufacturer technique promising to refund part of the sales price to the consumer upon receipt of proof of purchase. Synonymous with *rebate offer.*

refusal to deal: a stipulation that a manufacturer or distributor can refuse to sell to a buyer only if no joint action between them and other buyers exists. Attempts to eliminate any conspiracy to fix prices or to restrain trade.

refusal to sell: the right of a seller to choose the dealers that will handle his or her merchandise. Invoking this right, which is recognized by law, a seller may refuse to deal with firms that do not meet certain standards or qualifications. See *franchise.*

regional center: See *regional shopping center.*

regional chain: a chain store with involvement limited to a specific area or region of the nation.

regional department store: a department store, often with branches that services an area larger than a metropolitan area but not as large as the entire country. For example, the region might be taken to include the area between Boston and New York City.

regional manager: the individual working in a large retailing organization who is responsible for tasks of all the stores in a specific geographical area of the nation. Synonymous with *territory manager.*

regional mart: the central location where producers, importers, and others display their goods for store buyers and merchandise managers from within that general area of the nation (e.g., the Chicago Merchandise Mart).

regional shopping center: the largest type of shopping center with one or more full-line department stores and complemented by 50 to 150 (or more) smaller retail stores and related firms; attracts customers from a wide geographical area and requires perhaps as many as 100,000 purchasers to make it profitable. Road accessibility is critical.

regional store: a branch store, usually located far from the central store, that functions under the name of the parent store. In most cases, operates an autonomous unit. Cf. *branch store; regional department store.* Once synonymous with *parent store;* today, rarely used.

regional wholesaler: See *sectional wholesaler.*

regional wrap: See *central wrap.*

register:
(1) *general:* to record a trademark, patent, copyright, etc., with a governmental unit so as to claim exclusivity.
(2) *retailing:* a unit or machine for temporarily storing information while or until it is used (i.e., a store's cash register).

register audit: See *floor audit.*

registered trademark: See *trademark.*

register tape: the paper tape where all sales transactions performed by the store's cash register are recorded.

regular account: See *charge account.*

regular charge account: See *charge account.*

regular dating: terms of a sale under which the period for discount and the date on which payment is required are determined from the date of the invoice. Cf. *ROG dating.* See *ordinary terms.*

regularly unsought items: products that are regularly required by consumers, but which they will not go out of their way to purchase. For example, reference books for their children, insurance coverage. These items are often heavily promoted to increase consumer awareness and sales. Cf. *new unsought goods.*

regular merchandise allowance: See *returns and allowances.*

regular wholesaler: See *full-service wholesaler.*

Reilly's Law of Retail Gravitation: a theory stating that the relative pull of two competing shopping areas on potential customers resides between them; suggesting that customers are drawn from the intermediate town at or close to the point of equal probability, approximately in direct proportion to the populations of the two shopping areas and in inverse proportion to the squares of the distance between the town and the two shopping areas. See *point of equal probability.*

reinstatement:
(1) *general:* restoration of a worker to a former position without the loss of seniority or benefits.
(2) *retailing:* placement of a customer's record back into active status after being suspended, canceled, or becoming inactive.

related item display: See *cross merchandising.*

related merchandise: merchandise that complement or otherwise go with the item being bought by the customer.

related packaging: the coordination of package design and/or coloring for all items of a particular manufacturer to promote customer recognition.

relationship marketing: See *database marketing.*

reliability:

(1) *general:* accuracy and dependability.

(2) *retailing:* the consistency of performance of goods, i.e., a hair dryer is guaranteed to continue to work the same way over and over again until the warranty date passes. See *product reliability.*

remainder: goods that remain unsold at its original price because of a lack of demand; then sold at a lower price. Synonymous with *overstock.*

remarking:

(1) altering the price on the price tag of an item. Should the new price be lower than the original, both prices remain visible. Should a higher price replace a lower price, the older price is often covered. The Federal Trade Commission requires that both the old and the new price be accurate.

(2) replacing tickets on goods that are lost or mutilated or removed due to customer returns. New tickets are required to contain all of the original information for accurate inventory control.

remerchandising: an approach to improve the sale ability of a product while leaving the item, itself, unchanged. Alterations are made instead in the accompanying services such as standardization of product quality, improvement of product service, and the promotion of promotional guarantees.

reminder promotion: a sales promotion aimed at getting customers to stock up on certain merchandise before there is a price increase.

remittance: funds forwarded from one person to another as payment for purchased items or services.

remnant: a small piece of cloth, ribbon, or other yard goods that remain at the end of a bolt.

remote delivery: sending goods from a central warehouse to customers via area delivery stations located in the suburbs or by truck.

removal sale: a reduction in the cost of goods by the retailer who is in the process of relocating his or her place of work. Often storewide, and usually intended to lower inventories as much as possible before the relocation while providing liquid assets.

rented-goods service: involves the leasing of a good for a specified period of time.

reorder: a retailer's request for further goods from his or her vendor in order to replenish depleted stocks of fast moving items. Synonymous with *replenishment reorder.*

reorder number: a fast-selling item that retailers constantly replenish with more merchandise supplied by the vendor.

reorder period: the planned spacing of time between orders of a specific item.

reorder point: the pre-established minimum inventory level at which additional orders should be placed for a particular item; serves to replenish stock and to assure continued availability of the item to customers. See *Q-system.*

reorder system: See *Q-system.*

reorder unit: the amount of an item that can be reordered. For example, a dozen.

reorder window: in fashion merchandising, the time span when a style can be reordered with a degree of confidence that sufficient information has been gathered on sales to justify the reorder, and that sufficient time remains in the life of the style to sell further numbers without taking excessive markdowns.

rep: short for *representative*.

repeat demand: the demand created for items that are frequently requested and bought.

repeated event: See *repeat event*.

repeat event: a sales promotion featuring the sale of specially priced merchandise repeated after its initial success. Usually requires a reorder of the merchandise.

repeating technique: See *mirror response technique*.

repeat purchasing: purchasing the same item or service from the same source of supply over a given time period.

repeat sales: sales perpetuated by going back to the same store or retailer to make a purchase.

replacement branch: a new branch store replacing and substituting for an older facility of the same parent organization.

replacement potential: as measured in unit or dollars, the sales potential of merchandise to present consumers who will require replacing the item within a fixed time period.

replacement price: the current market price of an item that should be reordered.

replacement rate: the frequency with which merchandise is bought by consumers.

replenishment order: See *reorder*.

repossess: See *repossession*.

repossession: the reclaiming or taking back of items that were bought on an installment sales contract on which the buyer has fallen behind in payments.

repricing: making small markdowns to stimulate buying interest when many customers are still in the market. Repricing is critical when the replacement cost of items increases where goods on shelves must be marked up to cover the higher replacement cost.

repurchase rate: the repeat sales of an item, i.e., sales to people who are purchasing the product for the second or third time.

requisition: a written demand from a department to its purchasing department to release on a specific date materials to be used in a production process or other activity of consumption within an organization. See *store's requisition*.

requisition stock control: See *reserve system of stock control*.

resale: the selling of goods or services that have been bought by the seller from another person in essentially the same form.

resale price maintenance:

(1) the practice by a supplier of prescribing, and taking action to enforce, retail or wholesale prices for the resale of items.

(2) a supplier's control over the selling price of his or her goods at various stages of distribution by means of contractual arrangement under fair trade laws or other means. See *fair trade price; price fixing; retail price maintenance*.

reseller: See *jobber*.

reseller brand: See *private brand*.

reserve requisition: a written request that items located in a reserve or warehouse area be brought to the selling floor.

reserve requisition control: See *reserve system of stock control*.

reserves: See *reserve stock*.

reserve stock: goods on hand that serve as a cushion against stockouts because of unexpectedly high demand or delivery delays. Synonymous with *backup merchandise; buffer stock*.

reserve stock control: See *reserve system of stock control*.

reserve system of stock control: a method of unit control focusing on the stock in the reserve stockroom instead of on the selling floor. Records are retained of all goods sent to the selling floor and all goods received from vendors. The reserve stock is determined by subtracting all goods sent to the selling floor and adding new items received from vendors. An actual cost is not carried out.

resident buyer: any person or firm located in a market area who aids retailers in making market contracts and assists in their purchasing. Cf. *merchandise mart.*

resident buying office: See *buying office.*

resident salesperson: a supplier's salesperson located within the structure of one of the supplier's primary accounts. He or she provides full attention to the customer's needs.

resource:
(1) *general:* anything a country uses to produce goods and services (manpower, minerals, oil, etc.).
(2) *merchandising:* a producer or wholesaler from whom a merchant buys goods for resale. See *merchandise resource.* Cf. *vendor.*

resource analysis: the ongoing assessment of vendors to conclude which ones the retailer should continue purchasing goods from. Factors such as product line, reliability, delivery time, etc., are taken into account by means of the resource file. See *resource file.*

resource file: the gathering of information relating to each vendor with whom the store has done business. Facts include the performance of goods, delivery record, condition of goods, etc. See *resource analysis.*

resource rating: the measurement and assessment of vendors with whom the store has done business to determine each vendor's contribution to the retailer's sales volume and profits. See *resource analysis.*

restricted articles: articles that are handled only under certain conditions.

restrictive lease clause: the limiting section in a retailer's lease, especially dealing with shopping centers; attempts to control the type of items to be carried, discounting, hours and days the store is open, and employee parking.

retail:
(1) the sale of goods in small quantities to the ultimate consumer.
(2) merchandise sold at list price. See *list price.*
(3) See *retailing.*

retail accordion theory: a concept describing the evolution of retail institutions from general, broad-based outlets with wide assortments, to narrow-based institutions carrying specialized assortments, and back to general, broad-based assortments. Synonymous with *general-specific-general theory.*

retail accounting: See *retail method of accounting.*

retail advertising: The dissemination of sales messages by retail store operators through local media, such as newspapers and non-network radio and television, directed toward those consumers living within the trading area of the advertiser.

Retail Advertising Conference (RAC): located in Chicago, Illinois, an association of people involved in retail sales promotion, retail advertising, and serving retailers in a promotional capacity. Elects "Pro of the Year" to the Retail Advertising Hall of Fame.

Retail Advertising Hall of Fame: See *Retail Advertising Conference.*

retail assembly line: a conveyor belt system for retail mail-order firms to assemble customer orders. As merchandise is taken from stock, it is placed on conveyor belts and moved to a central location for shipping.

retail audit: the timely, systematic evaluation of a retail organization to determine the retailer's strengths and weaknesses, study its objectives, and improve performance. See *objective*.

retail brand: See *private brand*.

retail buyer: See *buyer*.

retail calendar: a retailer's planning calendar. It divides the year into four thirteen-week quarters where each week and month commences with a Sunday and ends with a Saturday. Synonymous with *4-5-4 calendar*.

retail catalog showroom: a discount retailer where consumers select merchandise from a catalog and shop at a warehouse-style location. Customers typically write up their own orders, products are usually stocked in a back room, and there are limited displays.

retail chain: involves the common ownership of multiple units. See *factory outlet*.

retail conglomerate: See *merchandising conglomerate*.

retail cooperative: a voluntary association of independent retailers who jointly own and operate their own wholesale facilities and often serve as a buying club to achieve the economies of large scale purchasing.

retail credit card: See *charge account; credit card*.

retail deal: an offering of goods at retail, either in the form of a price reduction or as multiple units at a special price. See *consumer deal; deal*.

retail display: See *display*.

retail display allowance: a decrease in the funds paid by the retailer to the manufacturer in exchange for a more favorable display of the item in the store or on the shelf.

retailer:
(1) a merchant whose primary activity is to sell directly to consumers.
(2) an intermediary that sells products primarily to ultimate consumers. There are store retailers—operators of department stores, outlets, supermarkets, boutiques—and nonstore retailers—firms that sell through mail-order catalogs, have direct-selling procedures, or operate vending machines.
(3) a firm that buys items from a manufacturer or wholesaler for resale to the goods' ultimate consumers at a profit; usually for personal and household consumption.
(4) See *affiliated retailer; general line retailer; general merchandise retailer; independent retailer; mail-order retailer; multiple retailers; noncompeting retailers; nonstore retailer; normal margin retailer; special-line retailers; specialty line retailer; store retailer; variable location retailers; wagon retailer*. See also *retailing*.

retailer brand: See *private brand*.

retailer coupon: See *coupon*.

retail franchising: a contractual agreement between a franchisor (a manufacturer, wholesaler, or service sponsor) and a retail franchise, which allows the franchisee to conduct a certain form of business under an establishment name and according to a specific set of rules.

retail hub: the center of retail activity where numerous retailers are found.

retailing:
(1) the activity of purchasing for resale to a customer.
(2) all activities undertaken by intermediaries whose primary function is to sell goods and services to ultimate consumers. The four functions of retailing are: (a) buying and storing merchandise; (b) transferring title of those items; (c) providing information on the nature and uses of those goods; and (d) in some situations, extending credit to buyers.
(3) See *catalog retailing; cooperative retailing; door-to-door retailing; electronic retailing; house-to-house*

retailing; in-home retailing; interactive retailing; international retailing; low-margin retailing; main-floor retailing; nonpersonal retailing; nonstore retailing; off-price retailing; outlet retailing; positioned retailing; rationalized retailing; round-the-clock retailing; self-service retailing; shop-at-home retailing; telephone retailing; television retailing; warehouse retailing; wheel of retailing. See also *retailer.* Cf. *wholesaling.*

retailing cooperative: See *retail cooperative.*

retailing cost: See *cost.*

retailing mix: the retail store's combination of controllable factors that create a unique image and position in the market. Factors include product, price, promotions, place, operating policy, purchasing, personnel, service, etc. Synonymous with *trade marketing mix.*

retailing strategy mix: See *retailing mix.*

retailing the invoice: where retail prices are indicated on the seller's invoice as approval for the markers in a receiving area. See *preretailing.*

retail installment credit account: See *all-purpose revolving account.*

retail life cycle: the evolution of a retail store from its inception to its decline, with four stages passed thru—innovation, accelerated development, maturity, and decline.

retail market audit: See *retail audit.*

retail marketing: where sales objectives are set based on market potential with heightened attention to the consumer's behavior; concerned with who is purchasing what and the underlying reasons for this action.

retail marketing research: the application of the principles of marketing research to the formulation of a retail strategy in the sale of goods and/or services to the consumer.

retail merchandising: the principles of merchandising as applied to the sale of merchandise to the consumer.

retail method of accounting: an accounting system where all percentages relate to the retail price of goods. Cf. *cost method of accounting.*

retail method of inventory: an accounting technique for recording all inventory inputs, including sales, purchases, markdowns, and so on, at their retail values. Purchased items are recorded at cost. See *markdown; markdown cancellation; markup; markup cancellation.* Cf. *cost method of inventory.*

retail organization:

(1) the arrangement and relationship of tasks within a store.

(2) the interrelationships between the units of a multi-unit retail operation (e.g., a parent store and its branches).

retail outlet: a store that sells directly to the customer.

retail personality: the way a store is defined in a consumer's mind. Many retailers go to great lengths to create an aura in their stores that can transform a visit into a unique adventure.

retail polarity: See *polarity of retail trade.*

retail policy: See *policy.*

retail price: the price at which goods are identified for sale or are sold.

retail price maintenance: allowing a manufacturer, under protection of state law, to set retail prices for his or her products. This is in accord with the terms of the fair trade acts. See *fair trade acts.*

retail promotion: See *sales promotion.*

retail reduction: the factors identified that cause a lower retail value of a retailer's inventory. Factors include markdowns, employee and other discounts, and stock shortages; expressed as the difference between the original retail value of the merchandise and net sales.

retail sale: the sale of items to the ultimate consumer.

retail salesperson: an individual who works inside a store, where customers come to him or her.

retail saturation: See *index of saturation; saturated area.*

retail security: the prevention and detection of goods and money shortages because of internal and external theft; includes guards, cameras, and detection devices.

retail space: See *selling area.*

retail store: a business that provides goods for sale to customers; buys, stores, promotes, and sells the items.

retail store cooperative: a store that is owned and operated by a number of people as a source of supply for at least a certain kind of product.

retail store strategy mix: consists of an integrated combination of hours, location, assortment, service, advertising, prices, and other factors retailers employ. See *strategy.*

retail strategy mix: See *retail store strategy mix.*

retail unit: the quantity of goods in a package sold by the retailer to the consumer.

Retail Virus Control Center: established in 1989 by the NRMA to collect and disseminate information on computer viruses.

retention cycle: the time an inactive customer's record is retained.

retrieval requests: See *chargebacks.*

return: See *returns; returns and allowances.*

return on assets: See *return on investment.*

return on investment (ROI): a measure of the profitability of a store or a department that compares the net profit to the amount of money needed to operate the store and, by extension, create a profit:

$$\text{ROI} = \frac{\text{net profit}}{\text{amount of investment}}$$

return on investment approach to advertising: a technique for setting the retailer's store's advertising budget by considering advertising a capital investment rather than a current expense. The profit generated by the advertising is compared to the amount of money required to advertise.

return per square foot: the dollar amount of sales contributed by a square foot of selling space within a department:

return per square foot =

$$\frac{\text{total sales for department}}{\text{number of square feet in department}}$$

return policy: regulations covering the return of goods by store customers; can include or exclude exchange, credit, cash refunds, and adjustments.

return room: that part of the store reserved for the inspection of damaged and unacceptable goods before it is returned to the vendor.

returns: goods returned to a supplier for credit, and sometimes, refunds. See *returns and allowances.*

returns and allowances: in retailing, the total dollar amounts of items that were returned to the seller by dissatisfied customers (returns) and the total price reductions/discounts that were granted to consumers by the seller (allowances). The monetary amount of returns and allowances deducted from the outlet's gross sales to arrive at total net sales. See *returns.* Synonymous with *vendor allowances.*

returns to vendor (RTV): merchandise returned to the vendor by a store for various reasons (e.g., damaged merchandise, lateness of delivery). See *vendor chargebacks.* Cf. *purchase allowance.* Synonymous with *vendor returns.*

reusable packaging: containers that have another use subsequent to their service as merchandise containers.

revenue: the grant total of all resources received from the sale of a firm's product or service during a stated period; not to be confused with general revenue.

revenue-and-expense budget: See *operations budgeting.*

reverse-order perception: the rate occurrence when consumers prefer to purchase the more expensive item because of the perception that the price is a better bargain. For example, an item market $19.95 may be thought to be a better buy than the same merchandise were it marked $16.50.

revision of retail downward: See *additional markup cancellation.*

revolving account: See *all-purpose revolving account; revolving charge account.*

revolving charge account: See *all-purpose revolving account.*

revolving credit: a regular 30-day charge account that is paid in full or in monthly installments. Paid in full within 30 days of the statement date will not commence any finance charge. Cf. *installment credit.*

rewrap: the provision of new packaging for goods should there be damage to the original container.

ribbon development: retail establishments found along a major highway containing, among other businesses, appliance and furniture stores, fast-food chains, gas stations, banks, etc.

rifle approach: See *rifle technique.*

rifle technique: the sales practice of concentrating on selling only a few items, using a carefully prepared style of presentation that will lead to a rapid decision. Cf. *shotgun approach.*

right of rescission: the privilege, guaranteed by the Truth in Lending Act, of canceling a contract under certain circumstances within three business days, without penalty and with full refund of all deposits that have been submitted. See *Truth in Lending Act of 1968.*

rights of consumers: a doctrine enunciated by President John F. Kennedy, stating that consumers have the right to be safe, to be informed, to choose, and to be heard.

rigidity of demand: the degree to which customers are willing or unwilling to accept a substitute for the desired product. The rigid variable can be an unbending attachment to size, color, style, price, etc.

rigid-limit plan: a type of revolving credit where the customer's credit limit is determined by the amount of the fixed monthly payment.

rigid pricing: See *one-price policy.*

ring of perishables: in supermarket retailing, the placement of perishable items, such as produce and dairy products, around the store's walls.

riser: a card or poster in the back of a display that extends over the goods and usually gives the retailer's message.

risk analysis: a strategic planning activity where the external threats of the marketplace are identified and evaluated in terms of their potential impact on the organization and the chances of occurrence.

risk reduction: the effort by a customer to solve a problem and make a purchase at the same time, cutting down on the uncertainties linked with a product or service. The customer is provided with a host of materials, information brochures, etc., to reduce this risk.

ROA (return on assets): See *return on investment.*

road buying: purchasing items directly from traveling salespeople.

Robinson-Patman Act of 1936: federal legislation, amending the Clayton Antitrust Act of 1914, in which price discrimination practices are more clearly identified. Quantity discounts in excess of the cost savings realized by selling in such quantities are declared illegal, as are false brokerage deals. Promotional allowances must be made to all buyers on a proportionately equal basis, and price discrimination is acceptable if it is done to meet a proper low price of a competitor and if the price does not restrict competition. Synonymous with *chain store law.* See *Colgate Doctrine of 1919; price discrimination; volume bonus.*

ROG: See *ROG dating.*

ROG dating: receipt-of-goods dating. Under this condition of sale, the date for payment and the discount period are determined from the date the buyer obtains shipment, rather than from the invoice date. This procedure is primarily employed when large shipping distances are involved. Cf. *regular dating.*

ROI: See *return on investment.*

roll-out:
(1) *general:* the expansion of a new item into previously unknown markets from a local introduction.
(2) *merchandising:* an approach to new-product introduction in which the product is launched in a series of geographic areas over an extended period.

rotated inventory control: See *rotated merchandise control.*

rotated merchandise control: counting a retailer's inventory on a rotated or staggered basis by scheduling counts on specific days.

rotation of products: See *product rotation.*

rounder: a circular display rack for large numbers of garments or other goods; can be rotated by the customer for greater convenience and accessibility to the merchandise.

round-the-clock retailing: where the retail store is open to customers on a 24-hour a day, seven-day a week basis.

round turn: in merchandising, synonymous with *turn.*

route selling: the sale of goods and services to customers on an established delivery schedule, i.e., milk delivery, diaper services.

routine sale: See *routine selling.*

routine selling: personal selling involving contact with customers prior to the customer's decision to buy, but does not require a great deal of technical knowledge on the part of the salesperson.

routing: the selection of a path and steps in the operation performed on materials during the manufacturing process. Salespeople use routing in the hope of ensuring that a territory is adequately covered at the lowest possible cost to the selling organization. Cf. *traffic.*

routing instructions: directions for the vendor attached to the purchase order by the buyer. These directions indicate the shipping instructions and preferred means of transport.

royalty: in retailing, the payment made by a franchisee to a franchisor.

RSA: See *Rack Service Association.*

RTV: See *returns to vendor.*

RTW: See *ready-to-wear.*

rubber banding: a return agreement for cosmetic items allowing the store to return the item to the manufacturer if not sold within a specified time period.

rub off: a sales increase, attained by the department, resulting from a promotion in another department.

runner: See *best seller; running.*

running: in merchandising, a best-selling item, especially one that is continually kept in stock because of its heavy sales volume. Cf. *sleeper.* See *best seller; fill-ins.*

run sizes: the number of items manufactured at one time in a given lot.

SA: See *Seventh Avenue.*

safety stock: See *cushion.*

salaried buying office: an independent resident buying office where a fixed fee is paid on an annual contractual basis by the retailers it represents.

salary plus commission: a compensation package where the worker receives a straight salary plus a percentage of his or her total sales during a given time period. See *commission.*

sale:
(1) *general:* the agreement to perform a service in return for cash or the expectation of cash payment.
(2) *retailing:* the offering of goods at a lower than regular price. See *sales.*

sale advertising: advertising where the low price is of primary importance and the expanding of store traffic a major objective.

sale-below-cost laws: See *unfair practices acts.*

sale merchandise:
(1) goods from regular stock with lowered prices.
(2) merchandise specially bought for the purpose of the sale.

sales:
(1) revenue received the sale of goods.
(2) final sales plus producer item sales.

(3) the occupation of being a salesperson.
(4) See *gross sales; net sales; sale; selling.*

sales agent: See *agent; selling agent.*

sales allowance: a lowering of the price of an item when merchandise delivered is not exactly what was ordered by a buyer.

sales analysis: an aspect of market research involving the systematic study and comparison of sales information; carried out for specific territories, products, or salespeople, quarterly, monthly, or annually. See *systems selling.* Cf. *cost analysis.*

sales anchors: concepts and statements used by sales representatives when attempting to overcome customer resistance.

sales aptitude: the capability to achieve success in the sales field, as acknowledged by a sales department and measured by means of interviews and recommendations.

sales audit: an audit that is a comprehensive assessment of sales strategy of fulfilling sales objectives with the aim to improve the overall effectiveness of the salespeople. This audit purports to determine whether or not the objectives set are realistic, appropriate, and reachable. It can also determine the store's sales plans and policies. Usually, a sales audit is carried out by an independent consulting organization.

sales-based pricing objectives: goals that orient a store's pricing strategy toward high sales volume and/or expanding its share of sales relative to competitors.

sales-below-cost laws: See *unfair practices acts.*

sales branch: a producer's outlet that maintains inventory and delivers to buyers from that stock.

sales broker: an agent who, though not physically handling merchandise that he or she deals with, nor has little control over the terms of a contract between principal and third party.

sales budget: a budget based on forecasted sales for a coming period; usually includes all marketing expenditures of which selling is only a part. Will have an impact on the funds provided to the sales department over a set time period.

sales call pattern: a pattern of effort where salespeople in the field call on prospective customers. The pattern evolves by: (a) the universe of target customers and their geographical distribution; (b) the frequency of calls required by each customer; (c) the cost-effectiveness of calling; and (d) the selling culture of, and competitive sales pattern in, the particular universe of customers.

sales check: the paper on which a sale is recorded by the salesperson.

sales check control: an inventory method where data is collected from sales checks rather than from other sources, such as price tag stubs.

sales clerk: an individual in a retail store who records the customers' purchases, who usually is responsible for maintaining stock, and who at times helps the customer in making a selection from the available stock. A minimum of salesmanship need be employed by a sales clerk.

sales closing: See *close.*

sales compensation: in retailing, money paid to store salespeople in the form of straight compensation, salary, or a combination of both. The three primary form of sales compensation are:

(a) straight salary—paying a salesperson a fixed annual amount.

(b) commission basis—compensation based on the salesperson's performance, e.g., as a percentage of sales that he or she generates.

(c) combination compensation—mixing a straight salary arrangement with a commission.

sales contest: a sponsored competition, usually by a dealer or manufacturer of an item, where outstanding sales efforts and results are rewarded.

sales demonstration: illustrating how an item functions and what its potential is. Demo used as shortened form. Synonymous with *demonstration.*

sales development: a selling plan that aspires to increase the flow of new customers.

sales discount: See *cash discount.*

sales efficiency: the correlation between sales volume or value and individual and total selling expenses.

sales era: involves hiring a salesforce and sometimes advertising to sell inventory, after production is maximized. The role of the salesforce and advertising is to make the desires of consumers fit the attributes of the products being manufactured.

sales exception reporting: where products are documented as either slow- or fast-selling.

salesforce: canvassers and sales representatives who contact potential purchasers of goods and attempt to persuade them that they should buy items being sold. These people are organized by geographic territory, type of merchandise, the market, or any combination of these factors. See *territory-structured salesforce.*

salesforce promotion: See *salesforce.*

sales forecast: a dollar or unit sales estimated made for a specified period in a store's campaign. See *forecasting.*

sales grabber: a salesperson who endeavors to wait on more buyers than his or her fellow salespeople in an effort to gain a disproportionately large share of sales.

sales incentive: offered by the manufacturer; traditionally money provided for a salesperson for exceeding some preset sales goal. Other perks include free trips, special prizes, etc.

sales invoice: the main written, typed, or computer-generated source of sales analysis data.

sales journal: a book in which records of sales are entered.

sales lead: providing the salesperson with information or a contact to assist in his or her selling efforts.

sales letter: a correspondence from a selling firm that is sent to prospective or existing customers; providing information on the product or service, with reasons for a quick reaction from the reader.

sales management: management activities in the development of a skilled salesforce. Involves recruiting, selecting and training, plus follow-up activities of supervision and motivation. See *sales analysis; sales audit; sales manager.*

sales manager: an executive responsible for planning, directing, and controlling the activities of sales personnel. The manager plans the store's sales objectives and strategies for achieving these objectives. Also organizes and directs efforts of the salesforce, develops sales programs, and monitors overall sales performance in relation to stated sales goals. See *sales management.* Cf. *product manager.*

salesmanship: the art of selling goods or services by creating a demand or need for a particular item or service and realizing an actual order. See *creative selling; hard sell; low-pressure selling; service selling.* Cf. *conmanship.*

sales manual: a book describing the product, merchandise, or service to be sold and suggesting approaches for selling to a customer.

sales mix: a combination of the various company products leading to a store's total sales.

sales objective: See *sales quota.*

sales office: a facility for taking orders and handling adjustments that serves as a contact point for suppliers and customers. No inventory is maintained at the office. Cf. *merchandise mart.*

sales penetration: the degree to which a store is achieving its sales potential as measured by:

$$\text{sales penetration} = \frac{\text{actual sales}}{\text{sales potential}}$$

sales per dollar invested in inventory: the dollar amount created by money invested in inventory.

salesperson:

(1) *general:* a person who practices salesmanship. Synonymous with *sales representative.*

(2) *retailing:* a person having the responsibility for actually selling merchandise, preparing a sales check, recording the sales, and receiving payment from the customer. See *clerk.*

salesperson wrap: covering of goods by the floor salesperson rather than by another individual in a central location; provides fast service to the customer, helps promote good will, and maintains the communication between the salesperson and the customer. See *package wrap.*

sales per square foot of gross space: the amount in dollars generated by merchandise or a line, or by a department or an entire store determined on an annual basis. All square footage in the store is used in making the computation including nonselling areas:

$$\frac{\text{gross sales}}{\text{square feet of space in store}} =$$

sales per square foot of gross space

sales per square foot of selling space: the dollars generated by merchandise or a line, or by a department or an entire store calculated on an annual basis. Only the square footage devoted to selling is used in making the computation:

$$\frac{\text{gross sales}}{\text{square feet of selling space}} =$$

sales per square foot selling space

sales pitch: a strong statement aimed at persuading a potential customer to buy the salesperson's product or service. See *pitch.*

sales plan: a merchandise budget that contains a detailed projection of sales for a given period, specifying the purchases, inventory, and so on, needed to achieve this goal.

sales planning: that part of marketing planning work concerned with making sales forecasts, devising programs for reaching the sales target, and evolving a sales budget.

sales potential: fulfilling the identified markets share or market objective with consumers. See *market potential; market share.*

sales potential forecast: a forecast of total potential sales for the firm for a specific time period.

sales presentation: the total selling process of describing to a potential customer the product or service, including the attempt to plan an order.

sales productivity method of space allocation: space that will be allocated to a product category based on the sales (or profits) the product has achieved in the past on a square foot basis.

sales promotion: the array of techniques that retailers use to stimulate immediate purchases, includes using coupons, rebates, continuity programs, price packs, premiums, samples, contests, sweepstakes, incentives, point-of-purchase advertising, and events marketing. See *promotion.* Synonymous with *demand creation; demand stimulation.*

sales promotion agency: the firm specializing in supplying broad sales promotion services to clients.

sales quota: a projected goal for sales of a product. Assessing a salesperson's performance is frequently based on the actual sales generated contrasted with a sales quota. Synonymous with *sales objective.* See *quota.*

sales record control: a system dealing with goods, used in unit control based on the analysis of sales ticket stubs, saleschecks, and other sales records which reflect an alteration of inventory.

sales register: See *register.*

sales reports: written reports summarizing back to management results of sales performance and salesperson's activities. These reports can detail customers' reactions to items, services, or company procedures, in addition to competitors' efforts.

sales representative: See *manufacturer's agent.*

sales resistance: the presenting of objections on the customer's part to the personal sales effort.

sales retail: the last sales price at retail, that is, the original retail price less discounts and allowances, shrinkage, and any markdowns.

sales, returns, and allowances: a contra-sales account in which the returns or allowances for previously sold merchandise are recorded.

sales revenue: total income derived from sales for a stated time period.

sales slip: the cash register receipt indicating money amounts, tax, and sales total, but without details of the transaction.

sales supporting services: store activities which are provided to support the profit-making segment of the business, for example, free alterations, free parking.

sales support staff: individuals who are not directly involved in selling goods, but whose performance assists the sales staff directly. For example, members of the sales promotion and publicity department, the fashion office staff, the display department.

sales tax: a tax levied by a state on items at the time of their purchase. It may be a tax on the sale of an item every time it changes hands or only upon its transfer of ownership at one specific time. The sales of manufacturers are taxed when the items are considered to be completed goods; the sales of wholesalers are taxed when their goods are sold to retailers; and retail sales are taxed when the goods are purchased by consumers.

sales terms: See *terms of sale.*

sales trainee: a recently hired sales representative who is engaged in learning the

basic concepts of selling. Usually the trainee receives a small salary during this period.

sales training: a firm's program for training sales personnel; may be carried out external to the institution, with the hiring of consultants or sending candidates to specialized programs or classes, or within the organization itself.

sales variance analysis: a method of data analysis in which data on actual sales are compared with quantitative sales objectives.

salon: a shop within a store for the selling of high-price apparel and accessories. Cf. *boutique.*

salutory items: where a consumer holds an item or service in low esteem because the high-priced item or service has yet to provide the satisfaction or benefit to the consumer.

salvage:
(1) *general:* equipment or property that is no longer used for its initial purpose.
(2) *merchandising:* goods that are soiled beyond reclamation for purposes of sale and thus usually disposed of by other means.

salvage merchandise: See *salvage (2).*

sample:
(1) *general:* items selected so that they represent the entire.
(2) *merchandising:* an item of a product which is a proper representative of all the units of that product.
(3) *retailing:* a portion of an item given away free to a prospective consumer. See *sampling.*

sample buyer: a person who buys at a special introductory rate or obtains at no cost a product sample. See *trial size.*

sample package: See *trial size.*

sample room:
(1) *general:* a room, usually adjoining the showroom of a manufacturer, in which representative models of the items offered for sale are presented for

inspection by the buyer. Sample rooms are common in the shoe industry.

(2) *retailing:* in a store, a room in which a manufacturer's samples are put on display.

sample selling: personal retail selling where the potential purchaser selects a sample of the item he or she wants (e.g., a shoe); takes it to a salesperson who, in turn, brings out the exact size and color from the reserve stock.

sampling: in retailing, the method where a market is exposed to new items in the store, packages, or package sizes by providing prospects with a miniature or actual unit of the item, hoping successful usage will lead to future purchases.

SANTA: See *Souvenir and Novelty Trade Association.*

satellite stores: smaller retailers, usually found in a shopping center, that are clustered around the large anchor stores.

satisfaction of demand: involves product availability, actual performance after purchase, perceptions of safety, after-sale service, and other factors.

satisficing: decision-making behavior in which the manager selects an alternative that is good enough (i.e., one that will yield a satisfactory return to the organization).

saturated area: a retail trading area in which there are just enough stores to provide goods and services for the population and not so many stores that they all cannot make a fair profit. See *index of saturation; saturated market.*

saturated market: a situation occurring when there is a greater supply of a particular item than there is demand for it. A store's item can gain market share at this point, only at the expense of another item. See *saturated area.*

saturation: when merchandise is no longer able to be sold because most consumers who are likely to be interested in it have already purchased it. Synonymous with *horizontal saturation.*

saturation interest: See *index of saturation.*

Savile Row: the London, England, street famous for its fine men's tailoring establishments.

SBD: See *secondary business district.*

SBUs: See *strategic business units.*

scan-it-yourself (SIY) technology: most developed in The Netherlands by applying hand-held laser scanners. Customers in Europe's largest grocery chain register to participate in the program and are issued an identification card with a mag strip. Customers enter the store, use the card to release one scanner from a locked rack storing 96 scanners. The customer uses the scanner, which contains an internal price look-up file and a display window, to scan and record each items as are placed in the shopping cart. The checkout procedure involves the printing of a receipt and the tendering of a payment.

scanner: in merchandising and retailing, an electronic instrument that reads bar codes and other graphic information found on product packages, coupons, and mailing envelopes. See *scanner market; Universal Product Code.*

scanner market: controlled market testing where products are offered for sale in stores where scanners have been installed, and special arrangements made to gather all relevant information about them and their buyers.

scanning: the electronic reading of a bar code that yields such product information as price, color, and size.

scarcity value: an increase in value caused by a demand for an item whose supply cannot be increased (e.g., works of art from the nineteenth century).

scare purchasing:

(1) purchasing to hoard.

(2) unusually heavy buying of merchandise in short supply.

schedule: a systematic plan for the retailer's future operation over a given period.

scheduling: the organization and control of the time needed to carry out a sales effort.

schlock (shlock): (slang) cheap, inferior items or services.

SCL: See *shipping container label.*

scorecard operation: a store characterized by the sales of shoddy, inferior, and sometimes meretricious goods.

scorecard credit system: a measure for the determination of credit worthiness. Applicants for retail credit are awarded points for various attributes. Points are totaled to give a final score that is used to determine approval or disapproval of a credit application.

scrambled merchandise: an approach by retail outlets of maintaining types of goods not normally found in those stores (e.g., clothing and large appliances sold in a drugstore); results in a wider variety of products being represented in the store. See *intertype competition.*

scrip coupon: See *due bill.*

SD/BL: See *sight draft/bill of lading.*

s-curve effect: occurs if sales of a product rise sharply after it is introduced because of heavy initial promotion effort (advertisements, coupons, samples, etc.), drops slightly as promotional support is reduced, and then rises again if a positive word-of-mouth communication takes place.

search: when buyers gather and interpret information enabling them to decide whether or not to purchase an item or service, including consideration for alternative items or services.

search goods: items the qualities of which are easily determined prior to purchase. See *experience items.*

season: in retailing, the selling period. Traditionally there are two seasons per year—spring, comprised of the 26 weeks from February through July, and fall, comprised of the 26 weeks of August through January.

seasonal dating: See *advance dating.*

seasonal demand: See *seasonality.*

seasonal department: a portion of the department store given over to goods that are closely related to a specific season, such as a Valentine Day decoration shop.

seasonal discount:

(1) a discount that is offered to customers who purchase a product or service during a season when the demand for that product or service is low.

(2) a price reduction given for purchases made out of season (e.g., ski equipment can usually be bought at a discount in the spring). Cf. *static inventory problem.*

seasonal employee: a worker who is employed for limited periods of activity (e.g., for working in a department store over the Christmas buying season).

seasonal fluctuations: regular and predictable shifts in business activity created by changes in the season (e.g., the selling of bathing suits during the summer).

seasonal forecast: changes in market demand that depend primarily on the time of year.

seasonal goods: See *seasonal merchandise.*

seasonal item: See *seasonal merchandise.*

seasonality: a time, the changing of the seasons, that is characteristic of a market, product or promotional campaign that indicates some variation in sales (e.g., trying to sell ski equipment in the summer may fail unless other incentives, such as bargain prices, are introduced). Synonymous with *seasonal demand.* Cf. *erratic demand.*

seasonal merchandise: items so closely identified with a specific season or holiday that they have a very short sales life (e.g., Easter candy and novelties).

season code: the letter or number-letter found on price tags enabling workers to tell when products were received by the store. Such information is used for inventory analysis and for planning markdowns.

season dating: See *advance dating.*

season letter: See *season code.*

secondary business district (SBD): See *secondary shopping district.*

secondary shopping district (SSD): a series of stores outside the urban center, but within the city limits, that services a larger population. Convenience items are particularly important in these stores.

secondary trading area: the zone outside the primary trading area from which customers are attracted to a store, but with increasing difficulty because of increasing distance from the store. See *fringe trading area; primary trading area.*

secondhand:

(1) *general:* not new.

(2) *retailing:* merchandise offered for sale that has already been used.

second line goods: a manufacturer's line of merchandise sold at a lower price than his or her regular line; can be of lower quality, but they are not seconds (i.e., they are not defective).

seconds: goods bearing defects that have possible effects on wearability and appearance. See *bargain store; shopworn.* Cf. *thirds.* Synonymous with *imperfects.*

second sale:

(1) a sale achieved by building on a customer's receptive mood following an initial purchase.

(2) an additional sale to the same person.

sectional wholesaler: a wholesaler who limits his or her activities to a fixed and small number of geographic areas, or states. Synonymous with *regional wholesaler.* Cf. *local wholesaler; national wholesaler.*

section manager: in a store, the supervisor having the responsibility for the efficient running of a specific part of the store, often several departments at one time.

secured distribution: a field warehousing technique where carload lots are shipped to a distributor's premises for release based on the bonded warehouse's arrangement as the distributor requires the items.

security: the department within the store having the responsibility for protecting the store against losses from pilferage, shoplifting, robbery, and other crimes against people and property.

security agreement: the agreement between a seller and a buyer that the seller shall have an interest in the goods. The security agreement must be signed by the buyer and must describe the goods.

see-through window: See *open display.*

segmentation: dividing a market into subunits with similar motivations and needs. Used to increase product or service acceptance by recognizing merchandise appeals. Demographics, geographics, personality, attitudes, values, and preferences are the most popular base for segmenting a market. Synonymous with *market cleavage.* Cf. *fragmentation.*

segmentation by city size: See *market segmentation.*

segmentation by degree of urbanization: See *market segmentation.*

segmentation by population density: See *market segmentation.*

segmentation pricing: when store prices are fixed at different levels for different segments of the population (e.g., in the airline industry which provides different classes of service).

segmentation strategy: See *differentiation.*

segmented merchandising: items for sale that were carefully selected to appeal to certain age groups, persons with similar social and economic backgrounds, and so on.

selection criteria:

(1) *general:* the basis for choosing a subset from a group.

(2) *retailing:* any quality inherent in merchandise which helps determine the customer's buying behavior.

selection factor: See *selection criteria.*

selective buying motive: an incentive or influence which contributes to a customer's purchasing behavior.

selective demand: the demand for a particular brand. See *primary demand.*

selective distribution:

(1) an approach to distribution that involves the use of a limited set of retail outlets in a given territory.

(2) choosing retail outlets that will be permitted to receive one's merchandise for sale; traditionally used with hard goods, such as appliances, VCRs, refrigerators, furniture, and so on. Permits manufacturers to maintain greater control over the way their merchandise is sold and reduces price competition among sellers of the items. See *exclusive distribution; intensive distribution; open distribution.* Synonymous with *limited distribution; selective selling.*

selective selling: See *selective distribution.*

selective stocking: balancing the cost of service with the expense of maintaining inventory to determine what merchandise should be stocked at every distribution center.

self-concept: See *self-image.*

self-concept theory: the notion that two factors influencing an individual's

purchasing behavior are how the person perceives himself or herself and how he or she wishes to be perceived by others. Cf. *motivation.*

self-image: peoples' concepts of themselves and their roles in relation to others. Synonymous with *self-concept.* See *ideal self-image; self-concept theory.*

self-liquidating display: in store display, the cost that the manufacturer passes along to the retailer.

self-liquidating offer: See *self-liquidating premium.*

self-liquidating premium: a premium for which the buyer pays all or part of the cost, where the advertiser offers something of value that enhances the item's image without incurring any cost. See *trade cards.*

self-liquidator: See *self-liquidating premium.*

self-selection selling: a merchandising approach that allows customers to make their choices without the initial assistance of sales help. Cf. *self-service retailing.*

self-service retailing: a sales outlet or store in which the customer chooses the items to be purchased, removes them from the shelves, carries them to a checkout counter for completion of the transaction, and carries or sends them to the place of use. Cf. *self-selection selling.*

seller's lien: the seller's privilege of holding on to certain items until the buyer has delivered payment. See *lien.*

sellers' market: exists at retail when the demand for goods have exceeded its supply. Synonymous with *tight market.*

seller's surplus: the difference between the price a seller actually receives and the lowest price that he or she would accept.

sell-in: the manufacturers' attempts to convince retailers to distribute and stock his or her merchandise. Cf. *sell-through.*

selling: the process of assisting and/or persuading a potential customer to buy merchandise or services, or to act favorably on an idea. See *sales.*

selling against the brand: when artificially inflated prices are kept on some items to increase sales on other items.

selling agent: an agent that handles the entire marketing function for a manufacturer; usually works on an extended contractual basis with the manufacturer and traditionally have full authority for setting prices; differs from sales agent, in that a sales agent does not have control or influence over prices and terms of sales and rarely gets involved in advertising and promotional activities. See *agent.*

selling area: the total floor space given over to selling activities, including aisles, fitting rooms, and adjacent stock rooms.

selling calendar: a schedule for promotions identifying specific dates for each intended special selling event.

selling costs: marketing costs (e.g., advertising, sales promotion) necessary to attract a potential buyer to an item or service.

selling days: the actual number of days in a given period that a store is open for business activities.

selling equipment: See *fixtures.*

selling error: when inappropriate, error-filled selling methods are employed; often leads to markdowns of goods. Cf. *buying error.*

selling expenses: See *selling costs.*

selling formula approach: a selling method that assumes that all consumers are alike or at least will respond in a predictable way to a set sales presentation.

selling price: the cash price that a customer must pay for purchased items or services.

selling: See *selling process.*

selling process: involves prospecting for customer leads, approaching customers, determining customer wants, giving a sales presentation, answering questions, closing the sale, and following up.

selling short: See *short selling.*

sell-off: See *sell-through.*

sell-out:
(1) *general:* to betray a person, organization, or cause, usually for profit or special treatment.
(2) *merchandising:* to dispose of an entire stock or set of products.

sell-through:
(1) the manufacturer's attempt to increase sales of merchandise at the retail level. Cf. *sell-in.*
(2) the amount of goods, expressed as a percentage of the total amount on hand, is sold over a given time period.

semi-direct expenses: costs which, although not directly chargeable to a store department, can be associated with that department.

semi-jobber: See *semi-jobbing.*

semi-jobbing: when the retailer makes wholesale sales or when the wholesaler makes retail sales.

semi-liquidator: a premium offer paid in part by the consumer. Synonymous with *purchase-privilege offer; semi-self liquidator.* See *self-liquidating premium.*

semi-precious stone: the largest of the gemstone categories; based on hardness, brilliance, abundance, and current fashion. Cf. *decorative stone; precious stone.*

semi-self liquidator: See *semi-liquidator.*

send transaction: a sale at retail that is to be delivered, or sent, to the buyer.

separate store organization: a branch store organization where each branch is treated as a separate unit with distinguishable buying responsibilities.

serial display: a series of display windows related to each other in terms of theme or overlapping merchandise.

series discount: taken on a base price that has already been lowered by a preceding discount. Usually they are granted by manufacturers to retail stores. See *chain discount.*

series trade discount: See *series discount.*

serpents in the garden: inducements and displays placed near the doors of a store to attract customers immediate attention.

service: a deed, act, or performance.

service area: See *accommodation area.*

service center: the portion of a store given over to activities such as watch repairs, appliance repairs.

service desk: a store location devoted to such customer service activities as making adjustments for returned merchandise, facilitating exchanges, and so on.

service marketing:
(1) efforts to raise the sale or delivery of a service.
(2) encompasses the rental of goods, the alteration or maintenance or repair of goods owned by consumers, and personal services.

service merchandiser: See *rack jobber.*

service mix: the range of customer services provided by the store.

service retailing organizations: retail organizations that sell services rather than merchandise or other tangible items.

services: privileges for customers of a store beyond the items themselves, such as credit, assortment, home delivery, gift wrapping. See *store services.*

service salesperson: usually interacts with customers after sales are completed. Delivery, installation, or other follow-up tasks are undertaken.

service selling: efforts by a salesperson who satisfies a consumer's needs and thus retains goodwill. See *salesmanship.*

service shopper: a worker of a retail store responsible for shopping other stores in order to report on the service features of the competition, feeding back information on sales personnel, cash and charge systems, delivery practices, etc. Cf. *comparison shopper.*

services marketing: See *service marketing.*

service wholesaler: See *full-service wholesaler.*

Seventh Avenue (SA): a street in New York City crossing the middle of its garment center, where some of America's ready-to-wear industry is located. See *garment center.*

shadow boxes: boxes that can display small item in retail stores; usually a framed box with tiny shelves.

shallow assortment: an assortment of items where each is stocked in small quantities.

shared business: that portion of a retailer's business which is generated by the proximity of neighboring stores.

share of the market: See with *market share.*

shelf exposure: the number of rows of shelf space a product requires.

shelf life: the time identified on the package or label that a certain item can remain in stock or on the shelf before deterioration of a significant nature occurs. When that date arrives, the product should not be sold to the consumer. See *stock rotation.* Synonymous with *product life.*

shelf miser: See *space miser.*

shelf stock: items available to store customers who remove what they desire from the shelves on which the merchandise are placed. See *floor stock; forward stock.*

shelf talker: printed advertisement hung from the shelf in a retail store, supermarket, or a variety store.

Sherman Act: See *price fixing.*

Sherman Antitrust Act: See *price fixing.*

shipment:
(1) *general:* delivery and transport of items by a carrier.

(2) *general:* a collection of items that are transported as a unit.

(3) *merchandising:* merchandise sent to a manufacturer to be processed, or items sent from the manufacturer to a wholesaler or retailer. See *drop shipper; middleperson.*

shipper's cooperative:

(1) a group of shippers who pool shipments of similar items in order to benefit from lower freight rates.

(2) an incorporated firm, owned by shippers of goods and run on a not-for-profit basis, that performs the functions of a foreign freight forwarder.

shipping container label (SCL): a key marker ingredient in making the cross-docking of containers in retail distribution centers possible and more cost effective.

shipping order: instructions of shippers to carriers for forwarding all goods; usually the duplicate copy of the bill of lading.

shipping permit: authority issued by a transportation line permitting the acceptance and forwarding of goods against the movement of which an embargo has been placed.

Shoe Retailer of the Year Award: See *National Shoe Retailers' Association.*

shop:

(1) *verb:* to study goods and/or services with the intention of making a purchase or for the purpose of making comparisons with other goods and services.

(2) *noun:* a small retail establishment or a clearly defined area in a large establishment where related items are sold. See *store.*

shop-at-home retailing: selling a service or item in a customer's residence at the customer's invitation (e.g., carpet and furniture cleaning).

shop layout: in a department store, how related items are to be placed in a carefully defined area.

shoplifter: the thief, amateur or professional, who steals merchandise from stores. See *booster; shoplifting.*

shoplifting: thievery of a store's items by a customer or employee. See *inventory shortage.* Cf. *pilferage.* See *shrinkage; shoplifter.*

shop merchandising: establishing certain locations in a store for serving buyers with special interests (e.g., tennis shop, teen-age corner).

shopper: the individual engaged in a search for goods or services. Synonymous with *pennysaver.*

shopping center:

(1) a cluster of stores and other related facilities (restaurants, rest rooms) planned and built to service a trading area.

(2) a group of retail stores at a single location that is planned, developed, and controlled by one organization. Cf. *superstore.* See *planned shopping center.*

shopping goods: consumer goods that are purchased only after the buyer compares the offerings of more than one store. See *convenience goods; specialty merchandise.*

shopping mall: See *mall.*

shopping mall intercept: a form of personal interview in which respondents are approached or intercepted as they pass a particular spot in a shopping mall.

shopping motivation: the reasons that buyers have for selecting a store to shop in.

shopping plaza: See *mall.*

shopping products: goods and services about which consumers will seek information before making a purchase.

shopping radius: the area around the store from which it usually attracts customers.

shopping report: See *shopping service.*

shopping service:
(1) an in-store department that aids people in selecting items for possible purchase.
(2) professional shoppers hired by large retailers to pose as customers for the purpose of assessing the store's sales staff.

shopping store: a retail outlet that is favored by consumers who are shopping for a certain type of product. See *store*.

shopworn: merchandise that has been handled to such a degree that it can no longer be sold as new. See *seconds*.

short: See *stock shortage*.

shortage:
(1) an excess of quantity demanded over quantity supplied, indicating that the price is below equilibrium. See *short merchandise*.
(2) a deficiency in quantity shipped. See *stock shortage*.

short delivery: items shipped that are less than the amount originally ordered and indicated on the invoice.

short hour: part-time workers who work during peak store hours.

short line: a portion of the vendor's complete line of items (e.g., certain specific styles chosen from a larger assortment).

short line distributor: See *specialty distributor*.

short merchandise:
(1) *general:* goods bought in small quantities, usually in extreme sizes, to complete an assortment.
(2) *merchandising:* purchased goods that were not included in a shipment. See *over, short, and damaged*.

short selling: selling items and purchasing them at a lower price to receive a profit. Synonymous with *selling short*.

short ship: See *short merchandise*.

short shipment: See *short delivery*.

short-time employee: an individual hired to work full-time, but over a short time period (e.g., Easter week).

shotgun approach: a disorganized approach to selling or advertising, aimed at reaching a large number of potential customers without expecting to make sales to all. Cf. *rifle technique*.

showcase: the class cabinet where goods are viewed, but, unless removed by a salesperson, not handled.

showing: See *fashion show*.

showroom: facilities maintained by manufacturers, suppliers, etc., for the purpose of displaying goods to buyers.

shrinkage: the gradual loss of inventory over time due to damage, misplacement, or theft. Shoplifting is a major cause of shrinkage. See *inventory shortage (shrinkage); shoplifting*. Cf. *wastage*.

SIC: See *Standard Industrial Classification System*.

sideline stores: stores whose primary interest is other than retailing (e.g., a wholesaler who also sells to the consumer as an accommodation).

sidewalk sale: the display of goods at a lower than usual price which is literally held outside the store on the sidewalk. Goods are placed on racks or in bins or on tables, usually at final prices.

sight draft/bill of lading (SD/BL): a type of COD selling in which the vendor, upon shipping goods to a buyer, sends the draft to the buyer's bank. The purchaser, before acquiring the goods pays the bank the amount on the invoice.

signage: the signs, posters, symbols, and other graphic forms for communicating with people both inside and outside of the store.

signature line: See *designer merchandise*.

signing: See *signage*.

silent saleperson: a POP display, direct mail item, or money used in a vending machine.

simplified selling:
(1) self-selection where customers have access to goods, making a selec-

tion, and taking it to a salesperson for final sales process.

(2) self-service where customers chooses goods and takes them to a check-out station where it is paid for.

simulated shopping environment: utilizing photographs or slide presentations of a manufacturer's product and competitive offerings; it allows customers to shop from an actual shelf fixture stocked with products. Cf. *virtual store.*

simulated test market: a type of market testing where consumer are presented with a simulated purchase situation to determine their reactions and feelings toward the merchandise.

single-item pricing: See *unit pricing.*

single-line store: a store that carries a wide variety of one type of goods.

single-line wholesaler: a full-service wholesaler that carries only one or two product lines, but offers considerable depth in each.

single-price policy: selling the entire assortment of a given category of items at one fixed price in order that the purchaser can concentrate only on the item offered (e.g., all gloves are $10.00). Cf. *one-price policy.*

sister-store concept: See *equal-store concept.*

SIY technology: See *scan-it-yourself technology.*

size lining: items, mostly apparel, grouped together in the store by size rather than by price or by lifestyle.

skimming: See *skimming price.*

skimming price: use of a high introductory price followed by a series of price reductions, designed to get all the trade the market will bear at one price level before lowering the store price and also to appeal to the more price-conscious consumer. Synonymous with *skim-the-cream price.* See *penetration pricing; penetration strategies; skip marking.* Cf. *creaming a list.*

skim-the-cream price: Synonymous with *skimming price.*

skip: in retailing, a store customer who moves from a known address without paying the bill of a business or utility.

skip loss: See *skip.*

skip marking: a price marking technique where each item is not separately marked.

SKU: See *stock keeping unit.*

slack filling: employing deceptively oversized boxes or other packages. An unlawful practice regulated by the Federal Trade Commission.

sleeper: a fast-selling item that has the potential to become a runner. Cf. *running.*

sliding scale: a reason for increasing or decreasing charges to a customer in relation to the volume of activity or usage over a stated time (e.g., a gas company may charge for gas on a sliding scale, with lower rates for greater consumption).

sliding scale tariff: a customs tariff in which rates of duty vary according to the price of a given import. Usually, as the price of the merchandise falls, the duty is lowered.

slippage:

(1) *general:* lost time.

(2) *merchandising:* people who purchase an item intending to redeem a coupon, request a rebate, or send in for a premium, and then fail to do so.

small order: small orders for merchandise. See *small-order problem.*

small-order problem: orders to purchase items which are so small that the transaction may not produce a profit.

small store person: the individual who is familiar with their various operations involved in running a smaller store.

SML: small, medium, large; abbreviations used in marking merchandise.

smorgasbord plan: a sales compensation method allowing the person to choose among salary, commissions, bonuses, and other fringe benefits which he or she prefers as a means to fulfilling individual needs.

snapper: an added incentive used to encourage prospects to buy a heavily promoted item or service.

snob impact: the degree to which demand for an item is discounted because too many other people use it.

SOB: store's own brand. See *private brand.*

social risk: the consumer-perceived risk that merchandise, if bought will cause embarrassment to the buyer.

soft goods: ready-to-wear clothing, piece goods, linens, towels, and small fashion accessories. Cf. *capital goods; dry goods; hard goods.* Synonymous with *nondurable goods; soft lines.*

soft lines: See *soft goods.*

soft sell: a selling technique that is convincing, subtle, and indirect. Cf. *hard sell.* See *consultative selling.*

SOH: stock on hand.

sort: to segregate merchandise into groups according to some definite rules, such as grade and quality. Cf. *assorting.*

sorting: a process in which products are brought together at one location and then divided up and moved in smaller quantities to locations closer to the ultimate buyers. See *sorting theory.*

sorting out: See *sort.*

sorting theory: a theory of buying behavior where people are perceived as problem solvers engaged in gathering an assortment of goods and services for themselves and their families. Following sorting, the consumer ends up with an assortment of goods and services.

souk: Arabic for marketplace; a resource for multiple resources; i.e., a showroom shared by a number of small manufacturers where retail buyers shop for what is often trend-setting merchandise.

source: See *vendor.*

source marking: See *source tagging; vendor premarking.*

source migration: an order pattern made by a customer over a time period where orders in response to varying promotions are made.

source tagging: when manufacturers label merchandise at the demand of their retail customers. See *vendor premarking.*

Souvenir and Novelty Trade Association (SANTA): based in Philadelphia, Pennsylvania, an association of manufacturers, wholesalers, distributors, retailers, and others involved in the souvenir and novelty industry.

space allocation: the quantity of shelf space in a retail store set aside for the display of merchandise.

space miser: a point-of-purchase display created to hold items that can be readily removed, as well as carry a promotional message. Frequently placed on a shelf where the item is available. Synonymous with *shelf miser.*

span of control: the extent of a supervisor's responsibility, usually identified in the organizational chart by lines of authority. Synonymous with *span of supervision.* See *evoked set.*

span of recall: the number of brands a person can name when asked to do so. See *evoked set.*

span of supervision: See *span of control.*

special: See *loss leader.*

special event: an activity held both inside and outside of the store to increase the flow of customers or to enhance the store's image.

special events director: the individual responsible for the development and staging of store activities such as fashion shows, demonstrations, etc.

special event pricing: promotional pricing where a sale is advertised, frequently linked with an event, or holiday. The goal is to bring inventories into line with consumer demand or to raise cash.

special merchandise: goods whose primary attraction are low price rather than stylishness and quality.

special order: an order that may be priced below the normal price in order to utilize excess capacity and thereby contribute to company profits.

special-line retailers: See *specialty stores.*

special purchase: goods purchased by the retailer at a lower than regular price.

specialty advertising counsellor: See *specialty distributor.*

specialty chain: chain specialty stores that sell apparel and are usually found in shopping centers. These stores do little advertising and offer few traditional customer services. They succeed by depending on the shopping center in its entirety to attract customers. They tend to be quite efficient and are able to target their market with usual accuracy.

specialty discount store: an outlet that carries a single item category and sells it at below regular retail prices.

specialty distributor: a wholesaler in the specialty advertising field; handles a variety of advertising novelties and assists in advertising campaigns of these items. Synonymous with *advertising specialty distributor; specialty advertising counsellor.* See *direct selling organizations.*

specialty goods: See *specialty merchandise.*

specialty line retailer: a limited-line retailer that carries only one or two product lines, but offers substantial depth and expertise in those lines.

specialty merchandise: consumer goods that have special features for which buyers are willing to make a major purchasing effort (e.g., imported foods, hi-fi equipment, cameras). Synonymous with *specialty goods.*

specialty-merchandise wholesalers: full-service merchant wholesalers that concentrate their efforts on a relatively narrow range of products and have an extensive assortment within that range. Synonymous with *limited-line wholesalers.*

specialty products: goods and services for which there are no acceptable substitutes in the consumer's mind (e.g., some luxury cars, consumer electronics equipment, designer fashions).

specialty salesperson: a salesperson, other than retail, who specializes in the sale of one product or a few products of a line of one or more manufacturers or producers.

specialty selling: usually the sale of products or services a person's home or place of work (i.e., the selling of insurance, encyclopedias, vacuum cleaners).

specialty services: See *specialty merchandise.*

specialty shopping center: contains stores that appeal to a restricted clientele. Goods are usually of high quality and high price, although some specialty shopping centers emphasize price and offer goods at a discount.

specialty shops: See *specialty stores.*

specialty stores: retail outlets that maintain a large selection in a limited line of merchandise (e.g., men's apparel stores). Synonymous with *special-line retailers; specialty shops.* See *store.*

specialty wholesaler: See *specialty distributor.*

specification buying: where the retail organization provides definite specifications to the manufacturer detailing how goods are to be made rather than shopping the market for items already bought.

specific identification: a method of valuing inventory and determining cost of goods sold whereby the actual cost of specific inventory items are assigned to those items of inventory on hand and to those that have been sold.

speculative buying: securing goods on the basis of an expected rise or fall in wholesale prices.

speculative purchasing: buying items when prices appear lowest, with the expectation that there will be a future price increase that will make a profit possible.

split item: merchandise that a firm both produces and purchases simultaneously.

split order: a large order that is separated into smaller units that are sold over a period of time. When purchasing or selling goods, a very large transaction could cause substantial price fluctuation, and the splitting is supposed to prevent this.

split rounder: an apparel display fixture composed of two hemispheres, one elevated above the other for greater 360-degree visibility.

split shipment: a partial shipment of merchandise from the vendor to the retailer, with the remainder to be back-ordered until available.

split ticket: a price tag perforated in order that at sale time, a portion—the stub—can be removed for inventory control purposes.

spoilage: merchandise found to be defective.

spot check: the inspection, usually in the receiving department, of a small sample of an incoming shipment of goods.

spot display: items clearly set down along store aisles with an attention-getting device attached.

spot shipment: a shipment of goods by railroad including instructions for the actual placing, or spotting, of the freight car on a siding at the consignee's facility.

spread:
(1) *general:* the differences between the bid and asked prices of an item.
(2) *retailing:* the difference between two prices.

SRAs (state retail associations): See *National Association of State Retail Association Executives.*

SRO method: in sales, a closing approach where the prospect is told that should the sale not be concluded immediately, the chances are small that the item will be available to the person at a later time. Considered an unethical practice.

SSD: See *secondary shopping district.*

ST: See *stock turnover.*

stacker: a freight handler who loads a vehicle.

staggered markdown policy: a price-reduction policy where markdowns appear in different stages.

standard classification of merchandise: an effort of the National Retail Merchants Association; a classification scheme where a store's merchandise and its operations are dividend into merchandise groups sufficiently specific in character to permit analysis of such matters as dollar sales, inventory, sales trends, etc.

Standard Container Acts of 1916 and 1928: federal legislation that fixed the standard sizes for baskets and containers for fruits and vegetables.

Standard Industrial Classification System (SIC): a numerical system developed by the U.S. Bureau of the Budget to classify establishments by type of activity for purposes of facilitating the collection, tabulation, presentation, and analysis of data relating to such establishments and for promoting uniformity within U.S. agencies. Retailing industries have code numbers 52 to 59. More specific forms of retailing are assigned three digit numbers (e.g., department stores have the code number 531).

standard merchandise classification: See *standard classification of merchandise.*

standard package: the quantity of an item usually shipped in just one carton.

standard volume: the expected sales over a given business cycle reduced to an annual basis.

standing order: an authority to a vendor to ship specific merchandise as available, or on a fixed-quantity basis per time interval.

staple items: See *staple stock*.

staples: See *staple stock*.

staple stock: goods on hand that are in continuous demand, such as milk, bread, sugar. Staple stock items are marketed primarily on the basis of price. Synonymous with *commodity products*. See *staple stock list*.

staple stock list: Synonymous with *bread-and-butter assortments*.

starting markup: See *initial markon*.

state-bonded warehouse: See *warehouse, state bonded*.

statement: a summary of transactions between a creditor and his or her debts or a presentation of names and amounts of accounts to show a financial condition (e.g., an IRS statement).

state retail associations (SRAs): See *National Association of State Retail Association Executives*.

static inventory problem: the tendency of items bought for a specific selling season to lose value, either partly or completely, because of changes in the market at the season's end. Cf. *seasonal discount*.

statistical demand analysis: statistical sales forecasting based on mathematical formulas incorporating such variables as the cost of the goods, the nature of the store's customers, etc., in order to project future sales.

status float occurrence: an attempt to explain the influence of fashion on different levels of social class. Numerous contradictions appear as to dress and code of dressing. See *horizontal flow theory*.

status quo prices: to minimize any price war among competitors, store prices are kept at the level charged in the mature stage of the product life cycle.

status symbol: an item or service purchased in the hope that it will communicate one's desired or real status to others.

step-up: See *upgrading*.

stickers: items that have not been purchased after a reasonable time and occupy space considered important for better-selling items. See *dead stock*.

stock:
(1) merchandise held for sale (e.g., inventory).
(2) material in inventory.

stock ahead: to maintain sufficient quantities of goods in inventory to cover an anticipated surge in future demand for the items.

stock alterations: alterations made to merchandise in inventory as contrasted with those made to goods sold to customers.

stock balance: See *balanced stock*.

stock book: a book, maintained by the buyer, in which are entered additions to stock in the form of merchandise received from vendors, and merchandise deductions which represent sales to customers.

stock clerk: an individual working in a store who is responsible for receiving and marking goods at they arrive, moving the items to the selling floor, maintaining inventory records, and other duties such as keeping the buyer informed on the status of the reserve stock.

stock condition: the amount of items available within the store.

stock control: See *inventory control*.

stock count: a periodic inventory where each piece of merchandise is counted and recorded, usually by unit price within a classification.

stock cover: the ratio of current average weekly sales to current stock, providing information on the quantity remaining in stock before new items need to be ordered.

stock depth: merchandise determined to be needed to maintain assortments without too many lost sales because of an out-of-stock situation. See *stockout.*

stockkeeping: See *housekeeping.*

stock keeping unit (SKU):
(1) a measure of an item of merchandise for inventory management.
(2) in inventory control and identification systems the stock keeping unit represents the smallest unit for which sales and stock records are maintained.

stockless purchasing: purchasing where financial responsibility for stock lies with the vendor. See *systems contracting.*

stock levels: the inventory carried by a retailer.

stock on hand (SOH): the amount of goods that is found in a store's inventory at a given time.

stockout: a condition that occurs when all inventory has been used or sold. Stockouts are very costly, as other inputs must then be utilized. See *stock depth.*

stock overage: a condition where the actual items on hand, as determined by physical inventory is greater than the amount indicated in the stock records. Synonymous with *inventory storage.*

stock room: the space off the selling floor where reserve stocks of goods are stored.

stock rotation: putting new incoming products behind those of the same kind already on the shelf, so that inventory remains fresh. See *shelf life.*

stock-sales ratio: the inventory retail value at the beginning of a given month, divided by sales for that month.

This relationship is used to control the sales and inventory balance:

$$\frac{\text{value of stock at retail (in \$)}}{\text{projected sales for month (in \$)}} =$$

$$\text{stock} - \text{sales ratio}$$

stock shortage:
(1) the amount of merchandise shortage through pilferage, bookkeeping errors, or mistakes at point-of-sale.
(2) a condition that occurs when the dollar value of the real inventory in stock is less than that which is shown on the inventory books. See *inventory shortage; shortage.*

stock spotting: where items are warehoused close to the customer instead of near the factory of production so as to lower delivery time and transportation expenses.

stock shrinkage: See *stock shortage.*

stock support: See *stock depth.*

stock-to-sale method: planning inventory levels from planned sales for a given month. The ratio of stock to sales of the same month in the prior year is used as a guide for the plan in the following year.

stock-turn: in retailing, synonymous with *turnover.*

stock turnover (ST): the number of times during the year that inventory turns; derived by dividing total sales by average value of inventory. See *turnover.* Cf. *inventory turnover.* Synonymous with *number of stock turns.*

stop and hold: the record status of an inactive customer; used when merchandise is undeliverable or when a cessation of service to the customer is needed.

storage: the holding of goods for future use.

store: any place where merchandise, goods, or services can be purchased, or a place for storage. Cf. *convenience store; supermarket; supercenter.* See *af-*

filiated store; anchor store; bantam store; bargain basement; bargain store; basement store; box store; branch store; budget store; business associated stores; cash-and-carry store; chain store; combination drugstore; combination store; combo store; commissary store; company store; consumer cooperative; convenience store; departmentized specialty store; department store; depot store; director of stores; discount house; dollar store; dominant store; downtown; express store; factory outlet; flagship store; franchise store; freestanding location; full-service store; general merchandise store; general store; independent store; instrumented store; isolated location; junior department store; limited assortment store; limited-line grocery store; limited-line stores; limited-service store; low-end merchandising; mill store; multi-price store; neighborhood store; nonpromotional store; off-price store; open-end discount store; package store; parasite store; parent store; pharmacy; proprietary store; redemption store; regional department store; regional store; retail store; satellite stores; shopping store; sideline stores; single-line store; single-price policy; specialty discount store; specialty stores; superstore; surplus store; traditional department store; twig store; unit store; upstairs store; variety store; warehouse store; window store.

store audit: a count of the merchandise carried and sold in a retail outlet.

store brand: a brand whose copyright is owned by the retailer, though the item may have been prepared for the store by a supplier. Usually the latter applies and a store label is affixed to the item. See *private brand.*

store cluster: a group of stores, that have off-street parking facilities on their premises, that services a community. Cf. *string street.*

store count distribution: a measure of distribution based on the number of stores. A product sold in 90 percent of all grocery stores would have 90 percent store count distribution.

store coupon: See *coupon.*

store credit: See *due bill.*

store credit record analysis: the analysis of a store's credit records to determine the trading area being served by the retailer. The residences of the credit customers provide some indication of the extent of the trading area.

Store Design Awards Competition: See *Institute of Store Planners.*

store division: See *division.*

store door delivery: See *drop shipment.*

store equipment: cash registers, trucks, elevators, and all other tools and equipment used inside and outside of the store.

store fixtures: See *fixtures.*

store front: the exterior face of a store (i.e., the facade, windows, entrances).

store generative power: the measure of a store's ability to draw people into the store. The stronger the retailer's generative power the greater the distance customers will travel to shop there.

store identity: See *store image.*

store image: the image of a store as perceived by customers or prospects. See *image.*

store induction: the informal orientation of a new retail workers to the particular store in which he or she intends to work.

store layout: See *layout.*

store load: the percentage that store owners add on to the landed cost of imported goods in order to compensate for lost markdown money usually received from domestic manufacturers.

store management division: See *operating division.*

store manager: the executive responsible for the profitable operation of the store, spending consider amount of time on the selling floor. He or she develops staff, contributes to the store's public relations effort, and supervises the maintenance of the store.

store money: See *due bill.*

store operations division: See *operating division.*

store owned buying office: See *cooperative buying office; corporate buying office; private buying office.*

store owned delivery service: a delivery system owned and operated by a particular retailer. For smaller retailers, a panel truck or station wagon may be adequate.

store ownership group: See *department store ownership group.*

store personality: See *store image.*

store redeemable coupon: a merchandise discount certificate that is redeemed in any retail outlet where the item is sold, as contrasted with a certificate that can only been redeemed through the mail.

store retailer: See *retailer.*

stores: plural of store. See *store.*

STORES: the monthly magazine of the National Retail Federation.

store saturation: See *saturated area.*

stores director: See *director of stores.*

store security: See *security.*

store services: intangible tasks or activities which benefit the consumer and which are provided by a retail establishment to attract customers. See *services.*

store's owned brand: See *private brand.*

store's requisition: the form for securing materials that are held in normal stock. It goes directly to the stores department from which materials are then supplied for use. See *requisition.*

store traffic: the number of customers coming and going in a store.

straight commission: where salespersons receive a fixed percentage of their total sales as their only compensation. Cf. *straight salary.*

straight lease: the simplest form of lease agreement where the retailer pays a fixed rent over the entire life of the lease without regard to the amount of business carried out in the store.

straight rebuy:

(1) a purchasing situation in which the organization has bought the item or service before and is likely to reorder from the same vendor.

(2) an undramatic repurchase of an item previously bought.

straight-rebuy purchase process: See *straight rebuy.*

straight salary: compensation for a salesperson based on a fixed rate and at regular intervals, independent of performance considerations. Cf. *straight commission.*

straight traffic flow: the movement of customers within a retail store in more or less straight lines due to the grid pattern employed in placing counters and different displays.

strategic business units (SBUs): one or more products, brands, divisions, or market segments that have something in common, such as the same distribution system. Each SBU has its own mission, it own set of competitors, and its own strategic plan.

strategic marketing: to make a store or company more customer oriented, the correlation between marketing activities and strategic planning activities are measured and provided with a greater percentage of the store's budget.

strategic partnering: in retailing, a meeting of the minds at every management level. Buyers and their vendor counterparts share information on sales, on orders, and inventory levels to eliminate duplication of effort and improve profitability for both.

strategic plan: a long-term plan covering a period of 3-,5-, or sometimes 10 years. See *strategic planning.*

strategic planning: in retailing, a basic type of planning by which a store formulates its long-range goals and selects activities for achieving those goals. Decisions include whether to enter a new untapped market, to grow an existing market, to dominate an existing market, or to dominate a small segment of an existing market by replacing competitors or by satisfying an unmet desire.

strategic planning gap: the difference between the present position of a store and its desired future position.

strategic window: the time period, as when the window is open, when a firm's abilities to produce items in demand by the public are matched with sales. When the window closes, such as when the store waits too long to act appropriately, the store may have lost its marketing opportunity.

strategy: in retailing, guidelines for making directional decisions that influence a store's long-run performance. See *retail store strategy mix.*

stratifying the market: determining the number of consumers who may purchase the item or service at various price levels.

street vendor: entrepreneurs working from stands, carts, or tables on the sidewalk who sell fruit, apparel, accessories, etc., to passers-by.

string street: a street with a large number of stores side by side, usually with curbside parking in front. Cf. *store cluster.*

strip center: an uncovered shopping center as contrasted with an enclosed mall, containing a single supermarket or a variety store. Synonymous with *neighborhood shopping center.*

strip shopping center: See *strip center.*

stripped down price: an item offered for sale at a lower price, and then upon visiting the store, the customer finds that the item contains fewer features than originally thought. For example, a stripped down car has no air-conditioning, or stereo.

strong market: a market that has a greater demand for purchasing than for selling.

stub: the portion of a price tag removed by a salesperson at the time of sale which is retained for inventory control purposes.

stuff: (slang) to sell goods that are not genuine or have been stolen.

style obsolescence: obsolescence that occurs when the physical appearance of a product is changed to make existing versions seem out of date.

style-out: identifying which characteristics of specific items attract customers purchasing attention by separating the fast-moving products from the slow-moving products and then studying the fast-moving products to uncover the common features which may be the explanation for the greater sales.

style piracy: See *knockoff.*

subjective price: a consumer's perception of the price of a good or service as being high, fair, or low.

substandard:
(1) *general:* conditions that make a risk less desirable than normal for its class.
(2) *retailing:* See *seconds.*

substitute goods: items that can easily replace one another either in production or in consumption (e.g., natural and synthetic fibers, strawberries and raspberries). An increase in the price of one substitute good encourages purchase of the other.

substitution law: the economic statement that if one product or service can be a replacement of another, the prices of the two must be very close to each other.

subteens: a specific segment of a store's customers whose member's age runs from around 9 to 13; usually girls.

suggested price: See *suggested retail price.*

suggested resale price: See *suggested retail price.*

suggested retail price: though not mandatory, the list price of merchandise as stated by the manufacturer as a fair price to be charged by the retailer. Manufacturers hope and expect that stores maintain a price close to their suggested retail price. Cf. *discount.* Synonymous with *recommended retail price.*

suggestion selling: See *suggestive selling.*

suggestive selling: the strategy of suggesting to a potential purchaser that he or she might have an additional need related to what has already been purchased (e.g., it might be suggested that a women who has bought a dress also select appropriate shoes or a sweater). See *complementary products.* Cf. *derived demand.*

Sunday hours: See *Sunday opening.*

Sunday opening: the availability of shopping seven days a week by opening the store on Sunday. This practice is in opposition to blue laws.

supercenter: a huge 110,000 square foot store, selling general merchandise and a broad array of food (40 percent) to nonfood (60 percent). Cf. *combination store; convenience store; conventional supermarket; express store; superstore.*

superette: See *bantam store; normal goods.*

superior goods: products and services that are demanded in larger quantities as incomes rise (e.g., expensive cars, caviar, fur coats). Synonymous with *normal goods.*

supermarket: a retail operation, having at least eight employees, occupying approximately 25,000 square feet, that sells food and nonfood items. Cf. *bantam store.* See *superstore.*

superstore: a combination of a general-merchandise discount operation and a supermarket; usually ranges in size from 50,000 square feet to 200,000 square feet. Established to fulfill all consumer needs for every type of food and nonfood-household item purchased on a regular basis. See *conventional supermarket; hypermarche; supercenter; supermarket.* Cf. *bantam store; combo store; convenience store; express store; shopping center.*

supplier: the firm that provides goods that are used in the manufacturing process but that are not included in the item itself. See *vendor.*

supplier/distribution intermediary contracts: focuses on price policies, conditions of sale, territorial rights, the services/responsibility mix, and contract length and conditions of termination.

supply: the quantity of items available for sale.

supply price: the lowest price needed to produce a specified output. It is the lowest price a seller will accept for the act of supplying a given quantity of a commodity.

supply schedule: a table of prices and corresponding quantities offered for sale in a given period.

supporting the market: placing purchasing orders at or somewhat below the prevailing market level in order to maintain and balance existing prices and to encourage a price rise.

support level: the point at which demand for a product or service is reached. It is the moment when the resistance level is overcome.

suprafirm: a retail organization where a large firm develops a relationship with a number of small stores (e.g., in a cooperative or voluntary chain, franchise system, shopping centers), in order to bring to the small stores the advantages of numbers. In return, the stores surrender some of their independence.

surplus: anything remaining or left over.

surplus store: a store which sells, along with other items of nongovernmental origin, merchandise which has been declared surplus by the U.S. government.

survey of buying power: a detailed demographic, geographic statistical study of consumer power to purchase goods of various types.

suspend: See *stop and hold.*

swap: to exchange or barter. Cf. *exchange.*

sweepstake: a sales promotion method where participants compete for awards by merely entering the contest. No skill or strategy on the part of the participant is required. A contestant merely submits an entry form with his or her name and address. Cf. *contest.*

swell allowance: a reduction from invoice cost to provide for the loss of item value due to damage in shipping.

swing shop: an area within department stores where trend-setting merchandise is featured.

switching customers: bringing in a sales specialist when the salesperson who originally served a customer is unable to close a sale.

switch selling: an unethical practice of using high-pressure tactics to sell an item that is more expensive than one advertised at a lower price. See *bait-and-switch merchandising.*

symbolic pricing: using price to create an impression about a product or a brand in the minds of consumers.

syndicate buying office: See *corporate buying office.*

syndicate office: See *corporate buying office.*

syndicated buying office: See *corporate buying office.*

systems buying/selling:

(1) purchasing or selling of a multifaceted product or service. Firms that participate in systems buying do not choose to make different buying decisions when purchasing a complex item, such as a telecommunications network. They prefer, instead, of coordinating their efforts with multiple groups or vendors, they deal with one contractor who is fully responsible for the bidding and assembling of subcontractors to provide the complete package.

(2) firms that provide systems selling market the capability to assemble all the items and services required by the purchaser. See *team selling.*

systems contracting: buying which permits for little or no stock to be handled by the purchaser. The purchase agreement is based on a catalog furnished by the supplier for the item agreed upon. Can benefit both the supplier and the purchaser. See *blanket order; stockless purchasing.* Cf. *systems selling.*

systems selling: the merchandising of a group of items that has some functional relationship to one another as a package, rather than as single items (e.g., matching tie and handkerchief sets). Cf. *systems contracting.* See *sales analysis, systems buying/selling.*

tag: See *Kimball tags; price tag.*

take: (slang) in retailing, the funds in the cash register of a retail store at the close of a business day.

take-and-pay contract: a guarantee to purchase an agreed amount of a product or service, provided that it is delivered.

take stock: to make an inventory of items on hand.

take transaction: See *carryouts.*

take-withs: See *carryouts.*

taking inventory: the procedure of counting all inventory on hand at a time set aside for this purpose. Cf. *unit control.*

tally card: a form used by salespeople to record their transactions. The form is usually printed on an envelope in which the tally (the following days starting amount of money) can be inserted.

tally envelope: See *tally card.*

talon: a special coupon (e.g., a voucher stub).

tame cat distributor: a wholesaler owned and controlled by a manufacturer.

tape plan: a promotional strategy, usually run by supermarkets, offering premiums in return for cash register tapes totaling a specified amount. Synonymous with *cash-register tape redemption plan.*

tare: an unproductive weight; an amount that is part of the gross weight of an article (e.g., the weight of a truck, a package, or any other container or vehicle). Net weight is gross weight less the tare. See *gross weight.*

target:

(1) the one to whom a selling message is addressed.

(2) a market where a selling effort is made. See *target market.*

target audience: See *target market.*

target customers: the people who are the objects of a store's total efforts to attract business. Cf. *market target.*

target market: those people whom are most likely to become customers and toward whom the retailer directs its promotional strategy. Synonymous with *target audience.*

target pricing: a technique of establishing prices to reach a profit objective.

target return on investment: an amount of income equivalent to a certain percentage of the firm's investment; this amount is set as a goal to be achieved through pricing. See *target return pricing.*

target return pricing: setting a product's price to yield a specific return on investment using the formula:

target return price = unit cost +

$$\frac{desired\ return\ \times\ invested\ capital}{unit\ sales}$$

See *target return on investment.*

taste level: in retailing, the subjective level of individual preference which includes a sense of quality, beauty, and relevance.

team selling: a selling technique using several salespeople, especially with highly technical or complex products since no one person could be expert in all the features of the offering. See *systems buying/selling.*

teaser plan: Synonymous with *campaign plan.*

teen board: teenagers employed by a retailer in a voluntary capacity who have a special interest in fashion. Cf. *college board; fashion board.*

tee-stand: See *T-stand.*

telemarketing:

(1) product and services sales using the telephone; carried out at both consumer and industrial levels of the marketplace. Such calls interrupt the consumer by requesting immediate attention and are not identifiable as a promotion before the consumer has been interrupted, thereby at times leading to an antagonized prospect. Cf. *teleshopping.*

(2) sales of items and services via an interactive system or two-way television. Prospects are often preselected such a current or prior customers or likely prospects selected from a rented list. See *outbound telemarketing.*

(3) Synonymous with *teleselling.* See *television retailing.*

telephone agency: a firm that makes and/or receives telemarketing calls for another organization or person.

telephone retailing: selling by telephone at the retail level, usually to the consumer. See *telemarketing; teleshopping.*

telephone selling: See *telephone retailing.*

telephone selling department (TSD): the department within the store responsible for all sales generated by telephone, either in the form of solicitation or as a response to some promotional campaign.

teleselling: See *telemarketing.*

teleshopping: when customers use telephones to secure products or services that have been seen in advertisements, or on radio and television. 800 telephone numbers are frequently employed for toll-free encouragement. Cf. *telemarketing.*

television retailing: See *electronic catalog; electronic direct marketing; electronic retailing; interactive television.*

tentative trade area: in retail site location, the geographic area around the site from which the store can reasonably expect to attract buyers.

term:

(1) the prescribed time a person has to make installment or other payments as identified in a loan or credit contract.

(2) the duration of an agreement, subscription, etc. See *terms of sale.*

terms file: the record maintained by a retailer of the terms of sale imposed by each vendor with whom he or she is doing business.

terms of credit: the obligations and conditions that a store sets down in granting consumer credit. Cf. *terms of sale.*

terms of occupancy: in retail site locations, terms placed on the physical structure that includes matters such as sale price or terms of lease, responsibility for repair, renovation, and maintenance, local ordinances, taxes, etc.

terms of purchase: See *terms of sale.*

terms of sale: identification of a vendor's given time to pay an invoice, any discounts offered, and other conditions of the sale. Synonymous with *sales terms.* Cf. *terms of credit.*

terms of trade: the number of units of items that must be surrendered for one unit of goods obtained by a group or nation that is a party to a transaction.

territorial departmentalization: organization of a department according to geographic location (e.g., a store with four major divisions: eastern, midwestern, western, and foreign.)

territorial potential: the full potential demand for a particular item within a defined area of territory.

territory manager: See *regional manager.*

territory screening: Synonymous with *canvass (2).*

territory-structured salesforce: an organization where each person is assigned an exclusive geographic area. It provides the salesperson with a clear knowledge of his or her responsibility; it increases the salesperson's chances for evolving closer relationships with prospects, customers, local businesspeople; and it saves on travel costs. See *salesforce.*

test:
(1) *general:* any instrument to identify a person's behavior or skills in a host of areas.
(2) *retailing:* to test merchandise by placing a small sample order on display to determine the customer's reaction before ordering a larger quantity.

testimonial: a statement by a satisfied customer praising a product or service that is used in advertising or sales promotion to influence others.

test market: See *test marketing.*

test marketing:
(1) trial distribution of a new product in a small market to determine its likely acceptance in the total market. Cf. *market fit.*
(2) the controlled introduction of a new product to carefully selected markets for the purpose of testing market acceptance and predicting future sales

of the product in that region. See *market fit.*

Textile Products Identification Act: federal legislation requiring that sellers of yarns and fabrics and household items made of these, which are made from natural or synthetic fibers other than wool, to attach labels to goods indicating the percent by weight of each fiber they contain and to list the fibers by generic name set by the Federal Trade Commission.

TFG: See *Fashion Group, The.*

theme/setting display: the retail display where the items to be sold are presented in an environment having a specific theme or subject orientation.

theme shopping center: a shopping center with a distinctive architectural design; carries over into the inner design and is often designed to associate with a historical event.

third-party plan: a retail credit plan promoted by a bank or some other credit-extending organization which, although accepted by the retailer, is usually administered by the credit granting agency.

thirds: goods of extremely poor quality, lower in grades than seconds. Cf. *seconds.*

13-month merchandising calendar: an annual calendar divided into "months" of four weeks.

13-month: the selling critical shopping period between Christmas and New Years.

30-day charge: See *charge account.*

thirty-three: (slang) a potential customer who refuses to make a purchase from one salesperson and is then turned over to another.

three Bs: See *Better Business Bureau.*

three Cs of credit: used to determine whether a person's credit is acceptable; character—as an indication of determination to pay; capacity—the measure of the ability to pay; and capital—a person's financial resources or net worth.

throughput: the distribution of merchandise via dealers and on to the consumer.

throughput agreement: an agreement to put a stated amount of merchandise through a production facility in an agreed time period, or if not, to pay for the availability of the facility.

throwout: the paper receipt descending from the cash register.

thumbnail: Synonymous with *esquisse.*

throwaways: Synonymous with *handbill.*

ticket: See *price tag.*

tickler file: a follow-up diary or folder containing memos, letters, and so on, ordered by future dates and pulled periodically for review and action.

tie-in agreement: paid for by the retailers who sponsor it and involves a retailer and a vendor of services, where the retailer sells the service under his or her own name and handles the billing while the vendor of the service actually performs the work.

tie-in promotion: displays and approaches that connect with an active promotional campaign to create immediate sales, assist in introducing merchandise. Synonymous with *cross-promotion.*

tie-in sales: sales that are limited so that a buyer cannot purchase one produce or service without purchasing something else from the same manufacturer. The Clayton Antitrust Act of 1914 made this practice illegal in interstate commerce. See *tie-in agreement; tying agreement; Clayton Antitrust Act of 1914; unfair practices acts.*

tight market: See *sellers' market.*

till: the cash drawer within the cash register.

time budgeting of purchases: in order to even out changes in prices of merchandise, small units of items are purchased over short periods. This will assure that the store's average price for each product will approximate the true average for the period. However, it tends to increase the total cost of purchasing.

time order: an order that becomes a market or limited price order at a specified time.

time payment: See *installment credit.*

time rate of demand: the quantity of an item which the market can absorb at a given price over a specified time.

time-series forecast: a method of forecasting in which historical trends are projected into the future.

time utility:

(1) the satisfaction that buyers receive from having a product or service available at the appropriate time.

(2) a feature of an item making it feasible to satisfy a desire or want based on time preference. Storage creates time utility. See *utility.*

tinge: (slang) a salesperson who specializes in the sale of undesirable merchandise that earn him or her bonus payments.

TL shipment: See *truck load shipment.*

toddlers: children in the age range from 18 months to about three years who wear sizes 1T through 4T.

token order:

(1) a small order placed to assess the desirability of an item.

(2) a small order placed as a means of getting rid of a bothersome salesperson.

tonnage: goods bought by retail buyers in large quantities which generates a high sales volume.

top credit: ready credit.

top down method: in retailing, a budget method where the budgeter commences with a gross amount and follows with specific amounts to designated classifications of merchandise. See *bottom-up technique.*

top out: the peak period of demand for a product or service, after which demand decreases.

to price out of the market: to charge prices for merchandise or services that are so high that one is no longer competitive.

top stock: goods shown on top of a counter; an open, as opposed to a closed display. See *closed display; open display.*

to shop a line: the inspection of a vendor's entire line of merchandise by the retailer with an intention of purchasing some or all of it.

to starve the stock: to have insufficient inventory to meet demand.

total cost: the sum of a store's total fixed costs and total variable costs. See *cost of goods sold.*

total-cost of goods sold: See *cost of goods sold.*

total loss: items that have been so badly damaged that they are not considered to be worth repairing (e.g., a car that has suffered a head-on collision with a truck, merchandise that is party destroyed by fire).

total merchandise cost: See *cost of goods sold.*

total merchandise handled: the sum of the value of opening inventory, further purchases, and any applicable transportation charges expressed as a dollar amount and calculated at cost prices.

total receipts: See *total revenue.*

total rent: in setting the total rent for a retail site in a planned shopping center, a number of considerations are taken into account. In addition to the monthly fee for the site itself (the rent), the prospective tenant must consider fees for the maintenance of common areas, dues to the center's merchants' association, and minimum lease guarantees.

total retail reductions: dropping of prices and inventory as shown by sales, mark-downs, employee, and other discounts, and stock shortages.

total revenue: total receipts of a store. It is equal to the price per unit times the number of units sold.

total sales: See *sales.*

total systems competition: a sophisticated and complete form of competition where the organization owns and/or controls sources of manufactured goods, storage/distribution systems, and a highly developed network of retail outlets. As a power, the organization effectively brings all its resources to bear on any competitive situation.

total variable costs: costs that change directly with the store's output, increasing as output rises over the total range of production, (e.g., labor, fuel).

to the trade only: used by wholesalers, vendors, dealers, indicating that they do not sell at retail.

to underorder: to order to few items in order to fulfill consumer demand.

to write: See *to write an order.*

to write an order: where the buyers write an order to the vendor for merchandise. Synonymous with *to write.*

tracer: a request to trace a shipment in order to determine its location, alter instructions, or affects its status.

tracking: monitoring inventory received, ordered, and bought, to maintain optimum levels for future purchases.

trade: transactions involving goods and/or services from profit between legal entities.

trade advertising:
(1) advertising directed at wholesalers or retailers.
(2) consumer-product advertising used for stimulating wholesalers and retailers to buy merchandise for resale to their customers.

trade allowances: incentives provided by the manufacturer to retailers and other channel intermediaries to stock, display, or promote the manufacturer's goods. See *trade promotion.*

trade area: See *trading area.*

trade cards: where retailers punch into a card the amount spent by a consumer until a total is reached qualifying the buyer to purchase a premium at a self-liquidating price. Synonymous with *purchase-privilege offer.* See *self-liquidating premium.*

trade channel: See *channel of distribution.*

trade credit: credit from producers and wholesalers to their customers on a short-term basis.

trade deal: See *deal (2).*

trade discount: a deduction from the agreed price, usually expressed as a percentage or a series of percentages, that is used in commerce to encourage prompt payment of bills; should not be entered in the books of account, nor should it be considered to be a type of earnings. Synonymous with *functional discount.*

trade down: See *trading down.*

trade in: to surrender an old product for a new one, accompanied by additional payment to make up for depreciation of the item traded in.

trade industry: wholesalers and retailers, who purchase for resale to others or for use in conducting their own business.

trademark: a distinctive identification of a manufactured product or a service in the form of a name, logo, motto, and so on. A trademarked brand has legal protection, and only the owner can use the mark. Organizations that file an application at the U.S. Patent Office and use the brand for five years may be granted a trademark. A firm may lose a trademark that has become generic. Generic names are those that consumers use to identify the product,

rather than to specify a particular brand (e.g., escalator, aspirin, nylon). See *Lanham Act of 1947.* Synonymous with *registered trademark.*

Trade-Mark Act of 1946: See *Lanham Act of 1947.*

trade marketing mix: See *retailing mix.*

trademark franchise: a franchiser with a recognized trade name and highly standardized method of operation. Examples are motel chains, car rental companies, fast-food outlets.

trademark infringement: See *infringement.*

trade name: the name under which an organization conducts business or by which the business or its goods and services are identified. It may or may not be registered as a trademark.

trade position discount: See *discount.*

trade premium: an incentive, such as vacations, prizes, free merchandise, etc., from a manufacturer to a retailer or wholesaler who achieves a specific level of sales of the manufacturer's merchandise. See *premium.*

trade price: the manufacturer's price to a middleperson.

trade promotion: sales promotion efforts directed towards retailers and wholesalers offering incentives, such as gifts, price-off discounts, trips, merchandise, etc., to middlepeople who will carry the manufacturer's items or will increase their inventory of the manufacturer. See *advertising allowance; dealer loader; promotion.*

trade puffery: See *puffery.*

trader: anyone who is engaged in trade or commerce.

trade rate: a special price given by wholesalers, distributors, or manufacturers, to retailers.

trade reference: a person or firm to which a seller is referred for credit data on a potential customer.

trade salesperson: a salesperson whose primary duties are promotional, by assisting customers to promote a firm's items or services. They write orders but spend most of their time dealing with established customers.

trade show: where manufacturers and/or wholesalers meet from a specific industry for the purpose of showing their merchandise; serves as a vehicle to generate new sales leads and to maintain existing customer relations.

trade specialty house: an industrial distributor who serves a specific type of customer, with a full line of items requested by him or her, (e.g., barbershop supplies, shoe repair supplies).

trade style: the unique manner in which a store displays its name in print in advertising and on letterheads.

trade up: See *trading up.*

trading across: when a store alters its marketing strategy to try to appeal to a different market segment. Shifting can be very difficult and expensive.

trading area: the region or shopping district whose limits are determined by the costs of delivering merchandise to the area.

trading area overlap: the area from which more than one store is drawing its customers. Cf. *trading area overlay.*

trading area overlay: a transparent plastic sheet onto which the store's trading areas are plotted. The sheet is superimposed over a city or town map. Used by retailers having more than one outlet in a region to determine areas from which the chain is not drawing customers. This method indicates where a new store can profitably be situated.

trading away: See *bait-and-switch merchandising.*

trading cards: See *trade cards.*

trading down: attempting to increase the market of a store or item with an established reputation by lowering price or quality or by changing promotional strategy to appeal to a larger potential market, which is frequently in a lower socioeconomic level. By trading down, the image of the item is often sacrificed for gains in profit. See *wheel of retailing.* Cf. *trading up.*

trading stamp: a promotional device; a stamp given to customers that is worth a small percentage of the total amount paid for purchases. When a large number of stamps have been accumulated, they can be redeemed at the store or at a warehouse for merchandise.

trading up: attempting to improve the image of a store or item by increasing prices or quality or by altering advertisement approaches, usually to appeal to a market in a higher socioeconomic level. See *wheel of retailing.* Cf. *trading down.*

traditional break-even analysis: determines the sales quantity in units or dollars that is needed for total revenues to equal total costs at a given price:

break-even point (Units) =

$$\frac{\text{total fixed costs}}{\text{price} - \text{variables cost (per unit)}}$$

break-even point (sales dollars) =

$$\frac{\text{total fixed costs}}{1 - \text{variable costs (per unit) price}}$$

traditional department store: a department store that has a great assortment of goods and services, provides many customer services, is a fashion leader, and often serves as an anchor store in a shopping district or shopping center. See *department store.*

traditional merchandise: goods that, in terms of style, change little from year to year. See *traditional department store.*

traditional supermarket: See *conventional supermarket.*

traffic:
(1) *general:* business done by a transportation or communications company.
(2) *retailing:* the flow of people who are exposed to a store's goods. Measurement of traffic (i.e., counting the people) is usually done as customers enter and leave the store's premises. Cf. *routing.*

traffic appliances: portable appliances, including toasters, blenders, irons, etc.

traffic builder:
(1) a low-cost premium offered as an inducement to enter a store for a demonstration of a product.
(2) a popular item whose price has been lowered to attract customers to the store or outlet. Synonymous with *giveaway.*

traffic building merchandise: See *traffic builder.*

traffic count:
(1) in retail stores, the process of counting customers as they enter a predetermined point.
(2) in site location studies, either pedestrian or vehicular traffic counted as a variable in locating a new retailer.

traffic items: consumer products that have a limited life and will in time attract consumers back into a store to purchase new replacement items.

traffic management: the planning, selection, and direction of all means of transportation involved in the movement of goods in the marketing process.

traffic manager: See *traffic management.*

transaction: any agreement between two or more parties that establishes a legal obligation.

transactions per square foot: the number of transactions per square foot of selling space in a retail store; computed by dividing the number of sales transactions by the number of square feet of selling space in the store.

transfer book: the book for recording which items have been transferred from one department to another.

transfer costs: the costs that a department accepts for items supplied by other departments.

transfer impact: a feature of an offering making it possible for that item or service to force a transfer of a consumer's allegiance to the offering source.

transfer-in: items moved into a department or branch from another part of the same retail operation.

transfer of title: the moment when ownership of merchandise is transferred from the seller to the purchaser.

transfer out: goods moved out of a department or branch to another part of the same retailer organization.

transfers: those items that are moved from department to department, or branch to branch, within a single retail organization.

transitional customer: a retail customer who bridges the gap between the traditional customer (one who has a practical approach to clothing) and the contemporary customer (who is more fashion conscious).

transition merchandise: merchandise sold to fulfill customer needs over two or more seasons.

transit privileges: the privilege offered a shipper by a shipping company of unloading merchandise in transit for a future processing, then reloaded and delivered to their destination without additional costs. Synonymous with *milling in transit; processing in transit.*

transit time: See *transit privileges.*

transportation costs: expenses involved in shipping goods from the vendor to the retailer.

transportation service companies: marketing specialists that predominantly handle the shipments of small and moderate-sized packages. The three major kinds of service companies are government parcel post, private parcel, and express.

transshipping:
(1) *general:* the transfer of items from one carrier to another.
(2) *retailing:* the shipment of merchandise by a dealer or distributor to another dealer or distributor beyond the usual selling area.

traveling sales representative: a salesperson who travels considerably to obtain orders.

tray pack: a point-of-purchase display where the top of the case of goods can be opened and folded back so that the case actually becomes a display tray that is readily placed on a shelf or counter in the store.

trend:
(1) *general:* the prevailing tendency or direction.
(2) *retailing:* in fashion, that which is currently popular and moving toward wide acceptability in the marketplace.

trend extension: forecasting sales for existing items based on previous data information and projecting that information to the future.

trend merchandising: the strategy where new items are presented in the store in such a fashion that they capitalize on evolving trends perceived by the merchandising staff.

trial: within the adoption process of a consumer, the period when a product is first used. This is a critical point in determining the continued acceptance of the item by consumers.

trial-and-error pricing: selling an item at varying prices in different locations and then assessing the response to each of the prices.

trial buyer: See *trial offer.*

trial offer: a soft-sell method permitting a first-time purchaser to examine, use, or test an item for a short period of time before deciding to buy or decline the opportunity to purchase the item; may also include a special reduced rate. Synonymous with *free examination offer; free trial offer.*

trial sampling: in sales promotion, encouraging a consumer to try an item, usually after being given a free sample. See *trial size.*

trial size: a package that is smaller than the usual manufactured package; often used as a giveaway or sample. Can be free or sold at a lower price to attract buyers. Trial-size packages are traditionally delivered by mail or are available in retail outlets. See *sample buyer.*

trickle-across theory: See *horizontal flow theory.*

trio of needs: basic motivations that make consumers purchase an item or service. They are needs for power, affiliation, and achievement. See *motivation.*

truck distributor: See *truck jobber.*

truck jobber: a middleperson who delivers at the time of sale (e.g., vendors of ice cream, lunch specialties, and other items that must be sold fresh). Synonymous with *truck distributor; truck wholesaler; wagon distributor; wagon jobber.* See *cash-and-carry wholesaler; jobber.*

truck-load shipment (TL shipment): a full truck load of merchandise shipped at the lower motor carrier rate than partial loads.

truck/wagon wholesalers: limited-service merchant wholesalers that generally have a regular sales route, offer items from the truck or wagon, and deliver goods at the same time they are sold.

truck wholesaler: See *truck jobber.*

trunk show: the display of a vendor's total line of merchandise before an audience that is gathered for the purpose of inspecting the wares.

trust receipt: where the dealer obtains merchandise that has been financed by a lending organization, by signing a receipt which obligates him or her to repay the lender. The dealer can or cannot take title to the merchandise in the course of the transaction.

truth in advertising: the requirement of a firm or store to truthfully explain the attributes and benefits of products within their advertising. Firms and stores that do not engage in truthful advertising can be cited for disciplinary action by the Federal Trade Commission. See *Truth in Lending Act of 1968.*

Truth in Lending Act of 1968: officially, the Consumer Credit Protection Act of 1968; requires that most categories of lenders disclose the true annual interest rate on virtually all types of loans and credit sales as well as the total dollar cost and other terms of a loan. See *Fair Credit Billing Act; right of rescission; truth in advertising.*

Truth in Packaging Act: See *Fair Packaging and Labeling Act of 1966.*

TSD: See *telephone selling department.*

TSIA (Association of Retail Marketing Services): based in Sea Bright, New Jersey, an association of firms issuing trading stamps which consumers redeem for premiums. Members also receive summaries of a survey dealing with retail marketing services.

T-stand: a free-standing display fixture in the shape of a T that is used for displaying hanging merchandise, usually apparel.

TTNF: See *Two/Ten National Foundation.*

tube system: obsolete; a series of pneumatic tube transport carriers which carry sales checks and cash to a central cashier's office. Once the cashier has made change or authorized a credit purchase, the carrier is returned through the tube system to the counter where the transaction began.

turn: in merchandising, turnover of items within an inventory. See *stock turnover.* Synonymous with *round turn.*

turnaround: the movement by a freight carrier in which the driver returns to the point of origin following the unloading and reloading of cargo.

turnkey: a contractual agreement between a customer and an organization to provide full services or a complete product.

turnover: in retailing, the frequency with which an inventory is sold and replaced over a stated period, usually determined by dividing the net sales for the period by the average retail value of the inventory during that period. See *demand sensitivity; stock turnover.* Synonymous with *stock turn.*

twig store: a small branch store carrying a selection of its parent store's goods, usually targeting a particular customer (e.g., a large specialty store can open a twig in a college town to carry merchandise that appeals to college-bound students, selected from the main store's college shop).

twin pack: traditionally sold at a lower cost, a retail product package of two containers of the same product bound under the same wrapping or in the same holder.

twofers: See *two-for-one sale.*

two-for-one sale: an offer to consumers of two units of merchandise for the regular price of one, made by a seller for the purpose of encouraging sampling of the product and to unload dealers' shelves. Synonymous with *twofers.*

Two/Ten National Foundation (TTNF): based in Boston, Massachusetts, an association of executives and managers of shoe manufacturing, wholesaling, and retail establishments.

tying agreement:

(1) a method of control over distribution in which the producer forces the dealer to buy additional products in order to secure one highly desired product.

(2) an agreement where the manufacturer requires a dealer or middleperson to buy certain items in order to purchase certain other items, or in which the manufacturer requires that the dealer not sell competing items. In turn, the dealer is often granted exclusive rights to sales of the manufacturer's items in a specified territory. See *tie-in sales.*

tying clause: See *tying agreement.*

tying contract: See *tying agreement.*

ultimate consumer: the individual who actually uses purchased items. See *consumer, user*. Synonymous with *final consumer*.

umbrella brands: See *family brands*.

umbrella pricing: See *predatory pricing*.

unbilled revenue: fees earned in a given period for which bills have not yet been sent to the customers.

unbranded merchandise: See *generic product*.

unbundled prices: a pricing method where customers are allowed to select specific merchandise and services on an optimal basis. Unbundling of prices is based on the concept that one price is no longer quoted for an item or service package.

unchanging list price: list prices that do not change over a determined time period, even when discounts from other competitors are offered. See *list price*.

undercharge: to charge less than the proper amount.

underpackaging: the use of packaging methods that are inadequate for the level of protection needed.

under-ring: a cash register error where the lower price than the actual price of the items is recorded on the register.

underselling: selling at a price lower than that listed by a competitor. See *price cutting; rate war*.

underselling store: See *discount house; underselling*.

understored area: a retail trading area where there are too few stores selling a particular item or service to properly fulfill the requirements of the people.

undiscounted: goods or services sold at the full price without discounts or any allowances. Such items or services are usually stable in demand and have little price elasticity.

uneven competition: a transaction where the customer returns a purchase and exchanges it for merchandise of a different value.

unfair competition: practices employed by a seller to increase profit by means of misleading promotion or advertising, selling below cost or dumping, obtaining rebates from suppliers, or utilizing other devices that unfairly take advantage of a competing firm.

unfair practices: the discriminatory commercial exchange activities of goods that are either unfairly subsidized or dumped, or are otherwise illegitimate, as with counterfeit items.

unfair practices acts: state regulations establishing minimum resale prices. Such laws stipulate that goods must be sold for cost plus some nominal percentage. In practice, there is little enforcement of these rulings. Cf. *fair trade acts.* Synonymous with *minimum markup laws; sales-below-cost laws; unfair sales acts; unfair trade practices acts.* See *tie-in sales.*

unfair sales acts: See *unfair practices acts.*

unfair trade practices acts: See *unfair practices acts.*

uniform delivered price: a pricing method whereby all the products are sold at the same delivery price in a stated area, without regard for delivery costs.

uniform markup: See *uniform percentage markup.*

uniform percentage markup: a pricing system where an attempt is made to apply a single markup percentage to all items offered for sale. If nearly all goods in a store are the same a uniform markup is possible, should various classifications generate widely varying selling costs, as in a supermarket, then a uniform markup cannot generate a reasonable profit.

Uniform Product Code Council (UPCC): located in Dayton, Ohio, an organization of retailers, processors, manufacturers, and wholesalers of items sold through high-volume checkstands. UPCC purports to develop a universal product code system for assigning a unique identification number to every product sold in the United States. Cf. *Universal Product Code.*

unitary demand: a situation in which a percentage change in price brings about an equal percentage change in quantity sold.

unitary elasticity: a pricing relationship where a percent change in price is shown in a corresponding percent change in demand for the item.

unitary falloff: a percentage drop in response or sales volume equal to the percentage increase in the price of a good or service.

unit billing: a list of all purchases by a customer, prepared on a single statement.

unit contribution margin: the excess of the sales price of one unit over its variable costs.

unit control: an approach for listing the quantity of goods bought, sold, in stock, and on order, with additional breakdowns as needed. Cf. *taking inventory.*

United Parcel Service (UPS): an independent delivery service whose trucks deliver parcels throughout numerous countries of the world. UPS packs up parcels at the retail store or distribution center according to schedule, takes them to a central warehouse, sorts them by routes, and delivers them according to schedule.

unitize: to combine a number of freight pieces into one large piece by banding, placing in a container, stacking, or any other means of assembling into a unit.

unit open-to-buy: See *open-to-buy.*

unit pricing:
(1) the quotation of prices given in terms of a standard of measurement (by weight, length, count, etc.). See *ton-mile.*
(2) the practice of pricing each product so that the price tag displays the price per unit of weight or volume in the package. Cf. *multiple-unit pricing.* Synonymous with *single-item pricing.*

unit store:
(1) an establishment of a company having but one place of business.
(2) a single store of a chain.

Universal Product Code (UPC): first adopted in 1973 by the food industry, UPC is a categorization where each item is given a ten-digit number, pre-marked on the package by the producer in the form of a bar code over ten corresponding numbers. The bar code is easily read by an optical scanner at the checkout counter, all controlled by a computer. The first six digits are the same for all of the manufacturer's items and represent the name of the maker. The following five refer to the item itself and are identified by the maker to the product of his or her choice. Retailers use this portion of the code to set prices on computers. The correct price is automatically pulled from the table and recorded on the register. The last digit of the UPC code is a check digit. See *bar code; scanner.* Cf. *Universal Vendor Marking.*

Universal Vendor Marking (UVM): a voluntary marking system where the producer attaches an identifying tag or label to his or her product on which is recorded information such as size, color, style, price, etc. Information can be read by eye or machine. Cf. *Universal Product Code.*

University of Shopping Centers: See *International Council of Shopping Centers.*

unloading:
(1) selling merchandise at a relatively low price. Slang for dumping. See *dumping.*
(2) the practice of stimulating the movement of consumer goods across retail counters by offering consumers inducements to purchase merchandise through such techniques as premium offers, contests, and two-for-one sales.

unpaid balance: on a credit purchase, the difference between the purchase price and the down payment or the value of a trade-in; on a cash loan, the difference between the total loan and the amount that is still owed.

unplanned business district: a retail location that exists where two or more stores are located close to one another without the use of prior planning as to the number and composition of stores. There are four kinds of unplanned districts: central business district, secondary business district, neighborhood business district, and string.

unsecured credit: credit given without collateral being required by the lender.

unselfish display: a form of altruistic display that also carries items not sold by the store.

unstuffing: unloading cargo from a container.

unsystematic freight equalization: meeting competitors' locational discount and delivered prices so as to retain market share. This is an unfair pricing practice if used with predatory intent. A company with high fixed costs and significant capacity can have no other price-setting choices.

unwholesome demand state: a demand situation where a harmful item yields marketing activities that attempt to discourage consumers from buying it, such as products of alcohol and cigarettes.

UPC: See *Universal Product Code.*

UPCC: See *Uniform Product Code Council.*

updated fashion: styles that are kept in the public's eye by the revising of lines, colors, fabrics, etc. Styles are new, but not so fashion-forward as avant-garde.

upgrade: See *upgrading.*

upgrading:
(1) *retailing:* offering superior goods and a greater assortment to customers.
(2) *merchandising:* an increase in the value of an order either at the time of the order or purchase or when a credit order is paid or when a second order is requested.

UPS: See *United Parcel Service.*

upscale: people and households of well above average income and education. For advertisers and manufacturers, such people are the best prospects for purchasing expensive items, such as luxury cars, jewelry, cruise tickets.

upscaling: See *upscale.*

upstairs store: level of the store which is, literally, above the basement floor, including the main- or street-level floor.

upward-flow theory: a fashion adoption theory where young, low-income, innovative people are the initiators of fashion movements that are often adopted by the general population at some future time.

upwardly mobile: people within a market who are striving for, and to some extent, achieve a higher socioeconomic position. Numerous products are geared for these people.

urgent consignments: merchandise that, because of its character, requires expeditious release by customs officials, e.g., perishable goods.

U.S. Customs bonded warehouse: See *warehouse, U.S. Customs bonded.*

useless quality: goods created with quality, dependability, and/or performance that is superior to that demanded by the public.

user: anyone who requires the services of a system or product or who employs a service. See *consumer; ultimate consumer.*

user calls: callbacks made by a sales representative to a customer who has already made a purchase from him or her or from the organization. Cf. *callback.*

user expectation: a sales forecast that is construed after a consumer survey or some other form of consumer research has been conducted.

use tax: a tax levied on the initial use of an item rather than on the merchandise when it is sold. Cf. *value-added tax.*

utility: the capability or power of an item to satisfy a need, as determined by the satisfaction one receives from consuming something. See *form utility; time utility.*

UVM: See *Universal Vendor Marking.*

valorization: government action leading to the establishment of a price or value for an item or service.

VALS: market information based on consumer's *values* and *lifestyles*. VALS data can be used to understand a persons' buying decision making. VALS data group consumers into segments of three categories:

(a) need directed—consumers who buy strictly on need.

(b) outer directed—consumers whose buying practices are influenced by how they believe other people will perceive them.

(c) inner directed—consumers whose buying practices are based primarily on satisfying their own psychological needs.

valuation: setting a value for anything.

valuation account: See *contra account.*

value:

(1) purchasing power.

(2) the worth of property, goods, services, etc.

value-added reseller (VAR): a reseller that purchases goods from a primary producer and adds value through product assembly, modification, and/or customization.

value-added tax (VAT):

(1) *general:* a government tax on the value added; a tax on the selling price of manufactured items less the cost of the materials and expenses used in their production.

(2) *retailing:* a tax that is levied every time a product is sold to another member of the distribution channel. For example, a retailer would be taxed on the difference between the wholesale price of merchandise and their retail price. Cf. *use tax.*

value in use: the value of goods to the individual who uses them.

value judgment: in merchandising, the result of a consumer's comparison of the attractiveness of two or more alternative items or services.

value of a customer: the total revenue coming from a buyer over time, minus all expenditures associated with obtaining that total revenue except the cost of advertising that is associated with securing the customer.

value pricing: when the price of a service is affected by the consumer's perception of its value, i.e., the price is based on what the market will bear without consideration for the actual retailer's costs.

values and lifestyles: See *VALS.*

van container: a standard trailer used to carry general cargo.

VAR: See *value-added reseller.*

variability in service quality: differing service performance from one purchase experience to another. Variations may be due to the service firm's difficulty in diagnosing a problem (for repairs), the inability of a customer to verbalize service needs, and the lack of standardization and mass production for many services.

variable budget: a budget that divides expenses into fixed costs and variable costs. The latter are allowed to vary on a predetermined basis with differing levels of output.

variable cost: a cost that is uniform per unit but changes in total in direct proportion to changes in the related total activity or volume. Cf. *fixed cost.*

variable expenses: expenses that vary with the level of factory output or plant capacity (e.g., the expenses of power, oils, and lubricants vary with the number of machines in operation). Generally, variable expenses are considered controllable.

variable leader pricing: a strategy where specific products are offered to consumers at prices so low that they produce little or no profit; these prices are frequently changed each week.

variable location retailers: people who sell on the street, such as street peddlers.

variable markup policy: a form of cost-based markup pricing whereby separate categories of goods and services receive different percentage markups; recognize that some items require greater personal selling efforts, customer service, alterations, and end-of-season markdown than others. See *markup.*

variable presentation: in retailing, an approach to setting prices by examining customers services, salesperson's knowledge of the product, store image, assortment and variety, competition factors, the prospect's satisfaction in order to determine that perfect combination to give the price the customer anticipates and is prepared to pay. Synonymous with *variable sales presentation.*

variable price policy: See *variable pricing.*

variable pricing: a method permitting a different price to be charged to differing prospects or at differing times; used especially at outdoor flea markets, antique stalls, street vendors, and the like. Its shortcoming is that at various times, customers may learn that others have paid less for the same item. In addition, federal and state regulations protect competing retailers from discriminatory pricing that gives competitors an unfair advantage. Cf. *flat rate.* Synonymous with *flexible pricing.* See *market-minus prices; negotiated price.*

variable sales presentation: See *variable presentation.*

variable slot location system: utilizing computers to keep track of where merchandise is kept, placing items in a warehouse by assigning newly brought merchandise to whatever place appears to be empty at that time.

variety: different types of merchandise sold to consumers. See *assortment.*

variety store: a retail operation that carries limited quantities of apparel and accessories for the family as well as other goods, with prices set somewhat lower than in retail stores, i.e., the five-and-ten store; the dime store.

varying price policy: See *variable pricing.*

VAT: See *value-added tax.*

vend: to offer to sell something.

vendee: the party who purchases or agrees to purchase something owned by another.

vending machine:
(1) *general:* selling merchandise with coin-operated equipment.
(2) *retailing:* a form of nonstore, self-service retailing through coin-operated equipment.

vendor: a manufacturer, wholesaler, or importer from whom goods or services are purchased. Cf. *resource.*

vendor allowances: See *returns and allowances.*

vendor analysis: the assessment of the strengths and weaknesses of current or new suppliers in terms of factors such as merchandise quality, customer service, reliability, and price.

vendor chargebacks: the return of goods or services to a vendor, accompanied by an adjusted invoice. Proof of delivery to the vendor is usually provided. See *returns to vendor.*

vendor coupon: See *coupon.*

vendor display: See *point-of-sale.*

vendor money: See *co-op money.*

vendor paid markdown: See *price guaranty.*

vendor premarking: where manufacturers who secure price tags and labels to goods enter into agreement based on the retailer's specifications. Synonymous with *vendor preticketing.* See *premarking; prepricing; source tagging.*

vendor preticketing: See *vendor premarking.*

vendor reliability: the capability of the seller to meet the conditions of the contract.

vendor returns: See *returns to vendor.*

vertical cooperative advertising: See *cooperative advertising.*

vertical price fixing: a form of price fixing in which marketers at different levels of the distribution system get together to set retail prices.

vertical shopping center: usually occupies the lower floors of a high-rise, multi-use structure, the upper floors of which are given over to offices and/or apartments; traditionally located in downtown city locations.

very profitable item (VPI): merchandise that a retailer believes is quite easy to convince consumers to purchase.

vest pocket supermarket: See *bantam store.*

VFRA: See *Volume Footwear Retailers of America.*

VICS: See *Voluntary Interindustry Communications Standard.*

video-shopping services: allows retailers to efficiently, conveniently, and promptly present information, receive orders, and process customer transactions. Its two basic categories are merchandise catalogs on videodiscs and videocassettes, and in-store and in-home ordering systems.

vignette: a display that stimulates a product in actual use.

virtual store: reality simulation offering a diverse array of research applications allowing retailers to explore customer behavior in a controlled setting. Applying graphics and three-dimensional modeling it creates the look and feel of a retail store on a computer screen. Cf. *simulated shopping environment.*

visibility: in retail store site location, the ability of a specific location to be seen by either pedestrian or vehicular traffic.

visible inventory control: See *eyeball control.*

visible shrinkage: stock shortage because of wear and tear or breakage of items. The shrinkage is accounted for in contrast to invisible shrinkage that is uncovered through physical inventory. Cf. *invisible shrinkage.*

visible supply: stock in distribution centers that has been brought there from production areas. Cf. *invisible supply.*

visual merchandise: in retailing, as a means for increasing sales, displaying items so that they are shown to their greatest advantage.

visual system of stock control: See *eyeball control.*

void:

(1) *general:* that which has no legal effect.

(2) *retailing:* an incorrectly prepared sales slip or cash register transaction. The mistake is corrected and voided slips retained for future audit.

voidable receipt: See *void (2).*

volume:

(1) *general:* a quantity, bulk, or amount.

(2) *retailing:* the total value of all retail sales for a given period, traditionally expressed in dollars.

volume bonus: a purchase incentive for customers who may be offered a discount on large purchases. See *Robinson-Patman Act of 1936.*

volume discount: See *bulk discount; patronage discount.*

volume fashion: See *mass fashion.*

Volume Footwear Retailers of America (VFRA): based in Washington, DC, an association of shoe chain stores.

volume merchandise allowance: a manufacturer's discount offered to a wholesaler or retailer for purchasing large volumes of goods.

volume price zone: See *volume zone.*

volume seller: items that sell in large amounts.

volume zone: the price range including mid-priced items aimed at customers who are moderately budget conscious, but who tend to purchase a significant amounts of goods if they determine it is affordable. Cf. *prestige zone; price zone.*

voluntary chain: a wholesaling organization established by independent retailers or wholesalers to gather increased purchasing power. See *affiliated wholesaler; chain store system; quasi-chain; voluntary wholesaler.* Synonymous with *wholesale-sponsored voluntary chain.*

voluntary cooperative: See *voluntary chain.*

Voluntary Interindustry Communications Standard (VICS): the retail sectors committee for standardizing the use of UPC and other information systems. See *Association for Retail Technology Standards.*

voluntary simplicity: a consumer lifestyle in which people have an ecological awareness, seek material simplicity and durability, strive for self-reliance, and purchase more inexpensive products.

voluntary wholesaler: a wholesaler who sponsors a voluntary chain that is active in supplying numerous members. See *voluntary chain.*

voucher: a written statement that bears witness or vouches for something (e.g., a voucher showing that services have been rendered or goods bought). See *due bill.*

VPI: See *very profitable item.*

WACA: See *Women's Apparel Chains Association.*

wagon distributor: See *truck jobber.*

wagon jobber: See *truck jobber.*

wagon retailer: a merchant middleperson engaged in selling anything for a profit.

walk: (slang) a customer who fails to purchase something and walks out of the store.

walk-out: See *walk.*

wall display: an interior display of posters and/or actual items that are suspended from the store's walls; intended to attract customer's attention and promote the sale of goods.

want book: See *want slip.*

want slip: written statements submitted to buyers by salespersons indicating merchandise not in stock that have been requested by customers. Synonymous with *want book.*

warehouse: a structure where merchandise is stored prior to distribution. See *warehouse terms below.*

warehouse, bulk: a storage facility for the tank storage of liquids and open, dry products.

warehouse, captive: See *warehouse, private.*

warehouse, commodity: a warehouse that stores commodity goods (cotton, wool, tobacco, and agricultural products).

warehouse, company: See *warehouse, private.*

warehouse, private: a warehouse operated by an owner, which holds his or her goods. Synonymous with *warehouse, captive; warehouse, company.*

warehouse, state-bonded: a public warehouse, under government supervision, that has been licensed by a state prior to operation. Merchandise is stored there without payment of duties or taxes until it is withdrawn from the warehouse.

warehouse, U.S. Customs-bonded: a federal warehouse where goods remain until duty has been collected from the importer. Goods under bond are also kept there.

warehouse and requisition plan: where the central buyer selected items in the market for a group of stores and has the initial stock for each store shipped to the store directly. Remaining goods are sent to a central warehouse to which the store managers send requisitions for further amounts needed to meet customer requirements.

warehouse club: a no-frills, cash-and-carry discount store. To shop there, the customer must become a member and pay dues.

warehouse control system: an inventory control technique where the retailer informs its warehouse of all sales so that the warehouse can adjust its inventory records to reflect such changes. In addition, the warehouse should be able to inform the store at any time as to how many items remain available.

warehouse discounter: See *warehouse store.*

warehouse receipt: an instrument listing the goods or commodities deposited in a warehouse. It is a receipt for the commodities listed, for which the warehouse is the bailee. Warehouse receipts may be either nonnegotiable or negotiable.

warehouse retailing: high-volume, low-overhead mass merchandising with few customer services.

warehouse showroom: a discount store that follows a strategy based on low overhead and high turnover; customers pay cash and must transport the merchandise themselves.

warehouse stock: goods held in quantity in a warehouse for reasons of economy.

warehouse store:
(1) a no-frills supermarket that stocks a wide variety of food and nonfood items and sells them at lower prices than the typical supermarket price.
(2) a simply furnished retail outlet that offers a limited assortment of items at discount prices as a result of special arrangements made with a producer. Synonymous with *box store.*

warehousing: involves the physical facilities used primarily for the storage of goods held in anticipation of sales and transfers within a distribution channel.

wares: items or commodities that are offered for sale.

warranty:
(1) *general:* a statement, either written, expressed, or implied, that a certain statement identified in a contract is true or will be true.
(2) *retailing:* a promise by a seller that the merchandise or that is being sold is as he or she has represented it. Usually a warranty is presented with the sold goods. See *caveat emptor; express warranty; implied warranty.* Cf. *guaranty; product liability.*

warranty price: the price established for an item that is deemed fair and just by both seller and buyer.

wash sale: a spurious sale in which the seller becomes the purchaser of what he or she sells. The purpose is to create activity in the item or to establish a market price; prohibited by law.

was-is-pricing: See *psychological discounting.*

wastage: wear of property; loss because of usage, deterioration, etc. Cf. *shrinkage.*

weak market: a situation characterized by a greater demand for selling than for purchasing.

wearout: the tendency of consumer response to a sales promotion to diminish over time.

Weber's Law: a retailing concept used in the understanding of people's perception of brands; suggests that consumers determine a product's value not on its separate characteristics but instead on their perceived differences between it and alternative brands. See *just noticeable difference.*

weed-out: to select and withdraw from stock those items that are slow selling.

week's supply technique: one of the four primary methods of retailers for stock planning. When sales shift considerably, this approach is not very helpful because it provides for the stock level to vary directly with sales, a situation that may not occur.

weighted average: a periodic inventory cost flow assumption whereby the cost of goods sold and the ending inventory are determined to be a weighted-average cost of all merchandise available for sale during the period.

WERA: See *Western/English Retailers of America.*

Western/English Retailers of America (WERA): based in Washington, DC, a division of Menswear Retailers of America. Members of WERA include retailers of Western and English tack, clothing, saddlery, and supplies.

wet goods: liquids.

Wheeler-Lea Amendment of 1938: federal legislation, amending the Federal Trade Commission Act of 1914, to protect the consumer against unfair trade practices in interstate commerce and against false or misleading advertising of foods, drugs, and cosmetics. See *phony list price.*

wheel of retailing: the theory that, when entering the market, new forms of retailing first emphasize lower prices but as time passes, the prices rise, making the merchandise subject to competition from newer organizations, which commence operations with lower prices. See *trading down; trading up.*

white goods:

(1) appliances of substantial size and cost (e.g., refrigerators, freezers, washing machines, stoves). Its name comes from the white enamel finish used. See *major appliances.*

(2) sheets, pillowcases, and lines. Its name comes from the early tradition of manufacturing these items in only white. Cf. *brown goods; orange goods; red goods; yellow goods.*

white mail: customer correspondence received in an envelope other than the one provided by the marketer; contains customer inquiries, complaints, or changes of address.

whole market approach: dealing with the full range of customers; does not recognize nor make an effort to appeal to the differences between various segments. See *market segmentation.*

wholesale: to sell goods in gross to retailers, who then sell the merchandise to customers.

wholesale club: See *closed door membership.*

wholesale cooperatives: full-service merchant wholesalers owned by member firms to economize functions and offer broad support. There are producer-owned and retailer-owned wholesale cooperatives.

wholesale merchant: See *wholesaler.*

wholesale price: the price for goods that is paid by retailers to suppliers.

wholesaler:

(1) *general:* an intermediary that distributes products primarily to commercial or professional users.

(2) *retailing:* an individual who buys and sells goods to retailers and other users but does not sell in significant amounts to the consumer. There are:

(a) full-service wholesalers—those who provide services such are carrying stock, maintaining sales forces, and offering management and credit assistance to purchasers.

(b) limited-service wholesalers—those who offer some, but not all, of the services provided by full-service wholesalers.

(3) Cf. *jobber; merchant wholesaler.* See *cash and carry wholesaler; rack jobber; truck jobber.* Synonymous with *distributor.*

wholesaler-sponsored retail franchise:
See *franchise.*

wholesale-sponsored voluntary chain:
See *voluntary chain.*

wholesaling:
(1) all of the activities provided by wholesaling intermediaries involved in selling merchandise to retailers; to industrial, institutional, farm, and professional businesses; or to other types of wholesaling intermediaries.
(2) selling merchandise to stores that purchase for reasons other than consumption, usually to resell the item for profit. See *merchandise mart; wholesaling intermediary.* Cf. *retailing.*

wholesaling intermediary: any firm that engages primarily in wholesaling activities. See *wholesaling.*

width of assortment: See *assortment breadth.*

will call: goods that are paid for in full by the customer and will be picked up at a future time.

window store: a store that attracts people primarily through its window displays.

Wine and Spirits Guild of America (WSGA): located in Minneapolis, Minnesota, an association of 500 retail wine and spirit outlets. WSGA promotes the exchange of information on merchandising, marketing, and buying of its products.

win-win situation: where both the purchaser and seller are pleased with their completed transaction.

wireless point-of-sale: See *noncabled point-of-sale.*

withdrawals: items sold or bought out of a consignment. Usually the consignee reports on and pays for these items on a periodic schedule.

without recourse: an agreement that a purchaser accepts all risks in the transaction and gives up all rights of recourse. See *caveat emptor.* Cf. *with recourse.*

with recourse: an agreement that if the seller is unable to meet his or her obligations, the purchaser has the right to endorse a claim against the seller for sustained damages. Cf. *without recourse.*

Women's Apparel Chains Association (WACA): located in New York City with affiliates in most states, an association of retail chain stores that sell women's clothing and discount stores selling women's, men's, and children's clothing, hard goods, domestics, and other goods.

Women's Wear Daily (WWD): the principal trade newspaper of the women's fashion industry.

Wool Products Labeling Act: federal legislation passed in 1939 and made effective in 1941; requires that items containing wool, with certain exceptions such as carpets and upholstery, must show labels on the merchandise indicating the percent of new wool, reused or reprocessed wool, and other fibers or fillers that are used.

working capital: the excess of current assets over current liabilities, representing the capital immediately available for the continued operation of a business.

workload analysis:
(1) estimating sales activities needed to fulfill the potential of a sales territory.
(2) an approach to salesforce design in which the size of the salesforce is determined by dividing the total workload in hours by the number of selling hours available from each salesperson.

workroom: in retailing, a nonselling area devoted to such support services as apparel alterations, placing names on purchased pens.

wrap: See *package wrap.*

wraparound: a decorative banner that is draped about or circles an in-store merchandise display; an example of point-of-purchase advertising.

wrapper:
(1) a label.
(2) the sheet of flexible material (paper, foil, etc.) or lamination used to cover a product for storage, sale, or shipment.

wrapping: See *package wrap.*

wrap-up: (slang) a customer who buys readily.

write-up: documentation of the making of a sale.

WSGA: See *Wine and Spirits Guild of America.*

WWD: See *Women's Wear Daily.*

yard goods: See *piece goods.*

yearly order: Synonymous with *blanket order.*

yellow goods: nonconsumable household items with a high profit margin, such as refrigerators, dishwashers, ovens, that are costly and replaced after many years of service. At times they are also called white goods. Cf. *brown goods; orange goods; red goods; white goods.*

yes, but technique: a sales approach to deal with objections, where the salesperson first sympathizes with the prospect, and then attempts to show how that point of view is inadequate. Synonymous with *agree and counterattack technique; agreeing and neutralizing technique.*

YMA: See *Young Menswear Association.*

young contemporary customers: a retail customer with significant fashion and clothes interest. Not a fashion pacesetter nor trend setters. Cf. *youth market; yuppies.*

Young Menswear Association (YMA): located in New York City, an association composed of people engaged in all aspects of the men's apparel industry. YMA promotes entry of new people into the field including providing scholarships to fashion design school; funds the YMA Men's Apparel Laboratory at the New York City based and world-famous Fashion Institute of Technology.

youth market: people between 14–25 years of age, who are often interested in merchandise that are different, unusual, or suggest values other than those held by older people. Cf. *young contemporary customers; youths; yuppies.*

youths: size ranges in teenage apparel for males in even numbers, ranging from 14 through 20. Cf. *youth market.*

yuppies: a creation of the 1980s, young urban professionals with money, who are in their mid-thirties and represent a target audience for some retailers. Cf. *youth market.*

ZBB: See *zero-based budgeting.*
zebra code: See *Universal Product Code.*
zero-based budgeting (ZBB):

(1) *general:* an approach to budgeting in which each part of the organization must justify each item in its budget before it will be granted the funds it needs.

(2) *retailing:* a means for determining the budget for the store which demands that each sales area or department justify each item of its expense budget.

zone delivered pricing: See *zoning price.*
zone pricing: See *zoning price.*
zoning price: a geographic pricing policy in which the seller divides a geographic area into zones and charges each buyer in a given zone the base price plus the standard freight rate for that zone. See *market segmentation.* Synonymous with *zone delivered pricing; zone pricing.*

ACRONYMS

AAMA	American Apparel Manufacturers Association
ABC	Audit Bureau of Circulations
ABF	American Buyers Federation
ACDS	Associated Chain Drug Stores
ACSMA	American Cloak and Suit Manufacturers Association
AFM	Associated Fur Manufacturers
AFMA	American Fur Merchants Association
AG	Apparel Guild
AGMAC	Association of General Merchandise Chains
AMOA	American Mail-order Association
ANSI	American National Standards Institute
APNRA	American Professional Needlework Retailers Associations
ARAE	American Retail Association Executives
ARF	American Retail Federation
ARTS	Association for Retail Technology Standards
ASCII	American Standard Code for Information Interchange
ATM	Asynchronous Transfer Mode
ATSOA	American Truck Stop Operators Association
AWBC	American Women Buyers Club
BAMA	Boys' and Young Men's Apparel Manufacturers
BBB	Better Business Bureau
BOM	Beginning of Month
BPS	Bits Per Second
BSNA	Bureau of Salesmen's National Associations
BTA	Best Times Available
BWSR	Bureau of Wholesale Sales Representatives
CAD	Cash Against Document
CAF	Cost and Freight
CAI	Career Apparel Institute

CAM	Common Area Maintenance
CBD	Cash Before Delivery
CEO	Chief Executive Officer
CEW	Cosmetic Executive Women
CFDA	Council of Fashion Designers of America
CIA	Cash in Advance
CIES	International Association of Chain Stores
CIF	Cost, Insurance and Freight
CL	Carload
CMA	Childrenswear Manufacturers Association
COD	Cash on Delivery/Collection on Delivery
COG	Customer Owned Goods
COM	Customer's Own Merchandise
CPI	Consumer Price Index
CPSA	Consumer Product Safety Act
CTFA	Cosmetic, Toiletry and Fragrance Association
CWO	Cash with Order
DCA	Diamond Council of America
DECA	Distributive Education Clubs of America
DGRA	Diamond and Gemstone Remarketing Association
DMA	Direct Marketing Association
DMM	Divisional Merchandise Manager
DOI	Date of Invoice
DOS	Department Operating Statement
DPP	Direct Product Profitability
EAS	Electronic Article Surveillance
EDM	Electronic Direct Marketing
EFFI	Educational Foundation for the Fashion Industries
EOM	(EOM Dating/Inventory) End of Month Terms
EOM/ROG	(Dating) End of Month, Receipt of Goods Dating
EOM	(Terms) End of Month Terms
EOQ	Economic Order Quantity Model
FAS	Free Alongside Ship
FAS	(Pricing) Free Alongside Ship Pricing
FC	Fixed Cost/Footwear Council
FCC	Federal Communications Commission
FIFO	First In-First Out

FISH	First In, Still Here
FOB	Free (Freight) On Board
FRM	Floor Ready Merchandise
FSA	Foreign Sales Agent
FTA	Free Trade Agreement
FTC	Federal Trade Commission
FTZ	Foreign (or Free) Trade Zone
GAA	Gift Association of America
GLA	Gross Leasable Area
GMROI	Gross Margin Return on Inventory Investment
GTC	Good 'til Canceled Order
GUI	Graphical User Interface
HABA	Health and Beauty Aids
HBA	Health and Beauty Aids
HCI	Home Center Institute
HVAC	Heating, Ventilation and Air-Conditioning
ICMAD	Independent Cosmetic Manufacturers and Distributors
ICSC	International Council of Shopping Centers
IDEA	International Downtown Executives Association
IMRA	International Mass Retailers Association
INP	Information-Need-Product
I/O	Input/Output
IRMA	Illinois Retail Merchants Association
ISDN	Integrated Services Digital Network
ISO	International Standards Organization
ISP	Institute of Store Planners
JA	Jewelers of America
JIT	(Purchasing) Just-In-Time Purchasing
JND	Just Noticeable Differences
KBI	Key Buying Influence
KBPS	Kilobits Per Second
KD	Knocked-Down
LAN	Local Area Network
L/C	Letter of Credit
LCD	Liquid Crystal Display
LCL	Less-Than-Carload Lot (on trains) Less-Than-Container Load (on ships)

LED	Light-emitting Diode
LIFO	Last In-First Out
LIMA	Licensing Industry Merchandiser's Association
LNO	Late Night Only
LTL	Less Than Truckload Lot
MADA	Money, Authority, Desire, Access
MAJAPS	Major Appliances
MBPS	Megabits Per Second
MFA	Men's Fashion Association of America
MFN	Most Favored Nation
MIPS	Millions of Instructions Per Second
MIS	Management Information System
	Marketing Information System
MMDA	Mass Merchandising Distributors' Association
MOAA	Mail Order Association of America
MOM	Middle of Month Dating
MOR	Merchandising and Operating Results
MR	Market Representative
MRA	Menswear Retailers of America
MSA	Museum Store Association
NACDS	National Association of Chain Drug Stores
NACS	National Association of College Stores
	National Association of Computer Stores
	National Association of Convenience Stores
NACSM	National Association of Catalog Showroom Merchandisers
NADI	National Association of Display Industries
NAFTA	North American Free Trade Agreement
NAGMR	National Association General Merchandise Representatives
NAM	National Association of Manufacturers
MANSB	National Association of Men's Sportswear Buyers
NARD	National Association of Retail Druggists
NARDA	National Association of Retail Dealers of America
NAS-RAE	National Association of State Retail Association Executives
NATAD	National Association of Textile and Apparel Distributors
NATSO	National Association of Truck Stop Operators
NAVS	National Association of Variety Stores
NBSCA	National Beauty Salon Chain Association

NFASG	National Fashion Accessories Salesperson's Guild
NGA	National Grocers' Association
NHFA	National Home Furnishings Association
NINFRA	National Independent Nursery Furniture Retailers Association
NLDA	National Luggage Dealers Association
NLSA	National Liquor Stores Association
NMRI	National Mass Retailing Institute
NRF	National Retail Federation
NRHA	National Retail Hardware Association
NRI	National Retail Institute
NRMA	National Retail Merchants Association
NRPSGA	National Retail Pet Store and Groomers' Association
NSRA	National Shoe Retailers' Association
NSTA	National Shoe Traveler's Association
OEM	Original Equipment Manufacturer
OS/2	IBM Operating System
OS&D	Over, Short and Damaged
OTD	Open-To-Buy
OTC	Over-The-Counter (Proprietary Drug)
PLC	Product Life Cycle
PLMA	Private Label Manufactures Association
PON	Plus Over Normal
POP	Point-of-Purchase
POS	Point-of-Sale
POST	Point-of-Sale Terminal
PP	Parcel Post
PX	Post Exchange
QR	Quick Response
RAC	Retail Advertising Conference
ROA	Return on Assets (Return of Investment)
ROD	Run of Time Schedule
ROG	ROG Dating
ROG	(Dating) Receipt-of-Goods Dating
ROI	Return on Investment
RSA	Rack Service Association
RTV	Returns to Vendor
RTW	Ready to Wear

SA	Seventh Avenue
SANTA	Souvenir and Novelty Trade Association
SBD	Secondary Business District
SBU	Strategic Business Units
SIY	Scan It Yourself Technology
SD/BL	Sight Draft/Bill of Lading
SIC	Standard Industrial Classification System
SKU	Stockkeeping Unit
SML	Small, Medium, Large
SNA	Systems Network Architecture (IBM)
SOB	Store's Own Brand
SOH	Stock on Hand
SRAs	State Retail Associations; Associated with the National Association of State Retail Association Executives
SRO	(Method) In sales, a closing approach where the prospect is told that should the sale not be concluded immediately, the chances are small that the item will be available to the person at a later time. Considered an unethical practice.
SSD	Secondary Shopping District
ST	Stock Turnover
TCP/IP	Transmission Control Protocol/Internet Protocol
TFG	The Fashion Group
TL	(Shipment) Truck Load Shipment
TSD	Telephone Selling Department
TSIA	Association of Retail Marketing Services
TTNF	Two-Ten National Foundation
UCC	Uniform Code Council
UPC	Universal Product Code
UPCC	Uniform Product Code Council
UPS	United Parcel Service
UVM	Universal Vendor Marking
VAR	Value-Added Reseller
VAT	Value-Added Tax
VFRA	Volume Footwear Retailers of America
VICS	Voluntary Interindustry Communications Standard
VLSI	Very-large-scale Integration
VPI	Very Profitable Item
VSAT	Very Small Aperture Terminal

WACA	Women's Apparel Chains Association
WAN	Wide Area Network
WATS	Wide Area Telephone Service
WERA	Western/English Retailers of America
WSGA	Wine and Spirits Guild of America
WWD	Women's Wear Daily
YMA	Young Menswear Association
ZBB	Zero-Based Budgeting